THE BIG TENT

THE BIG TENT

THE TRAVELING CIRCUS IN GEORGIA, 1820–1930

BY GREGORY J. RENOFF

THE UNIVERSITY OF GEORGIA PRESS : ATHENS & LONDON

Publication of this book was supported in part by the Kenneth Coleman Series in Georgia History and Culture.

Paperback edition, 2012
© 2008 by the University of Georgia Press
Athens, Georgia 30602
www.ugapress.org
All rights reserved
Set in New Caledonia by Bookcomp, Inc.

Printed digitally in the United States of America

The Library of Congress has cataloged the
hardcover edition of this book as follows:

Renoff, Gregory J., 1969–
The big tent: the traveling circus in Georgia, 1820–1930 /
by Gregory J. Renoff.
x, 235 p., [12] p. of plates : ill. ; 25 cm.
Includes bibliographic references (p. 209–226)
ISBN-13: 978-0-8203-2892-8 (hardcover : alk. paper)
ISBN-10: 0-8203-2892-8 (hardcover : alk. paper)
1. Circus—Georgia—History. 2. Circus—Social aspects—
Georgia. I. Title.
GV1803.R46 2008
791.309758—dc22   2008007281

British Library Cataloging-in-Publication Date available

Paperback ISBN-13: 978-0-8203-4437-9
         ISBN-10: 0-8203-4437-0

Frontispiece: "When the Circus Comes to Town" by A. B. Frost.
From the *Ladies' Home Journal* 18, no. 1 (December 1900).

In Memory of
George Miller Watkins Jr., MD
(1935–2003)
and
Laura Manning Watkins
(1969–2004)
In Coelo Quies Est

CONTENTS

Acknowledgments : *ix*

Introduction : *1*

1 Get the Show on the Road: Circus Trouping in the Old South : *11*

2 Selling Southernism: Showmen in Georgia, 1865–1874 : *33*

3 The Slow Embrace: Religion, Social Status, and Circus Attendance, 1865–1920 : *49*

4 Wait for the Big Show! The Economics of the Circus in Georgia, 1865–1920 : *67*

5 The Canvas City: Social Mixing on Circus Day, 1870–1920 : *85*

6 Performers in Bleachers: Audience Behavior and Social Interaction in Turn-of-the-Century Circus Tents : *109*

7 It's Showtime: The Cultural Content of the Circus, 1880–1920 : *132*

8 Sparks Circus and the Reinvention of Circus Day : *150*

Conclusion : *165*

Notes : *173*

Bibliography : *209*

Index : *227*

ACKNOWLEDGMENTS

Many people and institutions made the publication of this book possible. This work began as a Brandeis University PhD dissertation, and like all students in the American History program, I enjoyed four years of aid courtesy of Brandeis' Rose and Irving Crown Fellowship. More recently, I benefited from travel and research funds provided by Drury University. I would also like to thank my copyeditor, Molly Thompson; my indexers, DeAnna and Jeremy Millett; and the staff at the University of Georgia Press.

My pursuit of circus sources took me to archives located across the country. Particular thanks go to Erin Foley of the Circus World Museum's Robert L. Parkinson Library and Research Center and James M. Donovan of the University of Georgia's Alexander Campbell King Law Library. I also owe a debt of gratitude to the staffs of the Cincinnati Historical Society Library, the University of Georgia's Hargrett Rare Book and Manuscript Library, and the Ringling Museum of the Circus for their help and assistance during my visits to their institutions.

I also intellectually profited from the seemingly boundless knowledge and generosity of numerous circus scholars, including Steve Gossard, LaVahn Ho, John Polaseck, Richard J. Reynolds III, William Slout, and Stuart Thayer. I was particularly fortunate that Joseph T. Bradbury agreed to share his memories of his childhood visits to circuses in Athens, Georgia, with me in an oral interview, a conversation that proved essential as I formulated my argument about the nature of Circus Day. Yet above all, this book's scope and depth were made possible mostly by the incredible liberality of Robert H. Brisendine. After a single brief phone conversation in 2000, Robert graciously invited me into his Atlanta home, and gave me full access to his massive private archive of Georgia circus tour dates and newspaper clippings and transcriptions. Over the next two years, Robert granted me multiple opportunities to fully mine the amazing riches contained within his notebooks, folders, and scrapbooks. (These priceless source materials are now located in Emory University's Special Collections and Archives.) My only regret is that these two circus historians passed away before they could fully appreciate the contributions they made to my work.

My ability to bring this book to a conclusion depended in no small part on the guidance and support of a number of wonderful teachers and mentors, including James Livingston and David Oshinsky at Rutgers University; Alfred A. Moss Jr. and David Grimsted at the University of Maryland; Shelia Skemp, Charles Reagan Wilson, Ted Ownby, and the late Winthrop D. Jordan at the University of Mississippi; and finally and most importantly, my dissertation advisor, Jacqueline Jones of Brandeis University. Each in his or her own way shaped my interest in the study of the past and assisted me as I pursued graduate education and a career as a historian.

Finally, I want to offer special thanks to my friends and family for their love and support through good and bad times as I worked toward the goal of seeing this work in print. I am exceedingly grateful for the friendship of Tim Bass, Gale Boutwell, Julie Bydalek, Nick Chubrich, Andy Harris, Rob Heinrich, Nathan Hodge, John Inscoe, Tamasin Johnson, Paul T. McCartney, Max Matusevich, Hilary Moss, Terry Allen Shelton, Troy Smith, Amy Wood, and Diane Ziegler. I also have benefited from the love and support of my siblings, Michael and Maureen, and their families; my father, Richard; and my mother, Marion. I want all of you to know how blessed I am to have you in my life.

THE BIG TENT

> I been to the circus three or four times—lots of times.
> Church ain't shucks to a circus.
> —Twain, *The Adventures of Tom Sawyer*

INTRODUCTION

In his memoir of growing up in early twentieth-century Georgia, Jimmy Carter reminisces about the excitement surrounding the arrival of the circus in the small town of Plains. He recalls standing at a filling station as a child, listening to local men whisper that the coming circus "featured a striptease where the girls took off 'every stitch of clothes'" in a darkened corner of a sideshow tent. Although the town fathers decided to bar the risqué performance, Carter did see a range of other acts in the outfit's tents. Under the big top, he watched thrilling exhibitions of human and animal performers. In the sideshow, he stared at "deformed people and animals that were either alive or preserved in formaldehyde" and looked on as townspeople tested their luck at "various games of chance." But even as Carter took in the broad array of exhibits and games, he gazed at the nubile female circus employees, wondering which "might be the ones who performed in the more liberated communities."[1]

Carter's sense of wonder and curiosity about the show's "attractions" matched those of innumerable other Georgia men, women, and children who flocked to these traveling shows between 1820 and 1930. Indeed, the day that a circus performed in a particular location—the unofficial holiday of Circus Day—was a major event in the lives of southerners, drawing together people of all classes and colors at a time when the South was largely split along those lines. The scale of this event grew over time. While the earliest nineteenth-century forays by wagon shows into Georgia had drawn hundreds of individuals together to see a performance, by the 1870s, an appearance by a railroad circus could literally shut a town down. Starting at daybreak, thousands of excited people would line the main streets to await the grand daily circus parade. The occasion's mirthful atmosphere would continue throughout the day and into the night, ending only when the big top came down. The circus was arguably the only turn-of-the-century mass entertainment capable of attracting mammoth crowds into a single geographic location for an all-day celebration.[2]

Of course, this kind of community-wide event that encouraged people to join together in a festive style predated the emergence of the traveling circus, and in fact, European settlement in America. Circus Day in Georgia descended from what Mikhail Bakhtin, speaking of the premodern period, called the "ritual spectacle" of carnival. At their most basic levels, both Circus Day and carnival featured "open air amusements" as well as the "participation of giants, dwarfs, monsters and trained animals." Both also served to blur the line between performer and spectator. Most importantly, as Bakhtin notes, each produced a "second world" of existence that stood apart from the normal happenings of everyday life.[3]

Despite these premodern features, Circus Day also grew out of a convergence of economic and cultural trends in late nineteenth-century American life. More specifically, techniques of modern advertising—a concomitant of the rise of consumer capitalism—and the development of a national rail system served as the essential ingredients for the creation of Circus Day. By the time a railroad circus pulled into a town or city, thousands of people had already begun making their way to the show location, drawn there by the hundreds of huge color posters pasted up in the vicinity of the performance site by the outfit's advertising men. These circus fans left their homes with money in their pocket or with goods to sell in order to purchase the commodity of entertainment, thereby taking part in the national shift toward the commercialization of leisure. They traveled to town not just on horseback, by wagon, and on foot, but by train as well, thanks to excursion lines that offered cheap and easy transit to show locations. The circus industry's shift from wagon to rail transportation in 1872 allowed concerns to move tons of equipment and thousands of animals, workers, and performers efficiently and rapidly from place to place, facilitating the presentation of mammoth exhibitions that generated unparalleled popular excitement among Americans. In this sense, the circus participated in the trend in commercial entertainment that saw the nation's rail system carry burlesque, vaudeville, and theatrical companies into towns and cities across the United States.[4]

But Circus Day was a social event created by more than just amusements, advertising, and technological change. It was a product of the *people* who joined together in a "pressing throng," to use Bakhtin's phrase, to animate the event and give it its energy. Here I emphasize "people" because the circus of that era enthralled Americans of all stripes, even in a Georgia society divided along lines of class, race, and gender. As the *Atlanta Constitution* succinctly stated in 1894, "Everybody goes to see [the circus]. It is a highly democratic form of entertainment." Members of these different groups, as the title of this book suggests, came together under a single spread of canvas on Circus Day.[5]

Despite the circus' centrality to nineteenth-century popular culture, it has received scant attention from historians. Scholars of mass entertainment in the Gilded Age have investigated the social and cultural impact of Wild West shows, minstrelsy, amusement parks, vaudeville, burlesque, dance halls, motion pictures, and the theater. Even those works that have taken a broad view of the era's popular amusements tend to ignore the circus. Those scholars who have studied the circus have largely focused upon the life and career of its most important impresario, P. T. Barnum, rather than the wider industry. Nevertheless, the appearance of Janet Davis' *The Circus Age* suggests that a more expansive view of the circus can deliver important insights into the nature of turn-of-the-century American society and culture. She views the circus and its performances as one significant arena where discourses of race, power, and gender played out in the United States. Davis also uses the entertainment as a lens through which to view the broader historical transformations that America underwent during this period.[6]

This book takes a somewhat different approach by focusing on the impact of Circus Day on local communities in Georgia and the responses that the circus engendered in these places. That is, as much as it seeks to unpack the meanings embedded in the content of circus exhibitions, this book centers on the dynamics that took place *outside* of the tent before, during, and after the circus came to town for what they may reveal about a community's social, cultural, and economic life. For example, when northern-based circuses pitched their tents in the South during Reconstruction, they provided a staging ground for southern men to express their deep resentment of the presence of showmen hailing from above the Mason-Dixon line. Likewise, in the years immediately following the Civil War many Georgia community leaders bemoaned the moral impact of circus performances on their towns and cities. Yet by the turn of the century, most of the state's business owners and politicians applauded these exhibitions because they represented a singular opportunity to draw large crowds of eager shoppers into local stores. Significantly, they did so even though most religious and respectable people continued to assert that circuses offered morally dubious entertainment. In sum, the study of circus exhibitions offers an extraordinary window into issues central to southern life, including racial interaction, class formation, religious belief and behavior, popular culture, sectional identity, and the rise of consumerism.

Even though no southern state is a perfect "representative" of the region for the purposes of any academic investigation, Georgia features a number of factors that make it an ideal context in which to investigate the role of the circus in the South. First, the state's sizable black population permitted the detailed examination of issues surrounding racial segregation and mixing at circuses. Second, its large number of Baptist and Methodist congregations allowed for the study of evangelical southerners' attitudes toward the circus. Third, the varied economic activity in the state, ranging from the commercial activity of Atlanta to the cotton monoculture of the countryside, provided an opportunity to see how Georgians of vastly different life circumstances and economic outlooks might react to traveling shows. Fourth, the wide range of communities that hosted circus performances—ranging from, for instance, the large port city of Savannah to the small, isolated mountain town of Dahlonega—made possible a look at the ways that geographic location shaped local responses to tented entertainment. Finally, the significance of the railroad to Atlanta, and therefore to life in the state and region, was particularly advantageous to this study given this transportation network's essentialness to the circus industry.[7]

Conversely, a focus on Circus Day allowed for an examination of the state's unsettled developmental trajectory and, more broadly, of the contradictory nature of economic, cultural, and social activity in the New South. Despite the destruction of slavery, cotton production still defined the rhythm and texture of life in wide swaths of rural Georgia, trapping tenant farmers and sharecroppers in a web of debt to the state's planter and merchant class. Because few blacks owned land, these rural economic relationships helped reinforce white supremacy in many cases. At the same time, the South's commitment to staple-crop agriculture and extractive industries also limited the opportunities for agricultural diversification, or significant industrialization beyond the cotton mill, turpentine still, or lumber mill. Outside the world of work, evangelical churches called on their followers to endure life's hardships and to reject worldly pleasures in favor of the spiritual rewards of the afterlife. Considering these economic and cultural factors, the opportunities for commercial activity, including consumption and recreation, remained limited on the southern countryside.[8]

Still, a look at Georgia's large towns and cities suggests that much about life in the state had changed in the aftermath of the Civil War. The postwar rebuilding and expansion of Georgia's railroad network—a process that began in the late 1860s and moved forward in fits and starts until the 1880s—helped spur the growth of its towns and cities. By 1880, Georgia had five cities (Atlanta, Savannah, Columbus, Augusta, and Macon) with populations of ten thousand or more people and, between 1880 and 1890, Atlanta, Columbus, and Macon all saw their populations increase by seventy percent or more. Arguably, the state's large towns, rather than its larger urban areas, benefited most from this developmental process. For instance, while places like Rome, Dalton, Hawkinsville, Thomasville, Valdosta, and Griffin could not match the dynamism of the Gate City—or of major cotton centers like Macon and Augusta, for that matter—they all experienced significant economic and population growth in the wake of the post-Civil War railroad construction boom. During the Reconstruction and New South eras, thousands of black and white Georgians moved from rural areas into these places for the purposes of self-advancement, where they joined with local business elites, along with evangelicals and other social conservatives, in the town building project. Not coincidentally, Circus Day reached the height of its national popularity as Georgia underwent rapid changes in transportation, urbanization, and demographics.⁹

On Circus Day, the state's railroad towns and cities became the stage where these realms of country and city life converged. On a show day in a sizable community, a black sharecropper who spent the previous day staggering behind a mule and plow, and a white lawyer who spent the day before working in a well-appointed office, might stand alongside each other and watch a circus parade. Likewise, the most pious and the most commercially minded men and women shared the same streets and moved through the same show tents. More generally, on Circus Day black and white farmers and their families joined with townspeople drawn from across the racial and social spectrum to form the biggest gatherings that anyone had ever seen. As the varied members of the crowd waited for the parade to start or for the ticket wagon to open, they mixed with their social betters and lessers, stood in close quarters with unfamiliar members of the opposite sex, came face to face with friends, rivals, and strangers, and rubbed shoulders with persons of a different color. If Circus Day involved encountering novel and strange sights inside of show tents, then it also provided an opportunity for an unparalleled degree of social mixing.¹⁰

Despite its air of release, Circus Day also illuminated the tensions at the heart of southern life. For instance, the event offered evangelicals the opportunity to see the wonders of God's animal creation but also put them in close quarters with some of the most drunken and violent members of their communities. Similarly, it allowed middle-class farmers and townspeople to take in the "instructive" exhibits inside of a sideshow tent but also put them within eyeshot of lightly garbed "hoochie coochie" dancing girls and the enthralled men who longed to see them perform. Circus Day thus offers an exceptional opportunity to study the frictions that existed at the fault lines of identity and ideology in the New South.

Racial interaction took on a unique character on Georgia Circus Days as well. Although African Americans living in antebellum towns and cities had been excluded from many public and private facilities, including places of amusement, large numbers of slaves and free blacks watched circus performances, albeit from segregated seating areas. Beginning in the 1870s, however, the opportunities for racial mixing on circus lots actually increased as showmen added menagerie and sideshow tents, with their decided lack of seating areas or partitions, to their operations under canvas. Notably, this process occurred even as racial separation grew more rigid and more pervasive in the rest of southern society. Thus in the case of circuses, segregation became less rather than more severe from the end of the Civil War to the Great Depression.¹¹

Still, while Circus Day in Georgia did foster a singular sense of interactivity, it could not provide for the kind of broad-based and comparatively rapid social and cultural transformation that took place in northern cities between about 1890 and 1930. In the North, the circus was just one of many professional entertainments available to amusement patrons. Historians such as John Kasson, Kathy Peiss, and David Nasaw have demonstrated the function that commercial entertainments played in the late nineteenth-century breakdown of Victorian decorum among the North's urbanites. Collectively, their works suggest that amusement parks, theaters, dance halls, and nickelodeons provided spaces outside of the realms of home and family that gave staid middle-class men and women an opportunity to embrace novel and uninhibited ways of behaving in public. In fact, urban northerners had frequent chances for such self-expression at circus performances, given that the nation's biggest concerns often opened their turn-of-the-century tours in cities such as Chicago, New York, and Boston with stands that lasted as long as three weeks.[12]

As with so much between the two regions, the role that commercial amusements played in the South differed from the North. Most immediately, this stemmed from the relative dearth of outlets for professional entertainment in the South. On the countryside, few if any traveling shows other than circuses made regular appearances. In the case of circuses, a sizable southern community on a railroad line could, after the 1870s, expect two to three annual visits from shows large enough to draw a big crowd. Even the most dedicated Georgia circus aficionados would have found that only about a half-dozen troupes of any size appeared within a day's journey from their homes from year to year. But even in larger cities, entertainment choices beyond the circus remained limited. For instance, Gregory Waller notes that in 1896, Lexington, Kentucky, had no "arcade, dime museum, amusement park, burlesque house, or vaudeville theater." Likewise, Steve Goodson's study of public entertainment in turn-of-the-century Atlanta highlights the cultural and religious forces that helped slow the growth of commercial amusements in that key metropolis. Despite its irregular presence, then, the circus was the one entertainment that all rural and urban southerners could consistently patronize.[13]

Paradoxically, however, the infrequent nature of Circus Day in Georgia actually helped to provide its social power and to generate the popular excitement that surrounded it. Unlike the residents of large northern cities, Georgians could not casually choose the day they wanted to take in a circus performance during a show's multiweek stand. On the contrary, they clearly apprehended that a tour stop by a leading circus in the vicinity of their homes offered them one of their few annual chances to see the most awe-inspiring amusement of the Gilded Age. This helps explain why tens of thousands of them greedily seized their opportunities to take part in the happenings of Circus Day every time a big show raised its tents. Most Georgians, regardless of class or color, simply concluded that this was an event that was not to be missed, regardless of the time, money, and effort that it took to get to the show location. Indeed, a large number of them made this trip to town even though they lacked the funds—or the desire—to enter the tents of the traveling show. They came for the celebration in town as much as they did for the entertainment under canvas.

Thus, both inside and outside the tents, circuses in Georgia communities gave the state's residents the chance to challenge the New South's strictures of race, class, and religious belief and helped spur the social, cultural, and economic transformations that the state underwent between 1865 and 1930. Simply put, Circus Day allowed people to behave in new and unfamiliar ways. For instance, the state's "middling sort" could cast aside notions of moderation and self-denial while in town by spending to excess at local merchants and eating to excess at the snack stands that stood near the show lot. The respectable could test established ideas about virtue, whether that meant attending a circus at night for a woman or eyeing a lightly garbed female equestrian for a man. Evangelicals could press and exceed the boundaries of appropriate and moral behavior by attending an exhibition deemed sinful by their pastor, even though they had maintained to others that they would pay admission only to see the animals in the menagerie. The embrace of the circus as a "respectable" entertainment by almost all Georgians by the 1920s, and the eventual acceptance of behaviors such as female and evangelical circus-going and unfettered Circus Day consumption as a celebratory activity, are suggestive of the ways that the circus contributed to social and cultural change in the New South.

Scholars have long debated the question of change and continuity from the Old to New South. Here I want to suggest that Georgians could see and understand what was new about the New South when the circus came to town in the last quarter of the nineteenth century. Many of them made their way to the show location via the state's expanding railroad system, traveling much farther than they could have on foot or horseback. These shows frequently came off in the state's interior cotton centers, which had arisen along the sinews of narrow-gauge steel that snaked their way across the Georgia landscape. After alighting from their passenger cars, they browsed and shopped in stores filled with a variety of consumer goods and passed by or patronized snack stands operated by individuals who had been human property just a few decades earlier. Once they entered the show tents, they took in productions staged by outfits based in the northern states and, for the most part, managed and owned by men from the North. These shows, of course, ultimately took place because the community's business elite of bankers, editors, merchants, bookkeepers, and politicians had chosen to align themselves with the path of progress rather than conservative forces that would have liked to exclude the demoralizing influences of this cutting-edge form of American popular culture. On Circus Day, the South looked forward rather than backward.[14]

This work draws upon a variety of source materials. In researching this project, I quickly apprehended that newspapers would serve as a key resource in my effort to illuminate the circus's impact on life in Georgia. The arrival of a traveling show was newsworthy in any community; newspaper editors rarely failed to offer substantive coverage before, during, and after Circus Day. Accordingly, I mined a broad spectrum of daily and weekly papers published in places ranging from the state's largest cities to some of its smallest towns in an effort to grasp how people from all walks of life responded to circuses and behaved on Circus Day. Still, my reliance on these accounts does not mean that I assume that their content reflects the attitudes and viewpoints of all of the individuals in the wider community. Similarly, I do not believe that they offer the final word on what it was like to attend a circus in Georgia during this time period. Despite their limitations, however, they are the single best source of information available to the historian; the descriptions of Circus Day scripted by Georgia newspapermen are both vivid and detailed, and many of these individuals paid close attention to the events that are the larger concern of this work: the activities that took place on show dates in the streets and alleys beyond the circus grounds. Finally, while newspaper editors certainly should be counted among the elite in the communities they served, as this work attempts to demonstrate, they were not of one mind when it came to the subject of circuses. Simply put, while many enthusiastically embraced them, a significant number roundly condemned them. In this sense, then, their attitudes toward circuses resembled those held by members of Georgia society writ large.

Along with newspapers, I have utilized a range of other primary materials in my effort to recreate the fabric of life on Circus Day. Throughout the text, I interweave the personal reflections of individuals who attended circuses in Georgia and the South both before and after the Civil War. These accounts appear in the form of published and unpublished letters, diaries, memoirs, and oral interviews. To gain the perspective of circus men and women, I have used autobiographies, business records, circus yearbooks ("route books"), and articles from entertainment trade journals. Rounding out my body of sources are government documents, including census records and legal codes.

Structurally, this book examines its subject matter in eight chronologically arranged chapters. In the first chapter I argue that while a wide spectrum of people attended the circus, not everyone in the South welcomed these exhibitions. This opposition would serve as the stimulus for the antebellum and postwar efforts by circus owners and managers to broaden their entertainment's appeal. In chapter 2, "Selling Southernism," I look at the hostile reception circuses received during Reconstruction and show how northern circus men responded to a wave of violence by spotlighting any southern performers in their troupes as well as projecting a "southern" image for their shows.

The third chapter focuses on the efforts of showmen to address the more intractable problem of winning over some of their sharpest critics: evangelicals, women, and middle-class Georgians. To woo these anticircus folks, circus men worked to give their shows an air of religiosity and respectability, a strategy that met with some success. Chapter 4 considers the financial aspects of circuses and their performances in Georgia. Despite the persistence of economic hostility to circuses in many small towns, by the late nineteenth century, most large town and city leaders welcomed circuses for their monetary benefits to their communities. Significantly, this economic activity helped mute the cultural and religious opposition to circuses in these places.

Chapter 5 takes a wide view of the social activities that took place outside of the circus grounds before, during, and after an exhibition. On Circus Day, thousands of Georgians came to town to watch the parade, drink, feast, celebrate, and socialize, even before they stepped on the circus lot. In fact, a significant portion of every crowd came to town solely for these diversions since they knew that they would not be going to the show itself. In chapter 6, "Performers in Bleachers," I suggest that circuses produced a boisterous atmosphere among their patrons, thanks to the profoundly participatory nature of the entertainment and the limited exposure of rural Georgians to Victorian standards of public etiquette. Chapter 7 addresses the entertainment content of turn-of-the-century circus performances and reveals how these traveling shows offered a slate of attractions that appealed to both rural and urban customers, helping to make the circus a "democratic" entertainment.

The eighth and final chapter focuses on the city of Macon and its relationship with Sparks Circus, which spent winters there from 1919 to 1929. During those years, Sparks built a notably close relationship with the community and its leaders. This embrace of the circus by some of Georgia's most "respectable" residents suggests that their long-held view of tented entertainment as morally dubious had evolved to a point where they viewed it as an upright, if not uplifting diversion.

Ultimately, in the pages that follow I have attempted to capture the essence of the circus experience in Georgia from a range of perspectives. For example, I want to convey a sense of what it was like for circus workers to brawl with drunken southern men, for ticket agents to look out on a sea of faces and hands in front of their ticket windows, for performers to gaze on a segregated circus crowd, and for Yankee show owners to finalize arrangements with southern politicians to winter in their communities.

More importantly, however, I want to give the reader an understanding of what Georgia residents encountered on Circus Day, especially given that the occasion offered a singular opportunity for a sensory experience that diverged sharply from the workaday happenings of life in the state's countryside and communities. On Circus Day, people accustomed to noises no louder than a locomotive or steam powered cotton gin got to hear the tumult of a calliope as it trundled down a dusty street. Likewise, individuals whose diet centered on pork and pone got to sample the variety of scrumptious food and drink offered up at the snack stands. Rural people who rarely saw more than a few dozen people in the same place at the same time got to feel the press of a huge crowd on a midway packed with thousands of enthusiastic circus fans. In sum, the vivid colors of the performers' costumes, the raucous noises that emanated from the crowds and from circus bands, and the unfamiliar smells and cries of exotic animals made the circus a feast for the senses for all who attended, regardless of social position, gender, age, or color.[15]

> One day a circus came to town! It is impossible now to realize the frantic excitement aroused in those humdrum days by such an event. The riding of men and women, the gay dresses, the witticisms of the clown, the little dramatic plays, the bears, lions, camels, elephants were talked of for weeks before and weeks afterward. —Kemp Plummer Battle, *Memories of an Old-Time Tar Heel*

ONE

Get the Show on the Road
Circus Trouping in the Old South

In the Old South, men engaged in vigorous, competitive, and physical recreations. On muddy street corners, loafing townsmen laughed and yelled whether two men or two dogs tore at each other's throat in mortal combat. Out on harvested fields, crowds of boys and men cheered as jockeys lashed the flanks of sleek racehorses. Inside dusty barns, perspiring gamblers whispered soft prayers when they threw dice and shouted in thanksgiving when their lucky numbers came up. And in wooded groves, a fleet-fingered fiddler and a jug of strong whiskey offered sufficient motivation to get the feet of most men moving in time with the infectious music.

The popularity of such simple diversions testifies to the fact that southerners living outside of cities had few opportunities to patronize professional entertainment. Antebellum southern communities did host repertory and minstrel companies, but in Georgia, for example, only about a half-dozen towns possessed the two prerequisites for a tour stop: a theater building and a population large enough to merit a performance. Thus for country people who lived more than a day's ride from a large settlement, patronizing theatrical productions was an impractical endeavor.[1]

But the impresarios of one entertainment genre did take their troupes outside of cities and into the remote areas of the South. After the 1825 invention of a portable canvas show tent allowed showmen to break their dependence on theater buildings, circus owners began playing backwoods settlements, near taverns, or at key crossroads deep in the southern countryside as they moved between larger communities. "In the early days in the South," noted legendary circus owner William Cameron Coup, "the country was so sparsely settled that we did not content ourselves with showing in the towns, but were in the habit of putting our tents up on any large plantation which appeared to be centrally located." The average circus, traveling along poorly maintained southern roads, could move about fifteen miles in a day. To keep their operations solvent, showmen needed to perform six days a week, meaning that people who lived along the lengthy routes between towns and cities had the chance to see the same show as city folk. The circus, therefore, was the only professional amusement that rural people could consistently attend.[2]

Despite staunch and vocal charges from some quarters that circuses were immoral, men and women of both races and from all stations of southern society turned out for these shows. They came and paid good money to see an entertainment form that both mirrored and amplified southern culture and its recreational components. Circuses placed equestrianism firmly at the center of its entertainment, a skill both admired and practiced by southern auditors. In acts that did not involve horses, circus athletes offered demonstrations of gymnastic ability and physical strength to crowds filled with people who relied on muscle power for the completion of most work tasks. Circus clowns were practiced at the arts of the witty song and sally, a style of humor in tune with the South's oral culture. This method of merrymaking also involved clever exchanges with audience members, making the circus a decidedly interactive entertainment.

Outside of the tent, a circus performance afforded the opportunity for crowds to watch the free street parade, to mix and mingle, and on occasion, to brawl with circus roustabouts, a group of community outsiders. While a circus appearance in the Old South produced a joyous atmosphere wherever a troupe raised its tents, a low population density and a primitive transportation network meant that hundreds, and not thousands, of people would turn out for a show, making an antebellum Circus Day different in magnitude and scale from those of the New South period.

Still, the circus's appeal would steadily build over the course of the nineteenth century. America's circus showmen built their genre's popularity in the Old South from their first known southern appearances in the 1790s up through the middle of the century, when as many as seven shows might be touring the South in any given year. Through raw determination and despite difficulty, circus men—"Yankees" by birth and trade—brought their exhibitions into the southern states. Thus, the history of the American circus in the Old South reveals how an entertainment form promulgated by northerners came to be embraced by southerners of all classes, races, and ages.[3]

The circus first appeared in America in April 1793, when a talented Scottish rider named John Bill Ricketts put on an equestrian performance in Philadelphia. Along with his riding, Ricketts presented a ropewalker, clown, and acrobat within his circular performance ring, or "circus." This combination of acts drew enthusiastic crowds to his exhibitions and would help make Ricketts the most popular circus man in the Early Republic.[4]

The early circus was strictly an urban entertainment. Ricketts and his contemporaries performed in single cities for weeks at a time, playing in theaters or in temporary wooden structures they built for their shows. Ricketts put up his first pavilion in Philadelphia, and his show soon became a major attraction in the nation's capital. In 1794, he toured up and down the East Coast from Boston to Baltimore, and the next year he opened new pavilions in New York and Boston. Ricketts' popularity grew, but he suffered two devastating losses when his New York and Philadelphia amphitheaters burned in 1799. These conflagrations financially ruined Ricketts, and, after an ill-fated effort to bring his circus to the West Indies, he perished at sea in 1800 while sailing to England. Slipping under the waves with Ricketts were the fortunes of the American circus. As circus historian Stuart Thayer explains, "with Ricketts gone there was no entrepreneur with the talent and possibly the capital to maintain the genre at its previous level." In fact, no circuses operated in the United States between 1800 and 1807, and only two existed in 1812.[5]

Although the circus business was moribund, the American people soon developed a taste for a different kind of traveling attraction: the wild animal or menagerie show. Around 1808, a Somers, New York, farmer named Hackaliah Bailey bought a female African elephant from his sea captain brother and successfully exhibited it throughout the northeastern states. The popular acclaim surrounding "Old Bet" demonstrated to Bailey's equally ambitious neighbors that the display of wild animals was a highly profitable line of work. By 1813, these Somers farmers and merchants had begun securing exotic beasts of their own and soon took their newly formed menageries on tour.[6]

Over the next two decades, about forty of these animal shows were organized in the vicinity of Somers. The region's entertainment class expanded as the sons of showmen came of age and took to the trouping life. Other adventurous men abandoned their conventional careers as druggists, traveling salesmen, storeowners, hotel proprietors, and butchers to enter the entertainment industry. A central reason why so many local men became menagerie operators was financial; the initial capital investment needed to start a traveling concern was relatively modest and 60 percent annual returns were possible. In addition, the rental of large theaters or the construction of a pavilion was unnecessary because a local barn or stable sufficed, meaning that nearly every sizable community would have a suitable and inexpensive place to display a group of rare animals. By the late 1820s, the Somers area had become a hotbed of show business activity and would remain so for much of the century. In fact, about half of the circus owners who took their shows into Georgia after 1865 had roots in the region.[7]

Eventually, increased competition began to reduce the profits of menagerie owners. In response, Somers showmen turned to a sound nineteenth-century business practice: they formed a trust. On January 14, 1835, the most successful menagerie company, June, Titus, Angevine and Company, signed an agreement with eight lesser firms to create the Zoological Institute. The arrangement was signed by more than one hundred investors, and its total capitalization was $329,325.[8]

The Zoological Institute pooled their animals and distributed them among its outfits. The directors used seven separate menagerie companies to tour the United States. The largest of these shows stayed in New England, where population density was high and roads were good. This show had the highest overhead, and the directors accordingly sent it into the region where the largest number of stops could be played in a single season. By contrast, they sent the two smallest shows into the South. With bad roads and long distances between population centers, the southern market was well suited for lesser shows with low expenses.[9]

That the national market could support so many traveling animal shows in the 1820s and 1830s is a testament to their ability to draw customers from all economic and religious classes. Perhaps most importantly for the reputations and profits of menagerie owners, the cultured public embraced animal shows. They did so because these shows ostensibly offered edifying "instruction" rather than immoral "amusement." In other words, leading citizens brought their families to these exhibitions because they afforded invaluable opportunities to learn about the splendor of the natural world. Menagerie operators were quick to support this notion. The Waring and Company's Great Zoological Exhibition informed residents of Columbus, Georgia that menagerie attendance "furnishes subjects for investigation which have engaged the interest of the most gifted minds during a period of more than four thousand years."[10]

Evangelicals also patronized these itinerant exhibitions. Unlike the "worldly amusement" of the theater or the circus, a menagerie gave devout Christians the chance to further appreciate the wonder of God and His living creations. Again, showmen affirmed that they too thought this the case. The Waring management proclaimed that "a visit to a well arranged menagerie" enhanced a devout visitor's "veneration for the Author of all things" while remaining utterly free of "every moral objection frequently made use of against places of amusement in general."[11]

Of course, these shows held a similarly strong appeal for the less spiritual or genteel. At a time when zoos were nonexistent, traveling animal shows allowed people who spent their daily lives in direct contact with a variety of domesticated animals to examine lions, elephants, camels, and innumerable other exotic creatures. The thrill of such encounters must have made these shows almost irresistible. In sum, antebellum menageries offered attractions, like the late nineteenth century circus, that captured the imaginations of a broad array of individuals.

At the height of the menagerie's national popularity, a clever Somers showman named J. Purdy Brown challenged the industry's leading showmen by reconfiguring the relationship between the circus and menagerie. In 1828, Brown's circus was the first to include the exhibition of wild animals *and* the performances of clowns, riders, and acrobats, a formula that continues in the circus business to this day. Although the two genres would remain definably different throughout much of the antebellum period, ultimately it was this merger of both entertainment forms that allowed the circus to actually surpass rather than just compete with the menagerie.[12]

Despite the revolutionary nature of this new formula, Brown trod on dangerous ground when he fused these two elements. Many religious people who enjoyed attending menageries never went to the circus. These pious individuals and their leaders objected to circuses for several reasons. First, circuses, unlike menageries, were not "rational amusements," and thus no self-improvement came from seeing such performances. Second, they encouraged poor people to squander money on a useless diversion. Third, they attracted a rough and uncouth crowd, thereby fostering a demoralizing atmosphere in and around the tent. Fourth, during performances, clowns cracked vulgar jokes and females performed socially inappropriate "gymnastic feats" while dressed in revealing knee-length skirts. Fifth, the members of circus troupes purportedly lacked religious orientation. Finally, some circuses desecrated the Sabbath by assembling and performing on that holy day.[13]

Such indictments provided the justification for legislation in the states of Vermont, Connecticut, and Delaware in the eighteenth and nineteenth centuries that at least on paper, banned circuses from appearing in those locales. In these places, the Puritan tradition of hostility to amusements sustained, in varying degrees, throughout the antebellum period, leading to charges from authorities against circus companies ranging from immorality to witchcraft. In the southern states, by contrast, opposition to the circus flourished during the nineteenth century, especially among religious authorities, but it never manifested itself into outright bans by political bodies. As historian Samuel S. Hill has pointed out, southern evangelicals saw morality and sin as a personal, rather than societal, issue. Thus southern churches focused their energies on persuading individuals of the wickedness of circuses, rather than trying to pressure lawmakers to outlaw these shows.[14]

Political and religion opposition aside, the astute Brown tackled the problem of the circus's moral stigma in clever fashion. Rather than seamlessly integrating riding, acrobatics, and clowning with his wild animal collection, he displayed his exotic beasts prior to his circus entertainment so that the spiritually minded could buy a ticket, look at the animals in their cages, and exit his enclosure before the circus exhibition got underway. This solution drew the widest range of customers to Brown's ticket wagon on show day.[15]

Other shows quickly adopted this approach. In 1834, one circus gave Columbus, Georgia residents the option to see its elephant, lion, tiger, dromedary, hyena, badger, armadillo, and two kangaroos in the afternoon for twenty-five cents or to gain admittance to both its menagerie and circus performance at night for fifty cents. The New York Circus and Arena Company offered a similar arrangement in Savannah in 1840, but carried only a single giraffe, an animal so rarely seen in captivity that it alone could draw crowds. This successful marriage of wild animal displays and the circus marked the beginning of the end for the menagerie show. By 1838, there were only two menagerie concerns touring the United States.[16]

Apart from the conjunction of menagerie and circus, the circus industry owes another debt to the creativity of J. Purdy Brown. In 1825, Brown broke new ground when he deployed a canvas exhibition tent. This new type of enclosure was both portable and durable, and would allow circus showmen to dispense with the need to construct (and invest in) temporary wooden buildings or to rent theaters before performance stands could commence. This technical innovation would serve as the essential ingredient for staging circus performances for the next 131 years, and remains in use to this day.[17]

Brown's tent significantly enhanced the ability of circus companies to ambulate. Unlike menagerie owners, Ricketts and the circus showmen who followed him had been confined to cities. In a river-rich state such as Georgia, for instance, circuses might move from Augusta to Savannah by steamboat, although some traveled overland. Regardless, between 1801, when Georgia hosted its earliest documented circus performance in Savannah, and 1825, no circus had played further west than the short-lived state capital of Louisville. By using tents, shows could now potentially undertake more frequent and ambitious moves by wagon deep into the southern backcountry. In Georgia, circuses reached the interior towns of Athens, Macon, and Milledgeville by the late 1820s and the western town of Columbus by the early 1830s, giving rural people the opportunity to see the same performances that their urban counterparts had enjoyed for years.[18]

At first glance, it seems surprising that showmen decided to tour the southern interior. The South's road network was poor and its population diffused. But there was one immediate benefit to overland tour routes. Stuart Thayer points out that the rural South was a largely unexploited entertainment marketplace. In addition, he notes that backcountry routes permitted showmen to steer clear of the competition in more populated parts of the country, namely the Northeast. Touring through the less populated areas of the South also allowed circus showmen to avoid going head to head with theatrical impresarios, who, by necessity, remained bound to performing in towns and cities large enough to support theaters. Circuses, by contrast, could raise their tents at any well-traveled crossroads or isolated interior town. Despite their remoteness, these places frequently produced good business for showmen. According to John Robinson Circus manager Gil Robinson, people living in these small communities had few entertainment choices beyond "the 'spelling bee' and the occasional 'barn-floor' dances." As a result, "the coming of the circus . . . was a great event."[19]

Once begun in earnest in the 1830s, the rituals of trouping through Georgia and the South would change little until the circus industry embraced rail transport in the early 1870s. The showman's first task was to plan a tour route. Routing was, in the words of one nineteenth-century expert, of "paramount importance" and the "very first thing to be considered for any sort of success." To limit a troupe's exposure to cold weather, the approximately seven wagon shows that toured the South before the Civil War typically entered the region in the autumn after playing the West or North. If the show was on the road year-round, the troupe might be playing Georgia by late winter or early spring.[20]

Once the route was in place, the "advertiser," or advance agent, moved about two to three weeks ahead of the show on horseback. When he arrived in a town, he reserved lodging for the troupe, rented the show lot, and secured a performance license. He also placed advertising with any local newspapers in the community. But perhaps his most important task was to hang bills. In contradistinction to the veritable army of bill posters that the giant circuses of the late nineteenth century deployed in advance of their concerns, the advertising operations of antebellum wagon shows were much more primitive affairs. According to former circus performer M. B. Leavitt, "the first John Robinson show agent was placed in charge of an old mule with a pair of saddle bags containing six weeks' posters and six paper boxes of tacks. . . . On trees, barns, and every place available where tack hammers could be used the bills and posters were placed." Typically, these ads announced performance dates, described the show's attractions, and offered a solemn pledge of morality, such as, "Nothing shall transpire within the Pavilion, that can in any way shock the most refined." In communities where the pace of life was slow and unusual happenings uncommon, these colorful bills immediately drew a crowd. In one North Carolina town:

> The [posters] posted up at the taverns, had been daily inspected by scores of glistening eyes for weeks. . . . These edifying documents diffused a special glow of good humor over the faces of their hosts of readers. The representation of galloping horses, with the performers dancing upon the backs—the stacks of men, topped off with a little boy—the tumblers with their heels in the air—the "old clown" with his striped tights and spotted jacket—the grinning Cuffee, a-straddle of a barrel, with a banjo in his hand, etc., etc. were each severally commented upon in every variety of grave and wondering thought.

The speculation and excitement generated by bill posting helped assure a good turnout on Circus Day.[21]

With the route and advertising in place, it was time for the troupe to get the show on the road. During favorable times, touring with a circus did have an undeniable allure. "When the skies were blue and the air balmy, the grass green, and business good," Gil Robinson observed, "it was a life with many compensations." Although days were long under the best circumstances, showmen could enjoy an easy nighttime journey to the next town if the distance to the next lot was short and the roads in good shape.[22]

But as often was the case in the South, bad weather, execrable roads, and a long haul meant a terrible night ahead for showmen. When these conditions prevailed the troupe left town immediately after the show and traveled all through the night by wagon, at the pace of four miles an hour. Clown Robert Sherwood tells of the arduous nature of trouping by wagon: "No one outside the profession can conceive of the many hardships that fell to the lot of performers. There were no sleeping accommodations other than jolting wagons; a piece of canvas to shed the rain was the only covering." Beyond the physical discomfort, showmen especially dreaded inclement weather because "several days of rain make the highways in very bad condition, cutting up and washing away the roads."[23]

Moving along rutted, muddy, and poorly maintained roads made for a ride so jarring that show personnel actually used their belts to strap themselves to their wagons to avoid being thrown off while sleeping. When a wagon became stuck in a hole or in the mire, horses and men strained together to free it, and if that failed, troupes put any elephants owned by the show to work at the same task. At the base of steep hills, teamsters awakened the showmen and musicians so they could walk up the grade to relieve the burden on the laboring horses. All of this nocturnal activity meant that circus men slept only a couple hours a night, leaving all hands, in the words of M. B. Leavitt, "pretty well fagged out." No wonder Gil Robinson wrote that although there was a "glamour" surrounding the showman's life, "the circus people were often a sorry sight," exhausted and dirty after the trip between towns.[24]

Upon arrival at its destination, the caravan (other than the tent wagon, which continued on to the circus lot) halted at the outskirts of the community so the performers could make their horses, their wagons, and themselves presentable for the morning procession through town. Appearance mattered because while posters nailed to fences and barns could bring crowds of people into town, a pitiful display of exhausted steeds, battered wagons, and mud-splattered costumes encouraged few people to actually spend their money on admission.[25]

Parades commenced in the late morning. A trumpet blast heralding the appearance of the pageant interrupted the chatter and laughter of the crowd, the grunt and squeal of domestic animals, and the squeak and clatter of clapboard wagons. A bandwagon full of musicians followed behind the mounted trumpeter, their melodies competing with the cheers of the crowd as the procession rolled into town. Robinson and Eldred's Grand New York Circus transported its musicians on "a beautifully gilded chariot" pulled by "20 perfectly matched Cream horses, dressed in most superb style—the harness being plated with the richest silver plating." The best of these bands consisted of skilled musicians playing the most up-to-date compositions. In 1847, Stone and McCollum's Mammoth Great Western Circus signaled its arrival in Georgia towns with a fourteen-piece brass band comprised of musicians from "the Orchestras of the St. Charles, American and French Theaters, New Orleans." Bandmaster H. K. Gaul led his performers through "a varied and beautiful selection from the latest Operas of the day."[26]

The rest of the parade could include everything from male, female, and child performers on horseback to grander displays, like the Stone and McCollum's parade in Columbus that featured "near one hundred and fifty persons and horses, and twenty five gorgeous carriages." This "Grand Traveling Cavalcade," the proprietors promised, "with the beauty of the steeds and their caparisons, and the splendor of the trappings, will present in procession the most extensive and imposing spectacle ever witnessed on this continent." The show's animal cages brought up the rear, some open to reveal their untamed occupants, and others closed to encourage parade watchers to pay to see what awaited inside. All in all, such processions made for a striking and memorable experience, especially in sleepy towns and hamlets where little changed from day to day. When everything went well, a procession turned paráde-watchers into circus-goers as people fell in behind the last wagon and followed the concern to the show grounds. The parade over, the performers headed for the hotel to rest while the ticket agent opened his wagon for business.[27]

If the show offered a separate menagerie exhibit rather than a matinee circus performance, genteel and religious citizens interested in viewing the animals alone entered the tent in the afternoon. One traveling company informed the residents of Columbus, Georgia in 1834 that they could gain "admittance to see the animals during the day" for a quarter, while the "Animals and Circus" could be "seen at one and the same time" at night for fifty cents. In between the outside wall of the canvas round top and the bleachers that faced the ring, showmen arrayed their animal wagons, allowing visitors to walk from cage to cage at their leisure. Their examinations complete, they exited the tent, allowing the show's roustabouts to make any final preparations for the nighttime circus performance.[28]

As evening arrived, a throng, not unlike those that formed in southern towns on militia muster and hanging days, crowded around the ticket wagon that stood outside of the entrance to the show's tent. On or near the lot also stood the wooden stands erected by "camp followers": peddlers who trailed but were not connected to the circus itself. These individuals sold victuals and beverages, ran gambling operations, and sometimes offered other exhibits of oddities, making them the forerunners of late nineteenth-century circus sideshows. After patrons had secured a ticket and had their fill of these little stands and tents, they crowded in front of the tent flaps, pushing and shoving as they awaited its opening. When the flaps parted, young men and children scooted past slower moving spectators and raced into the tent.[29]

In comparison to the monstrous pavilions of later years, an antebellum circus tent was an intimate enclosure. The Barnum and Bailey Circus, for instance, raised a five-hundred-foot-long oval tent on its 1892 tour that seated approximately fourteen thousand people. In contrast, the average antebellum tent was round, measured one hundred feet in diameter, and held about two thousand people. Regardless of its size, the center of an antebellum tent held the standardized forty-foot-diameter circus ring.[30]

Circuses attracted customers from all stations of southern society. Leading citizens, especially in cities and large towns, came out for these shows. In Natchez, Mississippi, William Johnson recorded in his diary that "the Circus was in Performance and a Greate many of Our first Familys were thare with there Children. Aristocracy with Beauty and intelegence a plenty was thare." Most members of a Louisiana planter family patronized a circus in the town of Natchitoches in 1851, along with numerous "madams accompanied by their husbands and . . . young belles by their beaux." Yeoman farmers, along with their children, also attended circuses, as did poor whites. In 1836, P. T. Barnum stood in a tent in Georgia and watched it fill with "poor, thin, sallow-faced" women and a "pale, haggard set of uncombed, uncouth" men. Much to Barnum's disgust, nearly every male and female patron took great pleasure in variously smoking, dipping, or chewing tobacco as they watched the show.[31]

African Americans, both free and enslaved, joined whites at these shows. William Johnson, a free black barber, wrote in 1850 that he "was at the Circus to night and tis the Best performance of the Kind that I have seen for a long time if Ever." In the eighteenth century, George Washington allowed his bondsmen to attend a circus performance. Slaves continued to attend circuses in the antebellum years. Kentucky ex-slave William Emmons told a WPA interviewer that "we wuz let go to shows when dey come to Carlisle. I [re]member goin' to see Dan Rice's Circus dat use to come." Other slaves went to shows in the company of their masters. The circus vernacular of the time referred to this category of customers as "attending servants."[32]

These different groups all needed to be situated within the tight quarters of the tent. Consequently, circuses offered special reserved seats for middling and elite gentlemen, their wives or female family members, and their children for a charge of fifty cents per seat. The New York Circus reassured the better citizens of Columbus that "a portion of the boxes will be expressly reserved for the accommodation of those attending with ladies and families." Stone and McCollum's managers offered further security in the form of "ushers in attendance to wait on Ladies and family parties to seats." In addition to seating elites, ushers had the job of barring "unescorted women," or prostitutes, from the tent. Toward that end, Stone and McCollum announced in its advertising material, "No Ladies admitted unattended by gentlemen." Because of this stigma, respectable women rarely, if ever, attended circuses without male companionship before the Civil War.[33]

For twenty-five cents, lower-class white men, African Americans, street urchins, and the occasional prostitute could watch the show while standing in the "pit," the part of the tent that lacked seats. Most commonly, the pit was segregated, with whites on one side and blacks on the other. In 1823, a circus playing Savannah informed the public that it offered "seats on left hand side of pit for persons of color." Other shows reserved the pit entirely for black people. Regardless, Stuart Thayer explains that in that space,

> one either stood or sat on the ground. It was the practice to bring food and drink.... The pit audience ate, drank, cracked walnuts; they walked about, conversed, conducted business, there being nothing to confine them as seats do today. They were not above commenting loudly on the performance, the music and each other.

A description of an Atlanta circus audience provides a sense of the clientele confined to this part of the tent: "A fair specimen of Young America might have been seen at the circus on Saturday night last, two boys 8 or 10 years old, with high heeled boot[s] on, and a cigar in each of their mouths, puffing away at a 2:40 rate, before a large concourse of people, assuming an attitude of 'we are some pumpkins'—get out of the way old folks." Circuses would continue to provide spectator areas segmented by class and color well into the twentieth century.[34]

The band's opening overture interrupted the milling about in the pit and the talking in the bleachers. Although in the 1820s music was provided by a solo fiddler or hand organist, by the 1830s most sizable shows carried ten-piece or larger brass bands. A typical orchestra might consist of three clarinets, two horns, two trombones, a bugle, a serpent (a wind instrument), and percussion consisting of drums and cymbals. Bands of this size probably represented the biggest groups of instrumentalists that most small-town people ever heard or saw.[35]

The "grand entrée" appeared against this musical backdrop. Robinson and Eldred's Grand New York Circus described its opening pageant as being "headed by the Ladies, [it] will be ridden upon a great number of... Horses and Ponies—the dresses of the riders of a brilliant description, and the steeds most richly caparisoned, producing so gorgeous a spectacle, that the beholder is irresistibly carried back to the fanciful days of Aladdin and his wonderful Lamp." Other opening pageants of the era centered on displays of military drill, which certainly found receptive audiences among martial-minded southerners.[36]

A demonstration of acrobatics and tumbling typically followed the grand entrée. In 1850, Jerome Bachler of the Great Western Circus entertained Georgians with "Tremendous Somersets" through "Hoops of Daggers, Balloons on Fire, at the height of 12 and 15 feet from the ground, and lastly, his wonderful leap and somerset over a number of horses." (In the circus parlance of the time, a "balloon" denoted a hoop covered with paper.) To slowly build excitement in the tent, this act generally opened with five horses placed abreast in between a ramp and a landing area. After each successful attempt by a leaper with the troupe, a handler added an additional horse. If the circus included an elephant, the star athlete carried out the final leap and somersaulted over it and ten or so horses. This concluding jump featured a dramatic announcement by the ringmaster, adjustments of the horses as per the instructions of the leaper, then finally, a drum roll as the athlete sprinted toward the gap and flew into the air, his somersaults marked by the thump of a bass drum. "Still vaulting," or ground tumbling, was another popular gymnastic act. The vaulter entered the ring and proceeded to turn long series of backward somersaults. Robert Sherwood personally witnessed one star athlete turn eighty-nine consecutive somersaults. These kinds of athletic performances won favor among male southerners, who engaged in their own physical recreations in their leisure time.[37]

After all of the vaulting and tumbling acts came the first of the formal equestrian programs. Until the very end of the nineteenth century, equestrianism remained the centerpiece of circus performances. Americans of this era depended on horsepower for their transportation needs, but in the South, the vast majority of auditors had logged many an hour in the saddle rather than in a wagon or buggy. A "lack of good roads," William McPherson notes, "had compelled Southerners to ride from childhood, while most Northerners traveled on wheels *drawn* by horses." In the South, therefore, circus riders needed to impress audiences filled with experienced horsemen and horsewomen.[38]

One way to amaze such crowds was with child and female equestrians. At a time when children began laboring at a tender age, youths under ten years of age performing stunts garnered interest for their prodigy, not for their novelty. Georgians who visited the tent of the Welch, Nathans and Company's National Circus in 1851 enjoyed the performance of the "Infantile Equestrian" Emma Nathans, "whose daring feats startle and astonish all spectators, and the audience is kept in a thrill of fear as she bounds around the Ring, supporting her balance equal to a veteran rider, and performs her Poses and Equitations with an ease and grace which would put to blush practitioners of maturer years." Circuses would feature child stars throughout the nineteenth century and early twentieth century.[39]

Female riders, who raised as many eyebrows for their incredible feats on horseback as they did for their immodest dress, also had a featured role in the program. As early as 1833, a circus that visited the South gave top billing to a Mrs. Sizer, "the intrepid Female Equestrian." Like southern men, southern females were not easily impressed by feats of horsemanship. Women who rode frequently had personal experience with challenging riding since they depended "completely on their skill in balancing in a sidesaddle" rather than riding astride, as men did. Nevertheless, the equestrian abilities of female circus riders still amazed crowds. In 1856, a Columbus audience of men and women regaled a female rider with "great applause" for the "skill and agility" she demonstrated on horseback.[40]

Along with an appreciation for fine riding, southerners enjoyed watching ring equestrianism because it harmonized with their own recreational activities. Elite southern men enjoyed fox hunting, a demanding sport that called on riders to gallop after their prey through thickets, swamps, and ravines. For the less privileged, the sport of "gander pulling" offered males the chance to compete on horseback. Within an earthen circle, three men vied for the honor of being the first to separate a live goose's head from its body as the ill-fated animal struggled to free its feet from a cord connected to a pole. Before the match, the goose's neck was greased, making a firm grip difficult to achieve. Historian Frank L. Owsley writes that "to seize and hold the gander's slippery neck with three horses cavorting madly and three men reaching out at about the same time to grasp that neck was a supreme test of equestrian skill and co-ordination of hand and eye."[41]

Male equestrians, who followed female and child riders on the typical program, made their own demonstrations of balance and coordination on horseback. The most famous of antebellum riders was James Robinson. His act consisted of him "turning back summersets upon his bare back mare at full speed, flying backwards through balloons, striking attitudes on her at full speed . . . and performing a vast number of incomprehensible feats, which must be seen to be appreciated and believed." The best male bareback riders often received top billing on a circus program, and accordingly received the highest pay.[42]

Another popular equestrian act, Roman riding, made use of multiple mounts controlled by a single horseman. These performances involved a rider standing with his or her feet on the backs of unsaddled horses as they moved abreast around the ring. The founder, owner, and namesake of the John Robinson Circus performed a four-horse act of this variety that demonstrated his "dexterous management" of a team of supposedly "untameable steeds." Beyond the riding talent needed to pull off such a feat, his routine also helps illuminate why some religious southerners took offense to the circus. His son Gil Robinson explains that "Father's principal contribution to the circus performance . . . was a four-horse riding act. He appeared in a costume designed to make him look like the Devil. As he was billed as the 'Bottle Imp,' he wore skin-fitting tights of a dark-green color, enormous owl-like wings, talons or claws extending beyond his fingers and toes, a curling tail that ended in a spike, and a blood-red mask, surmounted by a vicious looking horn. In the midst of an accompaniment of stage thunder, blue lights, clanging brasses, and the roll of drums, he would dash into the ring astride four coal black horses." Gil Robinson confirms that this act made a significant impression on spectators, especially among the "ignorant" and "superstitious" in the audience.[43]

In between the equestrian performances, the clown took center stage to fill time as riders rested or prepared for their next act. Appearing in a striped outfit and whiteface, he sang songs, told jokes, conversed with the audience, and exchanged witty repartee with the ringmaster, who sported a whip and wore the traditional equestrian garb of a riding coat and leather boots.[44]

Antebellum clowning depended upon audience interaction. Unlike actors in theatrical exhibitions, clowns worked to efface the boundary between performer and spectator rather than trying to maintain it in an effort to keep order. One way that clowns engaged crowds was by poking fun at audience members. Circus historian David Carlyon relates this exchange between Dan Rice and an audience member inside a New Orleans tent: "Now, ladies and gentlemen, old and young, black and colored! [Ha! Ha! Ha! From a darkey in the pit] What are you?—Molasses colored gentleman? [Laughter and cries of Go on! Go on!]" A second way that clowns sought to connect with their audience was by joking about local events in an effort to give each performance a more intimate and personal feel. One experienced clown wrote, "I made haste, as soon as I reached a town, to get a local newspaper, find out what was going on, and then I made a reference to it in my clowning. It never failed to please the spectators." A third method involved mocking important local personages, such as politicians, and, in a more self-serving effort, complementing community businesses that the circus owed money for services rendered.[45]

The clown also spent his time sparring with the ringmaster. One stock exchange between legendary antebellum clown Dan Rice and his ringmaster went as follows:

> *Ring Master:* You are rude, and I feel that all my instruction is lost upon you.
> *Rice:* What have I done?
> *Ring Master:* You appear better fed than taught.
> *Rice:* Yes I feed myself, and you teach me. (Rice begins to exit [the ring], when the ringmaster pulled him back.)
> *Ring Master:* Remember, sir, I never follow a fool.
> *Rice:* All right, Master, I'm not so particular about it. I will.

When well delivered, verbal jesting like this always brought forth peals of laughter from the crowd. Humor in the Old South was transmitted mainly through speech, reflecting the strong oral orientation of the region's culture, and a funny sketch was always appreciated inside circus tents.[46]

Some observers suggested, however, that African Americans enjoyed clowning more than any other contingent under the canvas. After a night at Bailey and Company's circus, a west Georgia reporter wrote in 1858 that "the representation from Ethiopia was large and full, and were highly pleased with the performance, if we are to judge by the loud guffaws which greeted the funny man of the Circus."[47]

While white southerners would credit the "natural" frivolity of African Americans for this kind of enthusiastic response, in fact, African Americans enjoyed clown humor because they admired its verbal dexterity and appreciated its strong antiauthoritarian flavor. Before the Civil War, over 90 percent of black southerners were illiterate, making facility with the spoken word of great value in slave society. The clown's ability to come out on top after sparring with audience members, but especially with the white ringmaster, drew the approval of black patrons. With his haughty demeanor, formal dress, and bullwhip, the ringmaster signified authority and power within the circus ring. Slaves watching the exchanges between the lowly clown and the ring "master" could hardly have missed the parallels for their own existence.[48]

Reflecting the masculine character of the antebellum circus, clowns also produced laughs with jokes concerning women and their sexual habits. "Old maids," Robert Sherwood wrote, "were a target for at least seventy-five per cent of all the humorous dialogue between ringmaster and clown." Many of these jokes offered comparisons between the romantic proclivities of unmarried, married, and elderly ladies. The ubiquity of this subject matter is reflected in an 1858 account of the clowning at Bailey and Company's circus: "The ladies, as is usual, came in for the largest share of caricature." Females who attended antebellum circuses had to be prepared to endure dialogue that centered on their foibles.[49]

Not surprisingly, no verbatim accounts of the most salacious clown witticisms turn up in newspapers or diaries from the time. Still, Dan Rice biographer David Carlyon believes that the following was probably representative of a clown's "spicier fare." A newlywed bride "suggested that her husband stay in bed and rest a little. 'No,' he replied, 'I'll get up and rest a little.'" Wordplay of this nature, complete with a ribald gesture or two, was sure to bring an explosion of jeers and snickers from the pit while causing more than a slight blush on the cheeks of the ladies in the bleachers. Circuses continually promised that they would exclude "everything immoral or objectionable," but like the revealing dress of their riders, these jokes did challenge the social propriety of the day, encouraging large contingents of respectable ladies and religious citizens to shun tented exhibitions.[50]

A closing act that encapsulates the antebellum circus's ethos of interaction between audience and performer was the famous "countryman" or drunken rider routine. Robinson and Eldred's advertising claimed that their version of this "extraordinary metamorphose" act would produce "mirth" and "delight" among all who witnessed it. But more than any one circus troupe or performer, it was Mark Twain who immortalized this act for later generations. In *Huckleberry Finn*, Huck stands at the circus and watches as an apparently drunken farmer "tried to get into the ring—said he wanted to ride; said he could ride as well as anybody that ever was." After the crowd strenuously protests this interruption, the ringmaster "made a little speech, and said he hoped there wouldn't be no disturbance, and if the man would promise he wouldn't make no more trouble he would let him ride, if he thought he could stay on the horse. So everybody laughed and said all right, and the man got on." At first, the drunkard struggles to stay on the horse, but soon he stands erect on its back, "a-sailing around as easy and comfortable as if he warn't ever drunk in his life—and then he begun to pull off his clothes and sling them. He shed them so thick they kind of clogged up the air, and altogether he shed seventeen suits" until he reached the spangled tights that ultimately revealed that he was actually a member of the troupe, bringing the act, and the show, to a triumphant end.[51]

While individuals of all classes and colors attended the circus in the Old South, this fact should not be interpreted as evidence that opposition to the circus was insignificant during this time. In fact, many respectable women, evangelicals, and middle-class men absolutely refused to frequent an entertainment that they considered scandalously immoral. Certainly, for every individual that turned out for the show, another person remained at home rather than patronize an exhibition "offensive to both taste and morality."[52]

A vocal contingent of religious and secular leaders supported the views of these individuals by seizing every opportunity to denounce the circus. Protestant ministers took the lead in heaping obloquy on showmen and their entertainment product. Nineteenth-century Methodist, Presbyterian, and Baptist doctrine held that true Christians should eschew the circus, along with all other "worldly amusements," and accordingly, church authorities made clear that going to such shows was a sinful act. For instance, the Baptist church of LaGrange, Georgia announced in 1857 that attending the circus or other "popular amusements," was "unchristian and immoral," and "inconsistent with Gospel order." In short, if an entertainment "had no natural connection with religion," evangelical church members should avoid it.[53]

Along those lines, Presbyterian minister Thomas T. Skillman of Lexington, Kentucky lambasted an 1831 appearance of J. Purdy Brown's New York Circus in the pages of his weekly, the *Western Luminary*. He opened his attack by accusing the men and women of the show of having the "loosest morals" and of being criminals on the lam who now made their living by "preying on the community, deluding the ignorant and unwary." Yet Skillman also took aim at the spiritually minded residents of Lexington for tolerating such a cancer in their midst. "While we write," he proclaimed, "we blush for the morals of a Christian community that is willing to foster and cherish in its bosom an institution so corrupting and demoralizing. Where has virtue fled? Where is the morality, the philanthropy, the benevolence of our citizens?"[54]

During the antebellum years, such ministerial calls for the faithful to reject circuses would increasingly fall on deaf ears. If the lamentations of pastoral and lay authorities are to be believed, some well-to-do Protestant church members increasingly disregarded the intense anticircus rhetoric emanating from their leaders and turned out in growing numbers for the entertainment, a trend that seems to have accelerated in the 1840s and 1850s. Religious leaders believed that this mounting interest in "fashionable amusements" stemmed from wealth and worldliness, a poisonous combination that encouraged some to place social priorities over religious ones. Still, the number of antebellum evangelicals who went to the circus was probably a small, albeit highly visible and apparently growing, minority of southern church members.[55]

Leaders of higher education also worked to exclude circuses from their communities, and if that failed, they tried, with limited success, to keep their charges away from them. In 1848, the administration of Franklin College in Athens, Georgia "promptly & unanimously rejected" the request by a circus to raise their tent on school property. A year later, another circus was unceremoniously ejected from a campus lot after it tried to show without the school's permission. The faculty also barred its students from attending circuses. Some Athens scholars skirted this prohibition by blacking their faces and mixing in with the slaves in the pit, a scheme that did not fool the irate members of the college administration. Other educational institutions set down the same rule for their students. In 1857, the Georgia Military Institute expelled thirty cadets who attended G. N. Eldred's Great Southern Show.[56]

Notwithstanding these transgressions by the young, a goodly number of middle-class southerners joined evangelicals in their dislike for circuses. After an 1859 visit to the John Robinson Circus, North Carolina yeoman farmer Basil Armstrong Thomasson recorded in his diary that he "left before the close" because "it was mostly an exhibition of nonsense, very wicked and very disgusting." From that point forward, he "resolved to attend no more such shows." In 1846, a Virginia schoolteacher avoided a "wild animals circus" because he did not believe that such exhibitions bettered "the mind or the morals of a community." On Circus Day, an Alabama farmer complained that "the whole country is out for the circus, it is a damage to the county by taking out a large amt of money, neglect of farm labor and in its demoralizing effect."[57]

While some southern ladies did accompany their husbands to the circus, the strenuous efforts of showmen to solicit the patronage of women makes clear that many females steered clear of the entertainment when these traveling concerns came to town. The Stone and McCollum Circus sought to encourage female attendance by advertising in Georgia that "no word or action that would tend to cause a tint on the most modest cheek will be allowed within the ring." In another sign of women's unease with circus attendance, showmen tried to make such invitations more attractive through incessant promises of solicitous ushers and proper seating for ladies. These pleas demonstrate that showmen, unlike local theater owners, faced difficulties in convincing southern women that they would be contented and safe inside of an unfamiliar canvas tent staffed by total strangers. This also helps to explain why some southern women felt comfortable going to their local theater without male accompaniment, while few of them chose to go to the circus without a male escort. Finally, the female-focused humor of the clown, whether sexual or chaste, made for an atmosphere that must have made some ladies uncomfortable. In sum, while the majority of the southern people held attitudes toward the circus that ranged from indifference to enthusiasm, a sizeable minority—including church members, middle-class southerners, and respectable women—demonstrated their agreement with the anticircus views of religious and educational leaders by staying outside of circus pavilions.[58]

Another key reason why many southerners disliked circuses had little to do with entertainment content, seating, or staffing. Numerous observers drew attention to the fact that circuses fostered a general sense of disorder wherever they paraded and showed. Skillman provides the fullest portrait of this extracurricular activity and its effects on a community, and his vivid descriptions merit close study. After haranguing Brown's troupe and those Lexington Christians who did nothing to challenge its presence, Skillman complained of the broader social evils that circuses produced. He began by noting that Brown put up his tent not in a deserted field outside of Lexington, but right in town, in propinquity to the "dwellings of respectable citizens." These unfortunate homeowners endured daily parades by mounted performers, marked by "the sound of the trumpet." The show's public displays attracted "an immense concourse of boys and Negroes who follow after them, shouting with all the seeming power of their lungs." Before long, "servants are drawn from their work by these demonstrations and little children to the manifest danger of their limbs all rush after the procession." As the pageant, and the mob that followed, moved down the street, crowd members imposed upon the most delicate of pedestrians: "If a lady happens to be walking the street when the motley throng make their appearance, she must either make a precipitate retreat into the first house that offers or consent to be borne along with the excited rabble." Upon arrival at the circus lot, the aggregation grew through the addition of "slaves employed in the different bagging factories," persons that Skillman, and certainly many others in the community, thought had no business patronizing a circus.[59]

After all paying customers had squeezed into the tent, local residents suffered through a night of disorder and disturbance. The music and drumming that entertained those in the enclosure could be "heard over the greater part of the town" while "the boisterous, vulgar shouting and stamping of the excited and apparently highly gratified spectators" reverberated through the streets. For the "immense crowd of Negroes and white boys" who could not afford admission but enjoyed hanging around outside of the tent, the time during the performance was passed by the "occasional discharge of rockets and firearms" which contributed to this "unparalleled scene of uproar and confusion."

Even after the show concluded, many rowdy circus goers believed that evening's festivities should not yet come to an end. Skillman reported that "many of the individuals composing the audience, excited by the scenes they had just been witnessing, and probably in the case of some by the spirituous liquor drunk there . . . march through the streets with the sound of the drum," on their way to the "various tippling houses" located in the area, where they will "spend the greater part of the night in carousal." Taken as a whole, then, a night at the circus promoted "idleness, intemperate drinking, profanity, a taste for low company, [and] boisterous vulgarity." Religious elites like Skillman believed that no respectable and religious person would be caught dead anywhere near a circus.[60]

But southerners who did attend the circus did sometimes end up dead. The disorder that Skillman denounced sometimes escalated from noisy celebration to bloody confrontations between circus workers and local toughs. These brawls erupted with uncomfortable frequency in the early- to mid-nineteenth century. One circus man claimed that while on tour before the Civil War, troupes "used to have a fight with the 'rubes' two or three times a week." Geographically speaking, industrial and mining communities of the Old Northwest represented some of the more hazardous places for circuses to play. But the southern propensity for murderous violence gave the South a singular reputation for extreme danger. "As a general thing," one longtime circus employee recalled in 1882, "in the Middle and New England States sticks, stones and fists were the weapons and few men were killed, but down South, where its [sic] a knife or a gun, things were different. There has been many a man buried [on southern circus lots]."[61]

The catalysts for these violent incidents were numerous and varied, but the most salient causes included aggressive masculinity, the ubiquity of firearms, and the generous consumption of spirits. One circus man pointed out that "the Southern States generally yield good profits, but the crowds are more disorderly, often, than in any other section of the country. Guns protrude from many pockets and their owners are eager for a chance to brandish or discharge them. Inflamed by whiskey, these circus visitors are a constant menace to life and property." With bellies full of fire, armed southern men staggered up to the tent and demanded free admission. One old veteran told the *Chicago Times* that "it takes a man of nerve to attend a circus door, especially in the South." In 1838, a drunken man in St. Francisville, Louisiana wounded P. T. Barnum after the famous showman stopped him from entering his tent without a ticket. Once inside, troublemakers might attempt to cut the side ropes and bring the tent down. Other besotted rowdies sought to disrupt circus acts by throwing objects at performers. An incident of this type took place in Taylor's Bridge, North Carolina in 1851, bringing the show to a halt, and sparking a brawl between circus personnel and local ruffians that resulted in the death of one fighting patron.[62]

Of course, violent and uproarious behavior that spilled beyond the confines of the entertainment space proper was not exclusive to the circus; in particular, the antebellum period featured a number of public disturbances surrounding the theater, including New York's infamous and bloody Astor Place Riot of 1849. Richard Butsch notes that during these disturbances "working class [theater] crowds typically cast themselves as defenders against some insult or attack." As a result, these battles often pitted local theatergoers against the community "outsiders," or showmen.[63]

Butsch's point is particularly helpful in further illuminating the roots of circus violence. Although alcohol mixed with hot blood prompted local brawlers to battle circus men, the money-stealing tactics of circuses also drove southern men to attack show employees. P. T. Barnum wrote that circus workers included "a following of card sharpers, pickpockets, and swindlers generally, who were countenanced by some of the circus proprietors, with whom they shared their ill gotten gains." Another authority agreed in pointing out that these confidence men "traveled with the circus and kept in the favor of the fighters with the show by giving them a share of the money they would take away from the countrymen. When the fleeced native would insist on a return of his money, he would be met with the whole fighting force of the company." Southern men who turned out for circuses, like their counterparts in the North who attended the theater, reacted with violence against circus "outsiders" when they felt wronged.[64]

Showmen, then, like antebellum theater managers in the North, suffered through a contemporaneous period in which disorderly audiences sometimes attempted to seize control of their entertainment spaces. Yet circus audiences never achieved the hegemony that theatrical audiences did when they tore up the inside of theaters or attacked actors. This difference partly stems from the fact that theatrical impresarios simply did not respond to violence with violence. Indeed, a barrage of hurled objects and jeers by spectators often went unanswered by the staffs of theaters. Sometimes even police departments refrained from interfering with these disruptions, thereby "respecting public sentiment and the rights of audiences to declare its will."[65]

In decided contrast, circus men apparently made it a point of principle to aggressively confront disorder and violence, largely because as outsiders in unfamiliar communities far away from their homes, they had no choice but to fight when conflict erupted. As a retired circus man explained, "as soon as it commences they seize [the] first weapon that they can and fight as bull-dogs fight. No run there. They have to stay. If they run they are simply going away from home and assistance." In the late nineteenth century, circus veterans recounted the details of these brawls with a sense of pride. In 1882, one retired showman enumerated approximately thirty-five American communities where memorable battles had occurred over the years. Thus the crowds of rowdies that sought to disrupt circus performances never enjoyed a period of "audience sovereignty" as their counterparts who attended the theater in the North did from about 1825 through 1850.[66]

Sometimes, however, southern bullies targeted showmen just for sport. Historian Elliott Gorn has demonstrated that "rough and tumble fighting" between southern men of the lower orders was both highly ritualistic and deeply intertwined with the social and cultural life of the region. Similarly, John Hope Franklin has noted that antebellum southern communities contained local "champion" fighters, ever prepared to take on all challengers, especially during public celebrations like Election Day or the Fourth of July. The appearance of a circus tent, with its similar air of social release, represented an ideal occasion for the leading brawlers to test their mettle against new contenders, namely circus roustabouts.[67]

The new competition often proved stiff. Circus workers were hard, muscular men who made a living swinging sledgehammers six days a week. One animal trainer remembered that the workers with his show were "a husky lot, those fellows who took down the tents and watched around them. Six-footers mostly, broad-shouldered and heavy in proportion, with muscles that laughed at an eighteen pound sledge." In addition to being strong, many circus workers embraced a rough and tumble way of life. One performer called the laborers with his circus "a wicked set" and doubted whether there was any crime "that some of them had not been guilty of." Even circus performers stood ready to mix it up at any time. According to Gil Robinson, the entertainers were "expected to combine with their cleverness as riders, tumblers, or trapezists, the ability to fight hard." This union of pugilistic performers and workers meant that southern men often squared off against their equals in hand-to-hand combat.[68]

In many ways, this ritualistic violence was in harmony with the antebellum circus as a genre. At its core, the circus was a vigorous, physical, rough, and ribald entertainment that privileged body over mind. Although circus owners of the day might have believed otherwise, it did not constitute a cerebral diversion, which made it perfectly suited for the largely anti-intellectual populace of the South. Black and white men attended these shows to see athletes perform acts and stunts on horseback that even the most gifted local riders could not pull off and to hear jokes that took aim at female foibles or local personages of power. They also bought tickets to view more female flesh than was ever on display in southern communities. Women, too, entered circus enclosures to see such performances, but the fact that unaccompanied females rarely attended these shows without men makes clear that unlike the theater, the circus tent was very much a masculine domain.

This masculinity extended outside of the tent when circus men engaged local southern men in violent contests. While blood was spilled and men did lose their lives in these prewar southern encounters, ultimately the defining spirit of circus brawling remained as much about sport as it did about mortal combat. Right after the war, however, circus fighting would take on a new and much more savage character. Once southerners began seeing showmen not as outsiders, but as *Yankee* outsiders, violence at circuses intensified and became much more deadly. The perception of showmen as Yankees also promised to damage business prospects in the southern market. The response of showmen to the new realities of postwar trouping is the subject of the next chapter.

> It is a showman's place to supply what the public wants.
> —George Middleton, *Circus Memoirs*

Selling Southernism
Showmen in Georgia, 1865–1874

The evening air felt cool on clown Dan Castello's face as he dashed midperformance from the tent of S. B. Howe's Circus and entered the crowded streets of Columbus, Georgia on November 10, 1865. Heads turned to watch this costumed man race off in the direction of the city's United States Army command post. Reaching his destination, Castello burst into the military facility and immediately demanded an American flag, of all things, from the surprised officers. After repeated entreaties, he finally secured an "insignificant little flag" and ran back into the circus pavilion. In full view of the audience, Castello, who doubled as the show's manager, immediately raised the standard up the center pole and into the rigging at the top of the enclosure.

His task complete, he fixed his eyes on the groups of Union soldiers in the stands. With their faces registering approval, they slowly removed their hands from inside of their tunics. Simultaneously, the large contingent of southerners in the audience glared in disgust at the symbol of their defeat that now dangled from the rigging. Castello breathed a sigh of relief, retreated away from the tent pole, and resumed his performance.[1]

Castello's mad dash for the colors did not reflect a sudden surge of patriotism or a desire to humiliate his southern audience. In actuality, Castello simply sought to preserve the peace inside his tent. Just before the start of the show, he ascertained that almost all of the soldiers who had bought tickets had secreted lengths of wood under their coats that they planned to use to ignite the tent. Unbeknownst to the show manager, the name of his outfit had appeared insufficiently patriotic to Macon's military commander, especially when compared to another troupe in the vicinity, the Thayer and Noyes' United States Circus. Indignant at the Castello show's failure to pay tribute to Union victory, the officer telegraphed to troops in Columbus that the "European" circus "should not exhibit unless under the old stars and stripes." At the same time, the "firm Union men" of the Thayer circus had deviously passed word to Columbus' military contingent that Castello was a "rebel." Despite these efforts to sabotage his show, Castello successfully averted danger on this night.[2]

In the immediate aftermath of the Civil War, southerners and northerners in Georgia viewed circus men and their shows through a political lens. In the eyes of southerners, circus men were no longer just itinerant entertainers. They saw them as arrogant and money-grabbing Yankees, men worthy of contempt, suspicion, and hostility. Likewise, the enterprises they headed no longer appeared as mere frivolous amusements. To many, they now represented northern interests and Union victory. At the same time, Federal soldiers garrisoned in Georgia's towns and cities harbored suspicions about the political loyalties of circus men. After being absent from Georgia (and much of the South) for the duration of the war, showmen who toured these places in the fall of 1865 needed to walk a tightrope between paying homage to the nation and to the South in their public interactions.

By 1866, however, circus men had begun to lean to the southern side of this divide by making naked appeals to the native populace. They did so in three ways. First, showmen featured ring performances that offered both seemingly earnest and truly humorous tributes to the southern cause and the wartime sacrifices of Confederate soldiers. Second, they abandoned their nationalistic titles in favor of sectional names like "Great Southern" or "New Orleans." While some of these shows had legitimate ties to the South, most were northern operations that simply adopted southern-sounding names, thus following in the long circus tradition of stretching the truth, better known as "humbug." Finally, showmen began spotlighting the southern members of their troupes. In contrast to the use of southern show names, in almost all cases these performers were in fact native sons of Dixie.

This gravitation toward southern interests and themes stemmed from several factors. Circus men quickly learned that in contrast to the severe reactions of Union soldiers and officials in Columbus, few, if any, northerners in the state took umbrage at a circus's name or entertainment content after 1865. In addition, paying tribute to the South paid off at the box office, as evidenced by the fact that veteran, business-savvy circus owners utilized this southern strategy to one extent or another for several years. But most of all, the embrace of regionalism grew out of self-preservation. Showmen discovered that when they performed outside of towns and cities occupied by Union troops, they frequently came under attack from embittered former Confederates for their perceived connections to the North. In light of the violent encounters between rural southerners and showmen during the antebellum period, it is not surprising that circus men chose to give their shows a patina of "southernism."

It is tempting to link this shift toward sectionalism with the postwar southern effort to commemorate and sanctify the Confederate quest for a separate nation. Although it is true that a handful of the showmen who proclaimed their love of Dixie were in fact southern, the vast majority of the men who promulgated this regional message were Yankees, and therefore had little interest in the failed dream of southern nationalism. Unsurprisingly, these northern showmen acted not out of a noble or romantic attachment to the Lost Cause, but rather out of their desire to achieve business success and peaceable interactions when they toured the South. Still, these less than high-minded motivations do not diminish the fact that this campaign transmitted messages of southern cultural superiority to the people of the South in the wake of their overwhelming defeat on the battlefield, giving one key segment of southern popular culture a decidedly regional flavor at the height of Reconstruction.[3]

Late antebellum sectional conflict and the war itself had a demonstrable impact on the fortunes and futures of southern-bound circuses. With war looming on the horizon, almost all of the industry's impresarios chose in 1860 and early 1861 to keep their troupes either close to their northern homes or in the western states to avoid being trapped in the South if fighting did break out. In 1860, only the Robinson and Lake and Dan Rice shows played south of the Mason-Dixon line, and in 1861, the Rice outfit was the last circus to appear in the southern states before the shelling of Fort Sumter. It exited the region in early 1861.[4]

Rice's 1861 departure from Dixie, like almost everything he engaged in during his career, was not without controversy. While touring in Louisiana in January, Rice praised the region and its people, telling his audiences that the cause of the sectional conflict was the "fanatical people" of the North. But once the show had moved by riverboat up the Mississippi and back to the North, Rice changed his tune. In Erie, Pennsylvania, in April, he told an assemblage of Union recruits that they would "annihilate treason" and "subdue rebels" once the fighting started.[5]

As Union troops began capturing Confederate territory, circuses followed in their wake. Since overland itinerancy during wartime was highly dangerous, shows mostly moved by riverboat. In the late summer of 1863, Union soldiers occupying Vicksburg received a pleasant surprise when a circus arrived and performed in the city. As Union troops moved into Tennessee, showmen raised their tents in that state's urban areas. In November 1863, Lake and Company's circus played Nashville. In October 1864, Dan Castello's circus appeared in Memphis. While intrepid showmen faced the impressment of their animals by the Union Army, the occasional shelling of their tents by Confederate troops, and a handful of assaults by war-hardened Union soldiers, they experienced no significant hostility from natives, thanks to the presence of Union troops in these places.⁶

Lee's surrender at Appomattox fully reopened the southern market to circuses. The first outfits to enter Georgia in more than five years arrived in November 1865, when the Thayer and Noyes Great United States Circus and S. B. Howe's European Circus moved by rail into the state from points north. These two shows would undertake a limited tour of large communities along war-damaged, but operating, rail lines, appearing in the cities of Atlanta, Macon, Augusta, and Columbus. The troupes competed against each other by playing in "opposition," or in the same cities on the same dates.⁷

Both outfits had successful tours of Georgia. Even the provocatively titled Thayer and Noyes United States show experienced only minimal hostility from former Confederates. Although a correspondent to the entertainment weekly the *New York Clipper* claimed that the Thayer and Noyes show had suffered poor attendance in Macon after it flew the Stars and Stripes over its tent "in defiance of all secessionism," the show had a highly favorable stand at its next tour stop in Columbus. According to the *Columbus Sun and Times*, residents attended the show's performances in "very large" numbers and left the pavilion "well pleased" by what they saw. The attendance and reception for the Castello's concern in the same town was equally enthusiastic, with the masses "filling every nook and corner" of the show's tent. All in all, "thousands" crowded into the west Georgia community to see the two outfits. Unlike in Macon, an association with the triumphant Union seemed to matter little in Columbus.⁸

Notwithstanding Castello's memorable difficulties with Columbus' military garrison, there is little evidence that Union military personnel in Georgia looked upon circuses with disfavor. In late December 1865, army officers extended the curfew in Columbus from 9:30 to 10:30 to allow residents to attend the Stone, Rosston, and Murray circus. Unfortunately for the city's circus-goers, the show cancelled after a difficulty in shipping its equipment. A Union officer assigned to the Freedmen's Bureau in Americus wrote nothing more in his diary about a show's appearance in October 1866 than a "circus came to town [and] set nearly everyone crazy." In sum, the military did little to interfere with circuses in Georgia during Reconstruction, and in fact, its presence generally protected circus men when they played in occupied towns and cities.⁹

Showmen had toured Georgia's largest cities and had attracted big crowds, even with American flags flying over their tents. Still, they were under no illusion that strong attendance reflected southern hospitality for Yankee showmen. One animal trainer observed that despite the fact that his show was "popular and well patronized" by southerners during Reconstruction, "they looked on us as 'damned Yankees' and treated us accordingly." While touring the South in 1867, a Dan Castello show representative wrote to the *Clipper* that the show enjoyed good patronage but experienced daily reminders that southerners were "bitter towards the Yankees."[10]

Showmen initially tried to reduce this tension through humor. When funnyman Dan Rice mounted his trick pony in front of southern audiences after the war, he would first tell the animal, "Be careful, sir, Jefferson Davis is riding you." The pony would respond by loping gently around the ring as Rice hammed it up for the crowd. After a minute, the clown would halt the steed and make another proclamation: "Now, General Grant is riding you!" As the pony furiously bucked, the crowd would explode with cheers and laughter, not knowing that the words "be careful" and "now" served as cues to the animal to canter or kick. Rice also did not let on that he reversed the names for northern audiences.[11]

Showmen also offered seemingly sincere tributes to the Confederate cause. Immediately following the conflict, clown Pete Conklin had a circus act with a one-armed male performer. While above the Mason-Dixon line, Conklin realized that the injury might engender great sympathy from northern auditors if they believed that the man had bravely served the Union. This feeling, Conklin hoped, could also translate into increased sales of his songster, a souvenir book of his songs. Even though the man had not fought for the Union, Conklin clothed him in a blue uniform and sent him through northern crowds with an armful of books. Conklin narrated this heartrending scene by asking audience members to dip into their pockets not for him, "but for the benefit of a poor Union soldier who battled for his country" and had "lost his arm."

Conklin's scheme worked so well that he continued it in the South, only now the "soldier" wore Confederate gray and had "fought for no bounty, no pension, fought for the lost cause, [and] was a brave Southern soldier." The persuasive act even took in Robert E. Lee, who bought copies of Conklin's book in Lexington, Virginia. The clever clown felt quite self-satisfied until the concern left the South and headed back to the North to play more shows. After a District of Columbia performance, he heard that a former Confederate colonel had seen that evening's show *and* a show in Virginia and thus knew his secret. Concerned, Conklin met with the officer to determine his intentions. After several minutes of polite conversation, Conklin still feared that the military man planned to reveal his trick. As the color slowly drained from Conklin's face, the colonel smiled and told him not to worry, because "it's a good thing. I'll not say anything. Keep it up."[12]

While these skits entertained and fooled audiences, they did little to calm tensions in smaller and more isolated communities. In these places, the war seemed to have never ended when local men assaulted showmen and their property. Several attacks occurred in 1866 and 1867, bringing back vivid memories of antebellum southern brawls in the minds of circus personnel. Showmen across the nation could read of the latest outrages in the pages of the *Clipper*. In May 1866, the paper reported that about twenty self-styled "Regulators," or "returned rebel soldiers," had boasted that they would not allow the John Robinson Circus to perform in Crittenden County, Kentucky. As the show got underway the mob attempted to storm the Robinson tent but the showmen repelled them with hatchets in a pitched battle that left two Robinson men wounded and one dead. In December of that same year, a large Mississippi mob made good on a threat to attack Mike Lipman's Colossal Combination Circus by firing into the show's train as it left the town of Winona, killing one circus man and wounding another. The show's treasurer concluded in his letter to the *Clipper* that "the only cause that can be assigned for the outrage was that we had some Yankees in our company." In late 1867, the Orton Circus came under attack in Boston, Arkansas by a party of mounted "bushwackers" led by a former Confederate captain named Tom Duke. When the smoke cleared, two of the assailants, including Duke, lay dead and a total of thirteen locals and showmen were wounded. Finally, Dan Rice reaped the whirlwind of his pro-Union views on a Mississippi show lot when an inebriated and armed man screamed the ludicrous charge that the clown had led black troops into battle against the Confederacy, before proceeding to shoot at him. Luckily for Rice, the bullet entered and exited his coat without striking flesh. Without garrisons of Union troops to suppress southern hostility, circuses stood exposed in these isolated areas filled with embittered and aggressive southerners.[13]

Showmen bold or foolhardy enough to display Union symbols in rural areas only intensified the hostility of southerners. During its tour of small towns, one circus eventually abandoned the practice of flying the American flag after it sparked frequent attacks. But in the days before the show unfurled the Stars and Stripes for the last time, southern men would approach the management and ask them to remove the offending banner. If circus personnel refused the request, the men would attempt to take it down by force. Other times, attacks on the flag came "without any warning." Significantly, these mobs of former Confederates included not only local "roughs," but "substantial citizens" and "first class gentleman" as well. In another incident, showmen were at a loss to explain the cause of a fatal riot in Arkansas. Later, as the circus men explained to a northern newsman, they discovered that "the cause of all the trouble was the appearance of our principal clown, who thoughtlessly wore a red, white and blue suit with an American eagle on a shield at his breast." Perhaps naively, these showmen had previously thought of their show as "a Southern institution" because it originated from "a point south of the Ohio river."[14]

As they had in the antebellum era, showmen did their best to prepare for and respond to such assaults. The John Robinson Circus stacked a number of Civil War–era surplus muskets at the entrance of its tent to impress upon troublemakers that show members stood ready to use deadly force. Many of the show's employees carried holsters marked with three-digit numbers to give the impression that the show had hundreds of sidearms. When attacks came, the circus employees nearest to the perpetrators yelled "Hey Rube!"—"the 'S O S' call of the circus"—to alert their compatriots that rowdies threatened the troupe. All unarmed show personnel then made a beeline for the stake wagon, seized tent posts, and threw themselves into the fray. The improvised weapons they wielded, however, were not simple lengths of hickory. Showman W. C. Thompson writes that "the circus man's favorite weapon was the guy stake, a shaft of wood used to support chains and ropes. An iron ring circled one end, the other was pointed enough to penetrate the hardest ground."[15]

Nonetheless, such measures offered no real remedy for the rash of postwar depredations. Despite its very visible arsenal, the Robinson show came under attack from rural southerners several times during Reconstruction. Law enforcement personnel in these areas often did (or could do) next to nothing to protect showmen. Thompson remembered that "circuses expected and received little or no help from supine or frightened police, and learned to fight their own battles." The mortal dangers of such incidents aside, riots hurt business. Nothing scattered a crowd of customers more quickly than a mob of men shooting, stabbing, and bludgeoning each other. Clearly, showmen needed a more effective method of subduing southern audiences. This was not just a matter of profit but self-protection as well.[16]

Ultimately, showmen sought to obviate these assaults by advertising their ties with and support for the South. This process began as early as late 1865. The managers of the Thayer and Noyes circus divided their operation into two parts, sending the newly created C. W. Noyes Circus into the state of Texas. This new show, of course, consisted of former members of the "United States Circus," who now performed under the banner of the "Southern Circus." The show's manager—a native of Syracuse, New York—advertised with pride that his show was based out of the New Orleans Academy of Music. In February 1866, the northern managers of the Stone and Rosston and Company Circus "blew on their *Southern* feelings" in their advertising material while they toured Tennessee, Mississippi, Alabama, and Louisiana. In New Orleans, the concern billed itself as the "Great Southern Circus" and highlighted the Confederate military service of the troupe's director, who encouraged his former comrades-in-arms and their families to turn out for the show to see some "Southern entertainment." The show's management also announced that the outfit had spent the war years in Europe, even though it actually had been on the road in the North. With trenchant insight into the transparency of such a "humbug," the *Clipper* asked if the Stone managers had emphasized that they were "good Northern men" when they were above the Mason-Dixon line the previous summer. Still, the weekly's editors conceded that at that time it was "necessary for the success in the South of a meritorious show that its manager must have been identified with Confederate officers or Confederate interests."[17]

Other shows quickly followed this lead. In 1867, the legendary equestrian

James Robinson brought his Great Southwestern Circus into Georgia. Two years later, James Robinson dropped "Great Southwestern" from his title but explained in his ads that by playing the South he was doing so "in accordance with a long cherished desire to appear before the friends of his childhood." His Atlanta advertisements added the claim that the "Southern Boy" was returning to the "land of his birth, in the fond anticipation of receiving a *Southern Welcome*." The *Constitution* made him a veritable native son by dubbing him the "Georgia Boy." All of this identification with the South surely helped him sell tickets, but it could not change the fact that James Robinson was born in Boston, Massachusetts.[18]

Even though the show was a familiar presence in the South, the John Robinson Circus felt similarly compelled to profess its links to the region. In contrast to James Robinson's humbug about his origins, the John Robinson show drew attention to the Georgia birth and southern upbringing of its star clown. Johnny Lowlow began his career in the 1850s as a child performer in his native city of Savannah. Orphaned at age sixteen, he left home and joined the circus. Predictably, the John Robinson Circus wasted no time in reminding Savannah citizens, and people all over the state, that its clown was "a Savannah boy" who was "an old time favorite in the South." The show undertook a similar tactic in Milledgeville in 1869, informing the town's residents that its "Great Champion Leaper" Jerome Tuttle was a "Milledgeville boy as is well known." The proprietor of the Robinson show, John Robinson, offered no specific information about his roots in his advertising copy but did tell Georgians in his 1871 ads that he had "an experience of over fifty years in the South as owner of a menagerie and circus."[19]

The Robinson press campaign bore fruit on the pages of Georgia newspapers. Augusta's *Daily Chronicle and Sentinel* endorsed the show by writing that John Robinson "is well known in the South and his name is a guarantee that the exhibition is a good one." The editors of the *Athens North-East Georgian* paid Robinson an even higher compliment: "We have known Robinson for many years, he is a Southern man and a clever gentleman."[20]

Robinson was undoubtedly clever, but he was not a southerner. The legendary circus man was born in New York early in the century, and resided in Cincinnati for many years. In fact, Robinson would be a Republican candidate for mayor of that city in 1875. Yet it is no surprise that southerners mistook him as one of their own. Robinson's efforts to link himself with the South stretched back to the antebellum period when his Great Southern Circus made the rounds in Dixie, touring under the banner of "Southern horses, Southern riders and Southern enterprises against the world." As the erroneous labeling of James and John Robinson as southerners in Georgia newspapers demonstrates, these press campaigns convinced many in the South that these shows were homegrown.[21]

Still, Robinson's publicity campaign did not fool everyone in the South, especially after Robinson's competitors drew attention to the show's northern connections. On the day of Robinson's 1876 showing in Columbus, the owners of a rival concern assailed Robinson for his political loyalties in a large *Enquirer-Sun* newspaper notice that announced that he had "contributed . . . liberally to the support of Hayes and Wheeler." In the next day's paper, a reviewer labeled the Robinson show "the greatest humbug of the age" and curtly suggested that the owner not "come South with such an affair again." About a year later, the *Enquirer-Sun* editor resumed his attack on the show as it toured in the vicinity of Columbus, explaining that the owner of the "abominably poor" Robinson Circus was "one of the most noted of the Cincinnati Republicans." Luckily for Robinson, local newspapermen apparently did not know that during the Civil War the showman had operated his outfit in the northern states under the title of the "Great Union Combination" Circus. Despite previously playing Columbus in 1867, 1870, 1872, 1874, and 1876, the Robinson show left the community off its 1878 itinerary, and would not play the city again until 1921.[22]

The deceptions of some showmen aside, a few circuses had more meaningful ties to the South. After the Civil War, "Colonel" Clark T. Ames of New Orleans organized shows in the Crescent City, including his New Orleans Mammoth Circus and Menagerie. Ames and his managers celebrated their ties to the region. During the show's first year on the road, Ames' management informed Georgians that the show was the only troupe "equipped with Southern capital, managed and directed by Southern men, and its perambulations confined to the Southern States." Such claims appear to have helped the outfit make a positive impression on the Georgia press. The *Atlanta Daily New Era* told its readers that "Col. Ames is a Southern man, and his show is the only pure Southern circus traveling in this country. Of course, he will be patronized by our people." Similarly, the *Savannah Morning News* concluded that Ames "has been the most zealous and assiduous in catering to Southern taste and Southern notions. A gentleman himself of the old school, he never loses sight of those sensibilities so peculiar in 'rebeldom.'"[23]

To cater to these "peculiar" sensibilities, Ames offered entertainment with a regional flavor. A prominent member of his troupe was "Happy" Jack Lawton, who the show billed as "the Great Southern Clown." Along with southern performers, the show presented acts of particular interest to southern audiences. Capitalizing on the popularity of ring and lance tournaments among the region's gentry, Ames' opening pageant involved a "moral representation" of "a grand Tournament, in which ladies and gentlemen will participate in the sports of the arena. There will be a profusion of banners and armorial bearings, and the audience will insensibly be carried back to the days of chivalry." Ames also prominently featured the charger "Stonewall" in his performances. The appearance of this animal deeply affected Civil War veterans at an Atlanta performance: "We have always had a weakness for a noble horse, and have some touching memories connected with a rare thoroughbred that carried us through many a wild melee during the war—an animal that was shot under us, and on which we were shot one desperate day of Sherman's grand march, and Johnson's masterly retreat through Northern Georgia. Stonewall made us think of our old friend and war servant." However transparently patronizing such practices, performances, and proclamations appear today, these elements did resonate with many who attended circuses in Reconstruction-era Georgia.[24]

Being a southern circus also meant eschewing the distasteful but common tactic of promising attractions on the bills that showmen did not produce inside the tent at show time. With a nod to southern honor, the Ames show assured Georgians in 1868 that "this is strictly a Southern enterprise, and the proprietors and managers pledge themselves that the disreputable . . . style of advertising attractions they do not present shall in no instance be resorted to by them." Ames apparently kept this vow. A reviewer for the *Savannah Morning News* thought it remarkable that the circus "programme (which is seldom the case) was carried out in full accord with managerial promise."[25]

Ames offered an additional demonstration of how a southern circus should conduct itself to the people of Savannah on October 12, 1870. In midperformance, Ames received word that Confederate leader Robert E. Lee had died. With heavy heart, he respectfully informed the crowd of the general's passing. The *Morning News* reported that "the gallant proprietor stated that there would be no further exhibition. . . . As the crowd moved away the band played the 'Dead March from Saul.' This tribute of Col. Ames to the brave old hero of the 'Lost Cause' should be remembered by the people of the South, and will certainly endear him to the people of Savannah." Unfortunately for the city's circus fans, Ames had made his last appearance in Savannah. In November, ruffians shot and killed the circus owner in Dawson, Georgia as he tried to stop them from firing "indiscriminately" into a crowd that was waiting to enter his tent.[26]

Other than the Ames outfit, no circuses could make a better case for being southern than the various shows operated by Andrew Haight and P. Bowles Wooten from 1871 to 1874. Like James and John Robinson, Haight was born in the North, and like many in the circus business, he came from a merchant family. After forays into a variety of commercial enterprises, he entered the circus profession in early 1865 with a partner and by October had bought out his co-owner. In 1871, Haight purchased an elephant and several lions from the estate of Colonel Ames and the remnants of two circuses that had disbanded in Atlanta. By February 1871, he had met Atlanta livery stable owner P. Bowles Wooten. A native Georgian, Wooten had served in the Confederate Army and had worked as a mule dealer after the war. Together, the men formed the Haight and Wooten Circus in Atlanta.[27]

As the show's employees made pretour preparations, the *Atlanta Daily New Era* kept its readers abreast of their progress. The paper's coverage reveals the editors' interest in identifying the show with the city, state, and region and, more generally, exemplifies the promotion of southern enterprise by New South boosters. The *Herald*'s initial reports, for example, variously entitled the show as "The Georgia Circus Company," "The Atlanta Circus Company," and "The New Atlanta Circus." Moreover, the daily asserted that the outfit was "entirely a Southern institution, in fact an Atlanta institution." Along with an allegiance born of geography, the editor argued that the city's residents felt a particular connection to the show because a number of well-known local artisans were assembling and decorating the outfit's wagons. On the eve of the show's debut performance, the paper could barely contain its pride: "Atlanta is fast, one of the fastest cities in the South. It's [sic] latest sensation is a circus—a circus which is about to start from this city—a circus which has been organized in Atlanta, painted up in Atlanta, and now exercising in Atlanta. Our city has reached the acme of show business."[28]

After a series of Georgia dates, the show departed the state in early 1871 and traveled up the East Coast to points as far north as Newfoundland. When the show returned to Georgia in September, Haight and Wooten used their advertising to appeal to Georgians in three ways. First, they sought to capitalize on regional pride by announcing that the show was a "massive Southern combination" and "the only Southern establishment of the kind." Second, the showmen called on citizens to attend their exhibitions because unlike most circuses, the show's "troupe consists principally of natives to the manner [sic] born." Third, the two men tried to tap into the widespread feeling in the region that southerners were underdogs in the nation's economic and cultural endeavors. Their newspaper ads read in part: "A little less than one year ago, when this grand enterprise was organized in Atlanta, Georgia, many sagacious people predicted failure in its infancy; but the unprecedented success crowning it everywhere it has been, has satisfied them of the error of their judgment. . . . Throughout the Middle States and New England, the Dominions of New Brunswick, Nova Scotia, Prince Edward Island, Cape Breton and New Foundland, there has been but one voice from the press and public as to the merits intrinsic of this mammoth enterprise. Messrs. WOOTTEN & HAIGHT feel an excusable pride in referring to their repeated triumphs and the praise of the world." In this case, a southern outfit's invasion of the North had ended in triumph.[29]

Many in the Georgia press agreed that the circus's southern identity made it worthy of praise and patronage by locals. In accordance with its established editorial position, the *Atlanta Daily New Era* declared that the show's national success as a "Southern enterprise" was "a matter of pride to every citizen of Atlanta" since it had its "origin and development in the Gate City." Likewise, the troupe's capacity crowds in Atlanta—its "native hearth"—reflected a just reward for the circus, because as a "representative of the energy and enterprise and talent of Georgians," it was "doubly worthy of the support of the people." Along the coast, the *Savannah Morning News* endorsed the show as "a purely Southern affair, which should of itself be a recommendation from it to our people." In addition, the daily argued that it merited adulation and patronage because a "majority" of the performers were "Southern men." Yet most importantly, the *News* emphasized that the concern was "not a *Yankee humbug*, but a legitimate and deserving institution," staffed by men who "are Southern in sentiment" even though they are "engaged in what is generally conceded to be 'a Yankee calling.'"[30]

Sometime before the end of 1871, Wooten divested himself of his interest in the show over a disagreement with his partner, leaving Haight as the only name on the marquee. When the circus returned to Savannah in January 1872 to play more dates, it posted bills under the title "Haight & Co.'s Circus, Museum, and Menagerie." The tour continued on until mid-February, when the show's proprietor took it off the road in Atlanta. Almost immediately, Haight began reorganizing his business arrangements and enlarging his enterprise. He found a new partner in George W. DeHaven, one of the show's managers. The two men secured outside funding from two Atlanta bankers, using the fresh infusion of cash to defray the costs of new capital investments.[31]

Sometime around early March, the show concluded its activities in Atlanta and relocated to Cincinnati to make final preparations for its 1872 campaign. The new show opened in that city in early April under the banner of the "Great Eastern Menagerie, Museum, Aviary, Circus, Roman Hippodrome and Egyptian Caravan." The Great Eastern, however, differed from the previous incarnations of the show in more than just the length of its name. Instead of moving by wagon, the Great Eastern made use of several dozen rail cars. This new mode of transportation, first pioneered by P. T. Barnum and his partners that year, allowed the outfit to display a massive six-tent show that featured sixty entertainers, hundreds of laborers, horses, and exotic animals, and a large collection of attractions and curiosities. This great increase in scale came in response to the tremendous popular success that Barnum had enjoyed after using three monstrous exhibition tents, rather than the traditional single tent, on his 1871 tour. For the next six decades, the size of a show would be one of the most important competitive attributes in the circus business.[32]

Even though the Great Eastern did not publicly project a southern identity, the show's top staff included a large number of southerners. Out of seven American-born performers and managers profiled as "prominent members" of the show in its *Route Book*, five were southern by birth. Advertising agent A. R. Scott was born in Kentucky while Registering Agent Augustus Atkinson served in the Thirteenth North Carolina Volunteers before beginning a career in the circus business. Treasurer R. E. J. Miles was born in Virginia where he lived until ten years of age before moving to Covington, Kentucky. Equestrian Director W. B. Carroll was born in Knoxville, and principal clown and rider Sam Stickney was born in New Orleans.[33]

At least one southern member of the show's staff was not above trying to use animosity lingering from the war for competitive advantage. In early September, Sam Stickney lambasted the John Robinson Circus for the political loyalties of its owner and his family during at least two performances in North Carolina. He told the assembled thousands at Rocky Mount that the Robinson family members were "enemies to the south in the late war," and that the elder John Robinson had as part of his noncircus business pursuits "clothed the United States army while his son was a soldier in the same." While the crowd's reaction is not known, the editor of the *Rocky Mount Mail* found this speech highly distasteful, calling on the two sections to "'shake hands across the bloody chasm'" and for shows to pursue public favor through entertainment and not through appeals to "sectional feeling and prejudice."[34]

Proceeding south through the Carolinas, the show played its first Georgia date on September 12. During the month, the show would play twenty-one dates in the state, including in four of its largest communities, namely Savannah, Atlanta, Macon, and Columbus. With the tour winding down, Haight and DeHaven considered spending the off-season in Savannah, but eventually chose Selma, Alabama as a winter headquarters. The show played its final date of the season on December 14, having traveled more than nine thousand miles by rail.[35]

After its arrival in Selma, the show settled in at the city's fairgrounds, and proceeded to reorganize and enlarge its operations once again. Because the show remained an Atlanta institution in the eyes of many Gate City residents, the *Atlanta Constitution* reported on the show's off-season activities. These moves included the purchase of new exotic beasts, cages, and wagons from European sources and the dissolution of the partnership with DeHaven. Subsequently, Haight took on his brother and treasurer of the show, Jacob Haight, as his new partner. Prior to the resumption of touring, the two men claimed in their promotional material that they had spent over a million dollars in making the aggregation four times bigger than the previous year's production, drawing particular attention to their plan to use twelve exhibition tents while on tour.[36]

Despite the difficult financial conditions in the country, the Great Eastern toured the United States and Canada in 1873. The show opened its annual campaign in Selma in March and stayed on the road for the duration of the year, facing intense competition from other outfits, including the John Robinson Circus. When the circus reached Georgia in December, the Haight brothers found that the Atlanta press remained committed to claiming the show as a Gate City institution, even though it had spent the prior year's off-season in Alabama. "On Tuesday next," the *Atlanta Daily Herald* proclaimed, "the Great Eastern

Menagerie and Circus will arrive in its native city, Atlanta, returning victorious from many a wild[ly] contested fight with the most celebrated traveling exhibitions in the country."[37]

The daily also asserted that local pride in the show had not flagged. After witnessing the troupe's performances in front of capacity crowds, the paper's editors echoed its previous statements, writing, "the Great Eastern was first organized in Atlanta, [so] our citizens can congratulate themselves, since it is the most triumphant and largest of its character ever here." Furthermore, because "Atlanta is its home . . . our citizens manifest their pride in the manifold triumphs" of the outfit, so "to our friends all over the State we heartily and warmly endorse this emphatically best show on the road." After departing from the state's capital city, the Great Eastern moved through Georgia and Alabama during December. Its tour would continue without pause in the new year as the show headed west into Texas in the spring before traveling to the northeastern states.[38]

But Andrew Haight would not accompany the show on its 1874 campaign. Sometime in January of that year, he decided to terminate his professional relationship with the Great Eastern. With the tour proceeding apace, Jacob bade his brother farewell and continued on with the aggregation. Andrew, however, had different plans for the coming year. He moved his office to Newnan, Georgia, and immediately set out to organize a new, smaller show.[39]

It is quite possible that the actions of his former partner sparked his initial idea to operate an outfit that was less capital-intensive. On Christmas Day, 1873, P. Bowles Wooten unveiled his new concern, the Great Southern Zoological and Calisthenic Aggregation, in front of a sold-out crowd in Atlanta. But other than clowning by Jack Lawton and co-owner Billy Andrews, Wooten's outfit offered a peculiar variety of circus exhibition. The show omitted ring and equestrian performances—the traditional centerpieces of the circus—in favor of tumbling, aerial acrobatics, and gymnastics. This unusual program did not grow out of any novel aesthetic sensibilities. Instead, Wooten and Andrews sought to tiptoe around the wording of Georgia's circus tax statute, which particularly defined circuses as incorporating riding and ring work. Not coincidentally, Haight's troupe would follow this lead in the coming year by presenting a performance similarly free of such acts.[40]

In Newnan, Haight directly oversaw his new show's preparations. He purchased needed items from the town's merchants and employed numerous local blacksmiths, painters, and carpenters. The show's workers also spent their salaries "freely" at the town's retail businesses. The significance of this infusion of cash into the town's economy at the height of a nationwide depression was not lost on Newnan observers. The *Herald* declared that "the wintering and organization of this circus in our midst has brought a good deal of money into circulation, which we would not otherwise have had, which has aided not a little in relieving our monetary stringency." This economic boost prompted the Mayor and City Council, at the urging of "many" citizens, to waive any local license fees for the show's warm-up performance. The company's liberal spending also engendered the editorial support of the local paper, which like so many other Georgia dailies, encouraged citizens to support this "strictly Southern enterprise." By the turn of the century, when the wintering of circuses in Georgia would become more common, the economic benefits of having a show in winter quarters was one of the key factors that encouraged local political and business elites to fully embrace circuses.[41]

In the weeks leading up to the first performance of Haight's Great Southern, the show owner had the good fortune to find an undiscovered local talent named Sanders living less than ten miles from Newnan. Before he came to the impresario's attention, this eighteen-year-old had "practiced gymnastic and acrobatic evolutions" on his farm. Under Haight's guidance, he adopted the stage name Professor Sanders the Boneless Man and set out to translate his untutored athletic talents into the disciplines of contortionism and tumbling. Apparently, he proved to be a natural at such activities. During the show's first appearance in Atlanta, the *Constitution* called his abilities "truly wonderful." A few days later, the *New York Clipper* reported that this circus neophyte was "acknowledged by all" who witnessed his performance in Atlanta "to be the best contortionist and tumbler in the company."[42]

The two Georgia-based shows set out to tour the nation in 1874. Haight's Great Southern Circus traveled by rail through Georgia before entering Tennessee, Virginia, North Carolina, South Carolina, West Virginia, Maryland, Ohio, and Arkansas. At the same time, the Wooten and Andrews outfit moved by wagon through South Carolina, Kentucky, Virginia, and Tennessee. In February, the editors of the *Athens North-East Georgian* praised the Wooten and Andrews show for being "strictly a Southern exhibition" with a menagerie so moral that "the most strict churchman can look upon [it] without violating a single obligation of his or her church." In the months that followed, the *Clipper* reported that the Wooten concern was "doing a good business" and was so well received by residents of the Palmetto State that citizens from the town of Anderson presented its talented and "singularly attractive" star gymnast with an amethyst and diamond ring and a gold necklace. But the outfit's success was short-lived. On August 15, Wooten & Andrews' Great Southern Zoological and Calisthenic Aggregation "collapsed" in London, Tennessee. Haight's show, too, ran into trouble that same month in the Volunteer State. Some days after arriving in Memphis, Haight closed the show because he could not afford to pay the staff's salaries. With the death of these two shows, the brief era of "southern" circuses had come to an end.[43]

From one perspective, the way that circus men manipulated sectional difference reveals the ethos of the nineteenth-century showman: the truth was a malleable commodity, and ultimately it had to be sacrificed to preserve a show's bottom line. Impresarios presented skits that would amuse or please southerners, employed southern-sounding titles, and shone the spotlight on their southern performers when they toured in Georgia because it sold tickets and offered some modicum of protection against southern rowdies.

But the disingenuous actions of showmen should not be allowed to obscure the fact that they had tapped into the region's reigning cultural sentiment. Southerners' sense of damaged pride and defensiveness, of grievance and inferiority, made them very receptive to shows that trumpeted "southern" values during Reconstruction. The sense of self-satisfaction and ownership that characterized the response of Georgians to the Wooten and Haight enterprises of 1870 and 1871 demonstrates that there was more to this phenomenon than just an admixture of humbug and advertising. Progress-minded southerners, including business owners and newspaper editors, applauded the efforts of southern showmen because they improved local economies when they wintered in the South and offered evidence that the region could produce circus outfits that could successfully compete with northern-based shows. Circus men like Wooten, Haight, and Andrews, in turn, emphasized their national successes and southern identities in their advertising material because it worked to their benefit when they ambulated through the southern states.

Still, while showmen understood that professing links to the South (whether genuine or bogus) sold tickets and reduced violence, they also apprehended that they did nothing to draw many of the people who felt uncomfortable with circuses into their tents. To confront that problem, showmen would have to address the morality and propriety—rather than the political persuasion—of their shows.

One of the best hits of the season was made by the clown of Robinson's circus. He was about to walk a tight rope, and called to the ringmaster to chalk his foot to keep him from slipping. The process on one foot caused immense tickling and proportionate giggling; the chalking of the other was taken as quietly as a handsome coquette takes a proposal. Ringmaster asked why one did not tickle as much as the other. Clown replied: "one is my laughing foot, the other is my church foot; one came to see the circus, the other to see the animals."—*Columbus Sun and Times*, 17 December 1867

We know a good boy, some thirteen years of age, who is a member of a church whose rule[s] forbid attendance upon circuses. He, with others, was coming in for a free ticket. A gentleman, however, before delivering it, was impressing upon him the duty of "self denial," that denying himself forbidden pleasures in youth, would make him a stronger man. He listened very quietly, walked slowly out on the pavement, heard the circus band playing, and came back thoughtfully with the remark, "I can't deny myself." He continued. "You see Mr. ——, I said before the circus came that I would go if I got a free ticket, and now if I don't go I'll tell a lie, and that's worse than going to the circus." He was handed the ticket, such argument being unanswerable.
—*Columbus Daily Sun*, 27 November 1870

THREE

The Slow Embrace

Religion, Social Status, and Circus Attendance, 1865–1920

Circuses that played Georgia in the decade after the Civil War faced more than political opposition lingering from the war. Condemnations of the circus also came from some vocal community and spiritual leaders who opposed these traveling enterprises for cultural and religious reasons. L. F. W. Andrews, the editor of Macon's *Georgia Citizen*, regularly attacked shows in the pages of his paper and called on town leaders to assess a prohibitive circus tax of five hundred dollars per day. Pastor H. H. Parks of the Athens Methodist Church informed the community of his church's position on the circus in a newspaper notice published on the eve of an 1865 performance. He reported that fifteen of seventeen official members of the church had resolved that it is "very inexpedient and dangerous that *any church member should attend a Circus,* and deem it no place for them" and warned that attendance is grounds for dismissal from the Methodist Church. A southern Georgia editor's 1876 denunciation of "all such travelling dens of pollution and poison" accurately encapsulates the anticircus position of southern elites: "Of all demoralizing things ever permitted to run at large through any town, a circus takes the lead. It completely unjoints every particle of social, moral, or religious machinery in any small town."[1]

Even though the anticircus contingent never succeeded in its goal of excluding circuses from the state, the public condemnations of ministers and conservative editors could only serve to further degrade the reputation of such shows in the minds of some evangelical and middle-class southerners. These individuals avoided circuses because they disliked mixing with the "dregs" of southern society inside a tent while listening to off-color jokes punned by insolent clowns. The criticisms of anticircus leaders also resonated with genteel ladies who harbored an additional aversion to circus-going thanks to the rowdy and racially mixed crowds that surrounded ticket wagons and tent entrances. Although a wide range of Georgians attended circuses after the Civil War with little or no reservation, many elite women, church members from the town and country, and middle-class town dwellers considered these shows immoral and indecent, and therefore steered clear of them.

Reflexively, circus managers responded to such anticircus prejudices by reaffirming that their shows featured only virtuous and chaste entertainment. The management of Ames' Circus and Menagerie paid homage to Victorian domesticity when it vowed that patrons would "have no fear of either the ear or eye coming in contact with anything that might not be seen or heard with the nicest propriety at the fireside of the most refined."[2] The owners of Howes' Great London Circus similarly promised, "There is nothing ever presented that a gentleman would hesitate to bring his family to witness."[3]

But circus men had been making, and breaking, such pledges since the 1840s. The troupe that eschewed boorish jokes and other offensive content was an exception to the rule. "Unlike most other exhibitions of the kind," one southern auditor reported after a postwar show, "nothing was said or done in the performances that gave offence to the most fastidious person." The fear of hearing "*double entendre* and indelicate allusions," not to mention seeing scantily dressed performers, kept many people out of circus tents. From the showman's perspective, the problem was that they—unlike their contemporaries in the theatrical business—could not easily excise these morally dubious features without doing violence to the distinctiveness of the entertainment offered by their outfits. Simply put, lightly garbed riders and saucy clowns made a circus a circus in the mid-nineteenth century.[4]

While the seeming intractability of this fact probably tempted some showmen to simply write off the anticircus portion of the southern populace, more astute managers understood that they had to answer the charges leveled against their entertainments. By ignoring the pronouncements of southern ministers and editors, their most vocal critics, showmen risked political opposition that could manifest itself in increased regulation, including the higher taxes called for by editor Andrews. Additionally, circus managers recognized that the continued growth and acceptance of their industry in the South required addressing the prejudices of religious and respectable southerners who hesitated to enter the tents of traveling troupes. Although circus owners realized they would never win over all of those southerners who disapproved of tented entertainment, they set out to counter the arguments against their outfits and render their entertainment respectable through charity work, new ticketing and admission procedures, clever advertising, and a reorganization of their methods of presentation. By the turn of the century, showmen had generally succeeded in muting their critics and broadening their customer base even though many southerners would remain conflicted about the virtues of the circus.

From their first appearances in southern towns and cities after the war, northern circus owners and managers exhibited an interest in building relationships with potentially disaffected southerners. A central component of this effort was charity performances. Typically, circus men set aside one matinee performance of their multiday stands as a charity event, with all or sometimes half of the proceeds collected at the gate going to worthy local causes. At least one circus manager put on a charity show in almost every southern city his troupe performed in, and others put on benefit performances in many of the places they played.[5]

While showmen ostensibly wanted to alleviate hardship where they performed, these special exhibitions also served their interests. One immediate advantage they gained from these performances was the approval of local politicians. After the Dan Castello Circus put on a benefit show in Macon, mayor Steven Collins publicly thanked the show for its "liberality in tendering to the suffering poor." The generosity of the Stone, Rosston, and Murray Circus managers toward the Savannah Female Orphan Asylum won the plaudits of mayor R. D. Arnold, who proclaimed that it "reflects the highest credit on your benevolence." In Atlanta, a benefit for the underprivileged performed by the Haight and Chambers Circus garnered the public appreciation of the city council. In communities filled with destitute refugees and plagued by widespread poverty, circus charity work had the potential to improve conditions. Not incidentally, it also fostered better relations between southern politicians and Yankee showmen.[6]

Charity performances also reduced religious hostility to the circus among powerful members of the laity. Mayor Arnold of Savannah publicly pointed out that the "practical christianity" exhibited by the Stone and Rosston managers offered "an example for imitation which I hope will not be lost even on those who condemn public amusements." Even Atlanta's staunchly anticircus *Christian Index* felt obligated to inform its Baptist readership that "the receipts of yesterday afternoon's performance of Haight and Chambers' Circus were about $500, which sum was donated by the proprietors for the benefit of the poor of the city." The fact that charity could diminish religious opposition to the circus was a lesson that some showmen had learned before the war. After the Yankee Robinson Circus offered to contribute to the support of a young Atlanta widow in 1859, the editor of the *Atlanta Intelligencer* commented: "No matter how much, hither to, we may have been opposed to patronizing such places, we think that this is one of the times, everything considered, that even a [visit by a] church member would be excusable." When circus men displayed such munificence, lay authorities found it more difficult to plausibly claim that circus men represented an evil influence on Georgia society.[7]

In addition to countering religious arguments against the circus, charity events allowed circus men to "feminize" their entertainments in an effort to reach out to Georgia's elite ladies. While some genteel women had attended antebellum circuses, few, if any, had entered the tent without a male escort, especially at night when the most uncouth members of society would be in the audience. Typically, those who did patronize the circus preferred to go with their husbands and children to the more socially sedate afternoon exhibitions and sat in reserved seats or special family boxes. Performances for charitable purposes, however, helped redefine the inside of a circus tent from a space of rowdy masculinity to a more respectable realm suitable for elite women and children, even without male escorts. Thus, the *Savannah Daily Herald* pointed out that although the afternoon start of an 1866 Orphan's Benefit would keep many men from attending, "nothing will prevent the ladies and children from turning out in full numbers."[8]

Circus men furthered this redefinition when they extended a philanthropic hand to female benevolent organizations. Ever mindful of southern sensitivities, the Ames Circus and Menagerie sponsored a benefit performance for the beautification of Atlanta's Confederate Cemetery in 1869. To help assure the event's success, some high-minded "ladies" of the Gate City personally sold advance tickets to the show. In 1873, Andrew Haight of the Great Eastern Circus put on a show to support the Ladies Memorial Association of Atlanta. In this case, circus men provided a means for elite southern women to range beyond the confines of the home in their efforts to commemorate the Confederate cause, revealing both the growing respectability of circus entertainment and the rising interest of women in undertaking charitable work in the public sphere.[9]

Despite progress in this area, showmen understood that the occasional philanthropic performance did not represent a comprehensive solution to the problem of female attendance. While the deeply held belief that circuses were inherently immoral meant that some females—and males—would never go to a circus, a larger contingent of southern ladies might turn out for shows if they could avoid mixing in the crowds outside of the tent. To address these concerns, circus officials modified the way they sold tickets and admitted patrons. Although these actions did nothing to alter the morally questionable entertainment content that so many people found offensive, they did help change the conditions that discouraged some women from patronizing circuses.

The often arduous and unpleasant experience of purchasing tickets from a wagon on show day was one powerful deterrent to female circus-going. While a huge mob surrounding a ticket window warmed the hearts and the fattened the wallets of showmen, the town and city gentry, especially women with children, had little interest in being jostled in a crowd filled with their social lessers. Clearly, any delicate Athens females standing in the vicinity of the John Robinson Circus ticket wagon in 1872 were liable to be stampeded when sales commenced: "We never saw a people more eager for a show. As soon as the ticket office was opened crowds rushed to it to purchase their entrance to the canvas. The streets were crowded . . . with scores of whites, horses and mules, niggers and mares." No fashionable woman, regardless of the tears in the eyes of her disappointed children, wanted to fight her way through such a multitude in order to secure passage to a show.[10]

To obviate this problem, circuses made advance tickets available, sometimes for an additional fee, at local hotels or merchants beginning in the late 1860s. In 1871, the Stone and Murray Combination Circus advised Savannah residents that "for [the] convenience of ladies and families, tickets will be for sale a few days in advance of the Circus, at F. Grosclande's Jewelry Store, Bull Street, opposite Masonic Hall." The same year, the John Robinson Circus announced in Georgia that interested parties who have wanted to go to the circus but had been "heretofore deterred from doing so, on account of the annoyance and delay in procuring tickets at the ticket wagon," could buy tickets at a variety of local establishments. As an added inducement, James Robinson's Champion Circus allowed advance ticket holders "to enter the Circus before the opening of the Ticket Wagon." In other words, the proprietor arranged for his better class of customers to avoid having to spend time with the crowd outside of his tent.[11]

The success of this innovation meant that it soon became an expectation for the public. When showmen failed to provide an alternate method for ticket purchase, locals reminded them of the importance of the convenience. "In order to avoid confusion, delay and annoyance," the *Savannah Morning News* observed, "it is suggested that the managers of the circus company have tickets placed on sale at Bren's ticket office. Such an arrangement ... would be appreciated by hundreds who dread the crowd at the ticket wagon at the tent."[12]

A related postwar concern for white ladies—and the men who accompanied them to the circus—was the racial composition of the throng that collected around the tent before a show got under way. With the cessation of hostilities, white people living in Georgia towns and cities became increasingly uneasy about the growing number of former slaves relocating to their communities. African Americans living in Georgia, and all over the South, had departed the countryside for towns and cities in an effort to both exercise their freedom and escape the influence of their former owners. In Macon, for example, the number of African Americans had increased more than twofold by the end of 1865. This postwar migration prompted Georgia commentator Bill Arp to indignantly observe, "The whole of Africy has come to town."[13]

While this black influx was itself a concern, white southerners found the public behavior of freedmen particularly disturbing. Many city and town whites believed that the relative freedom afforded by life beyond the countryside undermined the etiquette of race relations that had been imposed under slavery, thereby eroding white supremacy and black submissiveness. African Americans seemed to grow increasingly assertive by the day, as they disregarded the long-standing restrictions that they should not drink or own weapons. In response to this growing sense of disorder, many southern whites angrily demanded that freedmen return to the farm.[14]

One new freedom that former slaves fully embraced while in town was circus-going. Denied the ability to freely socialize while on the countryside, African Americans enjoyed experiencing the excitement of Circus Day. According to one leading Fulton County citizen, African Americans were "fond of crowds and shows, and all such things as are going on in cities." Georgia observers rarely failed to point out the huge turnout of African Americans at these entertainments. The *Columbus Daily Sun* crudely highlighted this phenomenon by informing its white readers on the eve of a performance that "everybody who owes a nigger a quarter of a dollar must be prepared to 'fork over,' for Cuffee must see the circus." On Circus Day, former slaves, along with rambunctious street urchins of both races and local white workers, milled around the ticket wagon and tent before, during, and after the show.[15]

As they did with ticket buying, circus owners offered a remedy to white southerners who wanted to avoid coming in close contact with such crowds by providing separate entrances for whites and blacks. At least three circuses that visited Georgia in 1865–1866 offered such accommodations in addition to the segregated seating inside of their pavilions. Although the exact layout of these distinct entryways is unknown, it is probable that they funneled individuals of different races from outside of the tent directly to each group's designated segregated seats inside the arena.

While racial concerns shaped the thinking behind this new admission arrangement, issues of gender and class also drove the introduction of separate entrances. In 1866, the Stone, Rosston, and Murray's Grand Combination Southern Circus segregated their patrons by offering both "Freedman's Seats" and "Reserved Seats, particularly arranged for gentlemen accompanied by ladies." Moreover, the show's advertising particularly advised that "the Proprietors wish it distinctly understood that the entrance way to the Pavilion will be very commodious, [and] that the entrance to the different class seats will be separate."[16]

White southerners welcomed such precautions. The *Columbus Daily Sun* lauded Dan Castello's Great Show for its separate entrances, noting that this manner of admission "is a decided improvement on any circus that has yet visited Columbus." Similar praise came from an Alabama editor, who concluded that the Thayer and Noyes show had "perfected" an "admirable arrangement . . . by which Freedmen will be comfortably accommodated in a section of the pavilion, fitted up expressly for them, and entirely distinct from the rest of the *audience*, with a separate entrance" (italics in original). Of course, this method of admission allowed showmen to preserve the patronage of African Americans, who would prove to be some of the most consistently loyal southern circus fans.[17]

Without explanation, circus owners apparently phased out the use of separate entrances by the end of 1866. No advertised notices of the peculiar admission practice appear after that year, nor does any mention of the arrangement show up in other contemporaneous source material. It seems likely that as interactions between former slaves and white southerners became more settled in the wake of emancipation, circus owners sensed that the precaution was no longer necessary. The Georgia legislature agreed with this point of view, since during the time period covered by this study, it apparently never passed a law that mandated separate entrances, or separate seats, for the different races at circuses. In fact, in 1907 the Georgia House of Representatives, without explanation, rejected a bill that proposed that circuses give "separate performances for whites and negroes" when exhibiting in the state.[18]

These new ticketing and admission arrangements, when combined with the circus industry's charitable outreach efforts, motivated a larger proportion of Georgia's elite ladies to enter circus tents. Notably, they even patronized the circus at night. In Columbus, for example, the town's "most elegant and fastidious citizens" attended the John Robinson Circus's evening performance in December 1867. In particular, the elite contingent featured a high proportion of "ladies, [who] for the first time at an exhibition of this kind, turned out en masse." The next year, a similar turnout occurred, when "large numbers of ladies were in attendance" for the Dan Castello Circus's matinee and evening performances. And in 1872, the *Atlanta Sun* reported that fully half of the eight thousand people inside a Gate City circus tent comprised women. In the years following the war, Georgia's elite females decided that the circus was an entertainment worthy of their patronage.[19]

To be sure, however, increased female attendance right after the Civil War did not signal that the circus had become a genteel and chaste entertainment. In late 1865, one privileged Atlanta lady set out for her first circus. On her way to the show grounds, the young woman thought of her father's admonitions about attending such shows, but once she was "comfortably and cleanly" seated inside the Stone, Rosston, and Murray tent, her fears quickly subsided. "In the midst of the jolliest crowds of beaus in the city," she watched an "enchanted" and "splendid" performance by the troupe. "How unjustly I had been treated," she thought, "denied this pleasure all these years for a 'prejudice.' How much I had lost."

Less than a decade after the war, she attended another show. This time, she "boldly" strolled through the entrance with her male escort and servant. Yet her ebullience quickly dissipated after she found herself in close quarters with undesirable people and frightening beasts while in the show's menagerie tent. "Wild with horror and disgust," she struggled to escape the clutches of the dense crowd. Turning away from the "roaring and grinning" animals, the crowd pressed her "up against an old man, blear-eyed, whiskey-perfumed, with a pipe in his mouth." As she begged her escort to extricate them, the "old savage" asked her, "'Don't you like to be hugged by an old Confederate soldier?'"

After exiting the menagerie, her party made its way to the stands in the main arena. Unlike her prior "enchanted" experience as a circus spectator, she despised her time in the audience. Hemmed into a space so small that she needed to place her feet in her servant's lap, she endured "an avalanche of coarse jokes" from the show's boorish clowns. To make matters worse, the unreconstructed woman found herself seated right next to a Federal officer. In closing her tale of woe, which she provided in written form to the editor of the *Atlanta Herald*, she could only conclude: "If I felt myself in Fairyland at my first circus, I felt myself in the Black Hole of Calcutta or any other hot and dreadful place as this. When at last released with drooping feature[s] and troubled spirits, I marched home exclaiming, 'Thank heaven I am alive.'" Even if circus men had made inroads in the area of female attendance, the diverse character of circus crowds made circus-going a diversion that had the potential to produce highly unpleasant social interactions for those who shied away from mixing with their social lessers. Similarly, the entertainment content of many shows remained as bawdy as ever, which is perhaps what prompted this abashed woman to publicly relate her account under a pseudonym. Regardless, these factors taken together made the circus an amusement that gave many women pause.[20]

Showmen faced a more daunting project in trying to reduce the hostility of evangelical leaders. In the Reconstruction and New South periods, many religious and lay authorities remained staunchly opposed to worldly and fashionable diversions like the circus. In 1870, the Baptist church in Greensboro, Georgia decried the tendency of its members to frequent "bar rooms, billiard Saloons, . . . circuses, and dancing parties." "No Christian can follow Jesus," a Louisiana Baptist publication thundered in 1892, "and, then be found in a Circus." In the early twentieth century, one Methodist minister told his congregation in Dahlonega, Georgia that he would "rather hear the clods fall on his child's coffin" than take the youngster to a circus. More generally, almost all evangelical leaders would have agreed that a performance by a traveling show offered little that would enhance their social standard, as historian Donald G. Mathews puts it, of "a disciplined person within a disciplined community."[21]

Still, these rigid attitudes did soften after 1865. In 1867, one clergyman declared in an Athens newspaper that he supported "amusements if properly conducted." Likewise, a Savannah columnist told his readers in 1870 that "there is no very serious sin in seeking one's amusement, when tempered with moderation, seasoned with wisdom, and selected with that proper judgment ever kept in view by the well-thinking, moral-loving portion of humanity." And some ministers, albeit no more than a handful, did actually go to circuses after the Civil War.[22]

For their part, showmen reached out to pious patrons by continuing the antebellum practice of displaying their menagerie collections prior to the ring performance. This arrangement gave evangelicals or others uncomfortable with circus performances the freedom to see the animals and then depart the single tent before the other entertainment began. In 1866, Dan Castello's Great Show announced in Savannah that the display of the show's big cats "will take place prior to the commencing of the Circus performances . . . so that those who come specially to see the animals may return home with their families." Nonetheless, the number of people who actually rose from their seats and departed at any given performance was probably no more than a handful. A Columbus daily observed that "those who desire not to see the circus can retire after this [animal] exhibition, if they wish it. Few express such a wish by leaving." More than likely, those individuals most deeply offended by circuses did not enter the tent, menagerie or no menagerie, at all in the period right after the Civil War.[23]

But beginning in 1871, the fertile minds of P. T. Barnum and his two partners bestowed innovative new ways of soliciting the patronage of religious customers on the circus industry. In April of that year, Barnum, William Cameron Coup, and Dan Castello unveiled a circus of such massive and unprecedented scale that it necessitated three interconnected but separate tents, laid out in a line, to display all its attractions. Customers of P. T. Barnum's Great Traveling Museum, Menagerie, Caravan and Hippodrome entered through a single portal into the menagerie tent, before moving into the second tent, the "museum."

After finishing in the museum, patrons could continue into the last enclosure and take their seats under the big top, where they could enjoy entertainment presented within a single ring. To encourage the reluctant to enter the main tent, the three showmen promised patrons that their troupe would perform an entertainment free of vulgarisms and other offensive elements.[24]

Within these first two enclosures, Barnum and his partners displayed a diverse and expanded content. In their menagerie tent, they exhibited an assortment of exotic animals large enough to necessitate thirty cages. Their "museum" contained a variety of quasi-educational exhibits collected around the world including assorted relics, human "curiosities," and automations in the form of birds, men, and even a goat. The holdings in these two tents reflected the lessons that Barnum had learned as the proprietor of the immensely popular American Museum, an antebellum New York cultural institution that had demonstrated that there was a public demand for rational and respectable amusement that offered both "instruction" and "amusement."[25]

Although many in the industry thought the show's high operating costs would assure its failure, Barnum's organization met with such overwhelming success that other circus owners, including John Robinson and Andrew Haight, quickly scrambled to increase the number of tents carried by their own shows to include separate museum and menagerie enclosures. By the end of the 1871 season, the multiple-tent presentation had become the industry standard among the leading outfits. The Barnum show's three-tent arrangement and more comprehensive content had quickly revolutionized the circus industry.[26]

Even though the increased size of these shows stimulated much excitement among southern circus-goers, the multitent layout gave circus men a new and particularly effective way to attract southern evangelicals. With "entirely distinct and separate" pavilions partitioning the circus entertainment from the other attractions, pious customers could now be assured that they would not have to enter an enclosure where coarse banter and immodestly dressed performers held sway. To alert evangelicals to this fact, the John Robinson Circus made the following proclamation to the populace of Atlanta in 1872: "REMEMBER THE FOLLOWING—Each exhibition held under a SEPARATE TENT, and while one ticket and one price admits to all . . . the exits and entrances are so arranged, and the separation so complete, that a person visiting the Museum, or Menagerie, or Aviary in Tents 1, 2, and 3, neither see nor hear anything relative to the Circus in Tent No. 4." The Haight and Company's Empire City Circus specifically appealed to Christians by informing the public that its "Menagerie [is] in one [pavilion], the Museum [is] in the second and the Circus [is] in the third—those who desire to see the Creator's Wonders . . . can be accommodated without coming in contact with the Arenic entertainment." The directors of the Great Southern Menagerie, Museum, Aviary, Circus, Roman Hippodrome, and Egyptian Caravan noted that since "all good, religious people love to attend the menagerie," they had situated their tents so the circus enclosure stood "entirely separate from the zoological collection, birds, reptiles, etc." The *Savannah Morning News* praised this new system, emphasizing that it filled "a void which has hitherto existed in this class of entertainments, thus affording all a chance to see one exhibition without being compelled to witness the other."[27]

With separate tents serving as a bulwark against claims of immorality, circus men redoubled their efforts to depict their animal attractions as religious in nature. Their primary strategy involved the claim that their shows carried the full complement of God's animal creation. The John Robinson Circus, for example, quoted the book of Genesis in advertising that it possessed "the Largest and most Complete Menagerie, Aviary, and Aquarium in the World, Containing Living Specimens of our CREATOR'S GREAT HANDIWORK, of which *'They went in two and two, unto Noah into the Ark, the male and the female as God had commanded Noah'*" (italics in original). In their promotional material, the proprietors of the Great Southern Circus claimed that they would show the Earth's diverse creatures "just as God made them, in His infinite wisdom." While the managers of Van Amburg's Consolidated Show similarly stressed the size of their collection, they added that they had adorned their animal cages with "Biblical paintings from the famous collection of the eminent artist, Gustave Dore." More sophisticated church members undoubtedly knew of Dore's international reputation as a Biblical illustrator extraordinaire.[28]

Circus managers also singled out certain animals as particularly religious attractions. One perennial standby was the presentation of the hippopotamus as a living relic of Biblical times. One show put up giant posters in the South "which showed in four colors, a huge hippopotamus, with his mouth wide open and a number of wild eyed African natives fleeing to keep from being gulped down whole. Across the top of the poster ran a large streamer that read: 'The Blood Sweating Behemoth of Holy Writ,'" a reference to the huge beast described in the Book of Job. Ever creative circus managers did not limit their claims of sacred animals to just the hippo. During the 1870s alone, the resourceful team behind the John Robinson show gave top billing to "a 3 Horned and 3 eyed Bovine from the Holy Land," a "Sacred Bull," a "sacred ox," "sacred cattle," and the rhinoceros, "or unicorn of Holy Writ." Although more sophisticated southern evangelicals probably saw through such transparent attempts to entice them to enter the menagerie tent, the limited reach of the southern educational system meant that many devout Christians possessed a zeal for their faith but lacked a familiarity with the Earth's natural history. When the circus men promised to display hallowed animals collected from around the world, many less worldly evangelicals likely took them at their word.[29]

Yet even after weighing ministerial criticisms of the attractions, religious or otherwise, of the circus, larger numbers of evangelicals than ever before patronized traveling shows after the Civil War. For instance, even in the wake of

Methodist pastor Parks' public condemnation of circus-going, a leading citizen of Athens recalled that the "religious scruples on the part of church-goers were for the most part thrown aside" when much of his flock entered the show tent. To add insult to injury, the show's clown "impudently thanked" Parks during his act for the free publicity garnered from the published denunciation. Evangelical circus-going had become so commonplace by 1878 that a Columbus newspaper felt comfortable predicting that the audience at the upcoming circus would, as usual, feature a large number of "church members." As further evidence of softening evangelical attitudes toward the circus, historian Ted Ownby cites the ease with which church members moved from discussing the circus to discussing spirituality in their private correspondence and diaries. For instance, an Oglethorpe County woman wrote in her journal: "Went to the animal show & circus this afternoon. I think more persons attended then I ever saw in one in Athens. Some good actors very active & strong. Read in Galatians."[30]

Furthermore, despite the availability of "moral" attractions in the menagerie tent, there is little evidence that large numbers of evangelicals took advantage of the multiple-tent arrangement to preserve the purity of their souls. One west Georgia reporter informed his readers that although many people professed to attend the circus just to see the animals in the menagerie tent, he had "noticed that these menagerie visiting people always remain to see the circus." Thus, the intense advertising campaigns intended to get evangelicals under canvas had succeeded, but not in the way that circus men had expected. Promotional material that presented the menagerie as a chaste enclosure apparently provided Christians with one ready-made and entirely plausible explanation for why they would enter the tents of a circus. As one cynical circus manager noted, "preaching against us never diminished our receipts. You remember that we have the most moral menagerie in the world, and all at one price of admission." Whether caught up in the excitement of Circus Day or because they believed that the entertainment was not all that sinful, evangelicals who attended the circus moved through the menagerie tent and then headed into the big top for the main show.[31]

Still, the question of why evangelicals ignored the anticircus rhetoric of their leaders lingers. Ownby suggests two compelling reasons for why they concluded that circus attendance would not subject them to hellfire in the afterlife. First, most evangelical churches did not discipline their members for going to the circus. When measured against social evils like drinking, dancing, and cursing, circus patronage hardly seemed like a serious offense. Second, since the average Georgia town or city received visits from only two or three circus companies a year, few opportunities existed for Christians to engage in the spiritually dubious activity.[32]

Nonetheless, when evangelicals went to the circus, they did not exit the tent free from the burden of guilt. In 1877, University of Georgia student Edward T.

Bishop attended a circus performance in Athens. Afterward, the young Christian wrestled with his conscience as he wrote an account of his experience in his diary: "My pencil is even now tingling with shame; and if it was not so black it would be as red as a flush rose. I went to the circus last Thursday and having made this confession I shall subjoin a little sketch. But just—here I will add that it is not a regular habit of mine to attend such places." A north Georgia woman informed a family member in 1879 that she "was reforming rapidly, as I did not go to . . . [the] circus." Entering the tent of a traveling show placed Christians in close quarters with entertainment that their religious leaders and many of their spiritually-minded neighbors condemned as sinful to the core. Not surprisingly, remorse and shame lingered after the fact.[33]

In an effort to deal with these feelings, guilt-ridden southern evangelicals sought to rationalize their circus-going. The most common explanation they gave was that they went to the circus not to indulge themselves, but rather to please the juvenile members of their families. Bishop's diary entry (including his strike-though) reveals his strenuous efforts to justify his circus patronage: "By dint of much persuasion made the offer to pay my way for me I was prevailed upon by my relations to carry my little brothers to the circus." Although Bishop was the only adult in his party, a minister pointed out in an Athens newspaper that many people using this excuse often went to the circus in groups of several adults and a single child.[34]

Other Christians simply sought to conceal their circus attendance. One Georgia woman remembered that right after the Civil War "people were very strict" about circus-going. In fact, her congregation's pastor banned just two amusements as the "devil's own": dancing and circuses. While the woman's mother followed the pastor's lead by refusing to let her daughter dance, she did allow her to go to the circus. But "let me tell you," the woman remembered, "she kept it mighty quiet!"[35]

Of course, more secular-minded members of Georgia society could not pass up an opportunity to highlight the seeming hypocrisy of the most moralistic Georgians. Two days after a show, the *Thomasville Daily Times-Enterprise* pointed out "if every one who went to the circus will attend church to-day, there will be large congregations." In the wake of a well-attended performance, the *Tifton Gazette* informed the community, "Quite a number of church members—Baptists and Methodists—are now giving their excuses for attending the circus."[36]

At times, Georgia newsmen took an even more acid tone. The editor of the *Sandersville Herald* denounced one sanctimonious circus patron by writing: "we all know from friend Randall's moralizing about the circus, that he only attended to be able to rebuke the[m] more sharply, not that he cared anything about seeing the show—not at all." The *Tifton Gazette* scornfully reported, "The most popular excuse [among evangelicals] is 'I want to carry the children.'"

Scoffing at such a flimsy rationale, the editor curtly suggested that religious people "ought to go and carry their children to Sunday School too." Finally, a Columbus reporter sarcastically apologized to his readers for failing to examine the inside of a menagerie tent by noting that he had "no children to carry to the menagerie to serve as an excuse for seeing the circus."[37]

Frustrated by their inability to dissuade church members from visiting circuses, religious authorities likewise used the press to publicly criticize the circus-going habit. In 1884, one Mississippi publication investigated why so many "professors of Christianity," or church members, believed that the circus was "a good thing." In a sardonic accounting, the *Clinton Baptist Record* scrutinized some of the moral positives produced by circuses. For one, tented shows engendered "a spirit of enterprise" when circus-goers raised the money for tickets where they had formerly failed to find the funds for church dues. The circus also provided a "cure" for lameness when the "infirm," unable to travel to church, miraculously found themselves able to walk to the circus grounds. But most of all, the *Record* considered the circus a "great preacher." Since every church has members who "have the form of godliness but are servants of sin," the paper argued that circus attendance, like the sermons of any inspired preacher, might encourage these wayward members to take a true inventory of their sinfulness. The *Record* believed that the "coarse scenes" on display inside the tent might produce a true crisis of conscience. Only then would such transgressors "at last, seriously inquire whether they are fit for that Kingdom, where there will be no circuses."[38]

Even though religious leaders never stopped denouncing circus performances in the postbellum period, they made very little progress in halting the flow of Christians into circus tents. With "moral" animal collections and the circus-going desires of children as explanations for their actions, church members decided that the circus represented a relatively minor offense within the realm of sin. In the New South, many church-going Christians regularly attended circuses.

In the 1870s, circus men also turned their attentions to another hesitant group of circus patrons: the growing middle class in southern towns and cities. With poverty and the crop lien plaguing the agricultural economy in the wake of war, the sons of farmers and planters moved from the countryside to growing towns and cities to seek their fortunes as merchants, lawyers, clerks, and bookkeepers. These new positions required the adoption of the habits that were central to bourgeois life in Victorian America: industriousness, self-discipline, self-improvement, and piety. But the fact that they lacked established roots in their new surroundings produced a feeling of unease and made them cautious about their social behavior lest it damage their public sense of respectability. As historian Robert C. Allen notes in regards to popular culture and class formation, "the creation of the bourgeois self was predicated on the exclusion of . . . that which was not respectable, tasteful, or clean." Attending the circus involved taking a place in crowds and audiences filled with poor whites from the town and the countryside, perhaps serving as an uncomfortable reminder to some in the new middle class of their less than genteel background. In addition, the ribald entertainment content of a circus performance could beg the question of whether the middle-class auditor came *for* rather than in spite of such prurient content. The fear of being associated with lesser members of southern society and scandalous entertainment made some middle-class whites uneasy about going to the circus.[39]

To attract those Georgians who valued secular self-improvement as much as religious faith, circus men emphasized the "instructive" aspects of their museum and menagerie tents. The John Robinson Circus maintained that it would offer edification by displaying "the choicest excerpts from the realms of Zoology, Orthinology, Geology, Ichthyology, Conchology, Entomology, Anthropology, Mechanics, Numismatics, Science, Statuary, [and] Oil Paintings." The show's managers promised that such a diverse collection would garner the "admiration not only of Naturalists, but of Poets, Statesmen, Philosophers, and Divines." In his 1875 courier, P. T. Barnum pledged that his circus would present "rational, moral and instructive entertainment" to the public to make it "subservient to Christianity and enlightenment."[40]

Circus men particularly recommended their menageries to students of "natural history." Nineteenth-century Americans found the natural sciences especially fascinating, especially the relation of man to the animal world. Not surprisingly, then, the menagerie of the Great Eastern Circus won praise in Atlanta because it offered "valuable instruction to all seekers of lessons in natural history." An editor of the *Charlotte Observer* agreed that menageries were educational, noting that the Barnum and Bailey animal collection was "as solid, in point of instruction, as a book on natural philosophy."[41]

In fact, circuses did sell such "books" to their patrons. This practice began in the 1830s, and continued well into the post–Civil War era, when the Great Eastern Circus issued a thirty-two-page booklet that detailed the show's animals and their habits. For those customers who chose not to buy these volumes, shows attempted to explain the differences between species through the very layout of their menagerie tents. Reflecting the Victorian interest in organization and rationalization, the Ringling Brothers' Circus trumpeted the fact that it arranged the animal displays in its menagerie in a manner that echoed the taxonomic classification of the day. In this way, even the placement of cages within a menagerie could be edifying.[42]

The Barnum and London show utilized the endorsements of ministers, literary figures, and politicians to make the same point. In its 1886 advertising, the show offered approving statements from the Reverend Henry Ward Beecher, and poets William Cullen Bryant and Henry W. Longfellow. While Beecher highlighted the grand scale of the show, both Bryant and Longfellow emphasized the educational character of the troupe's exhibitions. In its Atlanta newspaper notices, the Barnum outfit added the acclamation of "one of the most distinguished and admired of southern gentlemen," Memphis mayor David P. Hadden. After praising the rational amusement provided by the show, Hadden extolled the fact that the production was "wonderful and incomparable in educational character, morality, discipline, and honesty." This statement represented a letter-perfect affirmation of how showmen hoped the respectable public would receive their shows.[43]

Adults were not the only Georgians who would educationally benefit from a visit to the circus. The John Robinson Circus's broad outreach to Atlanta parochial and public schools in 1872 reveals the interest that showmen had in encouraging the general public to view their shows as instructive. The concern called on adults to bring youths to the show by announcing, "Parents, Sabbath and Public School Teachers should bear in mind that No Public Exhibition ever instituted in America afforded a Tithe of the Practical Lessons of Intuition which are found in this Unique Exposition of Object Teaching." John Robinson himself extended a "special invitation" to students from the Sisters of Mercy Convent, who came to the show under the supervision of one Reverend Cullinan. The show also publicly stated to citizens of Atlanta that it would admit local orphans to the Robinson Zoological Institute, better known as its menagerie, for free.[44]

Other tented enterprises offered discounted tickets to large groups of schoolchildren. In a "Word to Schools" in its *Advance Courier*, Andrew Haight's Great Southern show noted in 1874 that if "teachers will make application to the Manager or Treasurer, they can always obtain liberal deduction in rates, where the school desires to attend in a body." Sometimes, a heightened sense of generosity—and the allure of free publicity—encouraged showmen to do more than offer group rate tickets to ordinary youths. After announcing in Augusta in 1877 that it would reduce the ticket price for school-age children, Howes' Great London Circus admitted a large number of these juveniles for free, which, according to the *Chronicle and Sentinel*, placed "hundreds of bright and grateful little faces" in the audience.[45]

Educated Georgians endorsed this activity because they too believed that circus menageries edified children. A Richmond County newsman noted that Howes' Great London Circus offered "one of the finest opportunities ever offered to the children of Augusta to witness a great moral and instructive entertainment. The collection of wild animals is one of the finest on the American continent, and there can be no possible harm in the children seeing them." Likewise, an Atlanta reporter noted that the animal collection of the John Robinson Circus, with its thirty-six different species, "offered much instruction to the young people as well as 'children of larger growth.'"[46]

While circus men welcomed this validation of the educational value of their shows, they took care not to allow secular concerns to overwhelm the broader Biblical context in which they sought to situate their menageries. The Great Southern called its "zoological and ornithological departments" the "pride and boast of the moral and religious classes." According to one press agent, "it matters not whether the [menagerie] visitor be a student of natural history or merely a casual observer of zoological subjects; whether adult or child; a grand universal lesson of his Creator's wisdom and goodness is before him, and fills him with indescribable admiration for the wonderful and diversely pattered creatures with which the Infinite has populated the earth." During this time period, leading showmen always sought to give their menageries an air of religiosity.[47]

The effort by circus officials to suggest that their menagerie tents provided a combination of worldly and sacred education continued into the twentieth century. In 1905, the John Robinson Circus seamlessly integrated secular and spiritual instruction by employing an actual minister, the Reverend William Sheak, as the show's Zoologist. To emphasize the show's moral priorities, the press agent placed a statement by Sheak in the opening pages of the Robinson circus's official *Route Book*. In a piece imbued with the language of religious didacticism, he called the menagerie "a university for instruction in Natural History" and argued that "the so called lower animals come next to man in the scale of creation, and we dishonor ourselves and dishonor our Creator in knowing so little about them." Although he did concede that the circus industry had its share of immoral and irresponsible people, he confidently held that with continued progress, "there is no reason why the circus cannot be made as moral as a Christian college."[48]

Despite decades of effort to elevate the character of the circus, many turn of the century middle class Georgians, like evangelicals, continued to feel uncomfortable and even embarrassed about their circus-going proclivities. This self-consciousness manifested itself in refusals to acknowledge to others that they had come to town to see the circus. In one south Georgia town in 1897, "there was lot [sic] of the good looking men and handsome women of Wayne [County] in Jesup Monday 'mostly' to see the show, so many of them we failed to get their names, and we know they don't want us to tell who they were and why they were here." Another way that these middling Georgians tried to conceal their interest in the circus was to claim that they had strolled into town for reasons other than the performance. A central Georgia newspaper poked gentle fun at the discomfort of these respectable people by predicting that "quite a number of our citizens will doubtless have business in Barnesville on the 21st," a day when it just so happened that a circus was scheduled to perform. Even as late as 1911, people in Statesboro on Circus Day explained to a local journalist that they had come to town primarily for "business." As the reporter noted with a touch of irony, such individuals "never come for the purpose of seeing the circus."[49]

When all else failed, middle-class townsfolk relied on the tried-and-true excuse that they went to the circus to please their children. In the central Georgia town of Jefferson, W. C. Clark's show "drew quite a large crowd. Of course, a great many people came only to bring the children." Likewise, in the west Georgia town of LaGrange, "everybody came" to the circus "and brought their children, and those that didn't have children borrowed one from somebody." A county sheriff perhaps explained it best: "You see it's this way. The grownups give as their excuse for coming to the circus the fact that they have to bring the kids. Now I have no small children, therefore I borrowed several of the neighbor's kiddies and brought them to Columbus, so I would have an excuse to come to the circus."[50]

Nineteenth-century circus managers never fully succeeded at the task of transforming the public image of their enterprises from morally questionable to chaste and educational entertainment. But showmen did succeed at getting the wavering segment among the anticircus contingent to pay to enter their shows. In the case of elite women, showmen sent the message that circuses represented a socially upright and safe diversion worthy of their attendance by offering charity shows, off-lot ticket outlets, and separate entrances. Although some respectable women remained resolute in their refusal to go to circuses, many more of the "best" ladies in Georgia considered the circus an appropriate amusement by the end of the century than had in the antebellum era. The actions of circus men, as much as broader social and cultural changes, gave rise to this slow embrace of tented entertainment.

In the case of evangelical and middle-class Georgians, many never felt comfortable enough with traveling shows to dispense with all pretense before and after they entered the circus tent. They felt it necessary to claim on Circus Day that they came to town for business rather than pleasure or that they went to the circus only because they wanted to "carry the children." But showmen, with their astute understanding of the prejudices and concerns of these highly self-conscious people, gave their shows an air of edification and religiosity sufficient enough to convince church members and middle-class townsfolk to buy tickets and enter their tents. The circus never became a morally upright diversion in the New South, but it did become a highly profitable one, thanks in part to the patronage of the most moral and respectable Georgians.

> I ain't opposed to spending money on circuses, when there ain't no other way, but there ain't no use in *wasting* it on them. —Twain, *The Adventures of Huckleberry Finn*

> Ginger bread, apples, pea-nuts, cake,
>   Lemonade and stronger take;
> The five cent market, active, firm,
>   Saving from a six month's term;
> Debtor and creditor side by side;
>   Move along with surging tide.
> So Humanity, from pole to pole
>   Plays his part and acts his role.
> Fun must be had, not minding cost—
>   To miss a circus all is lost.
> —"Bird's-Eye View of the Circus Crowd,"
> *Griffin Daily News*, 15 November 1885

FOUR

Wait for the Big Show!
The Economics of the Circus in Georgia, 1865–1920

In the spring of 1870, the John Robinson Circus embarked on its annual tour of Georgia. Although the show put on the same basic performance day after day, the response of city and town elites to the presence of the Robinson Circus varied widely. In the state capital of Atlanta, the *Constitution* called the troupe "unequaled, unapproachable, [and] peerless" and "the biggest and best show of the kind that ever came through this section of the country." But in the mountain town of Dalton, the *North Georgia Citizen* declared that "our people should abstain from patronizing such vagrant exhibitions, whose only object is to get money."[1]

This divergence of opinion did not stem from amusement-related matters such as the quality of the clowning or the skill of the riding. Rather, the comments reflect the understanding among Georgia merchants, storekeepers, businessmen, and politicians that even a few annual circus performances could have a significant economic impact on a local community. A successful tour stop by a large show could swallow up thousands of dollars that, in the eyes of local elites, might better be spent in plantation stores or general stores. On the other hand, circuses were an attraction worth traveling many miles to see. A well-known show could bring thousands of farmers with full pockets into towns and cities ready to spend not only at the circus, but also at retail outlets for provisions, supplies, and the like. For Georgia towns and cities, circuses could be a boon or a bust.

Circuses that played in Georgia after 1865 entered an economic system altered by the turmoil of the Civil War. On the countryside, planters took legal and extralegal actions to keep their labor force dependent and immobile. At the same time, the end of the factorage system and the expansion of the South's railroad network shifted the cotton economy's power base from river and coastal cities to inland towns and cities. Merchants became a new elite in these places, thanks to their involvement in the marketing and distribution of staple crops and their role as suppliers of commercial goods to rural consumers. The city of Atlanta benefited most from this new economic order. Georgia's other communities all slipped in relative importance as Atlanta became the region's major commercial center, thanks to its favorable geographic location and ambitious business class. Left behind were small, isolated villages without railroad access.[2]

In many of these smaller communities, economic hostility to the circus persisted into the twentieth century. Numerous small-town merchants and shop owners believed that circuses took a good deal more money out of town than they brought into it. These men pressed local lawmakers to set performance license fees high enough to discourage circuses from making a tour stop in their communities. Nonetheless, this economic hostility was not confined to rural areas. Savannah businessmen, for instance, had developed a sharp animosity to circuses by 1901 and actively worked to exclude them from the city and, eventually, from all of Chatham County.[3]

Despite these pockets of opposition, showmen did not face organized and widespread hostility for their business tactics or financial influence. The coming of a big show drew droves of Georgia farmers and their families into towns and cities where they joined with local residents to form huge crowds. In preparation, storekeepers ran circus-themed newspaper advertisements before show day and held sales to coincide with the arrival of the circus. Once in town, southerners energetically shopped before and after they patronized the circus, giving the two or three annual visits from circuses the potential to be some of the most lucrative days of the year for merchants. This economic activity often helped to drown out discourses about the moral implications of circuses for community life.

The shows themselves also paid dividends to larger communities. Georgia's businessmen enjoyed monetary windfalls when circuses restocked and show employees shopped while in town to perform. But perhaps the biggest financial boost came from a troupe in winter quarters. Because circuses needed to outlay thousands every month on equipment maintenance, feed, and other supplies, Georgia politicians offered showmen incentives to encourage the selection of their towns and cities as an off-season base of operations. Although the timing and responses varied, by the 1890s most Georgia town and city elites had come to recognize that Circus Day represented a significant opportunity for local businesses and rural southerners to enjoy the benefits of trade. When thousands of people crowded into groceries, taverns, restaurants, and stores to shop and spend on Circus Day in Georgia, the South looked very new indeed.

The first direct contact that Georgia's political and business elites had with showmen after the Civil War came in advance of Circus Day when circus owners or their representatives made contractual arrangements for their upcoming shows. Upon reacquainting themselves with these individuals, Georgians would have quickly grasped that men of northern roots continued to dominate the circus entrepreneurial class. For example, James A. Bailey of Barnum and Bailey fame was born in Detroit; Adam Forepaugh, who in the 1870s had a show rivaled only by Barnum, was born in Philadelphia; and William W. Cole, supposedly the circus industry's first millionaire, was born in New York City. One sociologist has described the circus owners and managers of this era as "shrewd, worldly, clever, and too adventurous to be confined to a single location." Culturally, Georgians would have identified them as Yankees, making them the antithesis of provincial rural southerners, whom the circus men viewed as easily duped "hayseeds" or "rubes." These men set profit as their primary goal, and few of them worried about whether it was earned honestly or dishonestly.[4]

The circus men had economic and cultural outlooks similar to those of the "new men" of Atlanta who rose to prominence after the Civil War. These politicians, merchants, financiers, and professionals were cosmopolitan, economically progressive in outlook, and interested in making money for money's sake. They embraced northern capital and business ways; in fact, about a quarter of them were born in the North. When one Macon journalist described "itinerant adventurers who come today, swindle somebody . . . and are off tomorrow," he was not talking about circus men, but the businessmen of postbellum Atlanta. These men recognized that circus performances increased commercial activity, the backbone of Atlanta's economy, and for that reason were happy to see the shows appear in the Gate City of the South.[5]

This harmony of interests between Atlanta's business class and the circus industry's owners and managers was consistent with the warm reception that circuses generally received from urban audiences between 1865 and 1930. These shows brought exotic animals and spectacular performers into the South, giving rural Georgians the chance to see an exhibition that may have played New York or Philadelphia just weeks before. Nevertheless, entertainment was only part of what drew farmers and their families into cities on Circus Day. In the fall of 1890, the *Savannah Morning News* concluded that many of the country people who came into the city "did not come with the intention of simply seeing the circus, but brought enough money along to lay in a supply of winter clothing and a quantity of other things of miscellaneous character, which can only be secured in a city market and on circus day." Consumerism, as much as an interest in tented amusement, brought big crowds to town on Circus Day in Georgia.[6]

This symbiotic relationship between urban merchants and traveling circuses went beyond embracing the visitors who shopped while in town to see the show. Store owners hung circus posters in their shop windows in exchange for free tickets. Many also sold advance tickets for circuses, thereby increasing foot traffic in their stores. To drum up business, urban storekeepers ran newspaper ads that mimicked circus advertisements. The J. B. White Dry Goods, Clothing, and Shoe Company of Augusta placed a full-page ad in 1883 with pictures of tents, bareback riders, and elephants across the top of the page to draw readers' attention to its advertisement for merchandise. In 1896, Atlanta's McClure's 10¢ Company sought to seize on the anticipatory excitement of an impending show with an ad that blared, "Wait for the Big Show!"[7]

Urban wholesalers and shop owners also profited from the purchases of circuses and their employees. The 1908 Ringling Brothers show bought provisions for one thousand people, six hundred horses, and dozens of exotic animals "whenever a big city is reached." The cook tent manager of the 1904 John Robinson Circus required a daily requisition of "nine hundred loaves of bread, 1,000 pounds of fresh meat, 10 barrels of potatoes, 40 pounds of coffee, 100 pounds of sugar, 25 pounds of butter, 100 dozen eggs, 50 pounds of dried fruit, 20 gallons of milk, 1 ton of ice, $100 worth of canned goods, [and] 200 pounds of smoked meat." Indeed, a Barnum and Bailey press agent estimated in 1894 that a "large part of what was taken in" in any southern city was paid out by the show in that metropolis to cover expenses. Showmen informed the public of this economic benefit by prominently noting their show's total "daily expenses" in their newspaper advertisements. Retail merchants enjoyed additional profits from the personal expenditures of circus workers. Because Atlanta was "the great shopping center of the South," circus employees—"notably generous and good spenders"—spent large sums in retail outlets when they passed through, or near, the Gate City.[8]

Showmen similarly suggested that farmers could profit from the coming of a big show. The Great Southern Circus informed the public that since it needed daily provisions for "almost one thousand men and horses" farmers had "an excellent chance . . . to dispose of large amounts of hay, corn, oats and fodder, butter, eggs, poultry, and any other articles which they may have on hand to sell." Likewise, the show pointed out that the "carnivorous wild beasts" and other animals required "meat . . . bread, eggs, honey, carrots, onions, milk, cabbages, and such like food." Georgians possessing these items simply needed to contact the show's agents in order to sell "them on reasonable terms."[9]

This lucrative business activity and forthright press campaign did not blind urban observers to the fact that circuses departed their cities with thousands of dollars. But instead of fretting over this cash drain, city editors expressed admiration for the pecuniary skills of show owners. After a brief stop, the John Robinson Circus "carried off $2,500 of Savannah's small change[,] a pretty good haul for two days." In the same city in 1882, "the expenses of the circus company were stated to be $2,000. It is estimated that the receipts for the two performances amounted to over $5,000, leaving a handsome margin." Along the same lines, the *Atlanta Daily Herald* stated that the owner of Lent's Circus "richly deserved the $3,000 he got last night." The retail business drummed up by circuses, along with the restocking done by these outfits, generally counteracted any sense that they profited too mightily from their visits to urban areas.[10]

Despite the broad enthusiasm among white urbanites for the economic impact of circuses, some conservative African Americans in Atlanta spoke out against spending at these amusements. After a 1907 visit by a large traveling show, the editor of the black newspaper the *Atlanta Independent* suggested that "it seems right and proper for one to see a show once a year, but the poor can ill afford to take in every one that comes along. It is all right to carry the young to see the animals, but as they grow older they ought to be taught that such habits do not feed, clothe, and house them. It is the poorest among us, always, who follow up these enticements." This call for financial restraint when the circus comes to town reflects the internalization of Victorian values among respectable African Americans in the South. Many middling and elite African Americans, like their white counterparts, continued to believe well into the twentieth century that the only thing worth paying for at most circuses was the menagerie. To attend frequently was a clear sign of being dissolute and spendthrift.[11]

This notion that circuses exacerbated poverty—and the attendant view that the poor had little ability to resist the circus—led an African American columnist writing in the same publication in 1917 to applaud the cancellation of a traveling show:

> The best thing that ever happened for Atlanta since I have been getting around the alleys and streets was for God to send a downpour of rain when the Circus came to town last week, which kept everybody at home. Usually the circus drains our poor people the same as a crushing mill makes oil out of cotton seeds, and there is nothing left but the hulls. This time, the Old Master sent the blessed rain.

Rain might be what was needed to keep the less fortunate away from circuses, because as one black preacher put it, such shows were "hard to resist."[12]

The divergent opinions that white and black journalists held concerning circuses can be explicated by considering the differing financial impacts that they had on white and black communities in the Gate City. For one thing, Atlanta's black businesses almost certainly did not share equally in the consumer-driven windfall from circus performances. On Circus Day, shoppers that came to the city to watch the parade from the sidewalk found themselves a few steps away from white, rather than black, retail outlets. In addition, it is likely that few if any circuses transacted their wholesale business with African American entrepreneurs. Finally, while the city's leading—and white-owned—dailies enjoyed advertising revenues from all the circus companies that played Atlanta, the city's black-owned newspaper, the *Independent,* featured few circus ads in its pages. Although some white leaders probably shared the paternalistic view that the poor attended circuses not out of rational choice but out of compulsion, the profitability of Circus Day for Atlanta's white business community helped mute their views in the public discourse surrounding the circus. [13]

Scholars have properly noted a difference in ambition and ideology between Atlanta's business elite and that of Georgia's smaller inland cities during the late nineteenth century. While the merchants, professionals, and politicians of a city such as Columbus were interested in enriching themselves and their town, both contemporary observers and modern historians agree that they were less economically aggressive and culturally more conservative than Atlanta's business class. Still, these men typically thought that circus performances had the potential to energize economic activity in retail and wholesale businesses, even if before the 1880s they had expressed qualms about the moral and financial influences that circuses had on their cities. By the 1890s, however, the economic outlook of these men was more closely in line with that of Atlanta's leaders.[14]

The free-spending habits of Columbus' poor people on Circus Day topped the local elite's list of complaints about the circus. This extravagance was particularly galling to their partners in the community-building project, the city's newspapermen. In the fall of 1865, the editor of the *Columbus Daily Sun* was shocked at the scene when the circus was in town. He and his party saw people at the show "who are living on charity; people who are unable to pay house rent; others who, on the morrow, could not tell where food for the day was to come from. . . . For a mere temporary gratification—a few hours of useless pleasure—whole days of misery are incurred." Six years later, a reporter observed that "notwithstanding hard times, nearly all who wanted to go [to the show] found the wherewithal to go. As usual, many doubtless attended who had but little to eat or wear at home." Wherewithal could come from many different sources. In 1879, a Columbus man pawned his false teeth to get the money needed to buy a ticket. "This is," the *Enquirer-Sun* dryly noted, "by far the greatest influence we ever knew a circus to have over an individual."[15]

In Columbus, these attitudes about profligacy and poverty quickly changed once it became evident that the excitement of a circus performance might prompt people to spend money both on the show *and* on consumer goods. In 1878, one reporter predicted that when the circus arrives "the country people will flock from all directions to spend their half dollars and to lay in their supplies. The merchants will do a brisk business." Two decades later, "after the parade was over the visitors to the city had an hour or more time to visit the stores and do their shopping. Many of the merchants enjoyed a large trade and the hotels and restaurants were overrun with customers." A Columbus editor summed up the calculus of the typical circus performance by writing in 1892: "Although it [the circus] took in a great deal of money, a very large sum was disbursed for provisions for the immense army of attaches and for the animals, and in addition, thousands were attracted to the city and retail stores were all benefited."[16]

Savannah's economic and political leaders eventually reached a different conclusion regarding the economic impact of the circus. Despite holding procircus views from the end of the Civil War through the 1890s, these leading citizens bucked the general trend of Georgia's city and large town elites becoming increasingly enthusiastic about the financial benefits of circus performances. By late 1901, Savannah's merchant community had reassessed the financial implications of these exhibitions and had begun to pressure local politicians to keep these shows out of the city.

Before 1890, there was little talk in Savannah of a link between the local economy and circuses. Big tops came and went, and public comment tended to simply compliment shows for their success in drawing customers. Yet during the last decade of the century, the store owners of the city began to connect consumer spending and circuses. After an 1894 Barnum and Bailey appearance, press reports indicated that the merchants "did a rushing business" on Circus Day. This commercial success led the *Savannah Morning News* to note that "while the circus took a good deal of money out of the city, it brought a good deal here, and a good many people who spent their money." Merchants said that the trade on Circus Day and the day after was the "best they have had in some time." Two years later, circus enthusiasts from the countryside "who had a little money left after paying their railroad fare, blew it in the Broughton and Congress Street stores, or in . . . bar-rooms." Taking the lead in applauding the convergence of circuses and consumerism was the city's Retail Merchants' Association (RMA), a politically active organization that promoted the interests of the city's storekeepers. In particular, the RMA's members celebrated the fact that rural people who had traveled to town to see the circus "had money to spend and spent it" in Savannah's retail outlets.[17]

By 1901, however, these businessmen had ceased viewing circuses as economically advantageous and began to lobby against their performances. In the final months of that year, the RMA petitioned the Savannah City Council to raise the five-hundred-dollar city license fee for circuses, since such organizations "take away a considerable amount of money which otherwise would legitimately circulate among the merchants of the city." Although the city council refused to increase the fee, in the years that followed the RMA and its members continued to support the idea that circuses damaged the local economy. In the wake of two circus tour stops in October 1904, the *Savannah Morning News* reported that "most" local merchants thought that "since the appearance of the two big shows business has been very dull." And echoing a popular viewpoint among Georgia's small-town merchants, Savannah shopkeepers concluded that "entirely too much money is taken away from a city in proportion to what's left" behind by traveling shows.[18]

The rejection of circuses by Savannah merchants did not mean that they believed that large-scale public entertainments lacked the ability to boost trade. As a stand in for circuses, city retailers and politicians began to support locally sponsored and controlled carnivals and fairs to stimulate economic activity in the city. Just months before its campaign against circuses began in earnest, the RMA declared that its members endorsed an upcoming Elks' Street Fair and Carnival because local shopkeepers support "their own interests and advance those of the city when they join a movement designed . . . to bring thousands of visitors to Savannah." Finally, in 1909, the RMA got its wish when the city council and the mayor passed a license fee of one thousand dollars per day for large circuses, an unusually high tax that effectively barred such shows from playing the metropolis. The mayor cited the fact that when circuses play "a great deal of money is taken away from the city" as one of the reasons why he backed the license increase. The anticircus position of merchants and city officials continued into the 1920s, when the only way that large circuses could perform in Savannah or in Chatham County proper was to play under the auspices of city- and county-sponsored extravaganzas like the Tri-County Fair or the Georgia State Fair. In this manner, Savannah's leaders came to more closely control who was to profit from a circus performance.[19]

At first glance, Savannah's turn toward protectionism is peculiar. Like Columbus, for example, the city had a significant number of shops that might benefit from circus performances in the city. In addition, Savannah visitors had demonstrated a willingness to shop and go to the circus on the same day, just as they had in the 1890s. But Savannah lacked some key economic and demographic advantages held by Columbus. With the rise of the railroad as the nation's main transportation network, southern seaport cities like Savannah found themselves at a true disadvantage when compared to the region's growing railroad cities. Savannah's economic fortunes suffered accordingly, making local retailers particularly aggressive about advocating for their financial interests. Once the RMA's leaders concluded that circuses were hurting their bottom line, they felt compelled to act.[20]

Ultimately, it was the number of would-be shoppers that dwelled in the hinterland surrounding Savannah, and not circuses themselves, that affected consumption on Circus Day. Excluding the population of the city of Savannah, the number of people dwelling in Chatham County and the adjacent counties of Effingham and Bryan numbered 31,451 in 1900. By contrast, the number of individuals living outside of Columbus in Muscogee County and the counties abutting it—Chattahoochee, Harris, Marion, and Talbot counties in Georgia and Lee County and Russell County in Alabama—totaled 117,207 in the same year. A circus that played Columbus, then, had the potential to attract nearly four times as many rural consumers as when it pitched its tent in Savannah. So while Columbus merchants welcomed crowds of country people eager to see a show and to shop while they were in town on Circus Day, Savannah shopkeepers faced throngs comprised largely of people who dwelled in Savannah itself. These Savannah circus aficionados, unlike Columbus circus-goers, felt no particular urgency to shop on Circus Day since they could visit city shops on any ordinary day of the week. For this reason, Savannah's merchant community decided to cast their lot with entertainments under local aegis that were certain not to "take all the money out of town."[21]

The urban exception of Savannah notwithstanding, elites in large towns offered more consistent complaints about the economic impact of traveling shows after the Civil War. These planters, merchants, and professionals were "profoundly conservative" but had an economically "similar outlook" to the elites of Atlanta. By the 1890s, most of these men had put their objections to circuses aside, choosing instead to focus on the advantages of thousands of potential shoppers lured into town by these outfits.[22]

In these towns in the 1870s and 1880s, local economies benefited when country people sold farm commodities to get funds to go to a show. One Athens observer was "amused" in 1873 by "the various articles brought in for sale by the different persons—some had chickens, some little sacks of loose cotton, some a load of wood, some dried fruit, cow hides, potatoes, apples, and most any other article that you could call for, which they disposed of to obtain the wherewith to enter the show." In the cotton town of Griffin, country people who needed money to attend John B. Doris' New Monster Shows sold butter and eggs to local residents in 1884. In the hours before an 1881 show in north Georgia, "people from the four quarters of the earth began to arrive, all bent on seeing the circus. Country produce, which had long been withheld from the Dalton market, was profusely abundant." The enticement of the circus stimulated much commerce on show day. Since these towns lacked broadly developed retail districts, circus performances helped put farm products into circulation.[23]

By the 1890s, larger numbers of merchants had opened stores in these towns, and the main benefit on Circus Day came not from farmers bringing goods to market, but rather from visitors shopping at local establishments. On Circus Day in Americus, "local businessmen reaped a good harvest of ready cash, for there were many things that were in constant demand, from items of larger variety on down to those of lesser importance. To sum up briefly, trade was very lively and profitable." LaGrange's "merchants did a good business" on Circus Day, with "everybody spending their money freely and enjoying life." Commentary in a Griffin paper summed up the notion that circuses boosted business: "A circus does not 'take all the money' as erroneously supposed. It is a distributing agency in which all reap a harvest. And besides the people like it."[24]

Predictably, showmen supported the idea that the circus was an economic boon to the circus owner and the shopkeeper. The press agent for the Forepaugh and Sells Brothers' Shows averred that "circus day is the biggest shopping day of the year. No one ever heard a storekeeper complain that a circus took too much money out of his town in one day." In a later piece, the same press agent wrote that on the way to see a show "father's pocket bulges with a roll . . . and mother has a list of things to be purchased" while in town. When local merchants charged that traveling outfits reduced their profits, circus men offered the "incontrovertible fact" that "the circus may, and probably does, take money out of the county, but it leaves more money in town than it takes out" so "every merchant in town is benefited by a visit of the circus." In this formulation, the circus aided the transfer of money from country folk to town merchants. Another creative circus man argued that shows only took in "idle" money that Georgians saved especially for amusements. In other words, circuses collected funds never intended for shop owners.[25]

These claims probably did little to change the minds of those small-town businessmen who felt that circuses hurt the local economy. As late as the 1920s, complaints still could be heard in relatively isolated or conservative small towns and villages about circuses siphoning off a large portion of the available spending money. Since these communities lacked the broad base of retail and wholesale outlets that would benefit from circuses, local businessmen found little reason to cheer when circuses pitched their tents nearby. As one Georgia man raised in the tiny plantation-belt town of Blakely recalled: "The coming of the circuses was not favored by our merchants because they took considerable money out of the community." Small-town shopkeepers understood that a "successful" circus performance at the height of harvest season could cause a short term but painful economic downturn.[26]

In the wake of circus exhibitions, many small-town editors decried the profit taking by circuses. In 1878, the *Monroe Advertiser* declared that the John Robinson Circus "gave three performances in Washington County and cleared one thousand dollars at each performance. Good for the circus but bad for the people." The *Swainsboro Forest Blade* complained that "the big show has gone and Emanuel County is $2,000 the worse by its coming." In the minds of these men, a cancelled performance merited more praise than an actual exhibition. An Upson County editor proclaimed, "We are truly glad that he [John Robinson] has given Upson the go by this year. There will be several thousand dollars here next spring and summer that would have been very absent if he had showed in the county." As the argument went, money spent at a traveling exhibition made the county poor and the circus men rich.[27]

A central reason for the hostility of many small-town merchants was the revenue-maximizing business methods used by showmen. People living in the vicinity of Tifton received the following preshow warning from their local paper: "The Sells & Rentfrow [Circus] have men connected to the show who will not only steal your money but your breath, if you give them half a chance." Such mercenary tactics even irritated people living in larger, more commercial towns. For instance, an Athens newspaperman expressed frustration in 1873 at the disjuncture between show bills that promised "'every thing seen for one price of admission'" and the "constant demand upon the purses of the audience." He noted that "there were 'side-shows,' concerts, song books, refreshments, fans and everything else that Yankee ingenuity could conceive to carry away money. . . . We never in our lives, saw so many attachments to a show to carry away money as there was to Lent's circus." The S. H. Barrett show's grandiose 1882 advertisements in Waynesboro deviated so greatly from the uninspired nature of the troupe's performance that the local reporter left the tent outraged at the "devious" lengths "these traveling nuisances" would go "to accumulate the 'almighty dollar.'" For southern observers used to more leisurely ways of doing business, deceptive advertising and seemingly incessant efforts to separate circus patrons from their money produced feelings of anger and resentment. By contrast, urban circus-goers who regularly rubbed shoulders with businessmen cut from the same cloth as circus owners and managers found little reason to grouse about the methods of showmen.[28]

The tendency of seedier shows to play small towns rather than big cities also helps illuminate why many townspeople disliked circuses. These disreputable outfits carried large contingents of gamblers and confidence men who were eager to defraud gullible countrymen. Although urban areas saw small-scale gaming and petty crime perpetrated by people following or connected to shows, dishonest circus men preferred showing in rural communities because law enforcement scrutiny was often limited or even nonexistent in these places, especially when lawmen turned a blind eye to rigged gambling operations run inside sideshow tents. After a representative show of this type raised its tents in Moultrie, a reviewer noted that it offered a "great big nothing" under its show tents but did feature a "great deal of gambling" that swindled locals. In 1905, the Van Amburg Circus carried into Statesboro "every type and form of a thief, pick pocket, cut throat, gambler and thug that was ever seen under one circus tent." Because money lost at the gambling table was money that would not circulate in the town's economy in the coming months, small-town businessmen had little love for circuses.[29]

But poor circus performances often left patrons feeling just as cheated as if they had been swindled out of their money in a rigged gambling game. In Athens, the Lent Brothers show "fell very far short of expectations," and "carried off a large amount of money, hard as the times are." At a Griffin circus, "the acrobats were sorry, the clowns were not funny and only the few animals acted like actors. Upon the whole the show was a disappointment and the few hundred people who gave good fifty cent pieces to see it were 'stung.'" The Norman Brothers' performance in the central Georgia village of Gray was "the biggest humbug that ever hit this place. They had a full house and carried away something like a hundred dollars for which they gave nothing like the value received. May all such pass us by in the future."[30]

The regular laments from small-town Georgians about money lost while gambling or spent on admission especially irked one group of local businessmen, newspaper editors. After hearing of heavy gaming losses at a show held in the tiny town of Powder Springs, one newspaperman carped that "some of these citizens who bet and lost would consider it a hardship to subscribe for [sic] their county paper." Perhaps with a touch of hyperbole, an Emanuel County editor reported that only one "man out of five hundred" who came to town to see a circus did not forget his pecuniary responsibilities to the local paper. After extending loans to several poor and hungry citizens who then entered the tents of a traveling concern, the staff of the *Dahlonega Nugget* fulminated about such behavior: "If people can raise money to attend a show they can do likewise in getting it to buy food. We have been helping along but will do it no more."[31]

This critique of circus spending as wasteful stemmed from the limited acceptance of the virtues of consumer spending in the South's rural areas. Many Georgians living outside of cities at the turn of the century still believed that careful accumulation, rather than self-indulgent consumption, represented sensible economic behavior. But the circus, with its daring performers, fantastic animals, and dazzling entertainment inspired many circus fans to spend with nary a thought for the long-term economic consequences. In order to not miss the big shows that appeared in the vicinity of Macon County, sharecroppers borrowed funds from their plantation landowner. Charles Belvin secured an advance of $1.25 in 1881 so he could take "Jenny" to the circus. In 1888, Hal Forhand borrowed seventy-five cents from his landowner for a show. The following year Jim Belvin took a $4.00 advance "for [a] circus." This type of debtor spending was not confined to African Americans. One white man in Dublin lacked the money to go to a show so he "tried to borrow it but failed. He then went to a merchant and bought a dollar's worth of coffee on credit, sold it for seventy-five cents cash, and was soon viewing the animals and the leapers with as much unconcern as the man who had to get a twenty dollar bill changed to purchase his ticket." Since circus entertainment hardly represented a necessity of life, many leading citizens believed that money spent at these shows was the height of extravagance.[32]

Despite the carping from small-town people about the profitability of circuses, several shows disbanded in the state when they went bankrupt. In one memorable instance, an 1889 circus bankruptcy enriched the lives of Georgia residents when an Atlanta businessman purchased its menagerie and donated it to the city's Grant Park. This group of animals became the basis of Atlanta's first zoo, providing a permanent site of instruction and amusement for the people of the city. When shows went bust in Georgia, local residents received object lessons in the financial challenges faced by traveling showmen.[33]

At first glance, the 1885 collapse of Colonel Giles' circus in a small central Georgia town seems to illustrate the same point. The show, apparently receiving a lukewarm welcome from Georgians, limped its way across the state in early December before arriving in Monroe on the twelfth of that month. On that day, the holder of its mortgages refused to extend any more loans to owner Giles Pullman, effectively stranding the show in Monroe. Over the next three weeks, people came from miles around to see the show's animals for free, in a daily procession that "would have done credit to a world's fair." In early January, however, the sheriff announced that the final day of this extended performance would take place on January 8, when he would oversee the liquidation of the show through public auction. In order to witness this singular event, huge numbers of people from the town and country gathered to form "one of the largest crowds ever seen in Monroe, hanging days not excepted." Among those who came to Monroe for the auction were some of the nation's wealthiest circus owners, namely, Adam Forepaugh, Lewis Sells, W. W. Cole, and John Robinson. These men wasted no time in demonstrating their financial reach, especially after some local citizens challenged the circus owners by offering bids on the available lions, horses, and elephant. Not surprisingly, Monroe residents quickly found themselves outbid by the showmen, who along with a few zookeepers, bought up all of the animals. As the country people watched Giles Pullman's dream sold off, they certainly apprehended that not all circus men got rich. But as the leading showmen of the Gilded Age bought it up, they also understood that many had found success beyond the wildest dreams of Monroe residents.[34]

Even if not all small-town residents found themselves sympathizing with the financial plight of the showman, sizable numbers of small- and large-town businessmen did ultimately reconcile themselves to the economics of Circus Day. Newspaper editors, for instance, frequently muted their criticisms of traveling shows once a troupe's advance agent appeared in the newspaper office offering cash and free tickets to pay for advertising. Making reference to the opinion held by many conservative Georgians that the animal collections carried by circuses represented their only uplifting aspects, the *Griffin Daily News* noted that a number of its competitors "are issuing supplements on account of a rush of circus advertising. Some of these papers, too, had previously taken occasion to express their strong disapproval of circuses. But then it may be that they were induced to accept the advertisements on account of the very moral menagerie."[35]

Town merchants, like urban shopkeepers, also demonstrated their understanding that circuses could be good for business by advertising sales that coincided with circus performances. In 1901, Tate, Eaton and Coffey's Wholesale and Retail Store in Dalton ran an ad entitled "The Big Show," encouraging potential shoppers from "out-of-town" to "come in" while "waiting for the noonday parade." The store announced: "WE WILL SHOW unprecedented bargains in brand new fall goods in every department." One Waynesboro dry goods store ran an advertisement a week prior to the arrival of a circus stating, "You will have to pay seventy-five cents to see the circus, but if you will go to the store of S. Schwarzweiss you will see the best display of Plaids, Sea Island Homespun, Prints ... at Prices So Low, they are astonishing." A Griffin grocery placed a front-page ad two weeks before an 1885 Sells Brothers performance announcing that "The Circus is Coming," but "G. W. Clark & Son have been here all the time, and have always kept the best line of groceries in the city." This practice of encouraging shopping on Circus Day through newspaper advertising continued well into the twentieth century.[36]

With so many towns benefiting from circus performances, community leaders in places that saw few traveling outfits appealed to showmen to add their municipalities to their annual tour routes. Town boosters placed notices in the entertainment trade journal *Billboard* in 1902 stating that "Cedartown, Ga., the county seat of Polk County, is a very good agricultural center. Just outside of the town's limits are located five cotton mills, employing about 3,000 people. It is a good field for tent shows, especially for circuses, and the latter would do well to include the town in their route when in that vicinity." The initial request unsuccessful, Cedartown representatives ran another call for circuses two years later, noting that the town's economy was booming and its citizens were "tent show hungry." A retired circus man turned fruit merchant made a similar request for the town of Cornelia in 1914.[37]

In spite of the potential rewards, local governments did not permit circuses to come to town on the whim of the showman. State, county, and municipal authorities in Georgia regulated circuses through performance license taxes. The State of Georgia taxed circuses as early as 1820, and the city of Atlanta levied taxes on circuses by 1847. Right after the Civil War, the high cost of license fees assessed by southern governmental bodies began to raise the ire of showmen. Georgia, along with Texas and Tennessee, often drew particular criticism. For instance, a circus man seeking to highlight exorbitant southern taxation in the pages of the *Clipper* gave the example of the small town of Cuthbert, Georgia, which charged "canvas shows" $200 per performance in 1866. By point of comparison, Columbus, which had more than three times as many residents as Cuthbert, charged $10 per performance during the same general time period.[38]

High southern circus taxes grew out of three factors. First, some conservative politicians voted for increased license fees out of "puritanical" motives, a legislative position denounced by the *Daily Atlanta Intelligencer* as reflective of a "spirit of intolerance." Second, the money-stealing schemes of crooked showmen encouraged some legislators to use license fees to deter circuses from appearing. One southern judge told a circus man in 1901 that after the Civil War "the majority of shows carried so many thieves and grafters with them, and robbed the ignorant farmers and innocent boys out of all the money they had that the communities considered that they were better off without the circus, and the high license was made for the sole purpose of keeping them away." Third, circus taxes offered an easy way for governmental bodies to raise revenue. In sum, licenses gave governments a measure of control over who showed within their boundaries, and allowed them to recoup some of the money that traveling concerns carried away.[39]

Circuses were taxed in Georgia through a variety of methods. Most counties, towns, and cities required payment of a flat fee that all shows would have to pay if they wanted to exhibit. Yet other more innovative systems were used as well. The State of Georgia assessed a fee based on the population of the community where the outfit performed. The greater the population, the more the circus would have to pay. Some towns and cities taxed a circus according to the number of railroad cars it used to transport itself. This type of law was designed to levy a higher tax on larger shows than on smaller shows.[40]

Other localities used a more personal and flexible approach. Reflecting the role that informal interactions between circus men and local politicians could play in determining the fee that a show would pay, regardless of the law on the books, the treasurer of the John Robinson Circus recorded in his ledger in 1909 that Carterville's "ordinance calls for 50.00 [but it] can be cut." Other communities wrote their circus tax laws to give their chief executives the freedom to assess a fee that he believed was appropriate. Stockbridge's statute called for the mayor to fix the price but set a range of one to ten dollars. Similarly, Savannah's 1880 law gave the city's elected leader the power to charge whatever "payment" he "deemed proper and expedient." Obviously, showmen who wanted to play Savannah sought to stay on friendly terms with the city's mayor.[41]

Taxation methods aside, the range of fees assessed by Georgia town and city councils demonstrates that these bodies understood that circus licenses represented a powerful tool for economic management. Community leaders that wanted to restrict circus performances set fees high. To keep circuses from competing with city-sponsored fairs, Savannah installed a seasonal $5000 circus license in the 1920s. Fitzgerald's city council passed a prohibitory law in 1914 that charged circuses $1000 per performance day. In 1911, a Jackson County editor laid bare the legislative intent behind this level of taxation when he railed against "cheap shows" that "are money getters . . . We trust that the Jefferson city council will put such a large tax on such performances that [it] will forever prohibit them from again showing inside the corporate limits of this town." Since these fees could easily surpass the net income of a single performance, circuses actively avoided places with steep licenses.[42]

Conversely, communities that wanted to encourage circus performances set low license fees. After the city's high license led to a circus drought from 1907 to 1909, Columbus politicians reduced the tax to make their municipality more attractive to shows. This cut rate was in effect until the mid-1920s. Similarly, the City Council of Newnan decreased its fee from $500 to $100 in 1916 because it was "anxious" to have a circus perform. The town of Washington lowered its license in 1922 after having had no circuses there for two years. Circuses could potentially "take all the money out of a town," but they could also provide an economic boost.[43]

Not surprisingly, circus officials frequently tried to evade taxation. In 1878, the John Robinson Circus undertook a tour of Georgia's small towns in an effort to circumvent the state law that taxed circuses according to community population. That same year, the Robinson show also tried to beat the state's tax by advertising that its admission fee was for access to the menagerie tent with free admission to the circus performance tent. The show did this so it might be classified as a menagerie and not a circus for taxation purposes since the menagerie tax was lower than the circus tax. Another tax-dodge method favored by showmen involved setting up their tents just outside the town line, so that the circus would only be liable for a county tax. McDonough, like many municipalities, wrote its license ordinance to take advantage of the fact that even if a show played out of town, it would still desire the free advertising provided by a circus parade though the center of town: "Each circus shall pay in advance for each performance a tax of $25. Circus parades, if exhibition is given outside of the city, $25.00."[44]

Some circuses petitioned city and town councils for license reductions. Typically, circus owners who publicly advertised that their shows were monstrous operations described their shows in much more modest terms when meeting with local lawmakers. In 1907, the managers of the sizable Hagenbeck-Wallace Circus told Savannah city officials that their show was "a very meek affair and nothing like a regular circus." On occasion, municipal bodies granted requests for reductions, as with the Barnum and Bailey petition presented to the Atlanta City Council in October 1903. But this approach could backfire. After the Sparks Circus appealed to the city of Dublin in 1917 for a reduction of the $200 circus license, the City Council doubled the fee.[45]

Some Georgia officials engaged in their own license trickery. In 1875, council members of some Georgia towns promised free licenses to the John Robinson

Circus prior to the show date only to appear on the circus grounds on the day of the performance demanding from $50 to $100. Presumably these visits occurred after the troupe had begun to set up so management had no choice but to pay.[46]

While Georgia leaders differed on whether they should encourage or discourage circuses from showing in their towns, there was no disagreement over the fact that a show in winter quarters financially benefited a community. Circuses and carnivals wintered in the southern states because of the region's mild weather and comprehensive transportation infrastructure. Impresario William Sells noted that Georgia, in particular, was especially "adapted by climate and water and railway facilities for wintering."[47]

A show's decision to dwell in a certain town or city for the winter could mean thousands for a local economy. For example, the Van Amburg Show wintered in Atlanta's Piedmont Park in 1905–6, and planned "to spend not less than $40,000 while located here, which means a good thing for Atlanta merchants." The spending habits of show employees also aided local economies. Harris Nickel Plate Show workers "had saved up their earnings in order to have enough to carry them through the winter months," so "Valdosta merchants will get a good many dollars out of what was paid out this morning and will get many more dollars out of the show people the four months that they will be here."[48]

A circus in winter quarters was so desirable that towns and cities often made the expensive capital improvements needed by shows. In 1916, Americus city officials gladly agreed to build the extra railroad sidetrack requested by John Robinson Circus officials. Yet circus men also understood the economic benefits of a show in winter quarters and did not shy away from pressing for a favorable deal. While deciding where in Georgia to winter in late 1900, William Sells told the Savannah press that officials have "offered no inducements" to his show to encourage him to choose their city. The Mayor of Macon, by contrast, had proposed giving the show "the exhibition place, free of charge, if we will winter there." Not incidentally, he also mentioned that his show would spend between $10,000 and $15,000 wherever it wintered. Two days later, the show came to an agreement with the City of Savannah for use of the old government hospital complex as an off-season headquarters.[49]

At the end of the Civil War, the former Confederacy was at a crossroads between the Old and New South. For traditionalists, the critique of the economics of Circus Day bolstered the cultural and religious case against the circus. In fact, the economic criticism proved to be the most durable of all the arguments against the circus by retaining its force in Georgia's small towns into the 1920s. The tension between the progressive-minded apostles of the "New South Creed" and the state's traditionalists remained central to the debate over the role and meaning of circuses in Georgia society.

But Georgia's ambitious business elites would hear nothing of looking to the past. They sought to improve the material condition of their communities and seized every opportunity to stimulate economic growth and development. These men welcomed circus appearances because they brought country people with full pockets and purses into town. Circuses also injected dollars into the state when they wintered in Georgia communities or just restocked while on tour. The New South's commercial class would dismiss those who would complain about the economic and cultural implications of dealing with these enterprises as hopelessly out of step with the new ways of doing business in the South.[50]

Undeniably, it was the promise of pulse-quickening entertainment that inspired Georgians from the countryside to make long trips into town on show day. But after arriving, these people also reveled in the experience of shopping at crowded stores filled with enticing merchandise at "Special Circus Day Bargain" prices. Like veteran circus men, local merchants understood that the celebratory excitement of Circus Day stimulated people to spend money in a way that they would not normally do, whether at the sideshow gambling table or in the dry goods store. Georgia citizens wanted to see the Gilded Age's most spectacular form of mass entertainment, and local business elites happily capitalized on the crowds that squeezed into their stores while waiting for the circus parade to start or the Big Top tent flaps to part. In the end, it was not morality or provincial culture that ruled the day when the circus was in town. In Georgia during these years, the economics of consumer spending and the attractions of popular culture in a nationalizing economy won out over southern regional culture.[51]

A view of P. T. Barnum's show lot, 1873. Barnum and his partners pioneered the use of multiple tents. Patrons offended by circus performances could see the show's animals and curiosities in the line of smaller canvas enclosures (on the left) without having to enter the show's big top (on the right). Courtesy of Circus World Museum, Baraboo, Wisconsin (BPT-np-73-1).

Black and white farmers gather around a cotton gin in Handy, Georgia, 1908. Circus bill posters frequently covered structures in rural areas with advertisements in order to spread the word of their show's upcoming performances to country people. Courtesy of the Georgia Archives, Vanishing Georgia Collection (cow-008).

A southern Circus Day parking lot, 1916. Rural people drove their wagons into town in the morning before a big show and parked them in the fields near the circus lot since the community's streets would be jammed with people awaiting the parade. Courtesy of Circus World Museum, Baraboo, Wisconsin (RB-np-16-48).

Black and white people in Atlanta stand shoulder-to-shoulder at the turn of the century as a circus wagon pulled by a team of horses trundles its way to the show lot. Courtesy of the Kenan Research Center at the Atlanta History Center (HGS1-26A).

Circus aficionados fill Atlanta streets, balconies, and windows as elephants lumber through the downtown area and stop cross traffic, circa 1895. Parade watchers shopped in local businesses located along the parade route before, during, and after the procession. Courtesy of the Kenan Research Center at the Atlanta History Center (PET 1-7).

Circus parade in Madison, Georgia, circa 1912. A successful procession transformed parade spectators into circus customers as they followed the steam calliope and other parade components from town to the show lot. Courtesy of the Georgia Archives, Vanishing Georgia Collection (mor-017-018).

Wooden framed snack stands surround a southern circus lot, 1916. Customers could feast on foods and beverages before and after they visited the circus lot proper. Courtesy of Circus World Museum, Baraboo, Wisconsin (RB-np-16-49).

The social scene around some snack stands in the South, 1916. Some religious and respectable African Americans congregated around these vendors on Circus Day in lieu of attending the morally questionable circus, although, as evidenced by the man and boy on the right, some white people spent time in this area as well. Courtesy of Circus World Museum, Baraboo, Wisconsin (RB-np-16-47).

"Yankee" circus men at a Barnum and Bailey ticket wagon, circa 1900. These showmen stood in windows located above the eye level of their customers, encouraging them to accidentally "walk away" from their change after receiving their means of admission. Courtesy of Circus World Museum, Baraboo, Wisconsin (B&B-np-04-19).

The "big push" of a crowd mobbing the ticket wagon on a Barnum and Bailey midway, 1906. For an additional dime, circus lot visitors could enter the "Annex," or sideshow, before going into the main complex of show tents. Courtesy of Circus World Museum, Baraboo, Wisconsin (B&B-np-06-7).

Ringling Bros. and Barnum & Bailey sideshow tent interior, 1924. Sideshows featured open viewing areas, making racial segregation or class separation unworkable. Once inside, patrons could observe and interact with the "exhibits" or their handlers. Courtesy of Circus World Museum, Baraboo, Wisconsin (RBB-np-24-33).

John Robinson Circus menagerie tent interior, circa 1929. Visitors, both black and white, could get close enough to wild animals, such as elephants, to feed them peanuts. They also could ask keepers, like the man standing between the pachyderms, questions about the animals under their charge. Courtesy of Circus World Museum, Baraboo, Wisconsin (JR-n45-30-7).

The view from the segregated seating area inside of a Ringling Bros. and Barnum & Bailey big top, 1924. Circuses placed black patrons, regardless of their social status, in the bleachers on one end of their show tents, forcing them to watch the performance from the worst seats in the house. In contrast, white customers, like those at the top of this picture, could choose from a range of seating options. Courtesy of Circus World Museum, Baraboo, Wisconsin (RBB-np-24-34).

"Trophy" photo of Valdosta Chief of Police Calvin Dampier atop the carcass of Gypsy the elephant, November 1902. After an overnight chase by a hunting party of Valdostians, Dampier killed the rampaging beast with a single shot from his high-powered military rifle. Locals later took souvenirs of bone and tusk from the dead animal as "relics" of the incident. Courtesy of the Georgia Archives, Vanishing Georgia Collection (low-49).

Sparks Circus parades through Macon for its 1928 season opener. By the early twentieth century, such processions became increasingly uncommon as automobiles, like those lining both sides of the parade route here, filled the streets of Georgia's towns and cities. Courtesy of Circus World Museum, Baraboo, Wisconsin (Sparks-np-28-16).

> We heard the following conversation [on the street] which is self-explanatory: Child to elderly female—"Auntie, please take me to the circus!" "No, my dear, I never visit such places." "Then Auntie, let's go home." "Well, my dear, we will, after the balloon has gone up and the man has walked the wire." —*Columbus Daily Sun*, 8 October 1871

> This show was here about twenty years ago.... Afternoon services at the Baptist church were dispensed with, giving all an opportunity of attending during the day so they could come back that night and pray for forgiveness for attending the show. —*Dahlonega Nugget*, 7 May 1920

FIVE

The Canvas City
Social Mixing on Circus Day, 1870–1920

The transformation of the grassy expanse of the show lot into a sea of white canvas literally happened overnight. Under the cover of darkness the Sells Brothers circus had arrived in the central Georgia textile town of Griffin, which meant that this November day in 1882 would transpire as the unofficial holiday of Circus Day. As circus workers scrambled to prepare for the day's performances, country people hailing from six different counties made their way along the roads into town by way of wagon, horse, and foot. By late morning, six separate passenger trains had arrived, disgorging eager excursionists from distant communities onto the streets, where they joined the throngs lining Griffin's main thoroughfare in anticipation of the free street parade. The assemblage, as usual on Circus Day in Georgia in the nineteenth century, consisted of people of all ages, classes, and colors. The *Griffin Daily News* observed the following day, "There is very little need of personal items this morning. Suffice it to say that everybody you know, or ever heard of, was in town yesterday."[1]

If asked, older Griffin citizens who had attended a circus thirty years prior would have testified that the traveling concerns of the late nineteenth century bore little resemblance to those that had existed "before the war." For instance, while a large circus of the 1850s had carried its approximately seventy employees and performers overland in thirty or so wagons, a big show of the 1880s transported its hundreds of staff members in fifty or more rail cars.[2]

Similarly, veteran circus-goers would have noted the changes in the social setting and nature of Circus Day. Movement by wagon had meant that a tiny hamlet was as likely to get a leading show as a large city. But movement by train restricted the top troupes to the growing towns and big cities along railroad lines. In these communities, several thousand people, rather than the thousand or so that appeared for an antebellum show, would gather on the two or three days a year when a big show pulled into town, doubling or even tripling the local population. Indeed, it was reported in Griffin that the assemblage was "the largest crowd in town that Griffin has ever known."[3]

Unquestionably, people turned out for these shows to enjoy the spectacle and excitement that waited for them inside the "city of tents" that showmen erected on circus lots. But people also came to experience the broader social aspects of Circus Day. In other words, they came to observe and participate in the events that took place beyond the confines of the show grounds. In fact, large numbers of poor and pious Georgians traveled to town knowing that they would not be entering the canvas enclosures. For example, along a parade route in Rome in 1894 "there were hundreds of little folks whose parents either could not or would not carry them to the circus." A Columbus daily noted the same phenomenon in 1906, writing that "many persons are content merely with seeing the street show . . . without attending a regular performance." On Circus Day, Georgians went to town to sightsee, visit, feast, and drink as much as they went to laugh at the clowns and gaze at the elephants.[4]

For regular Georgians and circus performers alike, participating in the day's happenings included taking up roles in the drama that played out in the streets, alleys, and open lots of a community. In his discussion of carnival, Bakhtin notes that it "is not a spectacle seen by the people; they live in it, and everyone participates because its very idea embraces all the people." Historian Jackson Lears amplifies this point in writing that on such occasions "open-air amusements of all kinds could turn the whole town into a theater, every actor a spectator, every spectator an actor." On Circus Day in Georgia, the entertaining antics of ordinary people who unwittingly became objects of amusement for onlookers were matched only by the actions of circus performers who posed as local farmers while awaiting their chance to spring a carefully planned prank on unsuspecting bystanders. The indistinct line between performer and observer contributed mightily to the day's lighthearted mood.[5]

Performers and performances aside, the excitement that came from joining a colossal Circus Day crowd helped foster a widespread sense of release among participants. One way people expressed those feelings was by energetically milling about town both before and after the circus parade. A spiritually minded man in Bainbridge responded to such a scene by suggesting that "the commotion on the square and streets reminded one of the pictures often drawn by fervid orators of the day of judgment." A Columbus journalist remarked that "the stir on the streets was something extraordinary" thanks to the "thousands of men, women, and children" who came to town for a show. This electric atmosphere produced—even in the hierarchical South—a particular sense of social equality. A Clarke County man concluded: "There is something about a crowd at a sporting event or a circus that appeals to me strongly—the free and easy, informal, democratic air that sweeps away all social barriers and makes everyone the same." A scribe for a Cartersville paper concurred in writing that Circus Day is an occasion "when people meet on a level and all are one. Whether viewing the street parade or beholding the nimble figures in their artful and daring evolutions under the tent, . . . [the] modern prince and peasant knock elbows amicably in the common shove." A circus's ability to captivate and stimulate almost all who came to town helps explain how such an event could temporarily relieve some—but not all—of the social tension that normally permeated southern society.[6]

But this release also produced less welcome aspects. Violent drunks stumbled down the streets with weapons secreted in their waistbands or coats. Fueled by liquor, these men slashed, stabbed, and shot each other in the midst of crowds filled with women and children. Townspeople, used to seeing the same faces day after day, suddenly encountered seemingly menacing strangers. And on rare but unforgettable occasions, escaped circus animals produced mayhem as people stampeded away from their clutches.

Despite these unpleasant components, Circus Day represented an event so compelling that even those who would not be patronizing the circus proper felt the need to take part. They did so by identifying, and then occupying, social spaces outside of the show tents befitting their particular religious, cultural, or economic limitations. Church members who thought circus attendance was immoral watched from the sidewalk as God's animal creation trundled down the street inside cage wagons during the street parade. Respectable African Americans who considered circuses indecent gathered with family and friends near the lines of snack stands that enterprising members of their race erected near the circus lot. Finally, poor black and white farmers who lacked the necessary funds to buy a ticket enjoyed taking in the free street parade, listening to the sideshow barkers, and indulging in delectable treats from the snack stands. Circus Day attracted the poor and the rich and the sinful and the pious because it provided a context in which could all take part in the celebration.

As they had in the antebellum period, Georgians took an interest in the coming circus from the very first day that bill posters went to work. Weeks before an Atlanta performance, "all the spare boys in town were around seeing that the circus posters were properly put up." In Columbus, members of a "crowd of Negroes" commented to each other about the colorful Barnum and Bailey lithographs as bill posters pasted them to walls. White and black farmers who frequented the gin and mill complex in the tiny hamlet of Handy could hardly avoid noticing the large, gaudy advertisements for an upcoming performance in Newnan plastered up by John Robinson bill posters. E. T. Bishop, surrounded everywhere he went in Athens by show posters, wrote: "Every body is talking about the circus. You cannot speak a word with a friend unless he or she asks you 'Are you going to the show [?]'" Whether in the town or country, circus bills sparked conversation and speculation about the coming show, and encouraged rural people to plan, and eventually undertake, a trip to town on Circus Day.[7]

In the hours before the show, hundreds of black and white country people came to town in a variety of ways. Some hitched up their wagons, loaded up their families, and began the long trip along moonlit roads. Other rural folk tacked up their horses or mules and started out for the show location. Amazingly, some had already completed the journey by the previous evening, and spent the night camped in warehouses or other places around town. In contrast, middle-class and elite Georgians from the countryside secured lodging in hotels.[8]

Railroads also carried people to town on Circus Day. Showmen made contractual arrangements with rail lines for special reserved trains, known as "excursions," that circus-goers could ride at a reduced price, or sometimes even for free. These trains gave people residing in distant places a quick and efficient way to get to the community where the circus was playing. For instance, the Great Eastern Circus sponsored a half-fare excursion from Thomasville to Savannah in 1872, a trip of approximately two hundred miles each way. Later that same decade, the Great Southern Circus announced, "Free trains to and from the performance will be chartered for the benefit" of interested excursionists. During the inbound train ride, passengers could purchase tickets for the performance "for the same price as if bought at the ticket wagon." Showmen subsidized these trains because they could transport huge numbers of circus customers. "The real crowds," on a Griffin Circus Day, "came with the arrival of the morning trains, bringing excited joy seekers from Forsyth, Barnesville, Hampton, Sunny Side, McDonough, Zebulon, and various town[s] in this section of the state. The morning Southern [Railroad] from Columbus was literally packed and jammed." In sum, excursions benefited both circus-goers living far away from a performance location and showmen eager to draw these people into their tents.[9]

To avoid running afoul of the state's Jim Crow law, excursion trains that operated in Georgia from 1891 onward needed to provide separate cars or compartments for their black and white passengers. A description of a "peculiar" segregated train provided to John Robinson Circus customers in Mississippi in 1903 gives a sense of the potential range of accommodations that excursionists could face: "The train was composed of eight box cars, two coal cars and two passenger coaches. The passenger coaches were crowded with white people and the box cars and coal cars were loaded with negroes."[10]

Regardless of the conditions endured along the way, people expended significant time and effort to get to town on show day. One black man walked sixty miles each way from his Florida residence to Thomasville, Georgia, to see a show. The dedicated circus fan left his home on a Tuesday and arrived on a Friday, the day before the performance. The local newspaper editor probably found few who disagreed with his pronouncement that the man "deserves a prominent place" right "behind the band wagon in the parade to-day." In 1896, a group of white boys made an overnight bicycle trip from Statesboro to Savannah to see a show. As they set off on their journey, locals in their hometown predicted, "They will not be in very good shape to enjoy a circus after the 50 mile ride." The great lengths that southerners like these went to get to a show is a testament to the drawing power of circuses of this era.[11]

Still, not all Georgians enjoyed complete freedom to travel to the circus. On the day before an 1884 circus exhibition, one Americus reporter on a plantation visit found it "amusing" to watch "the darkies try to get away to see the show. From 3 o' clock until 9 they were coming to the house for permission to go, but Mr. Clay had for once determined they should not go, and so they staid [sic] at home." Yet the next morning, the newspaperman passed "a stream of wagons nearly a mile long" on his return trip to town. These wagons carried scores of African Americans—"the laggards"—on their way to Americus to join those who had completed the journey the previous evening. "If there is any way in the world to go there," the reporter concluded, "the negroes are going to come to town on circus day."[12]

As dawn broke on the morning of a Georgia show, thousands of country people streamed into town. For an 1899 show, circus-goers "came in two-horse wagons, buggies, two-wheel carts and conveyances of all descriptions and kinds, and those who could not ride in, came in great numbers on foot, until it seems that all the people in this county and several adjacent counties had emptied their population into Marietta." In Griffin, thousands of "black deserters from the cotton patch . . . took advantage of the 'official holiday' declared by the circus" to come to town in 1913.[13]

As country visitors drove their vehicles into town, the avenues along the parade route soon became almost impassable. In Columbus "the middle of the streets was one mass of teams, wagons, buggies, horses, and mules" in the minutes before a 1901 procession. Once thoroughfares became jammed, circus fans parked their means of transportation outside of town and walked in.[14]

In most towns and cities, the arrival of a big show disrupted normal community routines. Schools regularly closed to allow students to watch the morning procession. In 1892, Columbus school officials dismissed their students "so that the children could get a red balloon and witness the big parade." Savannah's superintendent of public schools granted students an additional freedom when he let them go to both the Ringling Brothers' parade and show in 1912. But he bestowed this special privilege not after pressure from his young scholars, but rather from his normally "dignified pedagogues" who suddenly took an "interest" in seeing the matinee performance. According to the *Savannah Morning News*, this unexpected turn of events left him standing "alone" as the only person in the city who looked upon the occasion "with disapproval." He told a reporter that "I have no objection to circuses except that they disrupt the school work very much . . . [but] I am sincerely thankful that the next circus comes to town on Saturday."[15]

Since students merited time off, many politicians, local officials, and workers felt they did as well. In Thomasville, a circus "broke . . . up" the scheduled city council meeting in November 1895. The next year, an Atlanta City Council meeting came to an abrupt conclusion after a member moved for an adjournment "so that the members of the council could go to the circus." The *Constitution* reported that the body deemed this particularly important since "Ringling Bros. [had] provided the councilmen and city officials with passes" to the show. In the early twentieth century, a procession that moved past the courthouse in Dahlonega encouraged everyone inside the building "to leave the court except the engaged attorneys and jurors, and they got up on the benches while the street parade was marching around the courthouse. So the judge adjourned the court until the next day." Circuses even turned the proceedings of state government upside down, as in 1892 when the normally august Georgia legislature held a shortened session in Atlanta so members could attend the circus. Businessmen, other than those operating consumer enterprises, also dismissed their employees on show days. For a Barnum and Bailey Circus performance, Athens' Check and Lower factories, the local foundry, and "other enterprises" all closed so workers could spend the day at the show.[16]

In those instances when authorities refused to grant a holiday, the circus still tended to pull people away from their responsibilities. In October 1894, Atlanta educators unwisely chose to hold classes while a troupe performed in the city. Predictably, "very few scholars" appeared in the classroom, prompting the city's board of education to decide to shut schools at noon on all future show days. In Thomasville that same year, "the circus completely demoralized business." The editor of the *Americus Recorder* offered the following assessment of the general impact of traveling concerns on the labor rhythms in his town: "The regular channel of business is always diverted on show days. It is impossible to get your darkeys to do any work, and the white people are generally as much demoralized as the darkeys, so all hands drop work and go to the show."[17]

In the morning sunlight, schoolchildren, along with all the other town and country people, staked out viewing positions along the parade route. "Long before the hour appointed for the great street parade" in Americus, "the sidewalks and roadways were filled to overflowing with interested spectators." An Atlanta newsman who made his way to the parade route prior to the procession's appearance "found the streets bustling with people. By 8 o'clock the sidewalks of our principal thoroughfares were lined with all shades and sizes of our population, and it seemed as if Atlanta and all her environs had poured forth progenitor and progeny, feminine and masculine." The parade crowd in Barnesville grew so great in 1882 that "the whole business portion of the town was a living moving mass of people."[18]

As compared to a local community's actual population, the number of people in town often swelled to impressive proportions. In 1884, Griffin hosted an estimated "eight thousand country people" along its parade route when its official population was approximately 3,600. In 1897, the John Robinson and Franklin Brothers' Circus attracted ten thousand people to the town of Fitzgerald to form the "largest audience" the show had encountered during its Georgia tour. At that time, Fitzgerald's permanent residents numbered about 1,800.[19]

Confronted with the biggest crowds they had ever seen, southerners looked to the urban North as they tried to put their Circus Day experiences into words. An elite white woman named Evelyn Jackson Harden confided to her diary after an exciting Circus Day that "some say there were 20,000 people in Athens. I don't know, but I waited (like the man in New York City) two hours for the crowd to get by but at last gave that out & came through & arrived home safely." A Rome reporter also thought the comparison between Manhattan crowds and those in town on Circus Day was fitting: "Broad Street, Rome, had the appearance of Broadway, New York, and it was really difficult to make one's passage through the crowd." After experiencing a Circus Day crowd, only the throngs that filled the streets of northern cities seemed apt in comparison.[20]

Along with the size of the crowd, Georgians found the composition of these assemblages remarkable. One Columbus man looked approvingly in 1887 upon a "motley crowd" comprised of "elegantly dressed ladies, tow-headed urchins, Negroes, street gamins, countrymen and dudes . . . all mixed up together." In 1890, a Bainbridge journalist noted that locals enjoyed being part of a gathering consisting of people "old and young, big and little, [and] white and black." Nearly two decades later in the central Georgia town of Roberta, a reporter wrote that the "happy" multitude included "large people, small people, white people, black people, yaller people, old people, young people, halleluliah [sic] people, sober people, and all kinds of people and their brothers and sisters." Despite the South's hierarchies of race and class, Georgians of all stripes came together on Circus Day to boisterously share public spaces. The varied members of these throngs socialized, laughed, and generally celebrated a release from the responsibilities of life.[21]

While waiting for the parade to start, educated townspeople particularly enjoyed the pastime of people watching. The editor of the *Thomasville Daily Times Enterprise* noted that the "crowd itself was a show to one who was half inclined to study human nature." For the more sophisticated, ingenuous rural people became figures of fun as they wandered wide-eyed through the streets. A Griffin newsman noted in 1884 that "the severely rural lad with his equally rural sweetheart afforded some amusement" for locals. Similarly, a Savannah reporter thought that the antics of some country visitors offered "as much amusement to those around [town] as the clowns." E. T. Bishop, on the streets of Athens for a circus parade, recounted his people-watching experiences in his diary:

> The writer allowed his attention to be engaged by watching "his friends from the country." There were people of all descriptions, sizes, ages, colors, fashionable pretensions &c.
>
> Our city ladies have a very nice & pretty way of elevating their dress skirts especially on muddy days; it was quite amusing to view the country ladies attempting to surpass the city ladies by raising their under as well as outer skirts to a much greater height from the ground. This was very pretty & becoming in some cases but in all it was not.

The drama that played out on the streets furnished free entertainment for those who took the time to watch their fellow citizens participate in the extraordinary event of Circus Day.[22]

Sometimes, these impromptu "performances" could be less welcome and less amusing. Much to the chagrin of Columbus merchants, groups of "country bloods" puffed cheap cigars, gulped strong drinks, and generally made themselves "conspicuous" inside local establishments before an 1876 circus:

> About three out of six of these bloods profess to be musicians on some instrument or another. Of all the hideous and multiplied noises to be heard vibrate, were those we listened to in one of the book stores. Some were blowing harps and horns, while others were making fearful noises with violins, tambourines, and accordions. Each one—a King bee in his community—had his admirers around to praise his every piece. All were so elated. In the background stood the proprietor of the house with his clerks, and upon the face of each was pictured despair.

Young men from the countryside, enjoying a day free from toil, created their own amusement prior to the morning parade.[23]

The discomfort of Columbus shopkeepers hints at how the Circus Day fun of some could impinge upon the enjoyment of others. While in this case no real harm was done, in other instances, time spent in a crowd could be uncomfortable, frightening, and even dangerous. Visitors, excited by the sight of a parade or the opening of a ticket wagon, sometimes violently shoved their way through crowds. A Fulton County pundit found himself "very near smothering" while caught in a crush near an Atlanta circus. After a struggle, he secured a perch on a crate against a wall and watched as people "surged and pushed and made wild breaks, never a one caring for the other." Gatherings that encompassed people from all social stations brought elites into uncomfortably close quarters with their social lessers. In Athens, Harden described the ominous aspects of a town full of unfamiliar people in her diary in 1881:

> So many strangers negroes & tramps. One has already been in here in trying to beg from us but we soon dismissed her. She wore dresses but looked more like a man with short gray hair & long ugly teeth here & there. She was a frightful looking person said She was mrs. More from Gainesville had lost all her money since she arrived in Athens & wanted enough to send a dispatch home with but we dispatched her.

The diverse character of circus crowds often inspired bumptious excitement that sent emotions surging to joyous heights. At the same time, however, the informal nature of these gatherings produced more uncomfortable sensations.[24]

Falling victim to crime certainly made circus-goers uncomfortable. Pickpockets took advantage of the distraction of the circus parade to ply their illicit trade. In 1894, this "light-fingered gentry" reaped "a rich harvest from the large crowd" that assembled for a show in Rome. Two Athens factory workers named Bailey and Butler suffered a similar fate in 1885 when they had their pockets picked of $10.80 and $18.00, respectively, on Circus Day. Other criminals turned their attentions to local businesses. A Valdosta merchant suffered such a loss in 1901 when a "bold" thief entered his store and stole the contents of the cash register "while the clerks were watching the circus parade."[25]

The tendency of local inebriates to start tippling early in the morning of Circus Day also produced unpleasant and hazardous scenes on Georgia streets. In Rome, for instance, local law enforcement arrested an African American man after he "was reveling in a jag and told a good woman in a Broad street crowd that he didn't [care] if he did step on her dam[n] little kid." In the same community, a white man "showed up on Broad street full to the brim with some choice brand. He was particularly affectionate and during his journey through boozeland he grabbed hold of a respectable young girl . . . the girl screamed and the man was jerked away." Lastly, a Waynesboro man "made himself heard" on Circus Day "by firing his pistol off at random, shooting several ugly holes in the counters of the store of Messrs. Cates & MacKenzie."[26]

Despite the presence of rowdy rustics, petty criminals, and dangerous drunkards, most members of the New South's white elite and middle class joined the crowds on the streets on Circus Day. A gathering in Sylvania featured "merchants, and lawyers, and doctors, and bankers" rubbing elbows with town urchins and poor country people. Atlanta parade watchers witnessed the humorous sight of "a young M. D. with a piece of cheese in his hand tramping through the mud after a circus wagon." Circus Day's festive atmosphere allowed the New South's "best people" to drop some of their class-based pretense.[27]

Unlike the socially circumspect, "respectable" citizens who always claimed that they came to town on Circus Day for "business," some middle-class men made themselves conspicuous enough to end up in the social columns of local newspapers. In 1885, the *Griffin Daily News* informed its readers that "Dr. R. J. Arnold and J. T. Manley came down last night to attend the circus." The *Thomasville Daily Times* related in 1894 that "Mr. W. B. Dukes, Moultrie's leading merchant, came down yesterday, combining business with pleasure by attending the circus and attending to business." Other times, newspapermen facetiously questioned the "coincidental" arrival of a circus and prominent public officials at the same time and place. In 1875, the *Atlanta Daily Herald* speculated about the whereabouts of a former attorney general of the United States on Circus Day: "We don't know, and can't say for sure, but Hon. Amos T. Ackerman follows pretty closely after the elephants. He is in town."[28]

While a circus crowd was a place where bankers could rub up against bootblacks, elites—particularly ladies—preferred not to mix with the multitudes on the street. Instead, these socially connected and economically privileged people ensconced themselves on elevated balconies and windowsills as they waited for the parade to begin. Situated high above the street, these ladies talked with their companions as they drew gazes from those below them, behaving similarly to the fashionable northern urban women who had sat in antebellum theater boxes for the dual purposes of "self display" and of seeing the performance on stage.[29]

Male observers on the street took particular notice of alluring belles so visibly perched along the parade route. In Griffin, "the streets were crowded with the throngs of spectators to see the parade yesterday, while the windows of the *Daily News* office were graced with such beauty and chivalry as would have made a pageant of itself." As the "crowd surged on the pavements" in Atlanta, "every balcony and every window on the route was crowded with the beauty of the city." Likewise, a journalist swooned as he related that "the handsomest blonde ever seen in Griffin was on the balcony of the Agricultural Building during the parade." Watching the procession from elevated locations protected elite ladies from the crush of the crowd before they went into the tent, but it also placed them as much in the public eye as performers on parade.[30]

But not all privileged women who sought the sanctuary of a balcony did so for the sake of vanity and security. Evelyn Jackson Harden watched nearly every circus parade held in Athens between 1875 and 1926 from a terrace overlooking the town's main street. After a 1911 procession, she wrote in her journal: "Well our friends came & we saw the grand Parade of 37 elegant Chariots 22 Elephants about a Doz camels, Lions, Tigers, & c. with hundreds of horses & people in gay attire." But in the same entry, she made clear that there was a stark difference between the public display and the actual show inside the tent: "Barnum & Bailey Circus I never attend such wicked places, but don't

through the streets of another town a few days later, he knew that crowded snack stands and peanut shells and bologna rinds underfoot augured a heavy black presence in the tent of the show.[39]

Although evidence of southern whites eating at black-run stands is limited, the fact that some white observers did not distinguish customers by race strongly suggests that both southern blacks and whites ate at the stands. One Greenville, South Carolina, man noted around the turn of the century that "Negroes would have food stands along the street to the circus [grounds]. They cooked fish and sold it to the people going to the circus." And according to an account of a Bainbridge Circus Day, "the hash and fish stands from Jake Born's down below the Hook & Ladder Hall, were alive with customers. It is estimated that tons of hash and seven barrels of fish were destroyed by the hungry mob." Most whites probably followed racial etiquette by not congregating with the African Americans surrounding the stands. They purchased their food and then moved along to the grounds.[40]

Upon initial reflection, showmen Alf Ringling and Gil Robinson both thought that snack stand proprietors had their Circus Day priorities misaligned. Ringling found it inexplicable that these entrepreneurs "usually eat more than they sell." Robinson concurred, noting that "sales were apparently the last consideration in the minds of the 'snack venders.'" From the perspective of these profit-minded circus managers, undertaking a business venture without a focus on making money seemed careless at best and foolish at worst. But Robinson, who had spent a great deal of time among black southerners, did apprehend the broader purpose of the stands when he concluded that most of the operators had set up shop for "visiting" rather than for profit.[41]

This "visiting" done at snack stands by African Americans, like parade-watching from balconies by evangelical elites, is one key to understanding the social nature of Circus Day. In general, the area around the snack stands served as a social space for crowds of African Americans to greet old friends, visit with family, and chat with new acquaintances before they went into the tent. But particularly for poverty-stricken, pious, and elite African Americans, these eating booths, rather than the circus proper, became the central place where time could be pleasurably passed in lieu of going to the show.

In the case of the poor, their appetite for socializing at the stands is easy to appreciate once the percentages of African Americans who did not enter circus tents, but came to town, are considered. While racially differentiated attendance estimates by observers are rare, one man noted that a big top in Bainbridge admitted about two thousand Georgians, but less than 15 percent of the audience comprised black southerners, even though they "predominated" in the crowd in town. Perhaps equally as useful are the words of a *Columbus Enquirer Sun* reporter, who wrote that "it is a fact, almost proverbial, that a country negro too poor to pay his way into the circus, will walk ten miles to see a free parade." Here the journalist might have valuably asked how all these rural African Americans passed the time in town after the procession ended around 11 AM. On this holiday, African Americans who could not afford tickets could head over to the snack stands where they could spend a handful of nickels and savor a delicious meal, along with all the other free attractions available on Circus Day. One Americus journalist explained in 1885 how the typical poor black family "never missed a single sight that was free":

> They did not go inside the circus tent, but they had a good time nevertheless. They ate a frugal breakfast, saw every wagon hauled from the depot to the grounds, the tents erected, the grand parade, listened to the bands, the calliope, the loud-lunged ticket sellers, and feasted their eyes on the gorgeous pictures of the sideshow [banners]. They dissipated to the extent of a fish dinner and five cents worth of candy for the children. . . . Others might spend more money, but none secured more pleasure from the occasion.

Even if they did not go to the show, African Americans of limited means could extend the pleasures of the day by visiting with friends as they patronized the snack stands.[42]

The vicinity of the snack stands also may have served as a place for middle-class and elite African Americans to congregate after the parade. Photographs taken of southern snack stands show nattily-attired black men and women standing in front of tables of food and drink. Class sensitivities dictated that the "better" sort of African Americans not follow the lead of poor blacks by trying to race into the pavilions of every show that came to town. In 1909, the potential dangers lurking inside circus tents became all too real to African American parents from "some of the leading families" of Oglethorpe when they suffered the indignity of having their daughters elope and then depart with "attaches" of the Mighty Haag Circus after the girls became "stage struck." Faced with the prospect of a life with circus workers as sons-in-law, the horrified parents could only follow the show to its next tour stop in hopes of retrieving their kin. Elites like these could find sanctuary for themselves and their families in the vicinity of the snack stands.[43]

Although it is probable that many black evangelicals, like their white counterparts, attended the circus despite its immoral reputation, it is also likely that some sizeable African American church-going contingent followed the lead of black ministers who preached that the righteous should avoid traveling shows. Black congregations enforced this doctrinal position by continuing to punish their members for attending "worldly amusements" into the early twentieth century, long after white churches had stopped disciplining their followers for such activity. In a reflection of these stringent standards, one African American man remembered that as a child he had begged his mother to take him to the circus after watching a parade but she refused the request due to her "ortho-

mind seeing the Anamals [sic] God's creatures." For this Christian woman, the balcony, like a menagerie tent, served as a morally pure perch from which to observe and participate in Circus Day without coming in closer contact with the show.[31]

Harden was not alone in holding this view of parades. In 1920, the *Dahlonega Nugget* reported that "those who think it is [a] sin to attend anything about a show except to watch the rope walker and see the street parade and listen to the music were very much disappointed last Tuesday when the parade didn't take place." When parades did come off, some Christians situated along the street hewed to this restrictive standard. As a Kentucky woman sat in a wagon with her family along a procession route in her home state, an elderly black man approached her and offered to secure the family's wagon and horses while her party went to the circus. Recoiling, the mother sharply declined the man's proposal: "You-all's don't s'pose I'd take mah chil'len t' any low-down, disrespectful place as a circus; I jest aimed t' learn them chil'len somethin' about th' queer critters that Noah saved in th' ark. Now I'm goin' t' take them ou'ta town, right smart. That circus ban'll be a-playing in a minute, an' I ain't goin' t' have no husband or chi'llen of mine into temptation."[32]

Whether situated in a balcony or on the street, the attention of all turned to street level once the lead circus wagon appeared in the distance. Columbus parade-watchers turned their heads to look as "'It's coming; it's coming!' was heard on every side and loud shouts from the crowd went up as the first band wagon hove in sight." As the parade entered the business district of town, all activity save taking in the moving spectacle came to a halt. In enterprise-minded Atlanta, "business was suspended during the passing of the parade. Merchant princes and merchants who have not yet attained that rank stood elbow to elbow with their customers, sales girls and cash boys in the doorways. Typewriter and elevator boys looked out the same window."[33]

Since many people based their decision on whether or not to buy a ticket on the quality of a parade, the nation's top circus men invested much time, energy, and treasure in making their processions as spectacular and glamorous as possible, filling them with enough attractions to make them last as long as five hours. An especially vivid and precise description of the Ringling Brothers' 1896 procession through the streets of Atlanta provides some sense of what the leading shows of the day offered observers:

> The parade was a large one, consisting of sixty sections. . . . Following the first band wagon came three animal cages, each drawn by four splendid iron grays. Then the snake charmer, with the slimy reptiles twisting around her feet. The new woman, riding astraddle in bloomers was the next feature. . . . Following this up-to-date horsewoman came four animal cages. . . . Then came the cavaliers on horseback, shining in costumes of gold, red and white.

The first open cage contained two lionesses and two cubs, then came two hyenas, then two wild cats, then four black bears, then two leopards, then two jaguars, then two magnificent tigers, two large lions and a lioness. Drawn by six iron grays came the huge hippopotamus. Its keeper kept the crowd amused by throwing peanuts down its massive throat. . . .

A few animal cages followed then the tableau wagons passed. First was Columbia, escorted by soldiers in the colonial uniform. . . . Two horsemen followed, riding beside a wooden St. George and the Dragon. . . . Eight colossal animal cages separated St. George from the next wooden tableau figures, which represented Little Red Riding Hood, Jack the Giant Killer, [and] Robinson Crusoe. . . .

Equestriennes, accompanied by jockeys, in their loose satin skirts, came next, and excited the admiration of the crowd. The Roman chariots were next in line. . . .

More animal cages followed, and then came the third band wagon, tooting one of Sousa's marches. The lady horseback riders pranced up behind this bandwagon, and behind them came an equal number of cavaliers. Next came the clown wagon, with four white faced smilers making monkey shines for the amusement of the crowd.

The sixteen elephants and the tiny baby elephant came next; then the camels with their awkward tread. More animal cages, and then the grand finale—the calliope, steaming away and tooting out music that always pleases the crowd, with its odd melody, but disappoints them as the marker of the ended pageant.

Parades of this caliber, as much as the entertainment offered under the tent, drew Georgians into town on Circus Day.[34]

While a definable line between spectator and participant did exist during pageants, both showmen and parade-watchers acted at times to blur this boundary. Circus managers did so by sending "rube" clowns, disguised as farmers, out into the street during the parade to stage public confrontations. In 1901, the John Robinson Circus employed a "Rube" Newton and his "wife" to work the crowd but sometimes they did too good a job of imitating locals. The press agent for the show noted that the pair looked "so true to life that they have been arrested as often as three times in one week by conscientious policemen. On June 19 they were ordered off the street by Mr. Cole, advertising solicitor for the show, and a fake quarrel ensued. The people sympathized with Newton, and were fooled so strongly that Cole did well to get away without a good punching."[35]

Some showmen, however, preferred putting their rube clowns to work on the streets at a time and place when all eyes would be on them. In front of twenty thousand people on the sidewalks of Atlanta in 1891, "Mack" the Rube went into action at the head of the Forepaugh Circus parade:

Funnier than all else was the farmer driving as stubborn a mule as ever wore shoes. This red-headed spectacled granger, in an old, rattling cart, insisted on following, and his mule would balk ever few minutes. Right in front of the police station the old hayseed's mule balked and the procession had to stop. The two officers ordered the farmer to get out of the way. He began to argue with them and he said he was a tax-payer and the street a public thoroughfare. The police were nettled and caught hold of the mule's bridle.

"Let go that animal," yelled the old fellow.
"Drive out of this. Don't you see you're stopping the procession?"
"No, I can't see very well."
"Drive on."
"I can't do it. Anyway [I've] just as much right in this street as [you] have."
"No you haven't," one of the officers retorted.
"Well, I've just as much right here as this circus," shouted the farmer.

The police grew more and more mad. They pulled and jerked at the mule, which reared and struck at the officers. They turned from the mule to the owner and were about to pull him out and carry him into the station when he sang out: "I'm paid to do this. I belong to the show."

The crowd which had been watching the exciting scene yelled, the policemen took one disgusted look at Comedian Mack and stole off. They were badly sold, but they were not the only ones. Mack was arrested thirty times between the start and the finish. He said afterwards that he had not had so much fun with a crowd in a month.

On Circus Day, Georgians delighted at the sight of some "spectators" placing themselves into the procession.[36]

Some African Americans joined performers in this project. While middle-class and elite white and black Georgians tended to maintain the boundary between spectator and participant as wagons and animals moved down the street, many poorer black Georgians inserted themselves into the display. Circus bandmaster William Merrick noted that when a procession moved it was "no uncommon thing for a number of 'darkies' to start at the circus grounds and dance through the entire route of the parade; and when in doubling back on the main street . . . the band passes the steam calliope, . . . [and] the din caused by the mingling of the band-music with the shrill whistle of this instrument, seems to throw them into a veritable frenzy." In much the same way, "males and females of the colored way of doing things" mobbed the Great Eastern calliope in 1873 as it moved through Savannah's streets. Exotic animals on parade also attracted the attention of African Americans. That same year, a boisterous "crowd of negroes" marched alongside and behind a John Robinson Circus elephant as it lumbered through the streets of Columbus. Reflecting a cultural style that privileged expressive movement and energetic activity over stiff restraint at festive events, some African Americans in New South Georgia—like their counterparts in the colonial and antebellum periods—exhibited their enthusiasm for the parade with a raucous and participatory exuberance.[37]

Once the display had passed, many people followed behind it as moved toward the show grounds. On the boundaries of the circus lot, they encountered scores of black town-dwellers standing behind rows of snack stands set up to sell a variety of foods and drinks to the assembled crowds. These stands ranged from simple cloth-covered tables to more elaborate booths reinforced with wooden frames and shaded by canvas awnings. On a crowded Circus Day, these stands could number in the hundreds, making quite an impression on circus men. Showman W. C. Thompson offered this description of the stands:

> In the Southern States, "snack stands" line the limits of the circus lot. Colored people conduct them, and the food they provide is wholesome and wonderful in variety. No Northerner who has not witnessed circus day in the old Confederate section has any adequate conception of the extent to which these eating places flourish. The appetizing odor of food pervades the air, patrons are filled with the exuberance of the occasion, and the scene is one to add a measure to the joy of living. No dish often has a price exceeding five cents, and the ham and chicken and cakes and biscuits served have a particular charm of flavor, which sometimes even lures the showman from the canopied canvas of the "cook tent."

Like Thompson, Athens resident Susan Fan Tate recalled that "the most unforgettable smells would assail you" while passing the snack stands. But it was more than wonderful aromas wafting through the air that lured circus men and locals to these booths and tables. Alf Ringling observed that the "strength of lung power counts in running a 'snack stand.'" Hawkers solicited patronage with bellowed cries of "Hot fish, hot chicken, hot coffee-ee-ee!" and "Here's your nice hot wieners! They're red hot, they're red hot, they're steaming hot, they're boiling hot—they're hot! They're hot! They're hot-tot-tot-tot-tot." Such yells added to the boisterous atmosphere around the grounds, as people heading into the tent grabbed a quick snack while those who were not attending the matinee performance settled in for a leisurely meal.[38]

In light of the monotonous nature of the diet consumed by the average southerner, it is unsurprising that African Americans freely indulged in the diversity of novel foods offered at the stands. One Ringling attaché told a Chicago reporter traveling with the show during an 1899 tour through the Black Belt that he could predict afternoon attendance by the morning activity at the snack stands. On the days when "plantation negroes" have money, he stated, "you'll see them eating chicken, bananas, popcorn, bologna, stick candy, and all this other stuff from the snackstands." When the journalist took a morning walk

free parade." Here the journalist might have valuably asked how all these rural African Americans passed the time in town after the procession ended around 11 AM. On this holiday, African Americans who could not afford tickets could head over to the snack stands where they could spend a handful of nickels and savor a delicious meal, along with all the other free attractions available on Circus Day. One Americus journalist explained in 1885 how the typical poor black family "never missed a single sight that was free":

> They did not go inside the circus tent, but they had a good time nevertheless. They ate a frugal breakfast, saw every wagon hauled from the depot to the grounds, the tents erected, the grand parade, listened to the bands, the calliope, the loud-lunged ticket sellers, and feasted their eyes on the gorgeous pictures of the sideshow [banners]. They dissipated to the extent of a fish dinner and five cents worth of candy for the children.... Others might spend more money, but none secured more pleasure from the occasion.

Even if they did not go to the show, African Americans of limited means could extend the pleasures of the day by visiting with friends as they patronized the snack stands.[42]

The vicinity of the snack stands also may have served as a place for middle-class and elite African Americans to congregate after the parade. Photographs taken of southern snack stands show nattily-attired black men and women standing in front of tables of food and drink. Class sensitivities dictated that the "better" sort of African Americans not follow the lead of poor blacks by trying to race into the pavilions of every show that came to town. In 1909, the potential dangers lurking inside circus tents became all too real to African American parents from "some of the leading families" of Oglethorpe when they suffered the indignity of having their daughters elope and then depart with "attaches" of the Mighty Haag Circus after the girls became "stage struck." Faced with the prospect of a life with circus workers as sons-in-law, the horrified parents could only follow the show to its next tour stop in hopes of retrieving their kin. Elites like these could find sanctuary for themselves and their families in the vicinity of the snack stands.[43]

Although it is probable that many black evangelicals, like their white counterparts, attended the circus despite its immoral reputation, it is also likely that some sizeable African American church-going contingent followed the lead of black ministers who preached that the righteous should avoid traveling shows. Black congregations enforced this doctrinal position by continuing to punish their members for attending "worldly amusements" into the early twentieth century, long after white churches had stopped disciplining their followers for such activity. In a reflection of these stringent standards, one African American man remembered that as a child he had begged his mother to take him to the circus after watching a parade but she refused the request due to her "ortho-

through the streets of another town a few days later, he knew that crowded snack stands and peanut shells and bologna rinds underfoot augured a heavy black presence in the tent of the show.[39]

Although evidence of southern whites eating at black-run stands is limited, the fact that some white observers did not distinguish customers by race strongly suggests that both southern blacks and whites ate at the stands. One Greenville, South Carolina, man noted around the turn of the century that "Negroes would have food stands along the street to the circus [grounds]. They cooked fish and sold it to the people going to the circus." And according to an account of a Bainbridge Circus Day, "the hash and fish stands from Jake Born's down below the Hook & Ladder Hall, were alive with customers. It is estimated that tons of hash and seven barrels of fish were destroyed by the hungry mob." Most whites probably followed racial etiquette by not congregating with the African Americans surrounding the stands. They purchased their food and then moved along to the grounds.[40]

Upon initial reflection, showmen Alf Ringling and Gil Robinson both thought that snack stand proprietors had their Circus Day priorities misaligned. Ringling found it inexplicable that these entrepreneurs "usually eat more than they sell." Robinson concurred, noting that "sales were apparently the last consideration in the minds of the 'snack venders.'" From the perspective of these profit-minded circus managers, undertaking a business venture without a focus on making money seemed careless at best and foolish at worst. But Robinson, who had spent a great deal of time among black southerners, did apprehend the broader purpose of the stands when he concluded that most of the operators had set up shop for "visiting" rather than for profit.[41]

This "visiting" done at snack stands by African Americans, like parade-watching from balconies by evangelical elites, is one key to understanding the social nature of Circus Day. In general, the area around the snack stands served as a social space for crowds of African Americans to greet old friends, visit with family, and chat with new acquaintances before they went into the tent. But particularly for poverty-stricken, pious, and elite African Americans, these eating booths, rather than the circus proper, became the central place where time could be pleasurably passed in lieu of going to the show.

In the case of the poor, their appetite for socializing at the stands is easy to appreciate once the percentages of African Americans who did not enter circus tents, but came to town, are considered. While racially differentiated attendance estimates by observers are rare, one man noted that a big top in Bainbridge admitted about two thousand Georgians, but less than 15 percent of the audience comprised black southerners, even though they "predominated" in the crowd in town. Perhaps equally as useful are the words of a *Columbus Enquirer Sun* reporter, who wrote that "it is a fact, almost proverbial, that a country negro too poor to pay his way into the circus, will walk ten miles to see a

dox Methodist training." After the procession ended, black Christians hell-bent on staying out of circus tents could sustain the fun of the day by visiting with friends over by the snack stands. In this way, evangelical African Americans could reconcile their religious beliefs with their recreational interests.[44]

Those Georgians who wanted to practice their faith in a more immediate way on Circus Day got their chance when revivals and circuses operated at the same time and in the same place. For example, the *Valdosta Times* announced in 1894 that townspeople could avail themselves of both the "circus in town today" and the "services in the gospel tent on Creech Street." Such instances left citizens with a stark choice between tents of sacred and secular purposes. At times, circuses lost to revivals. In 1889, the John Robinson Circus squared off against a tent meeting in Rock Hill, South Carolina. An equestrian with the troupe scripted this account of the day's events in her diary: "One show. Poor business on account of big revival meetings in this place. Prayers from eleven till twelve for the poor sinful showmen."[45]

Unfortunately for revivalists, the victory in Rock Hill was an exception to the usual outcome of such contests. Two days after an 1894 Sells Brothers circus performance in Rome, a concerned citizen complained that "in the hurry of the business and the exciting scenes of the circus and other hurtful influences, the [Methodist] Tent Meeting . . . has to some extent been lost sight of." In 1890, a preacher running a weeklong gospel meeting in Waynesboro used his Sunday sermon to do "all in his power to keep the people away from the circus" due into town on the coming Tuesday. Despite the competing presence of the prayer tent, the show attracted a "large crowd," forcing the reverend to concede that his exhortations had been to "no avail."[46]

When Christians were not praying for showmen inside of revival tents, they begged God to save their town's inebriates and other sinners of varied stripes, who wandered around the streets in the afternoon and early evening, waiting for the night performance to commence. These prayers rang out with greater intensity when those who had begun to imbibe prodigious quantities of alcohol first thing in the morning began to fall victim to its ill effects. One "tall, bony fellow" started drinking rye on the streets of Columbus at daybreak and by noon "he was as happy as a lord." Unfortunately for this thirsty rural dweller, he passed out while splurging on a preshow shave and did not awake until after the troupe had departed. Other men celebrated the advent of the circus in local saloons and taverns. Thus in Barnesville, "the circus was about as profitable to the bar keepers last Wednesday as to Barrett & Co. [Circus]." Drinking even continued on crowded excursion trains departing Hawkinsville late in the evening, where groups of men "armed with black bottles" stood "swearing in the presence of everyone."[47]

But Circus Day tippling was not confined to a town's habitual drunks. As the editor of the *Griffin Daily News* noted: "We have known young men who would keep sober for months, or from one year's end to another, but could never take in a circus without getting a little 'off.' The crowd, the excitement, the brass band, the pomp and glitter of the circus procession seem to have a weakening effect upon [them]." Furthermore, many of these men drank even though experience taught that some would "lose a good position or squander the earnings of . . . twelve month[s]." The Griffin newsman's point is well taken; a Circus Day atmosphere of heady celebration did encourage even teetotalers to overindulge.[48]

Because almost all southerners viewed the day as an appropriate occasion to blow off some steam, both law enforcement and ordinary citizens tolerated men roaming the streets on Circus Day with a few drinks under their belts. "There was the usual number of plain drunks on the streets yesterday," the *Griffin Daily News* reported in 1885, "though only a few arrests were made." The Americus police force followed a similar procedure in 1894, arresting only the "'aggravated' cases" among the intoxicated in town. Even law enforcement officials sometimes succumbed to the temptation of the bottle. The treasurer of the John Robinson Circus scrawled a note in the show's 1911 account ledger documenting that LaGrange's "Sherif[f] [was] drunk at night." As long as inebriates did not make themselves particularly obnoxious or commit crimes, lawmen tended to look the other way, especially when they themselves drank to excess.[49]

Clearly, though, local officials who winked at Circus Day alcohol consumption recognized that widespread drinking fueled public disorder. After a Marietta show day passed without significant disturbance, authorities credited the dry city's lack of saloons. The *Marietta Journal* applauded this sober and law-abiding behavior by a circus crowd by writing that it "shows the good results of prohibition." But even after statewide prohibition passed in 1907, alcohol was often readily available on Circus Day. In 1914, a Milledgeville grocer running an illicit liquor operation, or "blind tiger," out of his establishment solicited business on the circus grounds. On occasion, showmen themselves served as the source for strong drink. In Alapaha, "one of the coaches of the circus train was a regular traveling bar room, and mean whiskey was freely dispensed" while corrupt town officials looked the other way. From whatever source it came, Georgia men in dry and wet towns drank when a show was in town, leaving the local circus grounds littered with "whiskey bottles to beat the band."[50]

The predictable result of such widespread bingeing was violent and bloody affrays, especially in Georgia's rapidly growing railroad towns. Sometimes, as in the antebellum period, circus men battled Georgians in these communities. An 1872 Valdosta appearance by the John Robinson Circus featured a "disturbance" between showmen and "citizens of the place, in which guns, pistols and brickbats were freely used." But by the 1880s, combat between locals and circus company members had become increasingly infrequent. Many large shows began carrying their own police and detective details who were charged with, among other security tasks, preempting such incidents. In addition, southern law enforcement professionalism did improve over time, giving showmen a better degree of protection. Lastly, sectional hostility ceased to manifest itself in attacks against circus men after 1880 as memories of the war began to slowly fade in the minds of white Georgians.[51]

With showmen more protected and white Georgia men less antagonistic toward circus personnel, Georgia circus-goers turned on each other. On a Circus Day that the *Valdosta Times* characterized as "not more disorderly than usual," a white man was stabbed, two white men squared off with firearms, and the owner of a local saloon "raised prominent bumps . . . on several heads while enforcing the rules of his place with a billiard cue." In Newnan, "several fights occurred on circus day. The principals in the most serious encounter were negroes, one of whom was carved in a way that resembled the scapelular [sic] work of a medical student on his first cadaver. About a spool of thread was required to sew him up." With good reason, the *Columbus Enquirer-Sun* made a plea for public order prior to an 1878 performance, reminding its readers, "on nearly every occasion of this kind some one either gets killed or mortally wounded." The *Americus Times Recorder* echoed that sentiment, writing in 1897: "Circus Day without a tragedy would be entirely contrary to the established custom." The New South was a violent place, but Circus Day's potent mix of extra-heavy alcohol consumption and general sense of release made for a particularly sanguinary occasion.[52]

Although most middle-class and elite Georgians would blame "country Negroes" and ignorant whites for the disorder of Circus Day, in actuality, a true cross section of the state's citizenry engaged in bloody affrays. White people would be quick to point to incidents like an 1897 fight between two black men in Americus that left one with "a goodly portion of his face" blown away by a shotgun blast. Since the assailant had successfully fled town, a reporter grimly noted that a verbal accounting of what transpired would not be forthcoming unless the grievously wounded man received "a new set of jaws, a tongue, and a dozen new teeth."[53]

But even members of the New South's white middle class were not above a Circus Day donnybrook. In late 1897, Georgians who came out for the Robinson and Franklin Circus in Cordele had the opportunity to observe a scrap between two of the town's leading citizens: "Mr. R. A. Rose, editor of the *Daily Sentinel*, and Mr. B. B. Pound, a prominent merchant of this place, engaged in a lively fight in the forenoon, in which Stepladders, knives, etc., played an important part, with the result that Mr. Rose is nursing several gashes on the back of his head and neck." Reassuringly, the local paper asserted that with the circus gone "everything is quiet today with no prospects of hostilities being renewed."[54]

Women, too, joined in interpersonal combat. In 1900, one white woman attacked another in Rome with a flagrant disregard for life: "Louisiana Booz cut Rose Jacobs over the left breast, administering a very bad wound. The Jacobs woman had her baby in her arms, and if some one had not snatched it away the child would have been killed." Twenty-one years later in the same town, a black woman named Lena Smith slashed another black woman, Cat Richardson, with a razor, "ripping up her arm and inflicting other cuts on various parts of her body." The cause of the dispute was "a quarrel over circus tickets."[55]

What also separated these baneful incidents from antebellum circus disturbances was that in many cases the parties involved knew each other and harbored long-standing, simmering resentments. An experienced animal trainer observed that Circus Day in the New South was an occasion that feuding parties considered "a good time to 'look for their man.'" In Valdosta, "Two farmers, John Hodges and Wash Bostwick, added their mite to the general excitement by reviving an old feud and attempting to 'shoot it out.'" On a day when "everybody you know, or ever heard of, was in town," revenge-seeking Georgians who encountered their rivals sought to resolve their differences through violence.[56]

Even though law enforcement officials did allow moderately drunk men to walk the streets, most police forces made a concerted effort to prevent serious crime. The Rome Police Department arrested thirty-seven individuals in 1911 for a variety of offenses committed during a John Robinson Circus tour stop in the city. Local law enforcement in Thomasville rounded up twenty-three suspects while the Valdosta police force arrested fifty-six people on their respective 1906 Circus Days. Police also relied on deterrence to prevent trouble before it started. In 1909, the *Crawford County News* credited the lack of trouble among aggressive drunks—"booze fighters" in the local vernacular—in the central Georgia community of Roberta to "the intimidating appearance of the wagon spokes which were used as clubs by the three heroic city detectives on duty for the momentous occasion."[57]

While violent clashes frequently occurred on Circus Day in Georgia, few exploded into the racially charged mobbing and vigilantism that regularly took place in the New South. Still, such ugly incidents did occasionally transpire. After a scrap between groups of white and black men, a white mob in the southern Georgia town of Cordele "loaded themselves up with shotguns and Winchesters and went on a general hunt for the dusky citizens and before their rampage was over they had shot one negro through the leg, drawn their guns on several, and made a goodly number 'burn the wind' for their homes." In Waynesboro, a white man who "wished to make himself conspicuous in some brutal way . . . endeavored to kill several negroes by shooting at their heads."[58]

Showmen had no enthusiasm for such episodes of southern white-on-black violence. As Gil Robinson noted, "there were always two things that circus men dreaded in the South; a shooting or a lynching." Continuing, he wrote that "in a section where very considerable of the audience was made up of Negroes who are particularly susceptible to the lure of the circus, anything that would drive the Negroes out of town [on] show day was a calamity." One John Robinson Circus appearance in Aberdeen, Mississippi was a huge financial loss for the show after a black man shot a white man during the morning procession. Almost immediately, the black parade watchers receded from town and in twenty minutes, "there wasn't a black man, woman, or child in sight." Most of the white people in Aberdeen quickly followed suit, leaving the streets "deserted." Even worse for receipts than gunplay, Robinson pointed out, was the mere "prospect" of a Circus Day lynching. But when a mob with murderous intentions began to form, the assembled mass of circus fans did not scatter, but instead headed for the spot where the killing was to occur. A lynching in the New South, it seems, was conceivably the only "counter attraction" that could outdraw a circus, making the traveling show "the financial sufferer." Circus Day was typically a joyous occasion, but it did have its darker moments.[59]

Perhaps the only other event that could disperse a crowd like a shooting or lynching was a real or imagined escape by a dangerous predator. To generate excitement, showmen had long displayed their big cats in a manner that straddled the line between pulse-pounding danger and primal fear. In 1866, Dan Castello's Great Show promised to let a lion "loose in the streets" during its parades. The troupe regularly made good on the claim by having its "intrepid" lion tamer Herr Lengel stand on top of the animal's cage wagon with the big cat on a leash. In Savannah, however, the acting chief of police prevented Lengel from removing the animal from its enclosure during the procession, "thinking that there was danger to the lives of the lookers on." Of course, Lengel himself faced the greatest danger from his feline performing partners. In the late 1870s, his luck ran out when a tiger tore him limb from limb during a show in the West Indies.[60]

The fear of a man-eater running free was so visceral that merely the thought that one had escaped sent Georgians racing away from the animal cages. In Albany, a cry of "the tiger has escaped" caused "thousands" to sprint from the circus grounds in sheer panic. In the process, "fences were broken down, people were trampled upon, mules and horses ran away, scattering wagons and contents." As people filed out of a tent after a Tifton performance by the Sparks Circus, the show's lighting system failed, plunging the circus grounds into darkness. Almost immediately, a disembodied voice yelled out of the gloom, "Lions are out." One resident remembered that "everyone made a wild scramble to get away and towards their homes as fast as possible. Those who did not hear the first report asked what the wild scramble was about. The answer was, 'The lions are out.' They joined in the race." Only after the fact would terrified locals learn that those within earshot had actually misheard the cry that dispersed the crowd. The person who called out had only sought to affirm that in fact the *lights* were out.[61]

Even though just the mere idea of a big cat on the loose struck fear into the hearts of circus patrons, an elephant parading down a street produced nary a thought in anyone's mind about any potential danger from these intelligent creatures. Crowds pushed closer to the massive animals when they promenaded through town and children eagerly fetched buckets of water for them on circus lots in exchange for free show tickets. Even when pachyderms "escaped" from their keepers in Georgia, they appeared entirely tractable. In 1895, an elephant "broke loose" at a Georgia fairground and "wandered off by himself. Coming to a restaurant he stuck his head in a window and after drinking several glasses of beer went back to his quarters." After a similar incident, an Augusta reporter informed his readers that it was "impossible" for them "to 'escape.' . . . Elephants just stray occasionally, like cows, and are driven back . . . without difficulty."[62]

In 1902, an extraordinary event in Valdosta shattered those widely held perceptions. On a Saturday evening immediately following the Harris Nickel Plate Shows' final performance of the season, trainer James O'Rourke mounted "Gypsy" the elephant and cued her to head to her barn at the outfit's winter quarters, which was located in Valdosta's Pine Park. O'Rourke was feverish from malaria and had been drinking whiskey during the day, but witnesses reported that he appeared steady atop the five-ton elephant. A short time later, several people on the city streets watched as Gypsy and O'Rourke headed away rather than towards the park. They called out to the trainer, but he did not respond, possibly because he was delirious from fever or intoxicated. On Toombs Street, the ailing man lost consciousness and tumbled off Gypsy's head into the roadway. To the horror of onlookers, Gypsy stopped, paused, and then kneeled on the motionless O'Rourke, killing him instantly.[63]

Minutes later, circus personnel arrived on the scene and had some initial success in controlling the enormous animal. But the excited crowd that had gathered appeared to "rattle" Gypsy, and she shook an electric pole, cutting the power along the street, and began tossing bricks and timber with her trunk. As the enraged pachyderm rampaged through the darkened downtown area, local residents fired numerous shots into the elephant, to little effect. After an hour or so, she headed toward Pine Park with a posse led by the chief of police in pursuit. Inside the park, Chief Dampier struck the animal with a few quick shots from a high-powered Krag-Jorgensen military rifle, but they did not disable her and she ran off into the inky night.

At daybreak on Sunday, a group of ten men resumed the chase and came upon the wounded animal six miles outside of town. There, Chief Dampier steadied himself and took aim with the military firearm from seventy-five yards away, firing a single shot that entered behind the elephant's ear, killing her instantly. Upon examination of the "huge bulk of inanimate flesh," the men discovered that the bullets from guns other than the Krag had "had only entered an inch or two and had probably done no more than tickle her." The one-shot kill, according to the *Valdosta Times*, "is a great advertisement for the Krag-Jorgensen army rifles, as well as for Chief Dampier." To commemorate the event, Dampier posed for a trophy photo atop Gypsy's massive carcass, with the deadly firearm perched proudly upon his hip.[64]

In the wake of the elephant rampage, the event remained a sensation to all in the vicinity. Over three thousand people came from miles around to stare at Gypsy's body before locals hacked it into pieces to ease the burial of all but the beast's "huge head, legs, and frame," which citizens cremated with gasoline. City residents had the chance to do another postmortem viewing at the local funeral parlor where morticians prepared O'Rourke for interment. In the weeks that followed, some citizens asserted with a touch of bravado that they had responded to the crisis by "getting down their guns and pouring buckshot by the hand-full into them," so they could give Gypsy a "warm reception" in case she headed their way. Others, perhaps more honestly, admitted that the sight of the vicious elephant trotting down their road on Sunday morning had sent them scurrying into their homes where "they locked the doors until the old brute was far beyond their places." Superstitious African Americans who lived outside of town told a newsman that they had seen "the ghost of the big creature almost every night" since Gypsy's death and blamed the week of intense rainstorms that followed the hunt on the animal's demise. Although the *Times* predicted "the story will live for years," townsmen sought to secure "the bones and white ivory tusks" as "relics" of the great event, in a manner not unlike the grisly souvenir-gathering done by white southerners in the wake of lynchings.[65]

A common complaint made by Georgia residents about circus performances was that they "were all the same." "When a circus takes it[s] departure," noted the *Savannah Morning News*, "those who patronized it generally say that they will never go to another." But just "like those after a hearty dinner declare that they feel they shall never want anything more to eat," such people soon "have a pretty keen appetite" for circuses when they return to town. To be fair, the initial impulse of these habitual circus patrons was correct. Circus performances did consist of conventions that showmen repeated show after show, year after year. Yet thousands upon thousands of people in Georgia came out for these performances as soon as circuses pitched their tents.[66]

Clearly, citizens gathered together on Circus Day because the tented entertainment provided thrills and excitement that the events of everyday life could not. But while the exhibitions repeated themselves, the happenings on the streets promised new adventures and sights for all who attended. Magnificent parades attracted hundreds, if not thousands, of people to town on each Circus Day. While waiting for the procession to start, people could smile at the laughable actions of some visitors and performers while trying to keep their distance from the town's bad actors. During the parade, rube clowns and African Americans who inserted themselves into the proceedings contributed to the lighthearted spirit of the day. At the end of the pageant, those who only planned on seeing the free display could head over to the snack stands for icy cold lemonade or a piping hot piece of fried catfish. In the final analysis, the popularity of circuses in turn-of-the-century Georgia stemmed as much from the action in town as the performance under the tent.

> CIRCUS, n. A place where horses, ponies and elephants are
> permitted to see men, women and children acting the fool.
> —Ambrose Bierce, *The Devil's Dictionary*

SIX

Performers in Bleachers
Audience Behavior and Social Interaction in Turn-of-the-Century Circus Tents

Like hundreds of his fellow Columbus citizens, a reporter for the *Enquirer Sun* took his seat inside of a John Robinson Circus big top one December evening in 1876. Yet as the show proceeded, the scribe found his attention drawn neither to the witticisms of the clowns nor the equitation of the riders in the center ring, but rather to the "incidental scenes" performed by a number of "country bloods" in the bleachers. He watched in exasperation as these young men abandoned their seats to crowd the ring, interjected "remarkable risibles" during performers' acts, filled the air with their "horse laugh[s]," and shouted "constantly" across the arena to their friends. After witnessing this display, he concluded that these individuals had achieved the acme of "their aspirations" when they resolved "to come to town, get new clothes, stick their pants in their red-topped boots, get tight, smoke a cigar and yell at the circus."[1]

These activities highlight the fact that circuses that played in postbellum Georgia continued to attract rough and rowdy patrons who eschewed polite standards of public decorum. Part of the explanation for this type of intemperate behavior lies in the cultural and economic identity of Georgia circus-goers. Historian John Kasson has demonstrated that the nineteenth-century trend toward improved public manners was largely an urban bourgeois phenomenon. On Circus Day in Georgia, a solid majority of circus customers hailed from rural areas (even at shows staged in cities) and were of modest economic means, making them much less familiar with Victorian standards of public comportment than the "respectable" southern middle class and elite. So while a contingent of mannered people from the country and the city attended almost every large circus that played in Georgia during this time period, the much bigger rural and poor portion of the crowd remained largely undisciplined.[2]

Moreover, the fact that the circus of this era was an essentially interactive entertainment helped assure that it would never become a diversion that turned circus-goers into "passive prisoners of their own excitement and bewilderment." While an increase in the standard number of performance rings (from two in 1872 to three in 1881) and the size of big tops did gradually silence the talking clown that had dominated the proceedings under canvas since the antebellum period, circus lot visitors had numerous opportunities to directly participate in acts and features. Inside of sideshow tents, they conversed with human oddities and played games of chance with circus confidence men. In menagerie tents, they queried zoological "lecturers" and fed wild animals. Even within cavernous main tents, customers came face to face with show personnel performing in the guise of audience members, rode trick mules, ran in footraces, and jumped from their seats and cheered as horse-drawn chariots dashed around the arena during hippodrome races. When Georgians went to the circus, the interactive nature of the performance joined with a boisterous behavioral ethos to produce energized audiences.[3]

Likewise, the fact that circus patronage involved being part of a moving crowd meant that customers of different classes interacted with each other as well as with performers. To be sure, circuses did not dispel all social etiquette or efface differences produced by class and gender. But circuses did foster social spaces where one could watch, just like an *Atlanta Journal* reporter did in 1890, as "the millionaire elbowed his way for a post of advantage with the day laborer and the woman with the pedigree did not scruple to contest her favorite position with the shawled disciple of working womanhood." Circus Day's atmosphere of social freedom permitted southerners to mix in ways that stood in marked contrast to that of everyday public life in the New South.[4]

The basic architecture of circus tents and lots furthered the occasion's sense of social possibility. The variety of entertainment areas on a circus lot meant that different patrons could, just as they did in the streets beyond the show grounds, find and occupy spaces to indulge their own Circus Day desires, whether they included a furtive gaze at the dancing girls in the sideshow or a wide-eyed gander at the wild animals in the menagerie. Moreover, although big top *seating* was segmented by class and segregated by race, circuses could enforce no separation on the midway—the open area in front of the main entrance to the big show—or inside the array of secondary tents they raised on circus lots, including their sideshow and menagerie enclosures. This meant that in crowded canvas pavilions black and white southerners found themselves in close quarters as they stood and walked through the same areas.

Still, historian Mark Schultz points out that in the New South, "black and white people did not interact as equals, however intimate their interactions." Indeed, black and white Georgians did not set aside their racial attitudes as they entered circus lots and retrieve them upon exiting. Racial subordination colored nearly every encounter—whether at a circus or in a cotton field—between black and white southerners in the age of Jim Crow. Nonetheless, Circus Day—and the circus itself—did provide a context where black and white Georgians could interact more equally at a time when segregation supposedly pervaded all aspects of southern life. Despite the discrimination that circus men showed toward their black customers, the circus in Jim Crow Georgia represented a place of pleasure and possibility rather than one of misery and limitation for black and white southerners during this era.[5]

As the last wagon of the circus parade passed through downtown, crowds along the parade route fell in behind the procession and followed it to the circus grounds. A large throng trailing a line of circus wagons meant that the rolling display had successfully drummed up business for the show. Before long, the crowd's progress slowed as large groups of people began to collect in the vicinity of the tents. After a grand display by the John Robinson Circus in Savannah, the two-block area near the lot was "one solid mass of crushing humanity."[6]

Upon finally reaching the circus grounds, crowd members squeezed onto the midway. To entice people onto the lot and to encourage ticket sales, circus managers turned this area into an entertainment space in its own right. On one side of the marquee, showmen placed their ticket wagons and concession areas. Across the way, they raised their sideshow tents.[7]

As visitors took in this scene, they caught the scent of enticing aromas drifting over from the refreshment stands. They heard the yells of the hot sausage, lemonade, and peanut "butchers"—"Buy your hot roasted here!"—over the cacophony of the crowd. They also listened to the bellows of the ticket vendors as they called out to the assemblage: "Buy your tickets here for the big show!" Perhaps most striking sight on the midway was the large, gaudily painted banners depicting the sideshow attractions, running one hundred feet in either direction from the elevated platform where silver-tongued "talkers" offered their descriptions of the sensational attractions in the sideshow. The midway experience, by design, stimulated all of the senses of those present.[8]

Despite the temptations of the refreshment stands and the sideshow, most circus-goers initially plunged into the teeming crowd surrounding the ticket wagon in order to secure admission for the show. As they drew closer to the wagon, those with sufficient funds for admission pressed toward the window while penniless folks loitered near the wagon in the hope of finding a way to obtain a ticket. Today, the telephone and Internet assure that people rarely have to wait in a long line for tickets for an entertainment or sporting event. But at a turn-of-the-century circus, crowds simply tended to dispense with lines and mob the wagon, making for a physically taxing experience where "people literally fought for tickets around the van window." In Columbus, "the wagon was situated some hundred yards from the main entrance, and this space between was completely thronged with those who were waiting for a chance to get to the box window. The crush was something awful, and at one time it was so great, that four people fainted." In an effort to control such large crowds, local police arrayed themselves around the wagon. During a Ringling Brothers appearance in Savannah, "it took the united efforts of fifteen policemen to keep the crowd from turning over the wagon and trampling upon each other in their anxiety to secure tickets."[9]

Although Louisiana passed legislation in the twentieth century that stipulated separate circus ticket wagons for blacks and whites, Georgia lawmakers allowed patrons of different races to intermingle as they pressed their way toward the ticket agents. Circuses rarely deviated from the practice of using single ticket wagons for both races, but in the wake of the 1906 Atlanta race riot, the Barnum and Bailey Circus took special precautions to prevent racial strife. The director of the show remembered that "we got into Atlanta just after the race riots there and the police were afraid that our coming might cause more trouble on account of the blacks and white[s] getting mixed up in the crowds at the show. So we had to sell tickets to the negroes from a separate wagon. We labeled it 'This Wagon for Blacks' so that the negroes couldn't jostle the white men." Still, it is important to note that it took a race riot for authorities to mandate segregated ticket windows; at all other times, apparently, circus tickets could be sold from a single window without coming into conflict with Jim Crow practices in Georgia.[10]

From his elevated position inside the wagon, the ticket seller looked out upon a sea of anxious people thrusting coins and bills in his direction. His goal was simple: sell the maximum number of tickets as quickly as possible, so individuals at the back of the crowd would not get discouraged by their lack of progress toward the wagon and decide not to go to the show. Clearly speed was of the essence here. One ticket seller estimated that at times he had sold as many as nine thousand tickets in less than an hour. The rapidity of the transactions carried out by agents amazed southern observers used to a more leisurely form of commerce. "Among the many wonders of the Great Eastern Circus is . . . Mr. George W. Zebold, properly termed the champion ticket seller," proclaimed the *Augusta Daily Chronicle and Sentinel*. The "readiness with which he handles the currency is not only remarkable but astonishing." Especially impressed was a contingent of that community's bankers, who thought that his lightening-fast ability to make the correct change regardless of the denomination presented meant that he "might profitably change his business."[11]

Despite the endorsement of Augusta's financiers, not all Georgians departed circus ticket wagons with the proper change. Some people were so eager to get from the wagon to the show's attractions that they simply "walked away" from their money at the counter after grabbing their tickets. Others suffered at the hands of dishonest vendors, who like other crooked members of the circus community, engaged in the widespread practice of grift, or the cheating of customers through short-changing and innumerable other schemes designed to separate patrons from their money. Ticket sellers could swindle customers by counting out change in a convoluted fashion or by simply passing back less money than was owed, knowing that most people would not pause to examine their change in the crush of a crowd. To make matters worse for customers, most ticket wagons featured transaction counters at eye level or higher, all the better to encourage people to wander off without taking the balance of their transactions. Unfortunately for the droves of small boys that turned out for circuses, these elevated counters kept the ticket agent literally out of reach, meaning that they often had to trust their handfuls of coins to strangers if they wanted to gain admission to the show.[12]

But not all southerners made themselves easy "marks," or victims, of ticket-wagon grifters. One veteran ticket seller recalled that some male heads of African American families had a smart strategy to avoid being tricked out of their money. They waited for the crowd to thin, and then made multiple trips to the wagon, buying one ticket at a time. The showman pointed out that "if there were fourteen in the family the man would bring up one [family member] at a time to buy a ticket and he always had the right change." This deliberate manner of securing admission was worth the time and effort to people who had been cheated in prior years by unscrupulous circus men.[13]

Some money-stealing schemes at the ticket wagon did not involve the ticket seller. On the midway of the Barnum and Bailey Circus in Atlanta, "a nice looking and gentlemanly young man" approached a group of young women and politely asked whether he could save them the trouble of fighting the crowds around the wagon. The ladies thanked the man for his thoughtful offer, and handed him a ten-dollar bill. The charming stranger then headed toward the window, but the ladies never saw him again. Later they would learn that this "gentleman crook" had victimized several other people that same day.[14]

Once patrons had their tickets in hand, they turned their attentions to the sideshow barker standing on the elevated platform in front of the lengthy and garish banner line. Commonly, circus managers placed a human exhibit (known in circus parlance as a "bally") on the dais to give the crowd a small taste of what awaited inside the tent. Cries rang out from the sharply dressed barker, or "talker," calling on those in the assemblage to look "this way for the great side show!" To those who hesitated, he yelled that there was "no extra charge to see the tattooed man with the body like a Sunday newspaper supplement. And the greatest of freaks, the three-legged boy! No fakes—all freaks!" Once some in the throng began paying their dimes and filing inside, the showman jabbed his finger toward the entrance and yelled: "They are going in! Look, look at the crowd; you can't afford to miss it! They have gone in to see the living skeleton. Positively his last appearance on this side of the ocean!"[15]

To stimulate further excitement among crowd members, showmen situated small brass bands on platforms in front of the sideshow tent. Racial custom in the circus industry dictated that black musicians would staff the sideshow band while the main band, comprised of all white musicians, provided the soundtrack for the big show. Joseph Bradbury of Athens, Georgia, remembered that in the 1920s "nearly every sideshow I knew had a black band, called colored back then; they would have a five piece band and . . . a couple of black girls would dance . . . something like clogging but a little different, you know. And they would put on a show."[16]

With few black circus performers included on show rosters, these segregated bands became the favorites of African Americans. One way they showed their appreciation for good performances was by crowding around the riser and dancing to the music. One circus route book informed its readers that the show's ticket agent "is the one to be envied [as] . . . he gets to hear the side show band and to see the colored people prance and caper." African Americans in Columbus found the Barnum and Bailey sideshow band's presentation so pleasurable that they seized the opportunity to "'pat time'" to the infectious music. These outdoor concerts, like street parades, inspired people to participate actively in events of the day.[17]

One reason for the enthusiastic response of black patrons was the great skill of the sideshow band musicians. O. A. Peterson, a white musician who toured with the Sells Brothers circus in 1882, admitted that his band mates thought themselves "far superior, as musicians" to the black sideshow band, but in fact "it would not have hurt any of us, had we followed the example of our humble brethren of the side show band" who practiced "faithfully every day." That band was led by "a saddle colored young man" named Hardy, who really "could sing those high ones on that E flat coronet." Peterson considered him "the best [cornetist] of his race until the days of P. G. Lowery." Lowery, the first African American graduate of the New England Conservatory of Music, got his start in minstrel shows before becoming the sideshow bandleader of the Ringling Brothers and Barnum and Bailey Circus in the 1920s.[18]

Those who paid admission to the sideshow entered an enclosure with elevated platforms arranged around the perimeter of the tent. On each of the stands was a person or animal possessed of unusual characteristics or abilities. Creatures with an extra appendage, shockingly hirsute women, extremely tall or short people, and skilled practitioners of legerdemain numbered among the attractions favored by circuses. In 1885, W. W. Cole's New Colossal Shows presented a representative collection that included a "double-headed cow, giants and midgets, the tattooed man, the albino woman, the ventriloquist and magician."[19]

Showmen also exploited American conceptions of "blackness" in their presentation of "exotic" acts in the sideshow. Drawing on deeply held cultural notions of African Americans as primitive, circus managers regularly linked blackness and savagery in their displays of non-Western "wild men." One circus shocked Savannah audiences with "a man monkey, from Africa, a singular looking semi-human creature." Similar attractions presented African Americans as less than fully human. One black man from Georgia went on the road in the late nineteenth century as a "horned" wild man. Yet Calvin Bird got his pointed projections courtesy not of nature, but rather thanks to an enterprising showman who placed two small plates under Bird's scalp with animal horns protruding from them. Once the hair grew around the plates, "the appearance was perfectly natural which made the subject look extremely wild."[20]

Notwithstanding the arrangement of the exhibits, the open observation areas of sideshow tents afforded no physical structures for racial segregation or class separation. Inside these enclosures, blacks and whites, both poor and rich, freely circulated among the displays. Joseph Bradbury recalled that "there were no seats, you know, on the circus sideshow. You just walked from platform to platform. Never any segregation [in] there." In this sense, the sideshow tent experience more resembled walking though the halls of a museum than sitting in the auditorium of a theater.[21]

Audience interactivity was central to the performance dynamics of the sideshow. Patrons assembled around the different platforms, listening to descriptions of the exhibits given by an "inside lecturer" or by the performers themselves. Some of the attractions depended on direct conversation with audience members, as with a Sells-Floto circus palm reader who, according to an account in *Billboard*, could tell visitors their ages, their thoughts, and the date of their future weddings "in such a way that leaves nothing but a lasting impression" on those who spoke to her. Further contact between the public and performers took place once the lecture and demonstrations concluded. Customers crowded around their favorite exhibits to purchase photographs and pamphlets from the performers themselves, who often autographed these souvenirs and inscribed them with personal messages.[22]

Sometimes, sideshow performers endured performances themselves. When two drunken Atlanta men engaged in fisticuffs directly in front of a bearded lady's platform, she "screamed a fine, delicate, soft scream, and placed her dainty feet on the chair rounds." In contrast to the woman's panic, the crowd in the vicinity "howled with keen delight" as this "side show within a sideshow" played itself out. At another Gate City circus, a similarly intoxicated man "talked too familiarly with the fat woman. He was ordered out, and failing to go, Patrolman Frank Whitley took hold of him. [The man] drew a pistol and would have shot the officer if the latter had not used his club." In a similarly unpleasant interaction between patron and performer, a Sells Brothers' "Hindoo warrior" punched a Thomasville spectator "in his mouth" in 1895, earning the entertainer a handcuffed appearance in front of a local judge.[23]

Trained animals offered another opportunity for participation by sideshow visitors. In Rome, the A. B. Rothschild and Company's Great Royal Victoria Menagerie, Caravan and Circus featured an "educated" hog that amazed those that gathered around his dais. He demonstrated his genius

> not only by means of card, would he carry on a conversation with his owner and do many tricks, but he actually played a game of euchre with a young Romanite that was present. After the cards were dealt, his owner showed each one of the hog's hand to him and then placed these cards, the hog's hand, on the platform. The game was thus played [with] the hog every time going to the right card when his time came to play, following suit when he could, or playing a trump—in fact he played the cards correctly; so well indeed, that he beat his opponent.

Although the reaction of the crowd members who watched this hapless man suffer defeat at the hooves of a barnyard animal was not noted in this account, one can imagine them laughing heartily with festive delight.[24]

In the sideshow tents of less reputable shows, defeat at a game of chance involved higher stakes than simple humiliation. Even though gamblers had maintained a presence on circus lots since the antebellum era, the rapid growth of the circus industry in the late nineteenth century encouraged greater numbers of unscrupulous owners to operate grift shows. In fact, one former circus confidence man estimated that perhaps half of the circuses on the road at the turn of the century engaged in grifting. These shows tended to play towns (rather than cities) where law enforcement was less professional and more limited in scope.[25]

Unlike the ethical business practices of showmen like the Ringling Brothers, who operated a circus so "clean" that their press agents proclaimed it a "Sunday School Show," managers of grift shows emphasized thievery over performance quality. In 1889, for example, one southern Georgia paper described a show of this type as "a ten cent circus charging 75 cents admission . . . with a large spread of canvas and very little exhibit and more swindling game tables than anything else."[26]

To arrange for these activities, grift circuses employed smooth-talking agents known as "fixers." These men were responsible for bribing local officials with tickets or cash to get them to look the other way while showmen ran rigged gambling games in a "wide open" fashion. The success of one fixer was in evidence at a Cordele, Georgia circus performance where the local paper reported that "some of the County officials and lawyers were royally treated by the manager of the show . . . while . . . the gambling machines were running full speed." This was not an isolated incident. A veteran fixer claimed that he encountered only three towns during a 1908 Georgia–to–British Columbia tour by the Yankee Robinson Circus that could not be "fixed." In the instances when town representatives balked, gamblers surreptitiously ran their activities knowing that law enforcement officers would be focused on the exigencies of policing a crowd of several thousand circus-goers. On the off chance that a visitor to the sideshow would "squawk" to lawmen about illicit gaming, the gambling apparatuses would quickly be broken down and the grifters would melt away into the crowd.[27]

Beneath the canvas of a grift circus sideshow tent, a few pitiful exhibits scattered around the interior provided plausible deniability for the real action, the show's gaming activities. While a handful of women and children studied the show's "freaks," groups of men crowded around the gambling tables. These black and white men fell into two, or sometimes three, categories. In the majority numbered naive and curious farmers, wholly ignorant of the grifting ways of the showmen. When well-dressed confidence men told of the great winnings that awaited players after a spin of the roulette wheel, many country people believed what they heard. A second smaller group consisted of the roughest and most disreputable men in the county. Occasionally, the assemblage also included "a professional man, a merchant, and a clerk" itching for a bit of gambling. Yet the social class of these southerners mattered little to the showmen. From their point of view, every visitor to the tent was a potential mark, an easy target for the money-stealing schemes hatched by the show's confidence men.[28]

The show's grifters stood behind collapsible tables and demonstrated the intricacies of the shell game, the three-card monte, and the wheel of fortune to the assembled crowd. But what their presentations did not reveal was that the confidence man had full control over the outcome of his game of "chance." For instance, shell game operators rigged their game as follows:

> The bean, which was not a bean at all, but a piece of composition which is very adhesive, was put down; and the walnut shells, the only thing genuine about the trick, were also put down, one of them covering the 'bean.' Then came the rapid shifting of the shells, while the 'bean,' during the process, was stuck securely under the operator's finger. The next step was the putting up of the money. If the man who had the game wanted his victim to win, there was nothing to do but put the 'bean' down by a little sleight of hand performance. If he wanted him to lose, which he generally did, he simply held to what he had for a while and made the bean show up under another shell.

Invariably, these demonstrations appeared to prove that large winnings were possible if not probable.[29]

After the showman had finished his explanation, men eager to test their luck stepped forward to play the game. To encourage players to risk large sums, grifters allowed some men to win significant amounts in order to inspire a false sense of confidence among those waiting to play. One central Georgia man won a reported $180 playing the "wheel of fortune" but not surprisingly, he was "more successful than others" who ended up contributing "to the wealth of the operator." In other cases, a confederate of the gambler, or "shill," posed as a citizen and quickly "won" large amounts of money. This had the immediate effect of encouraging those around the winning "gambler" to throw their cash down on the table. An even more devious method involved the showmen securing the assistance of locals willing to sell out their fellow citizens for money or tickets. An incensed south Georgia editor reported that "nearly a dozen different men . . . agreed, for a small pittance of one dollar and a free ticket to the show" to feign victory at gaming tables in order to lure "their neighbors and friends into risking and losing their money."[30]

The losses suffered by southern men in sideshow tents are staggering in light of the region's poverty. One former Confederate soldier was cheated out of $450 by a circus grifter "who said he was a veteran and had fought in the same battles" as the hapless man. Another Georgia man told a Dawson reporter that he had lost $500 to a shell man after watching a fellow player, later proven to be in league with the gambler, "win" hundreds of dollars. Unable to accept that their money was gone, other men sought to recoup heavy losses by heading straight from the tent to the bank to withdraw even more money to wager with at the gaming tables.[31]

The popularity of gambling at circuses reflects the longstanding love of southern men for games of chance. In the colonial period, the southern gentry sponsored horse races, card games, and cock fights to both entertain the lower orders and cement their own position on the top of the social hierarchy. This public gaming also provided a release of pent-up social tensions. In the nineteenth-century South, a wider number of southerners participated in gambling activities, with men betting on everything from dice to dog fighting. But by the end of that century, evangelicals, reform groups, and lawmakers had organized an antigambling campaign that resulted in legislation that banned gambling in several southern states, including Georgia. Thus the legal crackdown on gambling in the South coincided with an expansion of betting opportunities at circuses, making southern men all the more eager to enter the sideshow tents of grift shows.[32]

But the rigged nature of circus gambling put it at odds with southern notions of proper gaming. Historian Bertram Wyatt-Brown has pointed out that in the South gambling was a social activity intertwined with masculine ideals of honor. Southerners who gambled expected participants to "play by the rules," much as they would expect principals in a duel to behave during ritualized combat, even though in practice, neither activity always saw the engaged parties strictly adhere to the established standards. Still, when men cheated at games of chance, Wyatt-Brown notes, southerners viewed it as "the height of disgrace." Kenneth S. Greenberg adds that it was risk itself that gave gaming its status as an honorable diversion. Circus grifters, as professional gamblers operating rigged games, really risked nothing at all when they bet and thereby placed themselves outside the ethic of honor.[33]

Not surprisingly, southern communities, backed by law enforcement, aggressively challenged circus gamblers when they stole large sums from locals. A Milledgeville sheriff and his two deputies found themselves facing the business ends of "a dozen revolvers" when they tried to retrieve money lost by locals in a Sells and Rentfrow sideshow tent. After retreating, the outnumbered officers deputized a number of additional citizens, and along with an angry crowd of "several hundred people," confronted the grifters again. This show of force eventually encouraged them to hand over the "illegally acquired wealth, which was done under protest." In nearby Dillon, South Carolina, 250 armed men surrounded a Harris Nickel Plate Circus train as it tried to depart with the ill-gotten gains of a day of swindling. The circus men also brandished guns, but hastily agreed to grant "restitution ... one by one to victims" after concluding that the "opposing force was too strong." A similar set of events transpired in Bulloch County, Georgia. After citizens complained that they had been cheated, the local sheriff chained the wheels of the Van Amburg circus train to the tracks. The lawman did not let the show pull out of town until it made amends amounting to about one thousand dollars.[34]

Some showmen also indulged the prurient interests of southern men by offering them the chance to see "hoochie coochie" girls in the sideshow performing a dance "technique" first seen in America at Chicago's 1893 Columbian Exposition. *Billboard* related to its readers that the typical method of soliciting male customers for these salacious exhibitions involved an initial "mild performance" by the girls on a platform at the back of the tent before the barker brought the proceedings to a halt and called for the crowd's attention. He then "lines [the] cooch dancers up on platform ... and requests the ladies and children to go up to the front [of the tent], where they will be entertained. He repeats 'For men only' several times. He then makes a spiel that is positively vulgar." Joseph Bradbury recalled the stock announcement as "'Gentlemen we have children and ladies, we can't show you the type of show that you want. But you give another quarter [and] we'll go right in this little kit right here and you'll see a real show.'" After the showmen collected an additional twenty-five cents from the interested parties, the eager men crowded behind a curtained area free of children and "respectable" women to witness the risqué exhibition. The girls, dressed in ruffled dresses, soon reemerged and stepped onto a platform to shimmy and shake before beginning to ritually remove their clothing. Still, Bradbury points out that "the girls didn't completely strip.... They just stripped down to their pasties and G-strings."[35]

Most shows tried to keep some space between the girls and their customers, but regardless, some aroused individuals felt compelled to try to touch the women as they did their kicks, spins, and splits. Other circuses allowed even more intimate interactions. One southern journalist related to his readers that "the girls in the Side-Show were said to be very active in establishing close contact with the patrons." Unfortunately for the excited men, the reporter fully expected that now "a number of watches and pocketbooks are missing from local fellows." Dancing girls, like other sideshow performers, also made extra money by selling their pictures to the overheated "hicks."[36]

Southern men eagerly attended these shows for a couple of reasons. First, although prostitutes did dwell in southern towns, Glenda Gilmore notes that they "had long remained out of sight and unspoken of by whites." Men who enjoyed lustful stares at loose women would be hard pressed to indulge themselves outside of cities. This helps explain why a Sylvania, Georgia, paper reported that there was "a good deal of talk among the elders about the 'Salome dance'" offered by a circus. Second, with ideals of purity providing the foundation for white womanhood in the New South, southern men could not easily sexualize respectable white females at a time when racial radicals cited their passionless natures as part of the proof of an "epidemic" of black-on-white rapes. But circus dancing girls, typically "white" women cast as "Oriental" by circus men, could provide a ready resource for sexual entertainment for southern men.[37]

Both circus gambling and vice earned the opprobrium of middle-class Georgians. The editors of small-town papers expressed their community's outrage about the moral impact of these "features." After a Cole Brothers exhibition, the editor of the *Sparta Ishmaelite* wrote that "a gang of cut-throats and pickpockets gave one performance here Monday.... The best compliment we can pay either show or those in attendance is that 'they have gone.'" The *Statesboro News* lambasted the Great Van Amburg Circus for having "with it the famous hoochee coochee dancers and every imaginable rotten feature calculated to corrupt the morals and rob the pockets of the people who patronized them." Despite these condemnations, morally suspect entertainment flourished at circuses into the early 1920s, when newspaper exposés of "circus graft" finally encouraged showmen to begin to heed the calls of Charles Ringling to clean up the industry.[38]

About an hour before the matinee performance was to commence, circus workers opened the entrance into the main complex of tents. The crowds that had collected quickly sprang into action, as noted by E. T. Bishop during his Athens circus visit: "When the canvas doors of the tent were opened the crowd flocked in and a surging mass of humanity black & white yellow & brown young & old male & female continued to sardine themselves into the tents until they were 'packed full.'" A similar scene played out at a Sells Brothers show in Atlanta, where "the main entrance had a triple gate, and through the three gates crowds poured incessantly from one until half past two—a half hour after the show began."[39]

After passing through the entrance, circus-goers entered into the menagerie tent. Circuses placed their animal collections along the sides and in the center of the oval enclosure, with an elliptical aisle dividing the two groupings of living creatures. The John Robinson Circus offered a typical collection in 1876:

> At the right on entering, the first object that attracted our attention was the herd of elephants, four in number, a drove of camels, sacred cattle and other granivorous animals grouped in a corner together. Further on was [sic] the cages containing other animals, completely forming a circle around the tent, in the center of which was a large den containing sea lions. Among the special features in the cages was [sic] the rhinoceros or unicorn of Holy Writ, a monster animal, with skin of over one inch in thickness; a giant ostrich over ten feet high; one of the largest elands in America; a yak or grunting ox; a chinese or tawny bull, the only animal of its kind ever known to be on exhibition. A notable feature is the Japanese hog; this is a species of the hippopotamus, and often being advertised as that rare and curious animal by showmen who have no regard whatever for their reputation.

The oval arrangement was designed to allow patrons to pass from cage to cage and examine the animals. Of course, this layout, just like in the sideshow, allowed black and white customers to mix freely in menagerie tents. In decided contrast, Atlanta's city zoo featured segregated viewing areas for its black and white patrons.[40]

Although menagerie visitors could wander around the tent and come to their own conclusions about the animals, circus managers made staff members available to people who sought a more comprehensive and structured "educational" experience. For example, Georgians who entered the menagerie tent of Howes' Great London Circus learned about the show's animals from "Professor" Ellingham, the Zoological Lecturer, who presided over a veritable "School of Natural History." These lecturers and keepers gave detailed and animated descriptions of the different animals under their care. One woman noted in a letter to the *Atlanta Daily Herald* that members of her party enjoyed this energetic style of lecture since "the description given by the keeper is impressed upon our mind in such a way that we do not soon forget it." In later years, shows offered tours of their menageries.[41]

Animal keepers also took the opportunity to explain and demonstrate the habits and features of the animals. A Barnum and Bailey Circus hippo keeper widened the eyes of visitors with what appeared to be tangible evidence of the behemoth's blood-exuding ability. He dragged a blank white card along the animal's flank before holding it up for the crowd. To the amazement of those gathered around, the card had become stained red with "real blood." The attendant then presented the card to a lucky onlooker as a souvenir. In much the same way, the feeding of animals always captured the attention of patrons. One

Atlanta man stood in a menagerie tent in 1872 and marveled at the sight of a "monster" sea lion ingesting "whole buckets full of fish, with the voracity of a shark." In 1897, menagerie visitors in Thomasville thought it "quite a sight" to "see the animals fed."[42]

Patrons were similarly welcome to informally query staff members about their charges. Thus, customers in the Robinson menagerie in Athens sought to ask questions of the show's knowledgeable and "gentlemanly manager." But after months on the road, the endless litany of inquiries by spectators could begin to wear on nerves of keepers. One Ringling elephant handler especially dreaded facing the ubiquitous question: "Do you feed the animals raw meat or cooked meat?" Since telling credulous visitors that elephants were not carnivores would only continue the barrage of queries, the keeper often resorted to a stock answer of "roast quail," since this response "helped to increase the general wonder and relieved the strain on his patience."[43]

Unlike modern zoos, which tend to use moats or other barriers to place distance between animals and observers, circus patrons could closely examine or even touch the magnificent creatures carried by shows. Children seized the opportunity to feed peanuts to elephants and ginger cake to monkeys. One Athens resident, Susan Fan Tate, told an interviewer in the 1970s that when she was a child in the 1920s "you could walk right up to an elephant and give him a peanut, if you had the courage. . . . You would hold out the peanut in your hand and the elephant would stick out his trunk and pick it up, tuck it under his mouth." Troublemakers, however, set out to irritate and antagonize the animals. Naughty youngsters sometimes put pepper into monkey cages so they could laugh as the primates sneezed from the acrid powder. Handing a generous plug of chewing tobacco to an elephant seemed like a similarly funny prank, but only if the person who proffered the sweet leaf was out of the pachyderm's reach. In 1882, an African American man in Barnesville gave "an elephant at Barrett's Circus a chew of tobacco, for which the ungrateful beast caught him up in his trunk and injured him so he died the next day."[44]

Some shows also allowed visitors to tour their canvas horse stables. At a time when nearly every southerner depended on horses for their day-to-day transportation needs, a show's mounts garnered much attention. An *Augusta Chronicle and Sentinel* reporter asserted that "the stables connected with the Leviathan Exhibition constitute a veritable world horse fair. . . . A sight at [sic] this superb stud of royal blooded steeds is alone well worth the price of admission." An Americus newsman noted that "lovers of fine horseflesh found much to admire in the valuable stables owned by this circus. The number of horses runs into the hundreds and includes many very beautiful animals, perfectly matched teams, and thoroughbred Arabian coursers worth a small fortune." The John Robinson Circus invited Augusta residents to visit the show's "beautiful portable stables" in order to see "the largest and finest assemblage of imported thoroughbred

Circus stock in America." And just as in the menagerie tent, customers could discuss the merits and habits of the different types of equines with the show's grooms. To encourage these kinds of interactions, the Robinson show promised horse enthusiasts that "every attention will be shown [to] them by the attaches of the exhibition."[45]

As show time approached, the big top circus band began playing an up-tempo selection to signal to the crowds in the sideshow, menagerie, and horse tents that the circus performance was imminent. Soon after, a circus official "with a megaphone in his throat" stepped to the fore in the menagerie and announced that the big show was about to begin. These cues prompted people to head though the passage that connected the animal tent and the big top. Emerging from the short tunnel into the cavernous expanse of the main tent, even habitual circus-goers must have been continually struck by the steady growth in the size of big tops. For example, the two-ring Barnum show carried a 300-by-200-foot main tent in 1873, by far the largest enclosure ever used to that date. By 1894, however, the Ringling Brothers Circus presented a three-ring show beneath a big top measuring 600 feet by 200 feet, a truly mammoth pavilion.[46]

Circuses sold a range of tickets for seats inside the big top. Wealthier patrons could pay from seventy-five cents to two dollars per ticket for reserved seats. These seats faced the middle of three rings on either side of the tent and were considered the "best in the house." The Barnum and Bailey Circus, like so many circuses, numbered these seats on their 1894 tour—"exactly the same as in first-class theaters"—in order to guarantee that their privileged customers would never have to fight for a seat. The most expensive reserved tickets provided the added luxury of enclosed boxes. Showmen also placed a premium on comfort. In contrast to the hard, splintery benches in the general admission sections, circuses offered "Reserved Cushioned Opera Chairs" for an additional charge. These types of seats sometimes came with footrests as well.[47]

Bracketing these accommodations, on the far ends of the tent, were the non-reserved wooden bench or "bleacher" seats. Tickets for these seats cost between twenty-five and fifty cents, depending on the show's pricing. A correspondent to the *New York Clipper* accurately detailed the limitations of these general admission seats: "A seat in a circus show is usually a most uncomfortable affair, and after you have dangled your legs in empty space until you are tired, if you attempt to rest them you are very likely to soil somebody else's clothes and get into an unpleasant altercation." After the showmen managed to squeeze every possible person onto the bleachers, ushers seated late arrivals on the ground along the hippodrome track.[48]

Black customers, regardless of their economic means, had no such freedom to choose where to sit under the big top. From the antebellum era through the mid-twentieth century, circuses that played Georgia consistently segregated black patrons in their main performance tents. When showmen eliminated the "pit" after the Civil War, they began to place African Americans on one end of their circus tents. This sharp division between black and white in the stands that surrounded the circus rings presented a striking scene for performers, like equestrienne Dixie Willson, who were unfamiliar with the realities of southern segregation:

> I hadn't thought about the dividing color line, and no one had spoken of it. I had traveled halfway around the hippodrome track on the elephant in tournament, when suddenly I found myself facing a solid half circumference of black faces! I can't describe the impression of it—so unexpected! So much of it all together! So terrifically shady!

Showmen charged their corps of ushers with the task of enforcing segregation. Attaches scrutinized the general physiognomy of circus-goers to determine who was "black" and who was "white," and directed them to their respective seats. One white boy from north Georgia who attended the circus with one white and one black friend experienced this process firsthand: "We bought our tickets and went inside. The ticket-taker directed Vaston to the section of seats marked 'Colored Only.' Charlie and I were directed to the sections marked 'White Only.'"[49]

In most cases, attendants apparently completed this duty with little difficulty, but in some instances the complications inherent in using "racial" markers to segregate patrons into "black" and "white" sections came to the fore. Confronted with a man of Asian descent at a southern show, a flabbergasted John Robinson Circus attendant exclaimed to his superior: "You want the whites on one side and the blacks on the other, where the hell will I put this Chinaman?" Ushers faced similar challenges when they tried to prevent light-skinned biracial southerners who tried to "pass" as white from sitting outside of the Jim Crow section. A *Billboard* columnist wondered, "What usher has had the most difficulty in keeping some of the almost white 'high yallers' in their proper section while playing below the Mason-Dixon line?"[50]

Considering that well-to-do African Americans did not have access to reserved seating, it is unsurprising that some southerners of mixed racial origin attempted to "pass" as white. Regardless of social position, black Georgians who entered circus tents found themselves seated in the crowded, uncomfortable, and sometimes raucous segregated general admission area. Although the historical evidence is sketchy, at least some middle-class and elite African Americans seemed to have stayed out of circus tents. Most likely, a lack of suitable seating contributed to this trend.[51]

As patrons headed to their seats, circus performers interacted with them during the wait for the show to start. The entertainers did so in two guises. Clowns entered the crowd to make merriment with circus-goers. For instance, one circus's midget clown seized the arms of "stately, well dressed" women as they walked to their seats, much to their abashment and "the amusement of the onlookers." The more common method of mixing with customers inside the tent involved techniques that mirrored the antics of rube clowns and their street theater. During its 1894 tour, the Ringling Brothers circus staged a confrontation in the stands between an "immigrant" and an "upper class dandy." One male performer, masquerading as a "German, with a small string of 'sisages' and a loaf of bread for a lunch and a tin pail containing an amber-colored fluid resembling beer" sidled up to a dapper "dude" costumed "with eye-glass and cane, high collar and general extravagance of dress." The latter expended his energies flirting with attractive female audience members near his seat, but "every time the dude is looking his sweetest or has assumed his most charming pose, the German steals up behind him and knocks off his hat or purloins his cane or annoys him in some other way until the exasperated dude, losing his temper strikes at him 'real hard.'" The scuffle that followed sent sausages flying and the two men chasing each other around the arena. Only when the men departed the tent through the dressing room entrance did all in the laughing audience learn that the two were members of the troupe.[52]

Male clowns dressed in drag to pull off similar gags. Some clowns, costumed as frail old ladies, made their way through the audience looking for seats. To increase the believability of the bit, young boys connected to the show walked alongside the tottering "ladies" in depictions that *Billboard* called "so real that people seated ask the ushers to help the old woman and her boy." After enacting an altercation with a fellow performer posing as an audience member, the suddenly spry "woman" let the crowd in on the joke by running after her tormentor with "her skirts flying and her umbrella waving in air."[53]

A variation on this cross-dressing theme involved a male performer disguised as a flirtatious "aspiring debutante." In Savannah, a Sparks Circus performer successfully caught the eye of "all the good looking male patrons" walking with their female companions into the tent, sending onlookers into an uproar when the male circus customers learned that they had been eyeing a man dressed as a woman. Joseph Bradbury witnessed this type of skit during his childhood circus visits: "It would be a clown dressed in drag there, and he'd follow behind the man, [since] usually the lady would always go first. And he'd come behind, grabbing them, giving the 'come on' sign, and then give them the eye, you know that expression: 'You come on with me.' Most of the times, the lady wouldn't even look around . . . to get a sense of why everyone is laughing, then she would look around." The *Macon Daily Telegraph* likewise highlighted the fact that this trick produced chagrin for women as well as men: "It might well be mentioned for the satisfaction of some of the devoted wives who were surprised to see a red-haired woman flirting with their husbands before the show that the 'bewitching vamp' later pulled her hair off and revealed herself as himself." Of course, before the performer revealed his true gender, jealous Georgia women could only seethe as the costumed circus man cast sultry glances at their husbands and fiancés. The *Savannah Morning News* reported that female visitors to the Sparks tent "branded" the show's disguised clown as a "bold strumpet" for his "coyish, side-long glances and coquettish wink" that "supplied ground[s] for one and a hundred divorce suits and shattered engagements by tempting the beaux from their belles." Perhaps only within the carnivalesque context of Circus Day could southern men and women ultimately find a cross-dressing man in their midst an amusing—rather than shocking—inversion of established gender roles.[54]

Another favorite ploy exploited the eagerness of rural people to preserve their memories of their big visit to the circus. At one Thomasville exhibition, a performer dressed as a photographer set up a fake camera near the entrance inside the big top and after spotting a suitable target, "he would stop a countryman, or a groupe [*sic*] of them, have them remove their hats, and pose for a picture. After fixing their eyes on some object he would walk off, leaving them in a strained and conspicuous attitude for several minutes. Finally it would dawn on them that they were sold, and they would beat a hasty retreat, while the crowd would . . . yell at the ridiculousness of the thing."[55]

The effort to blur the line between audience and performer continued after the show began. On its 1901 tour, the Walter L. Main circus featured a footrace of local children drawn from the audience. At a matinee performance in Atlanta, "the footrace, in which about sixty small boys were entered, proved as exciting as it was humorous. The winner was a little negro, and the prize—a reserved seat to the evening performance." An even more amusing act involved audience members trying to ride a "trick" mule: an animal that appeared tractable but would violently buck soon after being mounted. At a Savannah show, the ringmaster of the Gentry Brothers' Circus promised three dollars to anyone who could remain on the back of the animal for three trips around the ring. Two black men from the audience took up the challenge, but each quickly flew from its back, much to the delight of the audience. At the conclusion of its show, the Gentry outfit also allowed children to ride its "ponies around the ring, and many of them accepted the invitation."[56]

Perhaps the most unusual circus audience participation stunt occurred in the east Georgia town of Thomson. In 1890, showman T. K. Burk advertised that he would give one hundred dollars to any couple that would marry during an exhibition by his show. A Mr. John Montgomery and a Miss Lena Hall agreed to be wed in the circus ring, and during the show's evening performance, the Reverend A. B. Thrasher, Ordinary, performed the ceremony in front of a "large audience." At its conclusion, Burk handed "over to the couple five $20 gold pieces and escorted them to a carriage amid great applause from the audience." While the involvement of patrons here is certainly notable, the audience's enthusiastic response to the taking of matrimonial vows in a show tent also reveals how Georgians' moral views on circuses had grown less severe since the antebellum period.[57]

When audience members were not playing a part in the performance itself, circus owners expected them to remain seated and orderly. But arguments and fights between patrons and the ushers and police charged with keeping the peace strained tempers and sometimes spilled blood. To be sure, these conflicts bore little resemblance to the postwar circus riots that pitted circus men against local rowdies, or for that matter, the disturbances that had surrounded antebellum theater going in the North. But the aggressive actions of some Georgia circus-goers reveals that many had failed to embrace Victorian standards of appropriate public behavior. Along with a place to fight, stands were seen by circus fans as a place to socialize with friends and even make contact with the opposite sex. They viewed certain exciting acts as an opportunity to stand and cheer, even if circus managers wanted them to remain seated. Despite the best efforts of circus managers to restrain rowdy behavior, Georgia circus audiences in the New South remained active, dynamic, and at times, unruly.

With crowds of up to fifteen thousand people filling circus tents, circus owners deployed large staffs of ushers and private detectives, sometimes supplemented by local police, to help maintain order and to try to silence "the usual fellow who yells." During the late nineteenth century, the Sells Brothers circus carried a staff of fifty "uniformed" attachés and kept a "number of special policemen" on duty to assist their ushers in controlling crowds. Howes' Great London offered even better security with a "special United States Detective Force" in place around its tents "for the protection of its patrons from impositions." In its advertising material, one show stressed the proactive nature of its security force: "Several detectives accompany the Sun Brothers shows on their travels, and they know every crook and thief of reputation in America."[58]

Sometimes, however, officious security personnel created more problems than they obviated. In the minutes before an 1894 Milledgeville performance,

> a serious difficulty was narrowly averted. A prominent citizen who had purchased a reserved seat, after seating his wife, left her for a short time. When he returned to occupy his seat he was stopped. He explained that he had paid for his seat. A dispute arose and the circus man knocked the citizen down. The citizen arose with a drawn knife and the circus man grabbed an axe. Several citizens rushed to the assistance of our townsman, and the circus man retreated. A number of pistols were drawn and excitement ran high for a few minutes.

In this case, bloodshed was prevented despite the fact that as per southern custom, the local man had armed himself before entering a public space.[59]

In not all instances did such encounters conclude peaceably. In 1915, trouble began brewing among circus-goers in Lavonia when one Cohen Davis slapped a man across the face after he allegedly called Davis a "vile name." When police officers confronted Davis in the stands, he and his two brothers tried to prevent the lawmen from arresting him. During the ensuing scuffle, a bystander pulled a gun and shot Cohen Davis' brother Tom twice at point-blank range. As Tom Davis lay dying, more firearms were drawn, and when the shooting stopped Cohen Davis was dead and the two police officers had suffered gunshot wounds. The bystander who fired first dashed from the tent and remained on the run until he was arrested in South Carolina some time later. A less gory but equally dangerous confrontation occurred in 1897 in a northern Georgia circus tent. The *Dahlonega Nugget* reported: "W. C. Thomas received a heavy blow across the head . . . at the show by Marshall [sic] Waters, who charged him with being drunk and disorderly. There was quite a nice display of pistols by some of the boys for a short while."[60]

When circus owners oversold their tents, they increased the difficulties faced by their security personnel. When the bleachers filled, ushers sat people on the ground along the ring banks. At the Main's Shows performance in Atlanta, "The tent was crowded beyond its capacity . . . canvas was spread on the ground and several thousand people sat there during the performance." With a reckless disregard for public safety, the Hagenbeck-Wallace Circus produced a "complete farce" in the same city when it squeezed people "into the tent until there was not standing room, to say nothing of room to sit in, and still the management took the people's hard cash. . . . People who had paid extra prices to secure reserved seats had no more chance of seeing the mediocre performance than a crippled grasshopper in a turkey pen." With the crowd encroaching on the exhibition area, "the police were urged on by diamond studded attendants to make the people sit down. They were laughed at." Finally, law enforcement personnel focused their attentions on the Jim Crow section in order to impress upon the crowd the importance of remaining seated: "A seething mass of Ethiopians was hemmed in on one end of the 'hippodrome.' A fly cop, goaded on by one of the management, waded into that sea of surging blackness, and wielding his club like a cavalryman at a tournament, cut a path through, leaving unprotesting broken and bloody heads in his wake." After enduring this unprovoked assault by the police, many African Americans departed the show before it had "half begun."[61]

Once the show did begin, circus ushers encouraged people to keep their seats. During the more mundane parts of the performance and in a tent that was less than full, circus fans did tend to stay seated. But when people along the ring bank blocked the views of those immediately behind them, crowd members would begin to stand section by section. Before long, the entire audience would be on its feet. At a central Georgia show, "All the seats were rapidly filled, and then a howling mob gathered about the ring and stood up to see the performance. Of course all on the bottom seats were compelled to get up and look over the heads of those between them and the ring. Then there was a general uprising—a kind of insurrection—and those on reserved top seats could see nothing."[62]

When standing patrons blocked the view or the show reached a lull, closely packed spectators socialized or partook in other forms of intercourse. The "Society" page of the *Savannah Morning News* reported that the circus "was not without its social aspect, and quite a fashionable audience graced the grandstand and the boxes. The season's debutantes, buds of last year, young married folks, and even sedater elders, family parties, and lively groups of four, six, or eight congenial friends mixed with the throng that filled the big tent last night. Everyone one might care to know was there, and in a gay good fellowship that made it seem like one big party." Other forms of contact occurred between spectators squeezed onto bleacher benches. A Hawkinsville editor took note of a "side show" performed by a "loving couple" seated right behind him: "He held her by the waist with his manly arm, to keep her from falling, and she twined her arms around his neck and ate peanuts out of his mouth—taking them out with her teeth." In neighboring Mississippi, the touching between a sixteen-year-old girl of "chaste character" and her adult neighbor in the stands of a show was much less welcome. After she rebuffed his first advance by knocking his roaming hand off of her back, he followed up by placing his hand on her leg just above the knee. This "indecent assault" earned the man thirty days in the county jail and a fifty-dollar fine.[63]

The bleachers could even become a place for a protest against the immorality of circus entertainment. In 1895, one railroad executive's wife agreed to enter the tent of a circus in Atlanta only because she did not want her party to miss the show "on account of staying outside with her." Once inside, however, the woman quickly made manifest how deeply she disdained this diversion by turning away from the exhibition area, so she could sit *"with her back to the performance the entire time!"* (italics in original). Undoubtedly, those in her party were not the only ones in the vicinity to take notice of this unique expression of circus antipathy.[64]

Circus protests aside, no part of the performance made more of a mockery of the showman's desire for crowds to remain orderly than "hippodrome races." At the close of the circus exhibition, showmen pitted mounted animals against one another on the oval track that surrounded the three main circus rings. Observers noted the fervor that these races inspired in Georgia audiences. As one news report declared, these contests "attract the crowd better than anything else." Although circus men wanted these competitions to electrify their customers, they remained mindful of the importance of crowd control, and thus specifically called on their patrons to remain seated. For example, the Ringling Brothers' 1894 program requested that audience members "retain their seats during the races."[65]

Nonetheless, few Georgia thrill-seekers followed these directives. A series of spirited competitions never failed to prompt patrons to "whoop and yell in an excitement caught from the work" of the racers. While watching these contests in Columbus, "people stood on seats," cheering as the contestants flew round and round the track at breakneck speeds. In contrast to the "monotonous features of a clown, with sayings that everybody has heard," the "stirring races" run by Buckley's Circus in 1874 "roused the whole being into enthusiasm and tightened the nerves to their utmost tension through excitement." And in 1912 in Columbus, "the hippodrome races were, as usual, quite thrilling, arousing the crowd to a high pitch of enthusiasm."[66]

The ability of these contests to completely absorb the attentions of spectators nearly caused a terrible tragedy at a 1913 Barnum and Bailey performance in Columbus. One enthralled man standing at the top of the bleachers in the "department for negroes" with an unlit cigarette dangling from his lips became so engrossed in the hippodrome competitions that he mindlessly held an ignited match "close to the tent over his head" during an "exciting stage of the races." The canvas burst into flame, sending thousands of people stampeding out of the burning tent, but amazingly, no one was killed or seriously injured on that day. Thirty-one years later, however, circus patrons in Hartford, Connecticut would not be so fortunate during a similar incident. After a Ringling Brothers and Barnum and Bailey Circus tent caught fire, 167 people died and nearly 500 were injured.[67]

Just as historians have lost sight of the fact that Circus Day fostered amusement spaces that extended outside of the big top to encompass community streets, many have incorrectly categorized the late nineteenth-century circus as a spectator activity comparable to theatrical performances. In point of fact, the open viewing areas of menagerie and sideshow tents coupled with the participative presentations contained within them helped make the circus an entertainment grounded upon audience interaction. In these enclosures, black and white patrons had the chance to intermingle and to create their own fun. After they grew tired of asking the fat lady how much she ate or feeding peanuts to the elephants, they could look their fellow citizens up and down, laughing at the drunk or ogling the handsome. The self-directed nature of a journey through these tents, and the informal way that the entertainment was presented, assured that customers could take an active role in the circus-going activity.[68]

Under the big top, the circus came closest to approximating a true spectator entertainment. But the limited reach of Victorian public etiquette in the South meant that many people under the big top thought nothing of standing up and blocking the view of others, cheering wildly, heckling performers, or even pulling a gun on a fellow patron, despite efforts by circus men to limit such unruly activity. Moreover, the highly enthusiastic responses of audiences to disguised performers in the stands and patrons riding trick mules virtually guaranteed that the circus would remain an interactive entertainment that at times blurred the line between spectator and performer. In this time and place, circus audiences were anything but passive. The nation's circus men would not have had it any other way.

> It is generally conceded that the circus is the national amusement.... In this very fact lies, in part at least, the secret of its appeal. While the opera appeals to the cultivated only and vaudeville has a limited following and there are time[s] when the play fails to satisfy, the circus has aggregated such a variety of startling things that the mind is fairly shocked into delight.—*Atlanta Journal*, 20 October 1906

SEVEN

It's Showtime
The Cultural Content of the Circus, 1880–1920

By the early twentieth century, the circus had reached its popular zenith. In Georgia, and all over the country, the industry's leading shows regularly played to massive, capacity crowds. In 1905, the *Atlanta News* reported that "between 35,000 and 40,000 people saw the afternoon and night performances" of the Ringling Brothers Circus. Showmen attracted audiences of this size by continually advertising that their shows represented the biggest and most novel productions ever staged under canvas. The Sells Brothers Circus promised that its 1895 show would be "BEYOND ALL COMPARISON—The Largest, Grandest, Best Exhibition ever seen in Atlanta, presenting all NEW EXCLUSIVE FEATURES." Eleven years later, Barnum & Bailey's advertising proclaimed that the outfit featured "NEW ARENIC ATTRACTIONS FROM EVERYWHERE, Presented in Three Rings, on Two Stages, in Mid-Air and Upon a Huge Hippodrome Racing Track, Under the Largest Tents Ever Constructed."[1]

To make good on these claims, showmen put on some of the most spectacular, audacious, and groundbreaking attractions ever conceived by the American amusement industry up to that time. These novel features, however, did not simply shape the diversions of the time. In fact, they helped pave the way for some of the most gripping and significant popular entertainments of the twentieth and twenty-first centuries. For instance, the huge historical spectacles, or "specs," that circus men staged in their tents in the 1890s can be seen as precursors to the early twentieth-century celluloid epics popularized by director Cecil B. DeMille. Along the same lines, by presenting bicycle, and then auto, "dips of death" that sent daring men and "new" women flying down ramps and through the air in front of breathless crowds, showmen anticipated the late twentieth-century embrace of "extreme" stunts and sports. Finally, hippodrome racing, with its speed—and specter of sudden crashes and falls—stands as a harbinger of the immense success and mass appeal that stock-car racing currently enjoys in the United States.[2]

Despite these novel and innovative additions, the new did not fully supersede the old in the turn-of-the-century circus. As it had been during the antebellum era, the circus of the Gilded Age remained an entertainment that emphasized vigorous physicality and glamorous sexuality. Showmen continued to draw crowds with their skilled equestrians, talented lion tamers, and scantily clad female performers. Moreover, the new dramatic specs were as likely to narrate time-honored classical and Biblical tales as contemporary political events. Through this fusion, America's circus showmen created neither a "low" amusement like the minstrel or burlesque show nor a "high" form of art like the opera or the refined theater. Instead, they gave birth to a "middlebrow" entertainment that reached out to all classes at a time when the region was still experiencing a cultural transformation from the Old to New South.[3]

As the rube clowns and the other imposters departed through the tunnel to the backstage area, the crowd's anticipation began to rise. Audience members fidgeted in their seats as they searched for signs that the show was about to begin. Finally, the conductor struck up the band, and the entertainment commenced. Into the 1880s, showmen often kicked off their shows with an opening pageant, or grand entrée, featuring all of their performers and many of their animals. The purpose of these types of displays was twofold. Showmen wanted to highlight the size and grandeur of their troupes while simultaneously elevating the energy level of the crowd. The account of an Atlanta spectator reveals how showmen often succeeded at both goals:

> The triumphant opening parade [was] ushered in by a crashing tune that set one's blood a tingle and caused queer, creepy feelings to crawl up one's spine, and a choking sensation in the throat . . . More music followed, and then the vast pageant got under full swing. First came the elephants and camels and other animals, followed by a vast array of equestrians of various kinds. How the horses did prance! What bewitching beauties, the gaudily-attired women, dashing cavaliers and armored knights! . . . The parade swept slowly around the arena . . . and deafening cheers arose from the crowd.

As the pageant proceeded, the performance area would slowly become filled with wild creatures, dashing riders, and spirited performers. Another eyewitness noted that "the band opened the show, of course, but with the first strains came the grand imposing spectacular entree. This was worked in two rings, on elevated stages, and on the hippodrome track, all at the same time. In both rings were riders in handsome costumes; on the stage was a fine band, while the hippodrome ring showed animals and actors in profusion." If all went well, the grand entrée would have audience members applauding wildly at its conclusion.[4]

As competition among the industry leaders intensified in the late 1880s, many of the leading impresarios began replacing or supplementing their entrées with dramatic specs. One basic reason for this change was that despite all the pomp and circumstance, the entrée was, in essence, just a street parade under canvas. In contrast, a well-produced and innovative spectacle offered showmen additional benefits beyond those they already enjoyed from the outside procession. For one thing, spectacles, unlike an entrée, allowed for claims of exclusivity. By staging an original spec, a circus owner could plausibly claim that his show was the only place in the world where it could be seen. In addition, most specs recounted familiar stories or events from the past, giving these shows an immediacy that entrées lacked. Finally, this narrative-based structure meant that specs could attract a class of people who might hesitate to go to the circus: sophisticated urban southerners who enjoyed theatrical productions.[5]

Even if these factors failed to sway all potential patrons, showmen felt confident that the great size and spectacular character of spectacles would give them a broad popular appeal. During the golden age of the spec (roughly 1890 to 1910), showmen staged shows with casts numbering upward of twelve hundred performers, clothing them all in beautiful costumes. They incorporated hundreds of horses and other more exotic animals into their productions. They constructed elaborate sets and employed "shifting machinery" to assist circus laborers in moving the set pieces. The biggest of these shows cost hundreds of thousands of dollars to produce. In this sense, these productions, with their lavish sets and large casts, represent the forerunners to DeMille's historical film epics, including *Joan the Woman* (1917), *The Ten Commandments* (1923), *Cleopatra* (1934), and *Sampson and Delilah* (1949).[6]

Some of the spectacles that showmen staged at the turn of the century dealt with America's role in contemporary international events. In the words of historian Janet Davis, impresarios produced shows that "portrayed the United States as a democratic republic whose style of government, economic system, and 'way of life' spread worldwide would herald a utopian age of unprecedented prosperity." She notes that some favored subjects included politically popular conflicts like the Spanish-American War or the Indian Wars.[7]

But impresarios also presented productions concerning more archaic historical events. Several leading circuses put on pageants that portrayed Biblical episodes or life in ancient cities. Although the specific reasons why individual showmen decided on one theme over another is not always known, classical and religious specs did offer showmen several benefits when seeking the patronage of southern audiences. First, these shows helped insulate impresarios from the charges of immorality made by some southern evangelicals and their religious leaders. Even if a show's female equestrians offended because they wore tights instead of more modest garb, show managers could point to a Biblical spec as evidence that they headed a virtuous enterprise. Second, religious-themed dramas could encourage evangelicals who might normally stay away from circuses to buy a ticket to a show. Third, these exhibitions had the merit of being largely uncontroversial. Apart from the most severe evangelicals, what citizen could plausibly oppose edifying reenactments of crucial scenes from the distant past? Showmen emphasized the historical "accuracy" of these dramas for this very reason: to underscore the idea that their entertainments continued to provide "instruction" as well as "amusement." These factors prompted circus owners to heavily publicize specs of this genre while they were in the South.[8]

The first major turn-of-the-century circus spec was a European import. "Nero, or the Destruction of Rome," was the brainchild of Hungarian theatrical impresario Imre Kiralfy. Initially performed in 1889, Kiralfy's grand production had made him the toast of European society, and James A. Bailey, ever with an eye for marketable entertainment, asked him to adopt the spectacle for his circus. Kiralfy agreed, and the Barnum and Bailey circus presented the drama on its 1890 tour. In Georgia, the show intended to stage the performance in Augusta, Atlanta, Savannah, and Athens, but a crash of the show's train forced the cancellation of the latter two stops, so only Augusta and Atlanta residents got a chance to see it.[9]

To minimize the time needed to put up and take down the production, the show performed "Nero" at the close of the matinee and at the opening of the evening show. The show's production team arranged the backdrop and set by placing the 450-foot-long stage on one side of arena, across from the audience of fifteen thousand. After the drop of a curtain, the drama opened with Nero's entry through the gates of Rome, "followed by scores of men-at arms, [and] a veritable army of followers." This "triumphal procession" included "the Gallic embassy and suite; a procession of priests, vestals, augurs and attendants; the Egyptian embassy, the emperor's favorite and her attendants, [and] Nero himself in his triumphal car," all set to the "sound of trumpets, the clash of cymbals, and the music of many voices."[10]

After a set change, the show proceeded with a "grand terpsichorean divertissement," or ballet, performed by "dozens of men and scores and scores of pretty girls" all pirouetting "within Nero's palace." Later scenes dramatized Roman marriages, Bacchanalian orgies, and sacrificial offerings staged by thespians portraying Christian martyrs, Roman Senators, slaves, vestal virgins, eunuchs, priests, and Praetorian Guards, all acting alongside camels, horses, and elephants. In addition, the show featured a re-creation of the Circus Maximus, complete with fierce gladiator combats and thrilling chariot races. Despite this dazzling array of features, the most gripping part of the show came at its conclusion when the burning of Rome was recreated with simulated, but fearsome-looking, flames.[11]

The show's dramatic effects certainly impressed Georgia spectators, but it was the "wicked deeds" of its protagonist that sent shivers down their spines. Nero truly was, as the *Atlanta Journal* pointed out, an "imperial tyrant." He practiced a pagan religion, abused his subjects, and even killed his own mother. But perhaps his greatest sin was his persecution of Christians. On the day of the Barnum and Bailey appearance in the Gate City, the *Journal* reminded its readers of the Roman leader's savage treatment of the pious: "Nero was the most cruel emperor of ancient Rome, and adhered so far to the tenets of barbarism that he gave a feast over which the light of Christianity was shed by means of living torches in the persons of so many living Christians. The victim was covered with solution of tar and pitch, the match was applied and for hours the barbaric guests of the imperial tyrant held high carnival uninterrupted save by the cries of Christians." Atlanta evangelicals who read this chronicle of cruelty must have felt both horror about the deaths of these martyrs and admiration for their willingness to die for their faith.[12]

In 1892, the Adam Forepaugh shows sought to capitalize on the success of "Nero" with the "Fall of Nineveh," a Biblical spectacular that reenacted the collapse of the "first great metropolis of the civilized world." The Forepaugh show presented it on the "largest and best equipped stage in the world, 300 feet long and 55 feet wide" with a cast of 1,000 men, women, and children costumed "in the most gorgeous array." And like the Nero production, "Nineveh" included a ballet and athletic competitions, and concluded with the destruction of a mighty city.[13]

Georgia reviewers applauded the Nineveh drama—as they had "Nero"—for its "almost realistic reproduction" of the past. The *Atlanta Constitution* pointed out that "Nineveh" had the power to transport spectators "back to the age of childhood" since it was an "old story which all had read in their infancy." In Columbus, the *Enquirer-Sun* reported that the audience enjoyed the dramatic renderings since "the chariot races before the populace reminds one of the famous description of Ben-Hur, and the running races are exciting to the extreme. The last scene where the hostile army breaks in upon the king and his court, and Sardanalapus mounts his throne and has the fires lighted and stands on the funeral pile and is consumed, is a fitting climax to an exhibition never equaled in Columbus."[14]

Unlike the single-season run of "Nineveh," the John Robinson Circus performed its "King Solomon and the Queen of Sheba" spec for the better part of two decades. Decidedly smaller than "Nero" or "Nineveh," the show featured about one hundred performers, including a clown who did double duty in the circus in the role of Solomon. The pageant opened with the entry of the king on a chariot and the queen on a litter. The two then took their thrones, and heard the pleas of two women who both claimed to be the mother of the same child, in a reenactment of the Old Testament's legendary "Judgment of Solomon."

During the drama, audiences also enjoyed the performance of a "ballet whose members were costumed elaborately and who danced and pirouetted through the figures of the Oriental dance . . . [to] fine effect" and a procession by the King, who rode around the hippodrome track on a water buffalo. For evening performances, the spec was "enhanced by the electric lights and colored by fire display, adding a more realistic and vivid hue to the gorgeous tournamental pageant."[15]

More than any of the other circuses that performed shows of this genre, the John Robinson Circus emphasized the religious aspects of its trademark pageant. In newspaper advertising used during its 1899 tour of Georgia, the show called the spec its "Grand Biblical Spectacle." In 1904, show manager Gil Robinson announced in the pages of the *Savannah Morning News* that "Sheba" was a veritable "Scriptural Tableaux."[16]

Robinson once commented to the Georgia press that the Sheba "act never fails to appeal to a certain class of spectators." Although the spec was "especially popular" with southerners, the "class" that Robinson referenced here particularly comprised religious southerners. Accordingly, the showman went to great lengths to spread word of the drama to the region's Christians. This included the dispatch of African American employees with "experience as exhorters" to local black churches located in towns along the outfit's southern tour route. These men sought, and regularly received, permission from the presiding pastors to speak to their congregations at Sunday services. "On the appointed Sunday," Robinson wrote in his memoir, "the visiting exhorter would announce a text from Chronicles or the Songs of Solomon. . . . [Then] the climax would come when the congregation had been stirred to the proper degree of enthusiasm and wonder. 'Alas, mah beloved brethren,' the speaker would cry, 'Alas, King Solomon has done passed away but his glories'" lived on at the John Robinson Circus. When the show employee stirred the assembled men, women, and children to this degree, "nothing short of an earthquake could have kept them away from the show."[17]

Despite the rectitude of their opening specs, circuses continued to face opposition at the turn of the century from some southern evangelicals. The three major sources of this hostility were the skimpy dress of circus athletes, the risqué nature of the female athletes' performances, and the persistent rumors that performers lived sexually promiscuous lifestyles while on the road. All three of these issues were fueled by the ways that circuses transgressed against established gender norms.

The moral taint of the promiscuity rumors, in particular, was severe enough that circus press agents found it necessary to regularly address the issue in their promotional materials. The main way they tried to debunk stories of turpitude was by claiming that most performers in their troupes were related by blood or marriage. After a "behind the scenes" visit to the Adam Forepaugh and Sells

Brothers Shows in the company of the outfit's press representatives, a *Savannah Morning News* reporter concluded that the circus profession does not make a show's talent a "degenerate class" since "almost every woman who was a performer in yesterday's show was either the wife or the daughter of some of the male performers."[18]

Circuses also took pains to disseminate the "stringent rules" that governed social interaction among their performers. But as Janet Davis observes, "many work rules applied exclusively to women." They included bans on fraternization between men and women and nightly bed checks for female performers. In spite of publicizing these regulations, press representatives still felt compelled to try to demonstrate that even if opportunities for promiscuity presented themselves, circus women could not indulge. One press agent contended that the arduous nature of circus athletics made it "impossible" for female athletes to "dissipate" since "not only their livelihood, but life itself, depends on a clear mind, firm muscles and steady nerves. . . . Their work is from early morning until late at night with no opportunity to gain any rest and recreation away from the show."[19]

Costuming and performance styles presented more intractable problems. In the antebellum era, female circus athletes wore skirts to the knee when they performed on the trapeze or on horseback, a daring display of flesh at a time when respectable women always ventured into public with their arms and legs covered. After the war, women performers dispensed with skirts and began wearing tights on their legs. While rarely singled out for censure, male performers also appeared lightly dressed. Along with the offensive nature of costumes, conservative southerners disapproved of female circus troupers because they "violated local taboos against riding astride, performing athletic feats and making public spectacles of themselves." Taken together, these controversial components stirred the ire of many conservative southerners.[20]

But they also stirred the libidos of Georgia men. Trapeze and tightrope actresses, performing high in the air, particularly offered a striking moral contrast to the subject matter of a show's spec. In his diary, seventeen-year-old E. T. Bishop recounted how he sat in a tent and watched as "two women dressed in tights with nicely trimmed satin waists put in an appearance. These blushing maidens run lithely into the ring and after kissing their dimpled hands to the audience they sprightly run up the ropes until they reach the top of the tent where is suspended a trapeze. There they perform various feats & come down kiss their hands again & as lithely run out." Bishop paid equally close attention to the dress of the female ropewalkers. He looked up at "a 'young lady' who impersonated a fairy, being very lightly clad in a short dress & perfectly fitting tights" as she walked a tightrope. Then came "another woman who being introduced to the audience (dressed like the others) ascends the rope or rather is hoisted by means of another woman who draws her up. She then performs various feats much like the others she then comes down the rope head forwards & goes out with the others." The revealing outfits worn by female circus athletes stood in such sharp contrast to the accepted sartorial standards of the day that they inevitably drew the interest of Georgia men.[21]

One north Georgia town's response to female performers demonstrates how these lightly garbed aerial athletes challenged Victorian sexual propriety. In his memoir, Clarence Hosch remembered that the first circus he saw as a child had put on a poor performance, so he resolved not to attend any more exhibitions. When the next show came to town, he did indeed skip the first night's show. But the next morning, he overheard his "fat, elderly" neighbor tell his mother what she had seen at the show: "In all mah bawn days Ah never seed sich scan'alous going-on! Them three young hussies swingin' on thuh trapeze bars with nothing on but them red tights! All thuh menfolks sittin' thar popeyed! Thuh Town Council oughta not allow sich going-on!" Upon hearing that report, he immediately resolved "not to miss the next performance."

When Hosch arrived at the show, he settled into the audience with the members of the town council and most other male members of the community. With "open-mouth admiration," he watched the three beautiful girls climb onto the trapeze. His "eyes followed the youngest as she flipped around a bar, swung with graceful ease from one to another, or dangled by her knees, by her toes. Jumping down lightly, the smiling young hussies bowed to the applause." At the turn of the century, the circus was a significant site for male erotic fantasy.[22]

Female bareback riders also attracted the male gaze. At a 1900 show, an Atlanta reporter took note of the "bewitching beauties" on horseback and in particular, the "ravishing creature in the pink tights [who] passed in a chariot drawn by four white horses." Even as early as 1872, a newsman felt it appropriate to complement a Barnum rider as "an accomplished equestrienne, having a beautiful face, [and] an elegant figure." Of course, not all females lived up to such standards of beauty. After scrutinizing circus posters that portrayed "beautiful young maidens standing on the bare backs of spirited horses as they galloped around the ring," Hosch and his friends were crestfallen when "the beautiful maidens . . . turned out to be one lone, short, fat woman in her thirties, who stood on the back of a tired-looking white horse as he ambled around the circle."[23]

Still, modesty did have its adherents among performers and audience members alike. Some acrobats and equestrians performed in fashionable gowns and suits. One turn-of-the-century acrobatic family, the Nelsons, carried out their act while garbed in what Ringling Brothers' press agents described as "evening dress." The troupe, which consisted of six men and three women, set themselves apart from their peers insofar as the "gentlemen wear evening costume and the ladies long skirts, and thus attired, turn single and double somersaults." Although the Nelsons risked injury by wearing constricting outfits that could hinder their ability to perform their stunts, the ironic effect of acrobats clad in the latest fashions outweighed these safety concerns. And for those less astute customers who did not pick up on the clever inversion of dress, the fact that the costumes covered the performers from head to toe protected the show from charges of immorality and pleased the more reserved people in the crowd. In 1910, the *Columbus Enquirer-Sun* reported that a different troupe of fully clothed acrobats "attracted attention" at the circus because the "close-fitting tights, so objectionable to some modest people, were not used at all."[24]

Most southerners understood that these conservatively attired performers stood as an exception to the rule. The circus was an arena where cultural norms could be challenged and overturned, and while modest by modern standards, these skimpy costumes resembled and thus represented the forerunners of early twentieth-century swimsuits. The dress and lifestyle of circus performers remained subjects that sparked not only outrage, but also the curiosity and sex drives of many southerners, as this newspaper account of the backstage scene at a 1910 circus in Atlanta demonstrates:

> In the women's dressing rooms the actresses are lined up in a semi-circle, each one with her trunk opened to form a dressing table, and before a tiny mirror she powders her nose, and laces with sure fingers the ribbons that make her fine costume attractive. With the speed born of long practice, a young performer will flash into the room dressed in short fluffy skirts, and before you can draw a breath scarcely, she is divested of all her garments and clothed in silken tights ready for another entrance in the ring.

Curiously, the male reporter never explained to *Constitution* readers how he could describe the female costume changing ritual in such exquisite detail. He left the answer to that question to the imagination.[25]

Well-trained performing animals represented the fulfillment of a different type of fantasy for Georgia audiences. For people who spent much of their lives in the company of headstrong barnyard animals, the sight of handlers compelling elephants to stand on their heads and lions to jump through hoops produced feelings of satisfaction and wonder among spectators. At its core, the deep interest that southerners had in this aspect of circus performances derived from the fact that the trainer's apparent mastery of their charges reaffirmed man's authority over the natural world. After an amazing demonstration that featured five elephants forming a pyramid and climbing ladders, the *Augusta Chronicle and Sentinel* declared: "The training of animals develops not only a high order of physical courage, but shows the power of intelligence, of mind over matter, that is worthy of the admiration of the most learned and cultivated. To see one man so far controlling five huge elephants at once . . . is to witness a triumph of human sagacity, intelligence and will that adds something to the dignity of human nature, as it demonstrates man's superiority over everything else in nature."[26]

Perhaps even more impressive than holding dominion over the world's biggest terrestrial beasts was controlling of some of the world's most dangerous animals, the big cats. The trainer of the Hagenbeck-Wallace shows thrilled crowds in Columbus when he "fed lions raw beef and placed his head in the mouth of one of them. Lions, tigers and leopards were also required to lie down together and there was never a move to indicate that he did not have the beast[s] under perfect control and they were as obedient as if human beings. The act of a lion riding a horse attracted especial attention, as there were a great many who doubted that this stunt which was advertised would be pulled off. Other unusual acts were a lion jumping through a burning hoop and riding an elephant."[27]

The popularity of acts that blurred the line between man and beast highlight the fact that these demonstrations of animal abilities had cultural implications beyond the circus ring. Although Charles Darwin's ideas concerning natural selection first appeared in 1859 in his *Origin of Species*, the dissemination of his more accessible views, most famously that man descended from apes, did not gain wide currency in American society until the last two decades of the nineteenth century. To be sure, antebellum circus trainers had succeeded in making an elephant walk a "tightrope," horses jump rope, and even a rhinoceros, a notoriously recalcitrant creature, ring a bell. But the anthropomorphism on display under turn-of-the-century big tops appeared against the backdrop of the Darwinian challenge to traditional biological classifications of man. To wit: did Divine creation make man wholly unique from other animals on the planet, or, as Darwin and his followers would have it, did man evolve from lesser life forms, thereby making humans just one living creature among many?[28]

Most Georgians remained committed to maintaining the ideological underpinnings of the hierarchy between man and animal. A Savannah newsman concluded that "the most interesting feature" of the show that he witnessed "was the trained seals and sea lions, animals of a low order of intelligence, that would perform unique and extraordinary tricks at the command of their master." Accordingly, Georgia citizens concluded that if trained animals possessed only modest cognitive abilities, the trainers themselves must be the truly gifted beings. Many handlers plied their trade under title of "Professor" to emphasize the didactic nature of their relationships with their charges. The animal act that "attracted more attention than any other" at a John Robinson show was "that of Prof. Winston's troupe of trained sea lions. The professor has succeeded in bringing his sea lions, which are among the hardest animals to educate, to a stage of development which is nothing short of wonderful."[29]

Yet other observers stressed the remarkable intelligence of circus animals. For example, one exclaimed that the seals of the Barnum and Bailey Circus did "stunts that would tax the ability of a man" while the show's huge elephants demonstrated that they possessed "almost human intelligence." An official with the Howes' Great London Show informed readers of the *Atlanta Constitution* of the particularly cerebral nature of the elephant: "There is no more intelligent animal than the elephant. . . . Once the trainer, Mr. Aratingstall, was sick, and a green hand tried to put them through their evolutions. We had forgotten the order in which the tricks came, and they got mixed up. The next time we just turned them into the ring and let them go it alone. They never made a bobble."[30]

Show impresarios and their trainers furthered the comparison between man and animal by staging acts that had wild creatures engage in humanlike activities. For instance, the Ringling Brothers Circus capitalized on the controversy surrounding evolutionary theory by billing the primate "star" of their 1910 menagerie as "Darwin, the man-chimpanzee." After a Gate City performance, the *Atlanta Georgian* confirmed that the chimp "is a bicycle rider and does equally well on roller skates." Elephants proved themselves similarly capable of acting out the latest human recreations. In 1913, the Sparks Circus offered a feature of elephants playing baseball. "Mary" the elephant was the star pitcher among the Sparks pachyderms, and reputedly sported a batting average of .400. Similarly, the 1911 Ringling Brothers Circus exhibited a herd of elephants that knocked down "ten pins" in a bowling demonstration. These giant animals could even demonstrate the delicate rituals of gentility, as in this 1886 skit by the Barnum and London Show: "When the clown and the little elephant both take a drink they pay the waiter. The elephant puts his trunk into his pocket, takes out the money, hands it to the waiter, takes back the change, then takes a napkin and wipes his mouth precisely as a human being would do. Then the clown reminds the elephant that he has his hat on, and the elephant takes it off. He almost seems to reason as a man would. His part in the dinner, in arranging the table, etc., is every whit as intelligent as the clown." By presenting acts that demonstrated the great "intelligence" of animals as they engaged in anthropomorphic activities, circus owners encouraged their audiences to ponder man's place in the great chain of being.[31]

Even though circus animals performed amazing tricks and even emulated the habits of the most mannered, they did occasionally wreak havoc in the ring, forcing handlers and Georgians alike to aggressively reassert their dominance. At an 1897 show in Macon, "Wallack" the lion stood in his cage in the center of the ring as the Harris Nickel Plate Circus trainer Harry Mozart put the show's other big cats through their paces. With Mozart's attention momentarily diverted, Wallack managed to pop the latch on the door of his cage, which allowed him to reach out a paw, grab his trainer "just above the eyebrows," and jerk him back against the cage. As the crowd screamed, "the plucky keeper drew his pistol and fired twice, which startled the lion. Some of the circus attendants seized the long wooden spikes which are always kept handy for such an emergency and so vigorously prodded the lion that he turned with rage upon them, which gave the keeper an opportunity to escape." Years earlier, Georgia men, rather than the keeper, had been the ones to draw their sidearms when an Ames' Circus elephant went "on a rampage" in an Atlanta tent. Only after show workers unleashed a flurry of blows with poles and clubs on the flanks of the furious animal did it cease its tantrum. No doubt, had the elephant menaced the throng filled with fainting women and yelling boys, the vigilant men in the audience would have pulled their triggers. Inside circus tents, man always conquered beast.[32]

Apart from wild creatures, the animal that garnered the most interest from circus goers was the horse. Horses were, as one east Georgia scribe put it, an attraction "dear to the true Southern heart." This love for equine performers meant that in Georgia, "the horses attached to the average big show are of more interest to a great many patrons than anything else under the canvas." At a time when nearly every southern man, woman, and child rode horses, residents of the state admired magnificent circus mounts in the same way today's automobile aficionados will admire a gleaming sports car. But southerners were not easily impressed when it came to horses. Unlike the giraffe or hippo, animals that attracted attention by virtue of their rarity, circus steeds needed to be particularly fine specimens to win plaudits because most southerners had seen their share of fine stallions and mares. That being said, locals did give credit to shows when they exhibited beautiful animals. For example, Howes' Great London Show earned the favor of a Griffin audience for its "handsome" steeds that looked "like a fine lot of special[ly] selected cavalry or race horses."[33]

Georgia residents were so attuned to the characteristics that made for an exceptional mount that they rated a show's overall quality by evaluating the grooming, health, and appearance of a show's horses. The occasional second-rate circus that paraded a herd of mangy horses through its show tents usually found this fact duly noted in the next day's paper. In Columbus, the John Robinson Circus drew criticism for not having not a single "sprightly horse" attached to its show. By contrast, the Coup circus won praise in Atlanta for its "sleek, fresh," and "spirited horses."[34]

Along with the physical appearance of equines, circus-goers paid particular attention to their responsiveness and training. A group of well-drilled mounts could always be counted on to win over a southern crowd. An Augusta journalist affirmed this truism when he wrote in the wake of a show that "the large number of elegant horses belonging to the establishment, so perfectly trained and under control, called out the spontaneous admiration of those who love horses, and who does not?" The numerous "lovers of horse-flesh" who attended the Barnum and Bailey Circus in Columbus found that "the acting of the trained horses was the most enjoyable part of the circus and it is safe to say that such an aggregation of show horses was never seen here before." Such demonstrations of discipline went beyond single riders on their steeds. "The strongest feature" of an Atlanta exhibition "was the seventy performing horses, performing in one ring under the command of John O'Brien. So smoothly did the horses and ponies work at the word of command that there appeared to be a revolving pyramid in the ring." This type of mastery over horses at liberty was sure to bring down the house.[35]

Nonetheless, the phenomenal athleticism of circus riders made them the true stars of the genre's equine features. One of the first postwar equestrian superstars was an African American boy named Lewis Willis. As a member of the John Robinson Circus from 1867 to 1878, Willis was billed as "Contraband Lewis," presumably because he had freed himself from the shackles of slavery during the Civil War. Yet the show's officials sometimes advertised Lewis as an "Ethiopian" rider to give him an aura of exoticism. Regardless of his nicknames, Lewis stood out from his peers because he was, in the words of circus historian William Slout, "one of the rare black riders America produced before the 20th century."[36]

Willis' specialties included hurdle leaping and bareback riding. After an 1867 appearance, the *Columbus Sun and Times* reported that "the hurdle act of the negro boy Lewis, the only negro equestrian in America, created enthusiasm. His riding was bold and rapid." A correspondent to the *New York Clipper* echoed this assessment after seeing him perform in New Orleans, claiming that for "daring while mounted on a bareback horse, rushing at a fearful pace, [he] excels any rider of the company." His rare talent and bold exploits made him a great favorite of African American southerners, who had few opportunities inside of circus tents to cheer members of their own race. In fact, his popularity was such that Gil Robinson claimed that "in the early 70's every colored person in the South knew that colored boy." Unfortunately for his southern fans, Willis' career was cut short when he died in 1881 at the age of 30.[37]

Standing head and shoulders above all other nineteenth-century riders was the greatest circus equestrian of all time, James Robinson. Robinson's unbelievable abilities never failed to astound audience members. One postwar observer concluded, "No words can describe the ease and grace and finish with which the superb equestrian performs hazardous feats. There is a dash and originality about his horsemanship which is as inimitable as it is thrilling." An 1886 performance in Savannah included a sequence whereby "with his horse at a rapid galop [sic] he leaped the banners backwards and forwards and sprang from one attitude to another rapidly and airily. Hoops which others merely jumped through he tumbled a somersault through and finished with a dash and a spirit that aroused the spectators to a tremendous burst of applause." Again, while almost all rural Georgians regularly rode with or without a saddle, the sight of bareback equestrians like Willis and Robinson leaping, tumbling, and flying over banners and through hoops with their mounts at a dead run impressed even the most experienced riders.[38]

By the 1890s, however, equestrians found themselves upstaged by a more sensational equine entertainment, hippodrome racing. In light of the region's longstanding love affair with horse racing, it is not surprising that southerners reacted favorably when the pastime was introduced into the circus context in the early 1880s. Southerners had enjoyed equine contests since the colonial period. This practice remained popular among the rich and the poor throughout the Old and New South eras. But to keep their racing entertainments fresh, circus owners did more than just pit jockey against jockey and horse against horse on the half-mile oval tracks that surrounded their three rings. For instance, in 1886 the Barnum and London show featured a spectrum of contests that included men's and women's races, wheelbarrow races, double bareback races, elephant races, flat races, hurdle races, steeple chase races, "monkey races, pony races, running races, trotting races, cattle races, foot races, camel races, [and] chariot races." Such dizzying lineups helped reinvigorate the circus genre because, as one Savannah journalist noted, races stood so far removed "from the old and hackneyed circus performances" that they drew "general commendation" from audiences.[39]

While Georgia spectators enjoyed the novelty of seeing camels and elephants race around the track, they found the horse contests especially engaging. In particular, they applauded the speed and vigor with which the jockeys ran their sprints. One correspondent pointed out that a Columbus crowd welcomed the way the "animals are sent around [the track] with whip and spur to their utmost speed." Daring riders of this variety, another newsman noted, "turn the sharp corners of the track with out any lessening of speed," proving "themselves to be splendid horsemen." A Savannah editor commented that "there was a genuine rivalry in all the hippodrome races, and the dust flew and the horses strained every nerve." Spirited competition won the affections of audiences because as every good southern man knew, "a 'feller' feels like going his whole pile on flying steeds." Just like today's NASCAR racing, demonstrations of speed stimulated and pleased southern auditors.[40]

Despite the appearance of heated rivalry, questions arose in the minds of skeptics about whether these races—like the "sports entertainment" of today's professional wrestling—had predetermined outcomes. The *Atlanta Georgian* confidently asserted that in every contest presented by the Ringling Brothers Circus "the horse to win is picked before the race." In Savannah, "a great many people" in the audience believed that the races run at the Barnum and Bailey Circus "were fakes, or rather that they amounted to nothing more than fast running." Showmen responded to these charges by citing the fact that they offered cash incentives to victorious jockeys.[41]

Regardless of whether the contests were staged or real, their dangerous nature made for enthralling entertainment. Riders, like one John Hunterson of the Barnum and London show, bore evidence of the risks they faced in the form of visible scars. But just as often, riders narrowly avoided serious injuries, agitating and arousing audience members as their emotional states lurched from horror to excitement. In the midst of a Columbus exhibition, "one of the horses stumbled and the rider was thrown violently to the ground. The moment was a thrilling one to the spectators, as it seemed that the man would certainly be crushed to death by the horses. It is fortunate, indeed that the horse which stumbled chanced to be on the inside of the ring, [or] else the fallen rider would almost certainly have been crushed to death. The other riders, by swerving their horses a little, managed to miss the man." An Atlanta performance by the Wallace show was marred when "two lady charioteers were racing; the chariot of one was turned over just before finishing the race. The driver was thrown at least 20 feet. Strange to say, except bruises, she was not hurt, though the horrified thousands who witnessed the accident thought she was killed." In an emotional roller-coaster ride familiar to every NASCAR fan, these types of brushes with death could send pulses surging, but they could also shake the emotional resolve of crowd members. In the case of the latter incident, the spectacular chariot crash so unnerved the show's patrons that many of them exited the tent before the show's conclusion.[42]

Beginning in the early twentieth century, circus owners moved hippodrome racing from its closing slot on the program and replaced it with more novel entertainments. These new "thrillers" utilized of some of the Gilded Age's latest technological innovations: the bicycle and the automobile. Although circuses had featured bicycle, or "velocipede," riders on tightropes and in the ring since the early 1880s, impresarios staged more elaborate—and more dangerous—entertainments when they constructed ramps and towers so their stunt drivers and riders could "loop the loop," vault gaps, and ascend and descend spiral ramps.[43]

The sensory impact of these new stunts on patrons far outstripped that of hippodrome racing. Certainly, chariots flying around narrow tracks had provided circus spectators with thrills. But the introduction of key components of modernity—mechanized speed, elevation, and the defiance of gravity—into the circus context proved much more effective in inspiring intense emotional shifts in those who witnessed them. Circus owners sought to heighten these sensations by emphasizing the increased risk that drivers and riders undertook when they performed these thrillers, as evidenced by acts entitled "The Dip of Death" and "Spanning Death's Arch." By inspiring palpable fear followed by delicious release, these performance components created an electrifying atmosphere inside circus tents that left audiences tingling with excitement.[44]

The growing popularity of cycling in the late nineteenth century inspired showmen to close their shows with seemingly suicidal bicycle stunts. The industry leader in this area was the Forepaugh–Sells Brothers Circus. In 1902, the show's operators presented the bicyclist Diavolo, whom they alliteratively billed as the "desperate daredevil." The outfit's press agents declared that his loop-the-loop stunt would "bring out the goose flesh and make the hair rise on one's head" when spectators watched the daring rider plummet down the ramp at fifty miles an hour. The show also featured Minting the unicyclist, whose act consisted of a ride up and down a forty-foot-high circular ramp in what one witness aptly called a "hazardous undertaking." Two years later, the show complemented Diavolo's act with "Prodigious Porthos, the Only Chasm-Vaulting Cyclist." If the pictorial representation of his trick is to be believed, Porthos, like a nineteenth-century Evel Knievel, would climb a tall ladder, mount his bicycle, speed down a steep incline, and soar over ten elephants before landing on the other ramp.[45]

These thrillers had the desired effect on Georgia audiences. In 1904 in Columbus, "the feat of Diavolo, when he looped-the-loop on his bicycle, made the greatest possible hit. This is as thrilling a bicycle feat as one could well perform, and the 8,000 people under the big tent fairly held their breath while the daring rider rode quickly around the loop with his heels above his head. . . . [T]he crowd realized the fact that it took great nerve to perform the feat, [since] if Diavolo had failed to control his wheel . . . he would have been sent hurtling" out of control and off the ramp at a high rate of speed. Another Columbus spectator concluded that although the stunt was over in just a few seconds, it still elevated anxiety levels because the audience felt "fearful that the daring rider is about to dash his brains out." Predictably, people reacted to these stunts with gasps, yells, and finally cheers. In 1904, the Diavolo and Porthos features "elicited screams from the ladies and children" in a Savannah audience.[46]

By 1904, circus owners had begun to phase out bicycle attractions in favor of automobile stunts. At that time, autos were a rare sight in the South, making these tricks especially novel to southern audiences. For example, there were only ninety-nine autos registered in Atlanta in 1904–05. The Ringling Brothers Circus took the lead in the area of auto attractions. Beginning in 1905, the show featured a loop-the-loop automobile act fittingly called the "Dip of Death." The Ringling Brothers, however, added a new twist to this variety of airborne stunt in 1905 by featuring a female rather than a male driver.[47]

Like wild animal performances, female drivers engendered conflicting social and cultural messages. For instance, Barnum and Bailey's management, along with the other showmen who adopted similar attractions, continually stressed that their female drivers were petite, glamorous, and "vulnerable." At the same time, however, the actions of these performers made them exemplars of the era's boundary breaking "New Woman." Their daring certainly impressed men who watched them in action. After seeing a Barnum and Bailey female driver's act, which involved her driving a car that plummeted down a ramp before "looping a wide gap upside down and landing with a tremendous crash on another incline," a male reporter confessed: "Miss Butler can have her job. Nobody else wants it."[48]

Since southern culture dictated that females needed protection from a world filled with menaces, Georgia audiences faced a more intense emotional experience when a woman climbed into the driver's seat to perform dangerous stunts like the Dip of Death. "When this feat is about to be performed," the *Atlanta Journal* noted, "the tension of those who watch it is so great that many people turn their backs or close their eyes until the thundering cheers of others assure them that the daring little woman has taken her seemingly fatal dive, and is safe on the ground again. How it is possible for one not magically endowed to seat herself in an automobile-like car, spin a dizzy loop high in the air and then after leaping downward to another spiral track, shoot unharmed to earth, is a marvel, but this is just what's done." Similarly, thousands of people in Savannah "held their breath as the automobile, in which a young woman was strapped, made its marvelous trip around the odd shaped track and sprang across a chasm to another circular roadway and thence through a chute like track until it was stopped."[49]

Both the bicycle and automobile stunts delivered the intended emotional payoff only when performers safely completed them. A crash could horrify and traumatize a crowd, and no circus manager wanted to expose their audiences to such disturbing scenes. Certainly, the Barnum and Bailey management remained ever cognizant of this fact after the woman driver who had performed the Dip of Death on the show's 1905 American tour died a violent and painful death when the stunt went terribly wrong in a European circus tent in early 1906. Residents of the southern Georgia town of Albany had their own encounter with this kind of nightmare in late 1902. While Minting balanced on his unicycle at the summit of his tower, part of the ramp groaned and then collapsed, sending him plummeting to the ground to suffer life-threatening injuries. In an unintended dose of black comedy, the *Columbus Enquirer-Sun* notified its readers in its postshow account, "It is understood that this is not the original Minting who fell from the tower and was killed several weeks ago."[50]

Georgians welcomed the coming of circuses for a whole host of reasons. Merchants applauded circuses because these shows drew large crowds of people who wanted to shop before they went into the tent. Town loafers loved Circus Day because they could stand on the corner, take a long pull from a bottle of bourbon, and cheer as the circus parade rolled down the street. Small boys jumped for joy when a circus came to town because they could crowd around the show lot as circus workers raised a city of tents in just a few short hours.

But ultimately country and city Georgians rich and poor, black and white, and young and old paid their hard-earned money so they could experience the thrill of seeing the big show put on under the big top. With "their keen understanding of what the public wants," circus owners attracted a true cross section of the populace by presenting both new, modern entertainments like the Dip of Death and venerable favorites such as bareback riding. Circus owners also had a particular talent for updating the best of the circus's traditional acts and repackaging them in a new form, as with hippodrome racing or dramatic specs. In sum, the circus's marriage of tradition and modernity gave these shows an appeal to country people eager to see newfangled automobile stunts and a grander version of the horse races run at the county fair. More urbane customers appreciated the compelling drama of the opening spectacles and the delightful irony of acrobatic performers garbed in the latest European fashions. In Georgia during this time period, the circus represented a truly democratic entertainment.[51]

> Circus performances are fit amusements for only
> children and negroes.
> —"Public Amusements and Social Enjoyments,"
> *DeBow's Review*, 1860

EIGHT

Sparks Circus and the Reinvention of Circus Day

At the beginning of the 1920s, the nation's economic and cultural climate gave circus owners reason for optimism about the coming decade. The 1918 Spanish flu epidemic, which had forced at least nine circuses to cancel all or part of their southern tours, had run its course. The postwar labor unrest of 1919, which saw more than four million workers walk off the job, had also ended by the close of that year. In 1920, the gross national product hit an all-time high. National prohibition contributed to a continued decline in disorder and violence at circuses. Finally, in another sign of changing moral attitudes toward the circus among religious authorities, approximately a third of America's Methodist ministers called for a revision of the *Methodist Book of Discipline*'s ban on amusements, including circuses. Taken as a whole, these factors helped produce conditions such that in 1920 the newly merged Ringling Brothers and Barnum and Bailey Circus could attract fifty thousand patrons to a single day's appearance in Atlanta.[1]

But the cumulative effects of other longstanding trends would soon temper this positive outlook. As early as 1904, a number of circus owners began phasing out the highly popular street parade, citing the oppressive costs of staging a daily procession and the opposition of urban merchants and officials who complained that parades blocked automobile traffic. This movement to eliminate the parade would gain momentum over the next two decades, meaning that the showman's best form of free advertising was disappearing. At the same time, circus license fees—always a source of frustration and expense for showmen—reached burdensome levels in many parts of the country, particularly in Georgia.[2]

To make matters worse, almost all of the circus world's legendary nineteenth-century impresarios—including John Robinson, P. T. Barnum, W. C. Coup, S. B. Howes, James Bailey, W. W. Cole, all four Sells brothers, and three of the five Ringling brothers—had died between 1888 and 1919. The impact of this loss of entrepreneurial talent and leadership is reflected in the 1921 formation of a circus trust, the American Circus Corporation (ACC). During the decade the ACC owned, among other shows, the John Robinson Circus, the Sells-Floto Circus, and the Hagenbeck-Wallace Circus. In effect, the ACC filled the void left by the deaths of the industry's giants. Its ascendance, however, came at a significant cost to the circus industry, for once a show joined the ACC roster, it stopped competing with other ACC outfits. This lack of competition, coupled with the deaths of the great showmen, gave rise to productions by ACC outfits that fell far short of the previous generation's standards for quality, innovation, and creativity. As one veteran circus observer tersely wrote in criticizing this crop of shows, "The secret to showmanship is originality, not imitation."[3]

Pressures also came from a range of diversions that competed with circuses for the attention of Americans. In the world of athletics, college football and professional baseball grew increasingly popular as spectator sports. Along the same lines, boxing enjoyed a wide appeal, with throngs of more than 100,000 people gathering to witness some championship bouts. In the realm of mass entertainment, motion pictures, first shown in nickelodeon houses at the end of the first decade of the twentieth century, became a fixture on the American entertainment landscape. Radio, introduced in 1920, quickly developed a national network of hundreds of broadcasters and millions of listeners. And amusement parks, popular since the turn-of-the-century, enjoyed growing attendance numbers. These factors help explain the circus's slide from its position of popular preeminence in America.[4]

Despite these difficulties, the circus maintained a prominent place in Georgia's entertainment landscape. In particular, the Macon-based Sparks Circus thrived during a decade when many troupes struggled to remain culturally relevant. The success that owner Charles Sparks had in winning the affections of the Georgia public stemmed from a combination of old and new strategies. Just as the previous generation of showmen had done in the wake of the Civil War, he had his circus perform numerous charity shows. These benefits secured both license reductions from Georgia municipalities and praise from its citizens. In addition, Sparks Circus earned the admiration of many Georgians by bucking the national trend toward the elimination of the street parade.[5]

But Charles Sparks also found novel ways to connect with the public. After making Macon his off-season headquarters in 1919, he formed substantive relationships with the city's political and business communities. One key reason why local leaders forged ties with Sparks Circus was that Charles Sparks, like the Ringling brothers, rejected the widespread practice of grift, which had long sullied the public reputations of circus men. This "clean" way of doing business also helped the show garner the endorsements of local and national religious leaders, most notably the evangelist Billy Sunday. On the statewide level, local fraternal and community organizations accepted the invitation of the Sparks proprietor to parade with his performers when these groups sponsored his circus, making a Sparks procession as much a display of civic pride as circus pageantry. Finally, the fine performances that Sparks Circus put on in the 1920s proved that Charles Sparks was a worthy successor to the great showmen of the nineteenth century.[6]

Nonetheless, the integration of Sparks Circus into the community of Macon in the 1920s and its general embrace by Georgians highlights how sharply cultural and religious views of the circus had changed since the turn of the century. Three decades prior, the circus had produced cutting-edge entertainment of a dubious morality. While its wondrous performances thrilled those who attended them, they also shocked the sensibilities of the respectable and challenged the moral standards of the religious. But by the 1920s, most Georgians, and for that matter most Americans, viewed circus entertainment as wholesome and inoffensive. The circus, for better or for worse, had become a tame and mainstream diversion.

But this shift grew more from wider cultural changes than from any actions taken by circus owners. On the national level, other entertainments, particularly motion pictures, supplanted tented shows as cultural products of artistic innovation and moral controversy during the Jazz Age. Even though circus owners had long sought to update their shows with newfangled acts and ever-larger tents, the core conventions of circus entertainment had changed little since the 1880s. Moreover, comparatively speaking, the moral content of circuses had actually improved between the 1880s and the 1920s while the wider culture grew seemingly more permissive with each passing decade. For instance, the elimination of talking clowns in the wake of circus tent growth removed their bawdy jokes from the circus arena. Likewise, while female costumes remained skimpy into the 1920s, they had not grown significantly more revealing over the course of the previous four decades. If part of an entertainment's power to effect social and cultural change stems from its ability to challenge cultural precepts and community standards, the circus had lost much of that power by the turn of the century.[7]

Circus Day had similarly changed. A turn-of-the-century Circus Day was an oppositional event, in which the actions of community outsiders compelled all those in town to make their peace with the circus as a cultural force. Yet the event's capacity to do so had dwindled by the 1920s, largely thanks to the gradual elimination of the street parade, a trend that produced smaller crowds and, consequently, less popular excitement in places where the circus performed. In the case of the Georgia Circus Days that featured Sparks Circus, they had become community-centered and sanctioned events that grew out of a union of interests between circus men and the "commercial-civic" elite who had assumed the mantle of leadership in Macon and across the South. Put another way, if a Circus Day in the late nineteenth century involved celebrating the arrival of a traveling show in a community, then a Sparks Circus Day in Georgia in the 1920s represented a celebration of the community itself, albeit with the circus at center stage. By the end of that decade, then, the circus had attained the position of respectability that showmen had pursued since the 1840s, in no small part because Circus Day had become a civic and tame, rather than an unofficial and electrifying, holiday.[8]

Sparks Circus became a part of the Macon community in December 1919, when it made this central Georgia town its permanent off-season home. As compared to the industry's biggest outfits, which used as many as ninety rail cars for transportation, the fifteen-car Sparks Circus of the 1920s was a modest outfit that had experienced slow but steady growth during its four decades of existence. The show got its start in 1889 when John H. Sparks and his adopted son Charles organized a small wagon show and began touring the country. By the turn of the century, the elder Sparks had switched the show to rails, using three cars to move his employees, stock, and performers. Around the same time, his younger son Clifton joined the show's management team. In 1903, John H. Sparks died, and the outfit passed into Charles' hands. Determined to carry on his father's work, Charles Sparks continued to enlarge and improve the show during the first decade of the twentieth century. The troupe spent off-seasons in Salisbury, North Carolina from 1910 until 1919, when Charles Sparks entered into negotiations with the City of Macon for use of its Central City Park as winter quarters.[9]

A closer look at the deal that Charles Sparks closed with Macon's leaders demonstrates why both the circus owner and city officials expected to benefit from the new pact. Charles Sparks surely felt particularly pleased that the city allowed his show to occupy the park's facilities for no fee, provided that the concern set up a free zoological park and a viewing area for locals to watch the show's performers train during the off-season for upcoming tours. But despite the lack of direct payment, this arrangement promised to pay dividends to the city of Macon as well. City officials, like those across the state, knew from past experience that a wintering circus provided a tidy financial return to the host community. Furthermore, the show's liberal visiting policies while in winter quarters would give residents new and unique recreational opportunities. Considering these potential advantages, it is easy to see why Macon's leaders welcomed the arrival of Sparks Circus.[10]

Still, Charles Sparks had to believe he had gotten the better of the deal.

While the free use of facilities was alluring, the park, and the city itself, boasted many other highly attractive attributes. Central City Park abutted a rail yard and featured a siding area for train car storage. In addition, the park stood next to the Ocmulgee River, a navigable waterway serviced by a steamship line. More broadly, Macon was experiencing rapid economic and demographic growth. This expansion was driven in no small measure by its advantageous central Georgia location and the five railroad lines that passed through the city. Macon's development was additionally aided by its mild climate and excellent water supply, which Georgia officials rated the "purest and best" in the state. Of course, these natural features provided particular benefits to anyone trying to care for exotic animals from temperate areas of the world. For all these reasons, the show moved to Macon.[11]

In contrast to the more perfunctory relationships that some other circuses maintained with locals while wintering in Georgia towns and cities, Charles Sparks worked from the outset to cultivate more meaningful connections with Macon's residents and institutions. This contrast is particularly evident when comparing Sparks to the previous tenants of Central City Park, the Sun Brothers' Circus, which had occupied the park's buildings for a decade before folding in 1918. Admittedly, the Sun management had maintained charitable and friendly relations with Macon's citizenry during its eleven years of residence in the city. For instance, the Sun show concluded its 1910 tour with a charity performance under the auspices of the local Shriners. Along with standard circus acts, the day's exhibition featured "many local acts and burlesque features" staged by members of the fraternal organization. In 1914, the Sun Brothers' opening day performance benefited the Macon Playgrounds Association. And just like Sparks would do in the 1920s, the outfit ran a "temporary zoo" that was open to the public during the winter months.[12]

Nonetheless, the community-outreach efforts of the Sparks brothers in Macon would go far beyond those of the Sun management. Within three months of the show's relocation, and before Sparks Circus had put on a single performance in Macon, Charles Sparks sponsored a parade especially for the city's children, featuring the show's elephants and camels. Youths who came out for the procession received special passes to visit the circus menagerie in winter quarters. In addition, the owner developed firm connections with local merchants, no doubt facilitated by the $35,000 the show injected into the local economy over the 1919–20 winter months. Finally, he publicly expressed his intention to make Macon the show's permanent winter home.[13]

Charles Sparks continued to extend his hand to locals as he prepared for the show's season-opening appearance in Macon. He agreed to have his show perform under the auspices of Al Slaah Temple Mystic Shrine, thereby inaugurating a policy of having the city's civic and fraternal organizations sponsor the circus's season openers. But even with the Shrine sponsorship in place, his plans for the upcoming opener remained incomplete until he informed the city of Macon that he intended to stage a street parade.

Of course, just two decades prior, a show never would have announced that it would parade before performing; simply put, a procession represented an essential element of Circus Day, and a show that failed to offer a public display let down the excited throngs who crowded along the pageant route. The *Columbus Enquirer-Sun* noted after a 1906 cancellation, "The public is grievously disappointed when the elephants and the chariots and the bands fail to come down the street in the grand official parade." This disappointment, according to a Griffin daily, was particularly acute for the "great many persons . . . who never attend a performance of a circus" but "will travel miles and miles to see the parade."[14]

Despite the popularity of processions, the opposition of municipal and business leaders to parades had prompted some showmen to begin to discuss eliminating the feature as early as 1904. In the early twentieth century, automobiles and streetcars, rather than wagons and horses, had begun to fill city thoroughfares, causing significant traffic problems as these locales raced to install stoplights and apply other traffic management methods. Within this environment, a public display by a traveling show simply brought the movement of vehicles to a grinding halt. In 1907, one press representative noted that many municipal officials opposed the circus parade in principle "because it blocks traffic." Another circus man explained that when processions did come off, "the traffic is so great that police officials do their best to keep the elephants and wagons from the streets on which the vehicular traffic is heavy, and if the parade does happen to be routed thru the congested district it is broken up into horrible fragments" as the display moved in fits and starts in order to allow cross street traffic to pass. Here, these circus officials might have added to their lists of complaints the damage caused by heavy circus wagons traveling along newly paved rather than dirt streets. In fact, the city of Savannah sued the Barnum and Bailey Circus in 1909 for damaging a thoroughfare while preparing for its appearance in that city. In the 1920s, city officials across the South would bar circus parades in order to protect freshly surfaced roads.[15]

Even more surprisingly, merchants added their voices to this chorus against circus parades. This shift in attitude is especially striking given that a generation prior, shopkeepers had considered the morning procession to be the key to drawing large crowds of customers into their stores on Circus Day. But the appearance of the speedy automobile on the American landscape meant that circus-goers no longer arrived in town well before show time in order to go to the circus *and* shop before and after the parade. In 1924, a circus press agent pointed out, "The folks from the country no more drive in the day before and camp near the lot or the unloading point to [a]wait the arrival of the show train. The farmer remains on his farm and does his day's work . . . and then cranks up the 'flivver' and drives to town to see the circus." Since the parade now failed to attract crowds of eager consumers, merchants increasingly saw the feature as an impediment to the habits of their automobile driving shoppers. In Atlanta, Whitehall and Peachtree Street merchants petitioned the city council in 1914 to prohibit circus displays on those thoroughfares. They called for the ban "because their business is brought to a standstill while the streets are so overrun with people viewing the procession." The previous year, a Sun Brothers manager voiced the same opinion, noting that city retailers "object to parades because they interrupt business and interfere with general traffic."[16]

Largely because of these attitudes, many in the industry had discarded the traditional start of Circus Day by the 1920s. No less of an authority than Charles Ringling announced to the public in 1924 that his show would no longer offer a street parade. He argued that it had become impractical for circuses to parade in many communities since "when one thinks of the difficulty of finding parking space in the business district of any city today . . . one can readily see how impossible it would be to move the big circus parade through such congestion, past stop signals now operating automatically . . . and especially thru all the unusual congestion caused by the heralded approach of the parade. For the big modern circus, exhibiting in the larger cities, the parade has passed forever."[17]

On the other hand, the problems presented by parading in urban areas did not exist in smaller locales. In these places, unpaved streets, few cars, and a lack of traffic signals produced a harmony of interests between circus fans who wanted to see a public display and merchants who "demand the procession as a stimulation to business." But from a financial and logistical perspective, circus managers recognized that it made no sense to equip a show with the intention of parading only in small towns and not in big cities. A show either planned to parade at each tour stop or not at all during its annual tour. As a result, showmen tended to dispense with the feature, even though many reported that the lack of a public procession could produce a noticeable number of empty seats under canvas.[18]

In the 1920s, however, Charles Sparks held a different view on the parade issue. Unlike the Sun Brothers' management, which had eliminated its daily procession, calling it "unnecessary" and an "extra expense," Charles Sparks believed that a morning display was essential for making Circus Day a communal celebration rather than an entertainment event confined to the circus lot itself. Still, his conception of a proper parade involved more than just having performers march down Main Street. In fact, Charles Sparks intended to directly involve local people in his pageants by effacing the conventional Circus Day boundary between parade spectator and performer.[19]

Macon residents got their first chance to witness this reinvention of the circus parade on the morning of April 5, 1920. Undoubtedly to the surprise of many along the route, Macon's mayor and his staff—rather than circus personnel—headed the procession in a camel-drawn carriage. Right behind the Mayor's conveyance came a group of Shriners on foot, followed by more members of the organization riding elephants and camels, all cheered on by "the largest crowd ever seen on Macon streets for a similar event." Of course, the pageant also featured the circus's gold-leafed tableau wagons, its marching band, and its calliope, with the latter two components emanating melodious tunes as the parade wended its way toward the show's tents. This joint parading by locals and performers would become the defining feature of Sparks performances in Macon during the 1920s.[20]

By 1922, Sparks Circus had succeeded in making the opening date of its tour into a singular occasion on the city's annual calendar. In the weeks leading up to the event, the mayor pronounced the day a civic holiday, a move applauded by the chamber of commerce. The junior chamber of commerce, the library council, and club women all sold advance tickets, with the latter group selling them in downtown businesses. The city draped the wires overhanging Main Street with flags and pennants in "honor of the circus and its manager," and the city's shopkeepers announced their intention to close their businesses during the afternoon performance. "All the community," the *Macon Telegraph* summarized on the eve of Circus Day, "has joined in making the circus Saturday a city wide event."[21]

That Saturday began with the departure of the circus parade from Central City Park. As it reached Macon's central thoroughfare, onlookers watched as "large delegations of the Chamber of Commerce, Rotary Club, Lions, and Kiwanians—1,500 strong" moved into line with the circus personnel. Next, the "Shrine Band of 35 musicians and Mercer College Band of 28 men," along with the Lanier High School band and three circus bands, "joined in the procession." According to show officials, this marked the first time in the history of the American circus that school and college bands marched in a circus parade.[22]

With the line of march formed, the display moved toward the Sparks tents. After arriving at the show grounds, members of the sponsoring organizations looked on with pride as over two thousand children, including "all orphans of the city," filed inside the canvas, thanks to the free tickets provided by the local clubs. This happy scene, along with all the day's happenings, made quite an impression on observers. *Billboard*'s reporter, for his part, wrote hyperbolically in the wake of the performance, "Never before has there been such a demonstration seen in the city of Macon."[23]

These early Sparks Circus Days in Macon reveal how dramatically the event had changed over the course of a generation. The very kinds of respectable and influential people who had eschewed the entertainment just a few decades prior now turned out not just for the parade and the circus, but also to march proudly in the procession and publicly declare their affection for the tented amusement. In addition, the community's involvement in the event stretched far beyond the day of the show, with fraternal and civic groups working together in the weeks before Circus Day to make the occasion a success. Finally, the fact that retail businesses would close during the parade reveals that the unofficial holiday no longer served as an engine for consumerism. Rather, it worked for the ends of community improvement and uplift rather than for economic development alone.

These tendencies intensified as the decade progressed. The 1923 opener saw an increase in the community's commitment to the annual event. Macon's banks, factories, and public schools all joined the shops in closing down for the afternoon performance. And for the first time, the city's two institutions of higher education, Mercer University and Wesleyan Female College, shut their doors in celebration of the Sparks opening. The morning parade again featured appearances by the Mayor, the city aldermen, and contingents from all the local civic organizations. Spectators enjoyed an expanded musical accompaniment, courtesy of the "bands from the different lodges," and the Mercer and Lanier high schools' marching bands. Yet perhaps most strikingly, by calling on Macon's schools and orphanages "to make as large [an] attendance as possible," city leaders signaled for the first time that the turnout in the Sparks big top was as important an indicator of civic pride as the parade itself.[24]

While it is unsurprising that Macon's politicians would view a full tent as a fitting capstone of the day's overall success, their desire for a sellout particularly highlights how locals had begun to associate the fortunes of the circus with the fortunes of the community. Clearly, one key reason for this convergence of interests was the charitable component of Sparks' Macon performances. Beginning in 1922, the show contributed a portion of the proceeds from its season opener to the construction of the city's Washington Memorial Library. This arrangement continued in later years, with Sparks Circus pledging as much as 20 percent of the gross receipts from its opening day's performances to the library. Starting in 1926, the show increased its generosity by giving the junior chamber of commerce and the chamber of commerce each 20 percent of the gross take from its opening performance. In an editorial, The *Macon Telegraph* praised this munificence by noting, "Mr. [Charles] Sparks has as good a circus as he has a civic interest."[25]

But the show's overall economic impact on the community also demonstrates how the goals of the city and the circus had become united. In 1921 alone, the Sparks ownership spent $83,000 at Macon businesses as the brothers worked to enlarge the show. By the mid-1920s, the outfit paid out an estimated $30,000 in annual upkeep and repairs during the winter months to local businesses and artisans, a figure that increased significantly in later years. The show kept anywhere from fifty to seventy-five employees on its off-season staff in any given year, and Macon shopkeepers benefited when these workers went shopping or dining while in winter quarters.[26]

To show its appreciation for their investment in the community, the Macon Chamber of Commerce made Charles and Clifton Sparks honorary members in 1925. In a further indication of the financial interconnections between Macon and Sparks Circus, the city's oldest bank made Charles a director in 1924. No wonder in 1925 the *Macon Telegraph* called Sparks "our own circus," declaring, "Macon feels a vital interest in Sparks Circus. It is as much a Macon business as any other business in town. Its owners and personnel have come to be good citizens among us." It had taken just a few short years, but by the mid-1920s the economic fortunes of Sparks Circus and the City of Macon had become conjoined.[27]

The city reaped an additional benefit from Sparks Circus in the form of the free publicity generated from having the show in winter quarters. In 1924 alone, four national publications, including *Collier's Weekly*, the *American Magazine*, and *McClure's Magazine*, ran stories profiling Sparks. These articles, in turn, also shined a spotlight on the city of Macon. Writing about this spate of features, the *Telegraph* asserted, "Charles Sparks and Sparks' Circus have done more in recent years and at present to place Macon at a point of vantage before the people of this continent than all the other [Macon] agencies combined." Along these same lines, Charles Sparks acceded to a Macon Chamber of Commerce request by hanging a large banner inside his show's big top that detailed the "advantages" of its home city. Finally, as the show moved from place to place along the nation's railways, onlookers could take notice of lettering painted on the sides of each of the show's train cars that read "Sparks' Circus, Macon, Ga."[28]

This elevation of Macon's national profile made the Sparks brothers and Sparks Circus particular favorites of Macon's business and civic leaders. These individuals showed their appreciation by making personal appearances at Central City Park when the show arrived home after completing its annual tours. In 1924, "a large delegation of business men" came out "to greet Charles and Clifton Sparks and their coworkers." The next year, the outfit was met by a "greeting party" of "bankers, representatives of the Chamber of Commerce, produce men, laundry men, packing house representatives and others." Businessmen also took out "special advertising merchants'" sections in the *Telegraph* to celebrate the opening and closing of the show's tours.[29]

These public displays and plaudits additionally reveal how the Macon elite's celebration of Sparks Circus gradually began to expand beyond the show's opening dates. For instance, during the week leading up to Sparks' 1926 opening, Charles and Clifton Sparks were the "guests of honor at several civic functions." These included a luncheon hosted by the Macon Elks Lodge given in tribute to the show's officials, and the two dances held in the Macon Hotel Ballroom in honor of the circus, with music provided by the Sparks' sideshow band. In the run up to the 1927 tour, the Elks Lodge hosted a pretour dinner and dance in honor of Sparks Circus while the local vaudeville house paid tribute to the show with a special "Sparks night." Lastly, Charles Sparks was the junior chamber of commerce's "honored guest" and keynote speaker for its weekly dinner at Macon's Hotel Dempsey in early April 1928.[30]

Although the relations between Sparks Circus and the city of Macon were singular in their warmth and depth, Charles Sparks also reached out to fraternal and social organizations located in other Georgia communities. In particular, the Shriners sponsored many of Sparks' early 1920s appearances in Atlanta and Marietta. In 1922, the morning parade in the Gate City saw Charles and Clifton Sparks and three local dignitaries head the procession in an automobile. This lead car was followed by two Shrine bands, about a dozen floats, four hundred ceremonially dressed Shriners on the march, "the big Sparks band, the clown band, the negro band and the two calliopes, one of the old fashioned steam variety and the other electrically equipped." Later that same week, the Marietta Shriners made Charles and Clifton Sparks honorary members of their temple, and presented Charles with a "gold-headed cane." In 1924, Marietta organizations had further opportunities to demonstrate their affection for Sparks Circus on a Sunday before the show's scheduled Monday performance. The Sparks Band spent its day off performing a public concert in the city park and afterward enjoyed a possum and chicken dinner courtesy of the Shriners. As a parting gift, the Ladies Club of Marietta delivered fifty cakes to the Sparks steward for the enjoyment of the show's employees.[31]

While the support of these Atlanta and Marietta organizations was impressive, perhaps Charles Sparks' biggest coup in the 1920s was winning approval from the Savannah City Council to show in that city. In late 1923, the Savannah Elks Lodge asked the municipal body to grant permission for Sparks to stage two benefit performances to support the fraternal organization's charity fund. As part of the arrangement, Charles Sparks would donate the proceeds from the matinee and evening shows to aid Savannah's "poor and unfortunate during the holiday season." The Elks also would purchase matinee tickets for hundreds of the city's orphans.[32] Despite its history of opposition to traveling shows, the city council agreed to waive the city license fee and allow the outfit to make an appearance in the city. The legislative body's decision meant that Savannah would have its first circus in more than four years.[33]

Without question, the charitable focus of the event helps explain why the Savannah City Council assented to a Sparks performance after snubbing the circus industry for so long. But other factors also influenced the council's decision. First, with the year's Tri-State Fair completed, the council members no longer needed to financially protect their project from a circus that might try to "take all the money out of the town." Second, the city's businessmen stood to profit from the show's visit to the city. Prior to the event, Charles Sparks made no secret of the fact that his outfit's final payday of the season would take place in Savannah, putting $22,644 into the hands of Sparks' employees after the matinee exhibition. This money, in the words of the *Savannah Morning News*, would then "be let loose in Savannah" as circus workers headed toward the city's shops and stores to spend their earnings between performances. Finally, as a leading press agent would later explain, since Sparks was "considered a Georgia institution by having winter quarters in the State," the council was more disposed toward granting Sparks a license waiver.[34]

The power of this final factor should not be underestimated when considering the success that Sparks Circus enjoyed in Georgia in the 1920s. Georgia reviewers of Sparks performances, like those who applauded the Atlanta-based circuses of the 1870s, rarely failed to note that Georgians felt a particular affection for the circus that hailed from their home state. In 1926, the *Augusta Chronicle* reported after a Sparks appearance that city residents wished the show "the best of luck, for this city has always had a tender feeling for this wholesome and home-like crowd of circus folks." In Columbus, an *Enquirer-Sun* newsman pointed out that Sparks enjoyed full tents—even though the ACC's Sells-Floto Circus was scheduled to appear in the city within days—thereby demonstrating that Columbus residents "are indeed loyal to Georgia's own circus—the Sparks show."[35]

Charles Sparks understood, like Andrew Haight and P. Bowles Wooten had fifty years prior, that home loyalty was a major selling point for his business in Georgia. Just in case state residents missed the "Macon, Georgia" lettering painted on the sides of the Sparks train cars, the owner ran newspaper advertisements detailing the show's relationship with its home state and its citizens. For instance, in 1924, the show's ads informed Dawson residents: "Remember—Sparks Circus is a Georgia Institution (Winter Home of Macon, Ga.) and every Georgian is proud of the success and vast growth of . . . 'their own Georgia circus.' Sparks Circus had [sic] advertised and carried the fame of Georgia into every state in the Union and every Province of Canada. Wait for the show you know. Beware of shows you never heard of."[36]

One important reason why Charles Sparks thought that Georgians needed to "beware" of unfamiliar shows was the widespread grifting that characterized the business methods of many of his competitors. The shows of the ACC were particularly egregious in this area. In the early 1920s, reports from across the nation accused employees of the ACC's John Robinson Circus, Sells-Floto Circus, and Hagenbeck-Wallace shows of engaging in systematic efforts to cheat their patrons. The citizens of Georgia, like those of all other states that these shows visited, fell victim to these schemes. In one notorious 1921 appearance, the John Robinson Circus unleashed "a carnival of lawlessness" in Rome, featuring numerous "flimflam and shortchange artists" as its main attractions.[37]

In stark contrast, Sparks earned the nickname "The Circus Immaculate" among showmen in the 1920s for its upright dealings with the public. Georgia journalists agreed. Commenting on the "unusually fine wholesomeness" of Sparks Circus, the *Macon Telegraph* noted that there was a "dignity and refinement about [the show] that are not always so greatly evident in attractions of this kind." Likewise, the *Augusta Chronicle* concluded that the operation was "clean and wholesome all the way through."[38]

Just as it did with its identity as a Georgia show, Sparks Circus used its ethical reputation as a selling point when it toured the state. A 1928 ad in Rome newspapers proclaimed that the Sparks outfit was "from every viewpoint the greatest circus achievement of the age—and above all, it's clean!" Along the same lines, an advertisement published in the *Columbus Enquirer-Sun* offered "A WARNING TO THE PUBLIC" that the Sparks Circus did not have a "short change artist, gambling games" or "any immoral or Oriental Dances, given . . . for men only." In contradistinction, the ad stated, the show did possess the "cleanest and [most] educational Circus in the world" staffed by "the most high class Circus performers of any show coming" to Columbus.[39]

This moral way of doing business won Sparks adherents among leading religious figures. In April 1926, evangelist Billy Sunday told a congregation in Staunton, Virginia, where Sparks Circus was appearing, "If you want to go to Sparks' circus, go in the afternoon and come [back] here at night. I don't blame you for wanting to go. If you didn't you wouldn't have thick red blood surging through your veins." A few days later in Georgia, Augusta newspapers ran a letter scripted by Sunday endorsing the show for its fine parade and performance.[40]

Like Sunday, Charles Sparks also thought people should hear the word of God. At the same time that the evangelist's encomium to Sparks Circus appeared in the Augusta papers, Charles Sparks told that city's residents who had gathered in his circus enclosure that there was another tent where they should make their presence felt that day: "Just before the people filed out of the big tent Mr. Sparks made a personal announcement regarding the John Brown revival now being conducted at the tabernacle on Reynolds street. He encouraged those who were in the audience [to] co-operate and lend their assistance to the revival by attending the meetings."[41]

Ultimately, though, Sparks Circus won popular acclaim in Georgia because it put on good shows. After watching a Sparks exhibition in Athens, a grizzled press agent concluded that the show's "close observance to [the] slightest detail manifests all through the performance, which is beautiful, nifty, classy and 'just right.'" Similarly, the *Columbus Enquirer-Sun* called the show "top notch," declaring in the wake of a Sparks visit that "one thing that was particularly noticeable . . . [was] that everybody seemed in fine spirits and full of pep, doing his or her best at every turn; the costuming is all new and clean, and the animals appear to be in the best kind of order, being sleek and glossy and well trained, and the tents all appear to be right new."[42]

Even as his show enjoyed almost universal critical and popular acclaim by the close of the 1920s, Charles Sparks' poor health forced him to consider retirement. Earlier in the decade, he had rejected offers from the ACC's owners to purchase his show, citing the grifting ways of their circuses. In late 1928, however, a veteran circus owner named Henry B. Gentry approached Sparks and offered to buy his show. Sparks pondered the proposition for several weeks before announcing on November 26 that he had agreed to transfer ownership to Gentry. But any sort of satisfaction that Sparks enjoyed from the lucrative sale of his circus dissipated within days of closing the deal. To his utter shock, Sparks discovered that Gentry had double-crossed him. As part of a prearranged move, Gentry planned to immediately sell the show to the ACC. According to an eyewitness, this turn of events drove Charles Sparks first to tears, and then into a rage. A seething Sparks confronted Gentry about the double-cross, reportedly saying to him: "You old scoundrel, if you weren't so old I'd take this cane and bash your head in."

Sparks walked away from Gentry that day without striking him, but even if he had done so, it would not have changed the fact that Sparks was now a "corporation" show. Yet the outfit's stint with the ACC was surprisingly short. After Sparks Circus toured in 1929 under ACC management, the corporation's owners sold the Sparks show, along with all other ACC properties, to John Ringling in late 1929. Ringling, possessed of ample winter facilities to house the circus in his hometown of Sarasota, Florida, moved the show's base of operations to that city in September of 1930, thus ending the decade-long relationship between Macon and Sparks Circus.[43]

To be sure, the wide appeal enjoyed by Sparks Circus during such a difficult period for the circus business proves the wisdom of Charles Sparks' contrarian formula for success. Sparks remained committed to staging a daily street parade at a time when other shows were abandoning the practice. He operated a clean show while his competitors' shows engaged in grift. Perhaps more than any other circus owner, he made charity shows a regular practice, a habit that in part earned him the chance to exhibit in the notoriously anticircus city of Savannah. And of course, he put on compelling performances as many of the nation's other concerns came under the control of a centralized company more interested in corporate profits than circus creativity.

In Macon, however, the foundation of his success ran deeper. From the outset of his decade-long tenure in the city, Charles Sparks worked to make his show an integral part of the local community. His outreach efforts included providing funding for the city's library and public access to his show's winter quarters during the off-season. He also forged links with Macon's municipal and business leaders. They quickly took to the presence of Sparks Circus, thanks to the revenue it generated for local businesses. Likewise, they valued Charles Sparks' willingness to sing the praises of Macon as his show toured the United States.

Yet it was Charles Sparks' determination to directly involve local citizens in the events of Circus Day that made a *Sparks* Circus Day a particularly joyous occasion. This participation included the sponsorship by Macon's fraternal and community organizations. By virtue of their organizations' support for Sparks, the members of these groups earned the chance to march in the parade alongside the show's performers. But Charles Sparks' willingness to include local marching bands and other nonsponsoring groups in his processions proves that he did not consider participation to be a reward for backing his circus. Rather, Charles Sparks believed that a relatively wide range of groups should play a central role in the community celebration better known as Circus Day. This broad-minded outlook helped make Charles Sparks and his circus into Macon institutions during the 1920s, even if Circus Day had evolved into a very different kind of public holiday.

Clearly, Charles Sparks' efforts toward community inclusion and charity had successfully reinvented Circus Day into a "safe and sane" holiday. All members of the community turned out for his shows in Macon, and religious leaders even endorsed his entertainment product. Moreover, prominent citizens who, a generation before, might have hesitated to be seen in the company of circus managers now publicly embraced Charles and Clifton Sparks, not just in Macon, but in places like Atlanta and Savannah as well. Nonetheless, Sparks Circus Days in Georgia generated a sense of popular excitement comparable to Circus Days of old, not because of tensions produced by a morally dubious yet enthralling entertainment taking over the streets of a community, but because of unusually close ties between the community and the show.[44]

> All the world's a stage,
> And all the men and women merely players:
> They have their exits and their entrances;
> And one man in his time plays many parts.
> —Shakespeare, *As You Like It*

CONCLUSION

In early April 1925, Atlanta residents received word that a troupe named the Fraternal Circus Company would make a weeklong stand in the city later that month. Undoubtedly, Gate City citizens welcomed the news that its performances, like many of those put on by Sparks Circus in the 1920s, would be under the auspices of a local organization and would serve philanthropic ends. But any popular enthusiasm that the outfit inspired would not be on display on the streets surrounding the show lot, since Atlanta's urban environment of paved roads, stoplights, and low hanging wires made a street parade a somewhat impractical endeavor. Still, once the circus's tent flaps parted in the early afternoon of the show's opening date, the enclosure filled with eager spectators, who, according to the *Atlanta Georgian*, gave "universal approval" of the performances. Of course, audience members also appreciated the charitable efforts of the sponsoring organization, the John B. Gordon Klan No. 91 of the Knights of the Ku Klux Klan.[1]

This episode illustrates two broad but interconnected points about the circus in Georgia from the end of the Civil War to the Great Depression. First, the fact that the leadership of an organization dedicated to the preservation of "traditional" American values including temperance, sexual purity, and more generally, the tenets of evangelical Protestantism, could view the circus as an ideal instrument for furthering its philanthropic goals demonstrates how drastically the image of the amusement had changed in the minds of conservative Georgians since the nineteenth century. Forty years prior, many religious and respectable citizens would have objected to almost any circus that came to town, thanks to the scantily attired female performers and ribald talking clowns who played leading roles in the tented entertainment of the day. But while American popular culture had grown gradually more permissive between 1880 and 1920, the moral content of circus entertainment had actually improved during that same time period. Indeed, by the 1920s, few southerners took offense at a diversion that included performers dressed not much differently than their predecessors had in the 1880s and clowns that refrained from offensive comments and gestures.[2]

Second, while southerners did base their evaluation of the circus's morality on the content of its performances, they additionally took the wider social context of Circus Day into account when considering the respectability of the diversion. From about 1872 to 1910, circus performances held in Georgia towns and cities attracted huge throngs of people who filled the streets before, during, and after the performances. These crowds contained numerous rowdy folks who came to town not only to see the show, but also to get drunk, leer at women, and fight with their enemies, all before the morning circus pageants even began. Yet once paved roads, automobile traffic, and disgruntled merchants prompted most showmen to abandon the parade feature, many of Circus Day's more unruly aspects simply disappeared, since large crowds—the natural environment for Circus Day rowdies—no longer collected on the streets before and after the circus performed. With the occasion's social milieu now largely limited to the circus tent and lot, Circus Day, and the circus by extension, lost much of its air of immorality and disorder. Unfortunately for the circus industry, this moral elevation came at the cost of the circus's popularity, since a great deal of the excitement surrounding the event disappeared as well once almost all of Circus Day's activities took place under canvas.

Clearly, the innate appeal of competing amusements did reduce public interest in circuses. Amusement parks, spectator sports, and motion pictures all offered their particular attractions, and southern patrons found themselves with more commercial leisure choices than ever before by the 1920s. Although the industry had faced sharp competition in the late nineteenth century from diversions like vaudeville, burlesque, and carnivals, the circus had handily dominated the era's national entertainment marketplace. This state of affairs, however, quickly changed as soon as the circus-going experience became more like that of other amusements. Of all entertainments, only the circus arguably had the ability during the late nineteenth and early twentieth centuries to transform the streets of towns and cities into amusement spaces where southerners could socialize, feast, drink, laugh, and fight. When the circus lost this particular and singular power, the industry saw its popularity slide.

Nonetheless, this development was not merely the result of changes within the entertainment industry. The rise and fall of Circus Day in Georgia grew from a set of interrelated historical processes that played out between 1820 and 1930. In the Old South, the nature of Circus Day reflected the impact of the anticircus views of evangelical and respectable southerners, the region's diffused population, and its poor transportation infrastructure. While the appearance of a canvas tent at a backcountry crossroads or small town attracted people from all social and racial groups, large contingents of conservative people refused to turn out for an entertainment they considered inherently sinful. In most cases, steering clear of the circus was just a matter of staying at home, since the vast majority of southerners lived all across the countryside rather than in towns and cities. This demographic fact, coupled with the South's poor road system, also served to keep many of those with an interest in attending the circus at home on the performance date. As a result, the typical circus exhibition in the Old South attracted hundreds, rather than thousands, of people to the show location.

Within a decade after the Civil War, a changed set of circumstances affected the character of Circus Day. Widespread and rapid railroad construction brought Georgia's towns and cities into a national network that connected the state's backcountry to its older settled areas, and more broadly, southern communities to northern communities. As the railroad spurred growth in towns situated along rail lines, the population of these locales expanded apace. In 1872, P. T. Barnum and his partners moved to capitalize upon both railroad expansion and demographic increase in these places by putting their show on rails. While this shift from wagon to train transport allowed them to put together a show of such unprecedented size that it required four large tents to hold all its attractions, it also confined their troupe, and all those that imitated its successful formula, to the growing towns and big cities along railroad lines. For rural Georgians, the journey to see the circus was now as much a part of the circus-going experience as the show itself. Farmers and their families left home hours and sometimes days in advance of a show and traveled to these places on foot, on horse, by wagon, and by excursion train. Upon arrival, the country people joined with town-dwellers of all classes and colors to create huge circus multitudes. With the streets of their towns and cities thronged with monstrous crowds, even those residents who disliked the circus for reasons of religion or respectability could no longer ignore its presence. The circus's ability to impact life beyond the show lot and tents forced everyone in the community on Circus Day to make their peace with the entertainment and its effects.[3]

In the eyes of progressive-minded community elites and showmen alike, these forward-looking towns and growing cities represented the perfect places to host circus performances. A lack of paved roads allowed circus wagons and heavy elephants to parade through town without damaging thoroughfares. Open lots, ideal for raising a "city of tents" near railroad depots, stood readily available. Town and city populations alone provided good potential audiences, but railroad access allowed showmen to run charters from distant communities directly to the show location, greatly enhancing the ability of Georgians to go to the circus. And the fact that Circus Day visitors, whether they came by train or by other means, enjoyed shopping along with seeing a good show meant that many longstanding critics of the circus, like newspaper editors and conservative politicians, fell silent as they watched their community's retail district bustle with eager customers before and after the day's exhibitions.

Although the shift from wagon to rail provided the means to bring circus entertainment to larger audiences and helped turn streets into places of play, the tremendous creativity of the era's showmen played an equally important role in making the circus a popular phenomenon in the late nineteenth century. Underneath ever-larger tents, circus owners like James Bailey, John Robinson, Adam Forepaugh, P. T. Barnum, and the Ringling brothers captured the public's imagination by regularly introducing new features like bicycle and auto stunts, hippodrome racing, and dramatic spectacles into their performances. At the same time, they remained committed to presenting the equestrian and athletic acts that had enthralled southerners since the 1820s. This blend of older and newer attractions proved to be the perfect recipe for commercial and popular dominance.

The circus industry, however, could not sustain this success. As the nation's leading circus men either died or retired from the profession, few impresarios—save Charles Sparks and the Ringling brothers—could competently fill their shoes. This lack of creative talent led to less inventive and engaging productions. In addition, showmen quickly found that one of their most powerful turn-of-the-century draws, the enormous size of their circus tents, had reached the point of diminishing returns in terms of cost and audience satisfaction. In sum, the failure of the new generation of showmen to approach, much less equal, the imaginative output of the industry's legends damaged the fortunes of the circus industry.

But modernization, especially in urban areas, perhaps dealt the sharpest blow to the circus business. As the population of America's cities grew in the early twentieth century, municipalities blocked parades to protect their newly paved streets and to prevent automobile and streetcar traffic from backing up all over town. Even urban merchants, who at one time had been some of the biggest supporters of Circus Day, wanted the free pageant eliminated since it prevented their customers—who now could easily shop on any day of the year in their nimble Model T's—from coming into business districts when the circus was in town. Once cities like Atlanta began to curtail or ban circus parades, many shows decided to abolish the feature altogether, meaning that even smaller communities that lacked the paved roads and traffic problems that made processions unworkable in cities would no longer see lines of elephants, wagons, and performers move through their streets in the early morning hours before a tented exhibition. In effect, this elimination of the circus parade changed the essential nature of Circus Day.

Still, these changes did not mean the end of the circus in America, or in Georgia. Despite its fall from its position as America's leading entertainment, the circus remains a successful and profitable amusement today, with shows playing to millions of customers annually in the United States alone. Yet out of all the concerns touring the nation, the industry leading Ringling Brothers and Barnum & Bailey Circus (RBBBC) represents the only outfit that can still claim direct links to some of the greatest showmen and circuses of the nineteenth and twentieth centuries and plausibly aver that its productions can match the grandeur of those staged by the leading shows of the Gilded Age.

Still, the middle decades of the twentieth century did not see the show continue to enjoy a period of uninterrupted triumph as it had throughout its peak years. During the Great Depression, the RBBBC and its principal owner, John Ringling North, endured seasons of sharply reduced attendance numbers and, consequently, episodes of financial crisis. In July 1944, the show's big top turned into an inferno in a matter of minutes on a Hartford, Connecticut circus lot, an unimaginable tragedy that killed 167 people and injured hundreds more. Just twelve years later, the show severed perhaps its most visible link to its past glories by playing its last show under canvas. Significantly, North's decision to perform indoors rather than in tents had its roots in the changes that the American landscape had undergone since the turn of the century, changes that had so fundamentally altered the character of Circus Day. As John's brother, Henry Ringling North, noted in 1956, "with the suburbs ringing every city in America from three to thirty miles in depth, where on earth could you still find a fifteen-acre lot that could be reached by public transportation or even conveniently by automobile? The answer was: virtually nowhere."[4]

Today, under the guidance and ownership of Feld Entertainment, the RBBBC offers three separate productions: the Red Unit, the Blue Unit, and the "Hometown," or Gold Unit. Each demonstrates how the circus, after decades of effort by nineteenth- and twentieth-century showmen, has become a fully "family friendly" entertainment and suggests that the performance models perfected back in the nineteenth century—a small, intimate one-ring show and a large, dazzling three-ring spectacle—are still viable today.

The Red Unit's production most closely resembles those of the giant three-ring shows of the late nineteenth and early twentieth centuries. The troupe presents its acts within three rings set not within a tent, but rather inside of a cavernous sports arena. In a reflection of the circus industry's adherence to tradition, the show opens with a modern version of the grand entrée, a feature with roots in the pre–Civil War era. The performances that follow include trapeze, acrobatic, and clowning acts, and much to the chagrin of animal rights activists, the performances of trained animals, including elephants, horses, zebras, dogs, cats, and tigers.[5]

Despite its massive size, the production also shows that the creative minds of Feld Entertainment understand that interactivity between performers and spectators must remain part of the circus experience. Ninety minutes before main performance commences, audience members are invited to come onto the arena floor for an "Animal Open House." This preshow segment offers customers the chance to experience something similar to visiting both a menagerie tent and the backstage area of a circus. While gathered around the outside of the performance rings, audience members can interact with clowns, try on performers' costumes, and chat with members of the show's production team. They can also touch an elephant as it lumbers its way around one of the rings.[6]

This drive for intimacy and interplay between the audience and performers has prompted the RBBBC to alter the makeup of its Blue Unit. Since the RBBBC divided its operations into two separate shows in 1969, the Blue show has featured a three-ring exhibition that closely resembled that of the Red show. In 2006, however, the RBBBC transformed its Blue unit by offering its first one-ring production since 1880. The CEO of Feld Entertainment, Kenneth Feld, noted that this change grew in part out of desire to allow audience members to be "part of a spectacle that is a bonding experience for their families." Moreover, he said that "getting rid of the rings gets rid of barriers, so that, in a visceral way, the audience is invited to be part of it all." The RBBBC attempts to enhance this sense that spectators can be part of the production in the Blue show by spotlighting the experiences of one "family" in the audience. Ostensibly, these lucky individuals are selected by a performer to take part in the acts because they have always wanted to be in the circus. As the show progresses, however, the audience discovers that these individuals, much like the performers that posed as ordinary citizens in turn-of-the-century circus tents, are actually members of the troupe.[7]

In 2004, the RBBBC looked to exploit smaller markets through the formation of its Gold Unit. As the RBBBC productions grew bigger in the twentieth century, the outfit dropped smaller cities that lacked large arenas off its tour itineraries. In an effort to revisit those communities, the RBBBC created its "Hometown Edition," a scaled down, one-ring production that would move from town to town by truck rather than by rail. For instance, this allowed the show to play Rome, Georgia in 2004 for the first time since the Second World War. By playing these lesser cities, RBBBC is, in effect, reversing the trend that began in 1872 that saw tour stops in smaller communities without railroad access dropped by the industry's leading concerns in favor of larger towns and cities located on railroad lines. In terms of its performance, the show features fewer clowns and trained animals than the larger Red Unit, but as with all RBBBC operations, the show centers on interplay between actors and audience members, with performers explaining the intricacies of their acts to the crowd.[8]

Although Rome was not visited by the RBBBC for sixty-four years, circuses continued to play a role in the lives of many Georgians throughout the twentieth century. Between 1930 and 1956, Macon's Central City Park hosted two different circuses over the winter months, and shows continued to tour the state in the decades that followed. Other Georgia cities where circuses wintered during the first half of the twentieth century include Americus, Atlanta, Augusta, Savannah, and Valdosta. More recently, Georgians have witnessed a rebirth of the circus in their state. For instance, the circus history of twenty-first-century Atlanta began in February 2000 with three separate shows playing in opposition in the Gate City, including the venerable RBBBC, New York's one-ring Big Apple Circus, and a newcomer to the circus scene, the Georgia-based UniverSoul Circus.[9]

The UniverSoul Circus, through its bold reinvention of the circus genre, has helped spearhead a popular resurgence of the circus in America since it debuted in Atlanta in 1994. This black-owned, one-ring show offers standard circus acts like clowning, acrobatics, and performing animals in its 2,500 seat tent but presents them with a distinctive African-American aesthetic, creating a production that its owners variously describe as "Hip Hop under the Big Top" and "The Most Soulful Show on Earth." Breaking with circus conventions, UniverSoul performers dance to the beat of rhythm and blues, salsa, gospel, jazz, and hip-hop, its clowns draw on the realities of urban life for their humor, and its "funkadelic" ringmaster dons a zoot suit and Converse sneakers rather than traditional equestrian finery and matching boots. Yet in a return to the intimacy and interactivity of the antebellum circus, the show brings audience members into the ring to dance and sing, and features call-and-response segments between the ringmaster and the children in the crowd.[10]

This trend in the circus industry back toward smaller productions makes it even more unlikely that Circus Days of grand street parades, bustling snack stands, and crowded excursion trains will ever reappear on the American scene. But despite Circus Day's disappearance as a ritual related to a circus's arrival in town, the social, economic, and cultural impulses that drove its creation have retained their force in American society, helping to assure that its celebratory features would reappear in other contexts. For example, New Orleans' annual Mardi Gras celebration sees thousands of people crowd into the streets of the French Quarter to parade, feast, and drink in a ritual with antecedents that extend back to premodern Europe. Other cities have, à la Memphis, Tennessee and its legendary Beale Street, turned thoroughfares into entertainment areas in their own right by closing them off to vehicular traffic, thereby allowing revelers to literally take over the streets, just as people had done when the circus was in town a century before. Not surprisingly, this effort to cultivate an atmosphere of release has produced mixed results. In an attempt to control traffic and boost business for its restaurants and bars, the city of Tampa, Florida closed Seventh Avenue in its historic Ybor City district to automobiles on weekend nights beginning in 1995. Yet in 2005, city legislators decided to lift the ban on vehicles after complaints that "allowing thousands of young nightclub and bar patrons to roam the street" had fostered "a rowdy, lawless atmosphere" in the downtown district.[11]

America's leading sporting events also attract people interested in merrymaking, but in a manner reminiscent of those Georgians who came out for Circus Day but had little interest in the circus proper, many of the attendees turn out as much for the party as for the sporting events themselves. For instance, on the day of a NASCAR race at Atlanta's Talladega Superspeedway, thousands of fans crowd into the huge open spaces on the inside of its track to cheer for their favorite drivers. But they also camp out in the infield to drink, flirt, and barbeque as part of a "pretty wild" giant party that *USA Today* noted "is not a place for young children." A similar dynamic occurs each May at Baltimore's Pimlico Race Course at the running of the second leg of horse racing's Triple Crown, the Preakness Stakes. Tens of thousands of celebrants jam into the track's vast infield beginning in the early morning for "one of the biggest beer bashes in the country," a celebration that lasts until the final race is run in the late afternoon. Significantly, large numbers of the individuals in the infield have no desire to see any of the equine contests and if asked will proudly proclaim that they have not seen a single horse all day.[12]

The circus and the individuals who made their living as showmen have demonstrated a remarkable degree of resilience over the more than two hundred years the circus has been in America. The pioneers of the industry survived both efforts to legislate it out of existence and fierce competition from menagerie shows. These same men adapted to playing in canvas tents on the countryside after always showing in wooden structures in urban areas. Later, their successors successfully shifted their operations from wagon to rail. But perhaps most impressively, showmen withstood the disappearance of Circus Day, an unofficial holiday wholly dedicated to celebrating the arrival of their concerns into a community. They did so because they oversaw an art form flexible enough to evolve to meet with cultural changes while still remaining recognizably a circus. So regardless of whether the wider culture calls for acrobats to garb themselves in formal dress or for performers to break-dance to hip-hop beats, people will still come to see risible clowns, incredible animals, and daring performers because the circus remains the only place in Georgia, and the world, where all of these things come together with such thrilling and happy results.

NOTES

Abbreviations

AAPSSA	*American Academy of Political and Social Science Annals*
AQ	*American Quarterly*
AR	*Americus Recorder*
ATR	*Americus Times Recorder*
AC	*Atlanta Constitution*
ACC	*Augusta Chronicle and Constitutionalist*
ACS	*Augusta Chronicle & Sentinel*
ADCS	*Augusta Daily Chronicle & Sentinel*
ADE	*Atlanta Daily Era*
ADH	*Atlanta Daily Herald*
ADNE	*Atlanta Daily New Era*
ADS	*Atlanta Daily Sun*
AEC	*Atlanta Evening Capitol*
AG	*Atlanta Georgian*
AGN	*Atlanta Georgian and News*
AHR	*American Historical Review*
AI	*Atlanta Independent*
AJ	*Atlanta Journal*
AN	*Atlanta News*
ANEG	*Athens North-East Georgian*
ASB	*Athens Southern Banner*
ASW	*Athens Southern Watchman*
BB	*Billboard*
BG	*Barnesville Gazette*
CDES	*Columbus Daily Enquirer-Sun*
CDS	*Columbus Daily Sun*
CDST	*Columbus Daily Sun & Times*
CE	*Columbus Enquirer*
CES	*Columbus Enquirer-Sun*
CST	*Columbus Sun and Times*

CT	*Columbus Times*
DAI	*Daily Atlanta Intelligencer*
DN	*Dahlonega Nugget*
DNGC	*Dalton North Georgia Citizen*
GHQ	*Georgia Historical Quarterly*
GDN	*Griffin Daily News*
GDNS	*Griffin Daily News and Sun*
GWN	*Griffin Weekly News*
HRBML	Hargrett Rare Book and Manuscript Library, University of Georgia, Athens, Georgia
HR	*Hustler of Rome*
JRCCR	John Robinson Circus Company Records, Cincinnati Historical Society Library, Cincinnati, Ohio
JAC	*Journal of American Culture*
JAH	*Journal of American History*
JNE	*Journal of Negro Education*
JNH	*Journal of Negro History*
JSH	*Journal of Southern History*
LKWL	*Lexington (KY) Western Luminary*
MJ	*Marietta Journal*
MDT	*Macon Daily Telegraph*
MT	*Macon Telegraph*
NYC	*New York Clipper*
NYT	*New York Times*
NH	*Newnan Herald*
RMC	Ringling Museum of the Circus, John and Mable Ringling Museum of Art, Sarasota, Florida
RBP	Robert Brisendine Papers, 1899–2002, Manuscript, Archives, and Rare Book Library, Emory University, Atlanta, Georgia
RLPLRC	Robert L. Parkinson Library and Research Center, Circus World Museum, Baraboo, Wisconsin
RTH	*Rome Tribune-Herald*
SH	*Sandersville Herald*
SDH	*Savannah Daily Herald*
SDNH	*Savannah Daily News & Herald*
SMN	*Savannah Morning News*
STNT	Stuart Thayer Newspaper Typescripts
TDTE	*Thomasville Daily Times Enterprise*
TG	*Tifton Gazette*
VDT	*Valdosta Daily Times*
VT	*Valdosta Times*
WTC	*Waynesboro True Citizen*
WMQ	*William & Mary Quarterly*

Introduction

1. Carter, *An Hour Before Daylight*, 159.
2. On Circus Day, see Davis, *Circus Age*, 1–36, esp. 13; Mishler, "The Greatest Show on Earth," 18–52.
3. Hallock, "The American Circus," 568; Bakhtin, *Rabelais and His World*, 5, 7.
4. Davis, *Circus Age*, 42–46; Slout, *Royal Coupling*, 10, 36; Richard Butsch, "Introduction: Leisure and Hegemony in America," in Butsch, *For Fun and Profit*, 14; Horowitz, *Morality of Spending*, 30; Nasaw, *Going Out*, 1–9; Rosenzweig, *Eight Hours for What We Will*, 171–221; Allen, *Horrible Prettiness*, 162–63; Butsch, *Making of American Audiences*, 108–9.
5. Bakhtin, *Rabelais and His World*, 7, 255; "It Was Circus Day," AC, 20 September 1894, RBP; Also see Waller, *Main Street Amusements*, 60–63.
6. Examples here include Kasson, Joy, *Buffalo Bill's Wild West*; Reddin, *Wild West Shows*; Kasson, John, *Amusing the Million*; Allen, *Horrible Prettiness*; Lott, *Love and Theft*; Kibler, *Rank Ladies*; Register, *The Kid of Coney Island*. Works that look at more than a single entertainment genre but largely ignore the circus include Click, *Spirit of the Times*; Goodson, *Highbrows, Hillbillies, and Hellfire*; Nasaw, *Going Out*; Peiss, *Cheap Amusements*; Rosenzweig, *Eight Hours*; Waller, *Main Street Amusements*. On Barnum see Adams, *E Pluribus Barnum*; Harris, *Humbug*; Saxon, *P. T. Barnum*.
7. Bureau of the Census, *Negro Population 1790–1915*, 108–36; Edwin S. Gaustad, "Religious Demography of the South," in Hill, *Religion and the Solid South*, 143–78; Charles E. Wynes, "1865–1890," in Coleman, *History of Georgia*, 225–37; Doyle, *New Men*, 39–41, 144–47.
8. Mandle, *Roots of Black Poverty*; Weiner, *Social Origins of the New South*; Ransom and Sutch, *One Kind of Freedom*; Woodward, *Origins*; Ownby, *Subduing Satan*; Ownby, *American Dreams*; Spain, *At Ease in Zion*; Loveland, *Southern Evangelicals*.
9. Broadly on these changes see Woodward, *Origins*, and Ayers, *Promise*. Also see Wynes, "1865–1890," in Coleman, *History of Georgia*, 232; Larsen, *Rise of the Urban South*, 22, 60–77, 149; Doyle, *New Men*, 39–41, 144–47; Howard N. Rabinowitz, "Continuity and Change: Southern Urban Development, 1860–1900," in Brownell and Goldfield, *The City in Southern History*, 92–122; Goldfield, *Cotton Fields and Skyscrapers*, 127–28. On population growth consult Larsen, *Rise of the Urban South*, 22, 149. Wetherington, *New South*, 232–33; William F. Holmes, "1890–1940," in Coleman, *History of Georgia*, 274–76; Ayers, *Promise*, 55, 61; Dorsey, *History of Hall County*, 208–9.
10. Stallybrass and White, *Politics and Poetics of Transgression*, 36–37.
11. On segregation, see Grace Elizabeth Hale, "'For Colored' and 'For White': Segregating Consumption in the South," in Dailey, Gilmore, and Simon, *Jumpin' Jim Crow*, 162–82; Rabinowitz, *Race Relations*; Woodward, *Strange Career*. On the larger historiographical issues, see Smith, *When Did Southern Segregation Begin?*
12. Kasson, *Amusing the Million*; Peiss, *Cheap Amusements*; Nasaw, *Going Out*. On these long stands refer to Apps, *Ringlingville USA*, 67, 71, 73, 75, 148. Also see Route Sheets of the Ringling Brothers Circus, 1895–1930; P. T. Barnum Circus, 1871–1880; Barnum & London Circus, 1881–1888; and Barnum & Bailey Circus, 1889–1897, 1903–1918, all at RLPLRC.

13. Waller, *Main Street Amusements*, 13; Goodson, *Highbrows, Hillbillies, and Hellfire*.

14. For detailed discussions of this debate, refer to Woodman, "Sequel to Slavery," 523–54; Harold D. Woodman, "Economic Reconstruction and the Rise of the New South, 1865–1900," in Boles and Nolen, *Interpreting Southern History*, 254–307; Joseph P. Reidy, "Economic Consequences of the Civil War and Reconstruction," in Boles, *Companion to the American South*, 303–17. Also see Ayers, *Promise*; Doyle, *New Men*; and Woodward, *Origins*.

15. Jordan, *Tumult and Silence*, 20–23.

Chapter 1. Get the Show on the Road: Circus Trouping in the Old South

1. These places include Athens, Atlanta, Augusta, Columbus, Savannah, Macon, and Milledgeville. See Dormon, *Theater*, 137–43, 167–71.

2. Coup, *Sawdust & Spangles*, 234; Thayer, *Traveling Showmen*, ix–x.

3. Thayer, *Traveling Showmen*, 30; Thayer, *Annals*, 1–14.

4. Culhane, *American Circus*, 3; Thayer, *Annals*, 1–2.

5. Thayer, *Traveling Showmen*, 1–2; Culhane, *American Circus*, 8–10; Thayer, *Annals*, 15, 28.

6. Thayer, *Traveling Showmen*, 7; Culhane, *American Circus*, 13–17.

7. Thayer, *Traveling Showmen*, 8–21; Slout, *Olympians*, 15, 45–46, 110–12, 178–79, 266–67, 275–76, 317–18, 370, 390–91, 402, 411, 485–86, 499–502, 519, 546, 560–63, 579–82, 592, 661–62, 667, 698, 754.

8. Culhane, *American Circus*, 16–17; Chindahl, *History of the Circus*, 29–33; Thayer, *Annals*, 148.

9. In addition to the seven menageries, this arrangement also created five separate circus-menagerie combination troupes. See Thayer, *Traveling Showmen*, 24–25.

10. "Waring & Co.'s Great Zoological Exhibition from the City of New York," CT, 31 December 1845, 4, RBP. On the tensions between "instruction" and "amusement" in nineteenth-century entertainments, see Altick, *Shows of London*, 3–4, and Click, *Spirit of the Times*, 4, 32–33.

11. Loveland, *Southern Evangelicals*, 97–101; Spain, *At Ease in Zion*, 201; "Waring & Co.'s Great Zoological Exhibition from the City of New York," CT, 31 December 1845, 4, RBP.

12. The first exhibition of this kind took place in Raleigh, North Carolina. See Thayer, *Annals*, 99, 131.

13. Carlyon, *Dan Rice*, 59–60; Thayer, *Annals*, 81, 157, 164, 174; Thayer, *Traveling Showmen*, 94; Clark, *Southern Country Editor*, 161; Barnum, *Struggles and Triumphs*, 2:792–98; Shippee, *Bishop Whipple's Southern Diary*, 99–101, 111, 119.

14. Thayer, *Traveling Showmen*, 27, 85; Thayer, "Legislating the Shows," 20–22; Thayer, *Annals*, 70, 81–82, 104, 175; Allen, *Horrible Prettiness*, 46–51; Samuel S. Hill, "Religion," in Wilson and Ferris, *Encyclopedia of Southern Culture*, 1269.

15. Thayer, *Annals*, 99; Thayer, *Traveling Showmen*, 6.

16. "Menagerie & Circus," CE, 15 March 1834, 3, RBP; Thayer, *Annals*, 186–87; Thayer, *Traveling Showmen*, 6.

17. Culhane, *American Circus*, 278. On Brown and his pavilion, consult Thayer, "Notes on the History of Circus Tents," 28–30; Thayer, *Traveling Showmen*, 1–4; Thayer, *Annals*, 75–76; Culhane, *American Circus*, 22–23.

18. Holmes, *Those Glorious Days*, 63; Hynds, *Antebellum Athens*, 129; Thayer, "Trouping in Alabama in 1827," 21; Bonner, *Milledgeville*, 74. The Savannah date of 10 February 1801 documented in the Homel L. DeGolyer Notebooks, Hertzberg Circus Collection, San Antonio Public Library, San Antonio, Texas; I thank Stuart Thayer for sharing this source with me. In 1819, one circus apparently traveled overland from Louisville, Kentucky, to Augusta, Georgia; refer to Thayer, *Annals*, 16, 49, 100.

19. F. N. Boney, "1820–1865," in Coleman, *History of Georgia*, 156; Phillips, *Slave Economy*, 158, 161–62; Thayer, *Traveling Showmen*, 26; Dormon, *Theater*, 44, 50, 86–87; Robinson, *Old Wagon Show Days*, 27.

20. Ashby Deering, "Routing a Twentieth Century Tent Show," *New York Telegraph*, 3 February 1907, 36, in *Barnum and Bailey Press Clipping Book 1906–07*, RMC; Thayer, *Traveling Showmen*, 30.

21. Thayer, *Traveling Showmen*, 35–44; Davis, *Circus Age*, 42–46; Leavitt, *Fifty Years*, 119; "Robinson & Eldred's Grand New York Circus," CE, 20 November 1849, 3, RBP; *Greensborough (NC) Patriot*, 27 September 1845, quoted in Thayer, *Annals*, 197.

22. Robinson, *Old Wagon Show Days*, 30.

23. "Circuses," NYC, 25 March 1865, 398; Thayer, *Traveling Showmen*, 13–16; Sherwood, *Here We Are Again*, 27; "Circuses," NYC, 18 July 1868, 118.

24. Cyrus D. Simpson, "J. Ed Long," BB 33 (10 December 1921): 99; John A. Dingess, Dingess Manuscript, 355, RLPLRC; Thayer, *Traveling Showmen*, 46; "Hey Rube! Hey Rube!" *Chicago Tribune* clipping, Charles & Nedra Gonzales Circus Scrap Book, (SBK-17), 1891, RLPLRC; Leavitt, *Fifty Years*, 118; Robinson, *Old Wagon Show Days*, 29.

25. Thayer, *Traveling Showmen*, 43.

26. Hallock, "The American Circus," 571; "Robinson and Eldred's Grand New York Circus," CE, 20 November 1849, 3, RBP; "Stone & McCollum's Mammoth Great Western Circus," CE, 30 March 1847, 1, RBP.

27. "Stone & McCollum's Mammoth Great Western Circus," CE, 14 March 1848, 3, RBP.

28. "Menagerie & Circus," CE, 15 March 1834, 3, RBP; Thayer, *Traveling Showmen*, 75.

29. Thayer, *Traveling Showmen*, 65–68, 73–75, 80; Slout, *Royal Coupling*, 45.

30. Chindahl, *History of the Circus*, 142; Carlyon, *Dan Rice*, 157; Thayer, *Traveling Showmen*, 61–62, 64.

31. Hogan and Davis, *William Johnson's Natchez*, 2:763, 1:351; *Daily Savannah Republican*, 23 January 1847, STNT, in author's possession; Saxon, *Old Louisiana*, 239; Crofts, *Cobb's Ordeal*, 121; Escott, *North Carolina Yeoman*, 205; Thayer, *Annals*, 594, 554; Barnum, *Struggles and Triumphs*, 1:156.

32. Hogan and Davis, *William Johnson's Natchez*, 2:707; Thayer, *Annals*, 42; William Emmons, WPA Ex-Slave Narrative, GR7999, 3, Ohio Historical Center Archives Library. Accessed online 28 July 2006 at http://dbs.ohiohistory.org/africanam/page.cfm?ID=13914; Thayer, *Traveling Showmen*, 74; "Spalding & Rogers," CE, 2 January 1855, 3, RBP.

33. Thayer, "Some Class Distinctions in the Early Circus Audience," 20–21; Thayer, "The Birth of the Blues," 24–26; "New York Circus," CE, 27 November 1844, 1, RBP; "Stone & McCollum's Mammoth Great Western Circus," CE, 7 November 1848, 3, RBP.

34. *Republican and Savannah Evening Register,* 15 December 1823; also refer to *Norfolk (VA) Gazette,* 16 April 1818, both STNT, in author's possession; "Stone & McCollum," CE, 7 November 1848, 3, RBP; Thayer, *Traveling Showmen,* 74–75; Thayer, *Annals,* 42; ADI, 11 January 1859, 3, RBP.

35. Leavitt, *Fifty Years,* 119; Robinson, *Old Wagon Show Days,* 31; Thayer, *Traveling Showmen,* 77; Greenwood, *Circus,* 113; Kitchen, "19th Century Circus Bands and Music," 14.

36. "Robinson & Eldred's Grand New York Circus," CE, 20 November 1849, 3, RBP; On grand entrées, see A. Morton Smith, "Spec-ology of the Circus," BB 55 (31 July 1943): 51.

37. "Great Western Circus," CT, 17 September 1850, 3, RBP; Sherwood, *Here We Are Again,* 37, 44–45; Ownby, *Subduing Satan,* 90–94; Owsley, *Plain Folk,* 107–14; Thayer, *Traveling Showmen,* 5; Thayer, *Annals,* 423. Also see Workers, *Atlanta,* 107.

38. Chindahl, *History of the Circus,* 195; McPherson, *Ordeal By Fire,* 190–91.

39. "Robinson & Eldred's Grand New York Circus," CE, 20 November 1849, 3, RBP; "Welch, Nathans & Co.'s National Circus," CE, 21 January 1851, 1, RBP; Davis, *Circus Age,* 98–99.

40. "Circus," CE, 11 May 1833, 3, RBP; "Amusements & C.," CE, 11 May 1833, 3, RBP; Owsley, *Plain Folk,* 123; "The Circus," CDS, 20 February 1856, 2, RBP.

41. Ownby, *Subduing Satan,* 23–26; Owsley, *Plain Folk,* 123–24.

42. "Robinson & Eldred's Grand New York Circus," CE, 20 November 1849, 3, RBP; Thayer, *Annals,* 128.

43. "Robinson & Eldred's Grand New York Circus," CE, 20 November 1849, 3, RBP; Robinson, *Old Wagon Show Days,* 59.

44. Root, *Ways of the Circus,* 242.

45. Click, *Spirit of the Times,* 42–43; Allen, *Horrible Prettiness,* 57; Butsch, *Making of American Audiences,* 50–52; Dormon, *Theater,* 241–43; Carlyon, *Dan Rice,* 154; Turnour, *Autobiography of a Clown,* 45–46; Hallock, "American Circus," 572. For more examples of audience interactivity at antebellum circuses, see Carlyon, *Dan Rice,* 35–38, 80–81, 154, 160.

46. Carlyon, *Dan Rice,* 55; Inge and Piacentino, *Humor of the Old South,* 5–7.

47. "Bailey's Circus," CDS, 29 December 1858, 3, RBP.

48. Blassingame, *Slave Community,* 114–48; James M. McPherson, "The Second American Revolution," in Perman, *Major Problems,* 439–40. Thayer writes that the ringmaster portrayed an "establishment figure" in the ring. See *Annals,* 58.

49. Sherwood, *Here We Are Again,* 71–73; "The Circus," CDS, 31 December 1858, 3, RBP.

50. Carlyon, *Dan Rice,* 199–200. No less of an authority than P. T. Barnum conceded that much of the circus's "fun consisted of the clown's vulgar jests, emphasized with still more vulgar and suggestive gestures, lest providentially the point might be lost."

See P. T. Barnum, "Piety in the Circus" clipping, RLPLRC. "New York Circus," CE, 27 November 1844, 1, RBP.

51. Thayer, *Annals,* 158; "Robinson & Eldred's Grand New York Circus," CE, 20 November 1849, 3, RBP; Twain, *Huckleberry Finn,* 111–13.

52. "Philadelphia Circus and Gymnastic Co.," *Charlotte (NC) Journal,* 6 October 1840, STNT, in author's possession.

53. Wills, *Democratic Religion,* 124–25; Loveland, *Southern Evangelicals,* 97–101; Spain, *At Ease in Zion,* 201.

54. "Sinful Amusements," LKWL, 10 August 1831, STNT, in author's possession; "Sinful Amusements Again," LKWL, 17 August 1831, STNT, in author's possession.

55. Crowley, *Primitive Baptists,* 50; Loveland, *Southern Evangelicals,* 97–101; Wills, *Democratic Religion,* 122–27.

56. Coulter, *College Life,* 288; Dyer, *University of Georgia,* 53; "Amusements," NYC, 4 July 1857, 86; Vaughan, "A Brief History of the Georgia Military Institute," 32–36; Thayer, *Annals,* 560–61.

57. Escott, *North Carolina Yeoman,* 205; Crofts, *Old Southampton,* 101. Mallory, born in 1807, wrote in regard to a circus that appeared in 1870, but his comments clearly reflect attitudes he formed during the pre–Civil War years. See McWhiney, Moore, and Pace, *"Fear God and Walk Humbly,"* 408.

58. "Stone & McCollum's Mammoth Great Western Circus," CE, 30 March 1847, 1, RBP; Click, *Spirit of the Times,* 35–36.

59. Thayer, *Traveling Showmen,* 84–85; "Sinful Amusements," LKWL, 24 August 1831, STNT, in author's possession; "Sinful Amusements Again," LKWL, 17 August 1831, STNT, in author's possession.

60. "Sinful Amusements," LKWL, 24 August 1831, STNT, in author's possession; "Circus and Theatrical Exhibitions," LKWL, 14 September 1831, STNT, in author's possession.

61. Thayer, *Traveling Showmen,* 90–91; P. A. Older letter, in *Barnum & Bailey Annual Route Book and Illustrated Tours, 1906* (Buffalo, N.Y.: Courier, 1906), 109, RLPLRC; Chipman, *"Hey Rube",* 15; Robinson, *Old Wagon Show Days,* 64; "An Old Veteran Relates the Memorable Fights Between Circus Men and Villagers," *Chicago Times* 3 December 1882, clipping in "Violence" folder, vertical files, RLPLRC.

62. Thompson, *On the Road,* 25–26; "An Old Veteran Relates the Memorable Fights," RLPLRC; Barnum, *Struggles and Triumphs,* 1:173; Thayer, *Annals,* 373.

63. Allen, *Horrible Prettiness,* 57–61, esp. 58; Butsch, *American Audiences,* 52–56.

64. Barnum, "Piety in the Circus," RLPLRC; "'Hey Rube!' The Cry," ca. 1897, clipping in "Violence" folder, vertical files, RLPLRC.

65. Butsch, *American Audiences,* 53; Kasson, *Rudeness and Civility,* 222.

66. Thayer, *Traveling Showmen,* 90–91; "An Old Veteran Relates the Memorable Fights," RLPLRC; Butsch, *American Audiences,* 44–65.

67. Gorn, "'Gouge,'" 18–43; Franklin, *Militant South,* 37–41; Thayer, *Traveling Showmen,* 90. Also see Nisbett and Cohen, *Culture of Honor,* 1–2.

68. Root, *Ways of the Circus,* 233; "Hey Rube! Hey Rube!" *Chicago Tribune* clipping, RLPLRC; Robinson, *Old Wagon Show Days,* 64.

Chapter 2. Selling Southernism: Showmen in Georgia, 1865–1874

1. "Dan Castello," AC, 11 April 1899, 8, RBP.
2. "Circuses," NYC, 25 November 1865, 263; "Circuses," NYC, 6 January 1866, 311. For another account of this incident see Slout, *Clowns and Cannons*, 208–10.
3. Regarding the Confederate "Lost Cause," see, for example, Wilson, *Baptized in Blood*; Foster, *Ghosts of the Confederacy*; Gallagher and Nolan, *Myth of the Lost Cause*.
4. Slout, *Clowns and Cannons*, xi, 55.
5. Carlyon, *Dan Rice*, 298; Slout, *Clowns and Cannons*, 57–58.
6. "The Great Show," *Memphis Daily Bulletin*, 6 October 1864, 3; Slout, *Clowns and Cannons*, 128, 131–32, 168–69, 170, 175–77, 179.
7. Slout, *Clowns and Cannons*, 208; Conway, *Reconstruction of Georgia*, 35–39; "Thayer & Noyes U. S. Circus," CST, 10 November 1865, 3; "Dan Castello's Great Circus," CDS, 11 November 1865, 3; "Circuses," NYC, 2 December 1865, 271. It is probable that the 11 February 1860 appearance of Robinson and Lake's Great Southern Menagerie and Circus was the final circus performance in Georgia before the Civil War; see Thayer, *Annals*, 558.
8. "Circuses," NYC, 25 November 1865, 263; "Thayer & Noyes U. S. Circus," CST, 10 November 1865, 3; "Dan Castello's Great Circus," CDS, 11 November 1865, 3; "Money in Columbus," CDS, 15 November 1865, 3.
9. "The Circus," CDST, 30 December 1865, 3, RBP; "The Circus," CDST, 29 December 1865, 3; "Regulations During Christmas Week," CDST, 24 December 1865, 3; "The Circus," CDST, 31 December 1865, 3, RBP; "Freedmen's Bureau Diary by George Wagner," 207. This circus was most likely the Haight and Chambers' Circus Company, which played Atlanta on October 10 and then headed south to Griffin for a show on the eleventh. Presumably the show continued on and played Americus on the sixteenth, as noted in the Wagner diary; see "The Circus," ADE, 11 October 1866, 3, RBP.
10. Root, *Ways of the Circus*, 235–36; "Circuses," NYC, 27 April 1867, 22.
11. Sherwood, *Here We Are Again*, 60–61.
12. Scott, "Some Personal Memories," 286; Pete Conklin, "How Conklin Sold Song Books," BB 26 (23 March 1914): 24; Root, *Ways of the Circus*, 244–45.
13. "Circuses," NYC, 5 May 1866, 31; Conover, *Give 'em a John Robinson*, 28; "Circuses," NYC, 19 January 1867, 327; "Circuses," NYC, 21 December 1867, 295; Carlyon, *Dan Rice*, 343–44. Also see "An Old Veteran Relates the Memorable Fights," RLPLRC; "Circuses," NYC, 18 March 1871, 399.
14. Root, *Ways of the Circus*, 235; "Hey Rube! Hey Rube!" *Chicago Tribune* clipping, RLPLRC.
15. Robinson, *Old Wagon Show Days*, 75; Root, *Ways of the Circus*, 234; Thompson, *On the Road with a Circus*, 162.
16. Robinson, *Old Wagon Show Days*, 64–76, *passim*; "Circuses," NYC, 4 February 1871, 351; "Georgia Items," ANEG, 22 November 1872, 2; Thompson, *On the Road with a Circus*, 161–62.
17. Slout, *Clowns and Cannons*, 200, 211–12; Slout, *Olympians*, 506–7; "Circuses," NYC, 24 February 1866, 367; "Circuses," NYC, 7 April 1866, 415.

18. "James Robinson's Great Southwestern Circus," ASW, 16 October 1867, 2; "James Robinson's Champion Circus," ASW, 10 February 1869, 2; "James Robinson's Champion Circus," SMN, 1 February 1869, 2; "Jim Robinson's Champion Circus," AC, 14 February 1869, 3; "Jim Robinson," AC, 16 February 1869, 3; "Famous Circus Bareback Rider," BB 28 (30 September 1916): 25.

19. "The Fame of a Clown," SMN, 8 November 1895, 3; Slout, *Olympians*, 415; "To Whom It May Concern," SMN, 9 November 1871, 3; "John Lowlow," AC, 14 November 1871, 3; "Old John Robinson Circus and Menagerie," *Milledgeville Federal Union*, 14 December 1869, 3; "Old John Robinson," AC, 14 November 1871, 2; "Old John Robinson," ADCS, 22 October 1871, 2.

20. "Old John Robinson's Circus and Menagerie," ADCS, 1 November 1871, 3; "The Circus," ANEG, 29 November 1872, 3.

21. "The Late John Robinson," NYC, 18 August 1888, 361; Slout, *Clowns and Cannons*, 29, 131, 186.

22. "Who is Old John Robinson?" CES, 8 December 1876, 4, RBP; "Old John Robinson's Circus," CES, 9 December 1876, 4, RBP; "Alabama News," CDES, 12 January 1878, 3, RBP; "Alabama News," CDES, 15 January 1878, 3, RBP; Slout, *Clowns and Cannons*, 131. On the Columbus appearances by the John Robinson Circus see notation by Robert H. Brisendine in "Incidental Scenes on the Streets and Under the Canvas," CES, 9 December 1876, 4, RBP.

23. "Col. C. T. Ames' New Orleans Circus and Menagerie," SMN, 16 June 1869, 3; "The Sensation Today," ADNE, 26 May 1868, 3, RBP; "Col. Ames' Circus & Menagerie," SMN, 12 October 1870, 3.

24. "Local Matters," SMN, 19 June 1869, 3; "Ames Circus," SMN, 8 October 1870, 3; "The Circus," AC, 29 May 1869, 3. For other circus horses with "Confederate" names, consult Ownby, *Subduing Satan*, 60.

25. "Col. C. T. Ames' New Orleans Menagerie, Circus," SDNH, 21 May 1868, 2; "Col. Ames Circus and Menagerie," SMN, 12 October 1870, 3.

26. "Col. Ames Tribute," SMN, 13 October 1870, 3; "The Killing of Mr. Ames," CDS, 11 November 1870, 3, RBP.

27. "The City," ADNE, 12 February 1871, 4, RBP; "The City," ADNE, 3 March 1871, 4, RBP; "The Circus," ADCS, 21 September 1871, 3; Slout, *Olympians*, 275–76, 754; "Circuses," NYC, 11 March 1871, 391; "The City," ADNE, 26 February 1871, 4, RBP.

28. Doyle, *New Men*, 136–58; Woodward, *Origins*, 142–74; "The City," ADNE, 5 March, 18 March, and 23 March 1871, 4, RBP; "The Circus," ADNE, 28 March 1871, 4, RBP.

29. "Haight's & Co.'s Circus, Museum and Menagerie," SMN, 25 December 1871, 3; "Haight's Southern Circus and Menagerie," SMN, 30 December 1871, 3; "The Circus is Coming," ASW, 7 February 1872, 3; "Wootten & Haight's Empire City Circus, Menagerie, and Balloon," ADCS, 10 September 1871, 2.

30. "Haight & Wooten's Circus," ADNE, 29 September 1871, 4, RBP; "Haight & Wooten's Circus," ADNE, 3 October 1871, 4, RBP; "Haight & Wooten's Circus," SMN, 7 September 1871, 3.

31. Despite the departure of Wooten, Haight remained committed to a southern image, as evidenced by ads that declared that the outfit was the "Only Southern Show" in existence. See "Haight & Co.'s Circus, Museum, and Menagerie," SMN, 2 January 1872,

2. "Haight's Circus," AC, 17 February 1872, 3, RBP; "Circuses," NYC, 17 February 1872, 367; "Circuses," NYC, 2 March 1872, 378; Slout, *Olympians*, 275–76, 754.

32. "Haight's Circus," AC, 17 February 1872, 3, RBP; "Great Eastern Menagerie," ADCS, 8 September 1872, 4; "Great Eastern Circus," AC, 2 December 1873, 4; "Circuses," NYC, 2 March 1872, 378; W. W. Durand, *Great Eastern Menagerie, Museum, Aviary, Circus, Roman Hippodrome and Egyptian Caravan Route and Organization of 1872* (Selma, Ala.: Jas. P. Armstrong, 1872), 26, photocopy in author's possession; Slout, *Royal Coupling*, 19–37.

33. Durand, *Great Eastern*, 5, 13, 16, 19, 20.

34. "Circuses," NYC, 21 September 1872, 199.

35. Durand, *Great Eastern,* 28–29; "Great Eastern," SMN, 16 September 1872, 2; "Circuses," NYC, 7 December 1872, 287; "Georgia Items," ADCS, 19 November 1872, 1.

36. "The Great Eastern Circus," AC, 2 December 1873, 3, RBP; "Great Eastern Menagerie and Circus," ADH, 29 November 1873, 4, RBP; "Great Eastern Menagerie and Circus," ADH, 4 December 1873, 4, RBP; Slout, *Olympians*, 276; "Circuses," NYC, 8 March 1873, 391–92.

37. "Great Eastern Menagerie and Circus," ADH, 29 November 1873, 4, RBP; "The Great Eastern Coming Home," ADH, 30 November 1873, 4, RBP.

38. "Great Eastern Menagerie and Circus," ADH, 3 December 1873, 4, RBP; "Great Eastern Menagerie and Circus," ADH, 4 December 1873, 4; "Circuses," NYC, 13 December 1873, 295; "Circuses," NYC, 21 March 1874; "Circuses," NYC, 18 April 1874; "Circuses," NYC, 15 August 1874.

39. Slout, *Olympians*, 276; "Great Southern Circus," NH, 10 April 1874, 3, RBP.

40. "Circuses," NYC, 3 January 1874, 319; "Great Southern Circus," NH, 10 April 1874, 3, RBP. For an example of this wording see Clark, Cobb, and Irwin, *Code of the State of Georgia*, 108.

41. "Circus," NH, 27 March 1874, 3, RBP.

42. "Haight's Southern Circus," AC, 8 April 1874, 3, RBP; "Circuses," NYC, 18 April 1874, 23.

43. "Circuses," NYC, 21 March 1874; "Circuses," NYC, 18 April 1874; "Circuses," NYC, 27 June 1874; "Circuses," NYC, 8 August 1874; "Wooten & Andrews," ANEG, 18 February 1874, 3; "Circuses," NYC, 15 August 1874; Stuart Thayer, "Haight's Great Southern Circus Route Sheet, 1874," typescript in author's possession. I thank William Slout for putting this source at my disposal.

Chapter 3. The Slow Embrace: Religion, Social Status, and Circus Attendance, 1865–1920

1. "Miscellaneous," NYC, 7 April 1866, 415; H. H. Parks, "The Circus," ASB, 20 December 1865, 3; "Circus," *Brunswick Advertiser*, 12 January 1876, 1.

2. "Col. Ames' Circus & Menagerie," SMN, 12 October 1870, 3.

3. "Howes' Great London Circus," SMN, 23 October 1875, 2.

4. "New York Circus," CE, 27 November 1844, 1, RBP; "Dan Castello's Circus," *Daily Richmond (VA) Examiner*, 11 September 1866, 3; "Dan Castello's Show," *Daily Rich-*

mond (VA) *Examiner*, 29 September 1866, 3. On the respectability project pursued by theater owners see Allen, *Horrible Prettiness*, 23–54, 73–78, 159–93; Butsch, *Making of American Audiences*, 68–71, 81–138; Click, *Spirit of the Times*, 34–56. On the moral content of circuses refer to Thayer, *Traveling Showmen*, 83–95.

5. "The Circus," SDH, 14 February 1866, 3. Also see Hope and Silverman, *Relief and Recovery*, 67–68.

6. "Castello's Mammoth Circus," CST, 10 November 1865, 3; "Benefit at the Circus for the Female Orphan Asylum," SDH, 13 November 1865, 3; "Receipts from the Circus," ADNE, 12 October 1866, 3, RBP; "The Benefit at the Circus for the Orphans," SDH, 20 November 1865, 3; "The Orphans Benefit," SDH, 17 February 1866, 3; Grant, *Way It Was in the South*, 96–97; Trowbridge, *The Desolate South*, 244; Conway, *Reconstruction of Georgia*, 21–23.

7. "The Benefit at the Circus for the Orphans," SDH, 20 November 1865, 3; "Local Intelligence," *Atlanta Christian Index and South-Western Baptist*, 11 October 1866, 3; "Circus," *Atlanta Intelligencer*, 7 January 1859, 3, RBP.

8. Butsch, *Making of American Audiences*, 72–74; Battle, *Memories of an Old-Time Tar Heel*, 9; Thayer, *Traveling Showmen*, 72; "Spalding and Rodgers," CE, 2 January 1855, 3, RBP; "Stickney's New Orleans Circus," CE, 3 July 1849, 3, RBP; "Stone and McCollum's," CE, 14 March 1848, 3, RBP; "The Orphans' Benefit at the Circus," SDH, 16 February 1866, 3. Also see "The Circus," SDH, 14 February 1866, 3; "The Circus," SMN, 21 October 1873, 3; "The Circus—'All Savannah' Under Canvas," SMN, 12 November 1879, 3.

9. "Proceedings of City Council," AC, 30 May 1869, 3; "Liberal," ADI, 1 June 1869, 3, RBP; "Ames Circus," AC, 4 June 1869, 3; "Great Eastern Menagerie and Circus," ADH, 3 December 1873, 4, RBP; "Handsome Benefit," AC, 4 December 1873, 3; Kathy Peiss, "Commercial Leisure and the 'Woman Question,'" in Butsch, *For Fun and Profit*, 108.

10. "The Circus," ANEG, 29 November 1872, 3.

11. "Stone and Murray's Combination Circus," SMN, 5 January 1871, 2; "Old John Robinson's Card—Tickets for Sale," SMN, 7 November 1871, 3; "James Robinson's Champion Circus," SMN, 1 February 1869, 2. Regarding the different methods of advance ticket sales see "James Robinson's Champion Circus," SMN, 1 February 1869, 2; "Van Amburg & Co.," SMN, 20 February 1878, 2; "Barnum and London United Shows," AC, 4 October 1886, 8; "Georgia and Florida," SMN, 5 October 1889, 6; "John Robinson Circus," SMN, 5 October 1919, 41; "Sparks Circus Pleases Large Crowds Here" GDN, 8 October 1927, 8, RBP.

12. "Matters and Things Laconically Noted," SMN, 10 November 1879, 3.

13. Foner, *Reconstruction*, 81–82; Litwack, *Been in the Storm So Long*, 310–16; Grant, *The Way It Was in the South*, 96–97; Trowbridge, *The Desolate South*, 244. Bill Arp quoted in Orville Vernon Burton, "The Rise and Fall of Afro-American Town Life: Town and Country in Reconstruction Edgefield, South Carolina," in Burton and McMath, *Toward a New South?*, 159.

14. Howard N. Rabinowitz, "Continuity and Change," in Brownell and Goldfield, *The City in Southern History*, 99.

15. William Burnet quoted in Rabinowitz, *Race Relations*, 22; "Circus To-Day," CDS, 12 October 1872, 3, RBP; "Caused a Scatteration," CDS, 28 December 1866, 3, RBP.

16. See ad for Stone, Rosston & Murray's Grand Combination Southern Circus, *Memphis Commercial Appeal*, 24 January 1866, 2, RBP.

17. "The Circus," CDS, 29 December 1866, 3, RBP. Here, Reid quotes a Montgomery, Alabama newspaper's discussion of the Thayer and Noyes Great United States Circus. The circus had traveled directly from Columbus, Georgia to Montgomery. See Reid, *After the War*, 377.

18. *Journal of House of Representatives of the State of Georgia*, 124–25. In 1917, the South Carolina legislature passed a law mandating separate entrances at "tent shows" for whites and blacks. Refer to Packard, *American Nightmare*, 92–93. On segregation at southern entertainment events, see Taylor, "The Negro Population," 249–50; Washington, "Recreational Facilities," 277; Konvitz, "Legally-Enforced Segregation," 431; Rabinowitz, "From Exclusion to Segregation," 328. The failed measure's sponsors may have been inspired by the successful passage of a 1905 Georgia state law that prohibited black and white people from using the same public parks. The reason for the proposed law's defeat does not appear in the source material, but since circuses that played in Georgia already offered segregated (albeit de facto) seating to their patrons, separate performances may have seemed unnecessary to Georgia legislators. See Wingo, "Race Relations," 140 and "Flood of New Bills Swamps Lower House," AC, 29 June 1907, 7. On Georgia's separate park law, see Franklin, "History of Racial Segregation in the United States," 8, and Dittmer, *Black Georgia*, 21.

19. "The Great Show," CST, 14 December 1867, 3, RBP; "John Robinson's Circus," CST, 15 December 1867, 3, RBP; "The Circus," CDS, 20 November 1868, 3, RBP; W. W. Durand, *Great Southern Advance Herald*, 1874, 7, RLPLRC; also see "The Circus," ADCS, 24 October 1873, 4; "W. W. Cole's Circus," CES, 1 December 1877, 4, RBP.

20. "Garathea," "A Racy Blast From a Clever Lady," ADH, 14 October 1875, 7, RBP. These themes are echoed in Porter, "The Circus," 36–41.

21. Wills, *Democratic Religion*, 125; *Ruston (LA) Baptist Chronicle*, 24 November 1892, quoted in Spain, *At Ease in Zion*, 201; "Local News," DN, 7 May 1920, 3, RBP; Mathews, *Religion in the Old South*, 40–46, 224. Also see Heyrman, *Southern Cross*, 249–52.

22. Click, *Spirit of the Times*, 5; ASW, 6 November 1867, 3; "Musical, Dramatic, & c.," SMN, 22 January 1870, 4; Ownby, *Subduing Satan*, 57, 64; Isenberg, *My Town and the Big Top*, 178, RLPLRC; Shuler, *Blood Mountain*, 115; "Local News," DN, 30 October 1908, 3, RBP.

23. Thayer, *Traveling Showmen*, 5–6, 75; "Dan Castello," SDH, 5 February 1866, 2; "The Circus is Here," CDS, 19 November 1867, 3, RBP. Also see "Col. Ames' Circus and Menagerie," SMN, 12 October 1870, 3.

24. A few large antebellum menagerie shows had used multiple tent arrangements to display all of their animals. See Thayer, *Annals*, 139. On the Barnum show and its multiple tents see Slout, *Royal Coupling*, 20, 45; Saxon, *Barnum*, 242; Kunhardt, Kunhardt, and Kunhardt, *P. T. Barnum*, 224, 229.

25. Slout, *Royal Coupling*, 21–23, 25; C. Fred Crosby, "The Early Days of Barnum's 'Greatest on Earth,'" BB 34 (21 January 1922): 49; Kunhardt, Kunhardt, and Kunhardt, *P. T. Barnum*, 107, 110, 222; Saxon, *P. T. Barnum*, 105–7; Allen Johnson, "Barnum, Phineas Taylor," in *Dictionary of American Biography*, 1964 ed.

26. Saxon, *Barnum*, 240–41; "All About a Circus," SMN, 14 September 1880, 3; Crosby, "The Early Days of Barnum's 'Greatest on Earth,'" 49. On the rapid adoption of the three-tent standard, see "Old John Robinson," SMN, 1 November 1871, 2; "Haight & Co's Circus, Museum, and Menagerie," SMN, 25 December 1871, 3; and "Haight & Co.'s Circus, Museum, and Menagerie," SMN, 2 January 1872, 2.

27. "Haight & Co.'s Circus, Museum, and Menagerie," SMN, 2 January 1872, 2; "'Old' John Robinson's Great Exposition," AC, 6 November 1872, 3; "Haight & Company's Empire City Circus," ASW, 7 February 1872, 2; Durand, *Great Southern*, 6, RLPLRC; "Haight & Co's Circus, Museum, and Menagerie," SMN, 25 December 1871, 3. Also see "The Coming Menagerie, Museum, and Circus," SMN, 3 January 1872, 3.

28. "Old John Robinson," ANEG, 25 November 1874, 3; Durand, *Great Southern*, 12, RLPLRC; "Van Amburg & Co.'s," SMN, 20 February 1878, 2; Dore, *Dore Bible Illustrations*.

29. Chipman, *"Hey Rube,"* 104–5; "The Mammoth Show," SMN, 6 December 1872, 3; "Old John Robinson's Great World's Exhibition," ANEG, 25 November 1874, 3; "Old John Robinson's Circus, SMN, 2 January 1875, 3; "John Robinson's Great Show," AC, 19 October 1876, 4, RBP; Wynes, "1865–1890," in Coleman, *History of Georgia*, 238–41.

30. Hull, *Annals of Athens*, 311; "Van Amburgh & Co's Circus," CES, 23 February 1878, 4, RBP; Ownby, *Subduing Satan*, 64; Francine Elizabeth Cox Greer King Diary (typescript), 1866–68, 6 November 1867, Oglethorpe County Diaries, ms. 3054, Box 1, HRBML.

31. "Coup's Circus," CES, 28 September 1880, 4, RBP; "The Circus! Details and Incidents of the Sawdust Arena," GDN, 30 October 1883, 1, RBP.

32. Ownby, *Subduing Satan*, 63–65. Also see Sparks, *On Jordan's Stormy Banks*, 146–73.

33. Edward T. Bishop Diary, 28 July 1877, Bishop Family Papers, 1857–1883, ms. 2345, Folder 1:31, HRBML; Jeannie Dubose quoted in Ownby, *Subduing Satan*, 63.

34. Edward T. Bishop Diary, 28 July 1877, Bishop Family Papers, HRBML; ASW, 6 November 1867, 3.

35. "My First Circus," *Atlanta Journal Sunday Magazine*, 31 October 1920, 1.

36. "Local Happenings," TDTE, 4 December 1897, 1; "Local Hotch Potch," TG, 13 November 1891, 1.

37. "Local Column," SH, 21 February 1878, 3; "Local Hotch Potch," TG, 13 November 1891, 1; "Coup's Circus," CES, 28 September 1880, 4, RBP.

38. "The Great Circus," *Clinton (MS) Baptist Record*, 27 November 1884. I thank Bland Whitley for supplying me with this source. Also see "Here You Have It," BB 22 (15 January 1910): 18, and Gladden, "Christianity and Popular Amusements," 384–92.

39. Ayers, *Promise*, 62–65, esp. 63; Kasson, *Amusing*, 4; Ezell, *South Since 1865*, 222–23; Dollard, *Caste and Class*, 76–77, Davis, Gardner, and Gardner, *Deep South*, 78–79; Allen, *Horrible Prettiness*, 146. Also see Stallybrass and White, *Politics and Poetics of Transgression*, 191–95, esp. 191.

40. See John Robinson ad in SMN, 3 December 1872, 2; *P. T. Barnum's Roman Hippodrome Advance Courier* quoted in Adams, *E Pluribus Barnum*, 32–33.

41. Saxon, *P. T. Barnum*, 97–98; "Great Eastern Menagerie and Circus," ADH, 3 December 1873, 4, RBP; Avery, *Idle Comments*, 36.

42. "19th Century Animal Booklets," 30–31; *Beneath White Tents: Official Route Book of the Ringling Brothers' World's Greatest Shows, Season of 1894* (Buffalo, N.Y.: Courier Co., 1894), 82–94, RLPLRC.

43. "Barnum and London United Shows," AC, 4 October 1886, 8; "A Big Compliment to Barnum," AC, 11 October 1886, 8.

44. "John Robinson," ASW, 23 October 1872, 3; "John Robinson," AC, 6 November 1872, 3; "Old John Robinson's Great Show," AC, 26 November 1872, 3; "City Intelligence," AC, 26 November 1872, 3.

45. Durand, *Great Southern*, 5, RLPLRC; "Howes' Circus," ACS, 10 April 1877, 4; "The Great Circus," ACS, 11 April 1877, 4.

46. "Howes' Circus," ACS, 10 April 1877, 4; "City Intelligence," AC, 28 November 1872, 3.

47. Durand, *Great Southern*, 2, RLPLRC; *Beneath White Tents*, 78–79, RLPLRC.

48. Reverend W. H. Sheak, "The Circus A Great Educational Institution," in *John Robinson's Route 1903: The Story of the Trip*, ed. "Punch" Wheeler (n.p., n.d.), 26, JRCCR. Also see "The John Robinson Shows," BB 17 (28 October 1905): 21.

49. *Wayne County News*, 18 November 1897, 3, RBP; "Pistol Shots," *Thomaston Middle Georgia Times*, 14 November 1885, 3, RBP; "Big Crowd Sees Circus in Statesboro," SMN, 19 October 1911, 5.

50. *Jackson Herald*, 15 October 1897, 3, RBP; "Big Crowd in Town," *LaGrange Reporter*, 21 October 1910, 5, RBP; "Many See Circus Here Saturday," CES, 22 October 1922, 11, RBP. Also refer to "Macon's Own Circus Opens Today," MDT, 5 April 1923, 1.

Chapter 4. Wait for the Big Show! The Economics of the Circus in Georgia, 1865–1920

1. "Robinson's Circus," AC, 2 March 1870, 3, RBP; "Around Town," DNGC, 28 April 1870, 3, RBP.

2. Cohen, *At Freedom's Edge*, 23–43; Foner, *Reconstruction*, 198–210; Ransom and Sutch, *One Kind of Freedom*, 116–20; Woodman, *King Cotton*, 269–77; Hahn, *Roots of Southern Populism*, 186–92; Doyle, *New Men*, 37–50; Russell, *Atlanta*, xvi, 109; Wetherington, *New South*, 47–62, 72–75; Ayers, *Promise*, 18–20, 58–59.

3. "A Great Crowd!" GDN, 4 November 1899, 1, RBP; "Record Crowd Came to Town to See Circus," ATR, 2 November 1911, 1, RBP.

4. Chindahl, *History*, 96–108; Slout, *Olympians*, 36, 130–31, 232–33; "The Late Adam Forepaugh," NYC, 1 February 1890, 774; "The Late John Robinson," NYC, 18 August 1888, 361; Bogdan, *Freak Show*, 81–83, quote appears on 83.

5. Doyle, *New Men*, 91; Russell, *Atlanta*, 128, 153–54.

6. "Came to See the Circus," SMN, 31 October 1890, 8.

7. "A Spirited Young Man," AC, 14 October 1890, 1; *Waynesboro True Citizen Extra*, 12 October 1883, 3; "Wait for the Big Show," AC, 6 September 1896, 6; "The Circus," SMN, 2 November 1890, 7. Also see "Dan Castello," SMN, 14 November 1868, 2; "Sells Brothers' Big Show," AC, 13 October 1895, 26; "Barnum & Bailey Greatest Show on Earth," AC, 14 October 1906, 8D; "John Robinson's 10 Big Shows," SMN, 23 October 1910, 39; Joseph T. Bradbury, author interview.

8. "Thousands Spent By Circus Here," AGN, 24 October 1908, 3, RBP; "Two Thousand People Turned Away from Robinson's Circus," SMN, 14 October 1904, 3; "It Takes Big Money," SMN, 12 October 1894, 8; Hugh F. Hoffman, comp., *John Robinson's Route: A Complete Compendium of the Tour and Incidents of John Robinson's Circus for the Season of 1901* (Jersey City, N.J.: Hoffman Brothers, 1901), 106, RLPLRC. For circuses and spending see "A City of Canvas," ANEG, 25 November 1873, 3, RBP; "All About a Circus," SMN, 14 September 1880, 3; "The Performance Last Night," CES, 21 October 1892, 4, RBP. For discussions of daily payouts by shows see advertisements for "Great Eastern," AC, 28 September 1872, 3; "John Robinson," AC, 3 October 1872, 2; "Barnum and London United Shows," AC, 4 October 1886, 8; "Old John Robinson's Great World Exposition," *Milledgeville Union & Recorder*, 2 December 1874, 3. For an example of small-town businessmen profiting from spending by a circus see "Chit Chat," SH, 21 February 1875, 3.

9. Durand, *Great Southern*, 2, RLPLRC.

10. "Matters and Things Laconically Noted," SMN, 4 January 1875, 3, and 25 October 1882, 4; "Lent's New York Circus," ADH, 31 October 1873, 4, RBP.

11. "Editorials," AI, 12 October 1907, 4; Gilmore, *Gender and Jim Crow*, 3–4.

12. "McHenry's Weekly Letter," AI, 13 October 1917, 5; Alf T. Ringling, "The Plantation Darkey at the Circus," in *With the Circus: A Route Book of Ringling Brothers World's Greatest Shows, Seasons of 1895 and 1896* (St. Louis: Great Western, n.d.), 112, RLPLRC.

13. An examination of the publication runs of the *Independent* from 1904 to 1913 and from 1916 to 1926 turned up advertisements for only three circuses, even though dozens of shows played the city during those years. See "Barnum and Bailey Show," AI, 13 October 1906, 6; "Robinson's Circus Here in Less Than One Week," AI, 1 October 1910, 1; "Barnum Circus in Atlanta," AI, 7 October 1911, 8.

14. Russell, *Atlanta*, 118, 127–28, 140, 260–63; Bartley, *Creation of Modern Georgia*, 110–11; Jensen, "Power and Progress," xii–xiii, 233, 238–39, 242–43; Blaine A. Brownell, "Urban South," in Brownell and Goldfield, *The City in Southern History*, 142; Woodward, *Origins*, 140–41, 150–53.

15. "Money in Columbus," CDS, 15 November 1865, 3; "The Circus," CE, 8 October 1871, 3, RBP; "Yesterday," CES, 18 November 1879, 4, RBP.

16. "Van Amburg & Co's Circus," CE, 23 February 1878, 4, RBP; "The Big Show Well Attended," CES, 12 November 1898, 3, RBP; "The Performance Last Night," CES, 21 October 1892, 4, RBP.

17. "Amusements in Savannah," SMN, September 20, 1871, 3; "Matters and Things Laconically Noted," SMN, 4 January 1875, 3, 12 November 1879, 3, and 25 October 1882, 4; "The News in the City," SMN, 10 November 1885, 8; "The Merchants Did Well," SMN, 11 October 1894, 8; "Merchants Ask Low Rates," SMN, 14 October 1894, 8; "The Day With the Circus," SMN, 15 November 1896, 8; Blaine A. Brownell, "Urban South," in Brownell and Goldfield, *The City in Southern History*, 142–43.

18. "A Study in Finance," BB 14 (11 January 1902): 8; "Merchants Say Circus Doesn't Benefit Town," SMN, 29 October 1904, 12.

19. "The Merchants Will Help," SMN, 7 October 1900, 19; "State Fair Would Pay Well," SMN, 13 December 1900, 10; "We Wonder Why," BB 22 (15 January 1910): 14;

"Amusement Enterprises and Circuses," BB 22 (29 January 1910): 14. On these other entertainments, see "Fair Opens to Eager Throngs," SMN, 9 November 1920, 5; "Circuses Barred by Prohibitive License," SMN, 1 October 1921, 12; "To Bar Tent Shows During Fair Season," SMN, 20 September 1923, 14; "Prohibitive Show Tax in Savannah, GA," BB 35 (20 October 1923): 80; "Robinson's Circus on Opening Day," SMN, 20 October 1927, 3; "The Georgia State Fair," and "Georgia State Fair Opens Today," SMN, 22 October 1928, 6 and 12.

20. Regarding Savannah's declining economic fortunes, see Steiner, "Changing Composition," 303, and Bartley, *Modern Georgia*, 105, 108.

21. "Merchants Ask Low Rates," SMN, 14 October 1894, 8; "Savannah's New Urban Population," BB 37 (11 July 1925): 58; U.S. Bureau of the Census, *Fourteenth Census of the United States*, 98–100, 192, 194; U.S. Bureau of the Census, *Thirteenth Census of the United States*, 30, 33. Concerning the population density in the vicinity of Columbus, see "Gossip Gathered Up," *Columbus Sunday Herald*, 28 November 1897, 3, RBP.

22. Bartley, *Modern Georgia*, 103–5; Shannon, *Politics in the New South*, 38–53. On the rise of a town business elite with an outlook similar to the state's urban economic boosters, see Wetherington, *New South*, 38–46.

23. "Lent's Circus," ANEG, 1 November 1873, 3; "Circus Circumstances," GWN, 7 November 1884, 10, RBP; "The Circurious," DNGC, 27 October 1881, 3.

24. "Record Crowd Came to Town to See Circus," ATR, 2 November 1911, 1, RBP; "Big Crowd in Town," *LaGrange Reporter*, 21 October 1910, 5, RBP; "Record Crowd Fills Griffin to Overflowing," GDNS, 17 October 1913, 1, RBP. On the sharp rise in the number of merchants in southern towns between 1870 and 1880, see Hahn, *Roots of Southern Populism*, 176–86 and Woodman, *King Cotton*, 325–28. For the merchant's role in southern towns, see Bull, "The General Merchant," 42 and Clark, *Pills, Petticoats and Plows*. On Circus Day commerce also see "The Day After the Circus," GDN, 29 October 1882, 6; "The Show Yesterday," GDN, 25 October 1890, 4, RBP; BB 34 (11 November 1922): 72; and "Rome Once More has a Circus Day," RTH, 22 September 1921, 5; thanks to Amy Louise Wood for sources from the *Tribune-Herald*.

25. Jay Rial, "Circus Day," BB 19 (2 February 1907): 8; Jay Rial, "What the Modern Circus Represents," BB 23 (15 April 1911): 10; "Gossip," BB 13 (23 March 1901): 5; "A Great Crowd!" GDN, 4 November 1899, 1, RBP; "The Circus Tax," BB 11 (1 November 1899): 2. Also see Gil Robinson, *Old Wagon Show Days*, 101 and "Does the Circus Pay?" BB 26 (10 January 1914): 65.

26. Powell, *I Can Go Home Again*, 73. For examples of small-town complaints about shows taking away too much money, see "Local Hotch-Potch," TG, 6 November 1891, 1; "The Show," *Sylvania Telephone*, 29 September 1911, 4, RBP; "Local News," DN, 31 May 1929, 3; "Local News," DN, 20 September 1929, 3, RBP; "Local News," DN, 4 October 1929, 3, RBP; "Live and Let Live," BB 38 (5 June 1926): 45.

27. *Monroe Advertiser*, 5 March 1878, 2, RBP; "Local News Briefly Told," *Swainsboro Forest Blade*, 12 November 1903, 3; "Local Matter," *Thomaston Herald*, 2 February 1878, 3, RBP.

28. "Local Hotch-Potch," TG, 23 December 1892, 1; "Lent's Circus," ANEG, 1 November 1873, 3; "The Circus," WTC, 24 October 1882, 5.

29. "Local News," *Moultrie Weekly Observer*, 3 January 1895, 3, RBP; "Big Show was

a Big Fake," *Statesboro News*, 8 December 1905, 1, RBP. In 1889, Sumner officials provided a "license" permitting Howe's circus to run rigged gambling operations while the show was in town to perform; see "Howe's New London Show," *Sumner Worth Local*, 12 January 1889, 2, RBP.

30. "Lent's Circus and Menagerie," ASW, 29 October 1872, 3; "Mighty Haag Show a Mighty Fraud," GDN, 24 November 1909, 4, RBP; *Jones County News,* 27 October 1921, 5, RBP.

31. Clark, *Southern Country Editor*, 34–38; "Local Leaflets," MJ, 26 November 1885, 3; "Local News Briefly Told," *Swainsboro Forest Blade*, 12 November 1903, 3; "Locals and Other News," DN, 31 May 1929, 2.

32. Horowitz, *Morality of Spending*; Ayers, *Promise*, 92–93; Ownby, *American Dreams*, 76–81; "Charles Belvin" entry in *Diary, 1880–82* and "Hal Forhand" and "Jim Belvin" entries in *Diary, 1888–1892*, both in James Daniel Frederick Collection, ms. 79, Box 1, HRBML; "How He Got to See the Circus," *Dublin Post*, 7 December 1881, 1.

33. For examples of circus bankruptcies, see "In the Arena," ACS, 18 January 1877, 4; "Richmond County Sheriff's Sale," ACS, 19 January 1877, 3; "A Circus Sold," ACS, 30 January 1877, 4; "A Show in Trouble," AJ, 18 March 1889, 3, RBP; "A Circus in Court," AC, 19 March 1889, 7, RBP; "Another Circus Sale," AC, 8 January 1886, 7, RBP and "Disposing of the Animals," AC, 20 January 1886, 2. On the creation of the Atlanta Zoo, see "The Stranded Circus," AJ, 20 March 1889, 3, RBP; "A Circus at Auction," AJ, 28 March 1889, 1, RBP; "Will Have a Zoo," AC, 29 March 1889, 5, RBP; "Gress' Generosity," AC, 30 March 1889, 8, RBP; and "Atlanta's Zoo," AJ, 30 March 1889, 4, RBP.

34. "Colonel Giles's Circus," AC, 16 December 1885, 7; "The Circus Sold," AC, 8 January 1886, 2. For the broader history of this episode, including the postauction overland walk of the elephant and two camels from Monroe to Atlanta, see Sams, *Wayfarers in Walton*, 231–37.

35. Clark, *Southern Country Editor*, 153, 155–57; GDN, 8 November 1885, 1.

36. DNGC, 19 September 1901, 1; "S. Schwarzweiss," *Waynesboro True Citizen Extra*, 17 October 1882, 1; GDN, 30 October 1885, 1; "The Hub," WTC, 16 October 1920, 5. More generally, see Ownby, *American Dreams*, 89–90 and Davis, *Circus Age*, 29.

37. "Circus Gossip," BB 14 (October 4, 1902): 11; "Circus Gossip," BB 14 (November 1, 1902): 12; "Circus Gossip," BB 16 (October 1, 1904): 25; "Wants a Circus," BB 16 (October 1, 1904): 11; "Cornelia (GA.) Wants A Circus," BB 26 (18 July 1914): 28.

38. "The Passing Throng," AC, 30 November 1901, 3, RBP; Chas. Bernard, "Cause and Effect in Georgia," BB 36 (12 January 1924): 76; Foster, *Digest of the Laws of the State of Georgia*, 327–28; "No Decision Yet on Circus Tax Question," SMN, 17 September 1923, 12; Garrett, *Atlanta*, 1: 246–47; "Circuses," NYC, 16 July 1870, 119; "Circuses," NYC, 27 May 1871, 62; "Circuses," NYC, 8 February 1873, 359; "Circuses," NYC, 27 June 1874; "Miscellaneous," NYC, 3 March 1866, 37; "The Stage and the Arena," ADNE, 10 March 1870, 3, RBP; U.S. Department of the Interior, *Ninth Census*, 105.

39. "The Circus is Coming—Tax Upon it," DAI, 12 February 1869, 1, RBP; Harris, *Humbug*, 255–56; Capt. W. D. Ament, "High License," BB 13 (13 April 1901): 6; "A Circus Pays $1010 in Taxes," AJ, 27 October 1903, 5, RBP; "The Circus Tax," BB 11 (1 November 1899): 2.

40. "The Circus is Coming—Tax Upon it," DAI, 12 February 1869, 1, RBP; "Tax on

Circuses," DAI, 17 February 1869, 3, RBP. The Georgia state law of 1869 called for circuses that appeared in cities of over 10,000 people to pay $100, cities of 5,000 to 10,000 to pay $50, and towns to pay $25. See "Georgia Legislature," AC, 10, 11, 12, and 13 February 1869, 1. The city of Rome used the "rail car" method in the 1920s, charging for less than 15 cars, $100; 15 to 40 cars, $150; over 40 cars, $200; see Bernard, "Cause and Effect," 76.

41. "Cartersville, Georgia—9-25-09," Series III, Box 15, Folder 35, JRCCR; "City Ordinances—Town of Stockbridge, Ga.," *Henry County Weekly*, 14 September 1900, 2, RBP; "City Government," SMN, 16 September 1880, 3.

42. "Prohibitive Show Tax in Savannah, GA," BB 35 (20 October 1923): 80; "City Government," SMN, 13 October 1923, 12; "Cigarettes, Carnivals, and Circuses are Outlawed," *Fitzgerald Leader Enterprise*, 21 January 1914, 1; "Cheap Shows and their Damage to a Town," *Jackson Herald,* 5 October 1911, 4, RBP.

43. "Howe's Great London Show," CES, 11 November 1909, 8, RBP; "Why Big Circus Doesn't Come," CES, 14 October 1908, 3, RBP; "Circus Taxes Were Reduced," CES, 6 January 1910, 6, RBP; Bernard, "Cause and Effect," 76; Circus Solly, "Under the Marquee," BB 28 (4 November 1916): 23; "Circus License," BB 34 (11 February 1922): 97; "Washington (Ga.) Tax," BB 35 (10 February 1923): 74; Washington (Ga.) Tax," BB 36 (2 February 1924): 76; "Washington, GA Licenses," BB 38 (30 January 1926): 100.

44. "Local Leaflets," MJ, 26 November 1885, 3; "Georgia News," CDES, 29 January 1878, 3; 30 January 1878, 3; 7 February 1878, 3; and 5 February 1878, 3, RBP; "Sparks Shows," *Dublin Times*, 19 December 1904, 6; "City Ordinances for 1902," *Henry County Weekly*, 7 March 1902, 4, RBP; "Special Tax Ordinances, McDonough, Ga. 1910," *Henry County Weekly*, 8 April 1910, 4, RBP. The town of Barnesville had a similar clause but charged $50. Refer to "License Ordinances for Year 1912–1913," BG, 26 September 1912, 6, RBP.

45. "Heavy Animal Tax May Keep Animal Show Away," SMN, 5 October 1907, 12; "A Circus Pays $1010 in Taxes," AJ, 27 October 1903, 5, RBP; "Dublin Doubles Circus License," *Fitzgerald Leader-Enterprise and Press,* 19 September 1917, 8; Circus Solly, "Under the Marquee," BB 29 (20 October 1917): 29.

46. "The Wolf Book," BB 13 (12 January 1901): 8.

47. Eckley, *American Circus*, 26; "A Big Circus," SMN, 24 November 1900, 6. Also see "Circus Preparing to Move," SMN, 25 March 1901, 8.

48. The financial benefits of a wintering show for the host community are discussed in "Circus," NH, 27 March 1874, 3, RBP; "Sun Show May Winter Here," AJ, 11 November 1901, 3, RBP; "Show Will Winter Here," *Oglethorpe Echo*, 15 January 1904, 1, RBP; "Circus Winters at Piedmont," AN, 20 December 1905, 2, RBP; "Circus Comes to the City," VDT, 12 December 1907, 5, RBP; "Circus Will Make its Home in Valdosta," VT, 4 March 1912, 1, RBP; "Deal Closed for Robinson Circus to Winter in Americus," ATR, 3 November 1916, 1, RBP.

49. "Deal Closed for Robinson Circus to Winter in Americus," ATR, 3 November 1916, 1, RBP. Also see "Circus Will Make its Home in Valdosta," VT, 4 March 1912, 1, RBP. "Circus May Move On," SMN, 31 December 1900, 8; "Circus Will Remain Here," SMN, 2 January 1901, 8; "Circus in Winter Quarters," SMN, 14 January 1901, 8; "Circus

Gossip," BB 13 (2 February 1901): 7; "Sells & Gray's Circus Here," VT, 27 November 1900, 8, RBP.

50. For an example of this variety of New South boosterism, see "Why Some Towns Grow," *Toccoa Record*, 26 February 1914, 6.

51. "Levy's Jewelry Store," MDT, 5 April 1923, 10.

Chapter 5. The Canvas City: Social Mixing on Circus Day, 1870–1920

1. "In the City," GDN, 28 October 1882, 8; "The Day After the Circus," GDN, 29 October 1882, 6.

2. Thayer, *Traveling Showmen*, 16, 19; "Barnum and London United Shows," AC, 4 October 1886, 8; "Barnum's Show," AC, 13 October 1886, 8.

3. Durand, *Great Southern*, 5, RLPLRC; "Great Eastern," SMN, 16 September 1872, 2; Thayer, *Traveling Showmen,* 69–72; "The Day After the Circus," GDN, 29 October 1882, 6.

4. "A Welcome Visitor," AC, 7 October 1886, 8; HR, 17 October 1894, 7; "Circus Day Drew Thousands to City," CES, 26 October 1906, 6. Also see "W. W. Cole's," SMN, 1 November 1879, 3.

5. Bakhtin, *Rabelais and His World*, 7; Lears, *Fables of Abundance*, 23.

6. "The Circus," *Bainbridge Democrat*, 23 October 1890, 2; "Yesterday," CES, 18 November 1879, 4; Mell Marshall Barrett quoted in Ownby, *Subduing Satan*, 58; "It Has Come and Gone," *Cartersville News and Courant*, 26 September 1901, 1. On the "buoyant democracy" of Circus Day see Ownby, *Subduing Satan*, 58.

7. "Town Topics," AC, 25 September 1875, 3, RBP; "His Dates Mixed," BB 14 (1 March 1902): 5; Georgia Department of Archives and History, *Vanishing Georgia*, 6; Edward T. Bishop Diary, 28 July 1877, Bishop Family Papers, HRBML; Shettles, *Recollections*, 45; "The Great Wallace Circus," CES, 31 October 1901, 8, RBP; "The Circus," CES, 3 November 1883, 4, RBP; Thomason, *Trying Times*, 98.

8. "The Circus Yesterday," CES, 16 November 1887, 4, RBP; "The Circus," TDTE, 19 November 1895, 1; "The Crowd Yesterday," CES, 22 October 1881, 4, RBP; "The Circus," HR, 18 September 1894, 1; "Round A-Bout," GDN, 14 November 1885, 4; "The Circus," CES, 3 November 1883, 4, RBP; "The Circus," CES, 28 November 1877, 4, RBP; "Come to the Circus," CES, 29 November 1877, 4, RBP; "Forepaugh's Circus," CES, 10 November 1882, 4, RBP; "City Brevities," SMN, 31 October 1890, 8; "Circus Comes To-morrow," SMN, 24 October 1902, 6.

9. *Beneath White Tents*, 35–36, RLPLRC; "Great Eastern," SMN, 16 September 1872, 2; Durand, *Great Southern*, 8, RLPLRC; "Record Crowd Fills Griffin to Overflowing," GDNS, 17 October 1913, 1, RBP; "We Missed the Circus," ATR, 10 October 1894, 4.

10. Wynes, "1865–1890," in Coleman, *History of Georgia*, 247; "Circus Gossip," BB 15 (31 October 1903): 9.

11. "Local Happenings," TDTE, 2 December 1897, 1; "Town and Country," *Bulloch Times*, 12 November 1896, 5, RBP.

12. "Going to the Show," AR, 31 October 1884, 7.

13. "The Crowd Yesterday," CES, 22 October 1881, 4, RBP; "Circus Today in Mari-

etta," AJ, 13 October 1899, 4, RBP; "Record Crowd Fills Griffin to Overflowing," GDNS, 17 October 1913, 1, RBP. Also see "Barnum & Bailey," HR, 16 October 1894, 1.

14. "The Great Wallace Circus," CES, 31 October 1901, 8, RBP; "Circus Was a Great Day in Columbus," CES, 4 November 1905, 3, RBP.

15. "Here, There and Everywhere," CES, 21 October 1892, 4, RBP; "All School Children See Circus Parade," SMN, 19 October 1912, 12.

16. "Local Happenings," TDTE, 20 November 1895, 1; "To See the Circus," AC, 3 November 1896, 7; "Local News," DN, 7 May 1920, 3; "Circus Day in Atlanta," SMN, 29 October 1892, 2; "Georgia and Florida," SMN, 30 October 1890, 6.

17. "Almost a Riot," AJ, 15 October 1894, 1, RBP; TDTE, 17 November 1894, 3; "Pen Points," AR, 31 October 1884, 5.

18. "Vast Crowd at Circus," ATR, 30 November 1897, 4, RBP; "Cole's Circus," AEC, 31 October 1885, 3, RBP; "The Circus," BG, 16 November 1882, 3.

19. "Circus Circumstances," GWN, 7 November 1884, 10, RBP; U.S. Department of the Interior, *Eleventh Census*, 96; "An Old Ocilla Paper," *Ocilla Star*, 10 December 1909, 1; U.S. Bureau of the Census, *Fourteenth Census of the United States*, 192.

20. Cf. Waller, *Main Street Amusements*, 61; Evelyn Harden Jackson Diary, 1885–1887, 4 November 1885, Harden-Jackson-Carithers Collection, ms. 45, Box 4, Folder 5, HRBML; "The Big Show Yesterday," *Rome Weekly Commercial*, 13 October 1875, 4.

21. "The Circus Yesterday," CES, 16 November 1887, 4, RBP; "The Circus," *Bainbridge Democrat*, 23 October 1890, 2; "Big Crown [sic] Saw Big Show," *Crawford County News*, 19 November 1909, 1, RBP. Also see "Barnum's Show," AC, 13 October 1886, 8.

22. "Old Time Circus," TDTE, 14 October 1894, 1; "Circus Circumstances," GWN, 7 November 1884, 10, RBP; "Cole's Success," SMN, 10 November 1885, 8; Edward T. Bishop Diary, 28 July 1877, Bishop Family Papers, HRBML. For plebian European fairgoers becoming the "object of the respectable gaze," see Stallybrass and White, *Politics and Poetics of Transgression*, 42.

23. "Incidental Scenes on the Streets and Under the Canvas," CES, 9 December 1876, 4, RBP.

24. "Sarge Plunkett," AC, 7 October 1900, 24; Evelyn Harden Jackson Diary, 1879–1881, 27 October 1881, Harden-Jackson-Carithers Collection, ms. 45, Box 4, Folder 4, HRBML.

25. "Circus Crowds Were Disappointed," SMN, 21 October 1913, 14; "Circus Day," CDES, 23 February 1878, 4; "Pick Pockets," HR, 17 October 1894, 2; "Georgia and Florida," SMN, 13 November 1885, 5; "The News of Valdosta," SMN, 26 October 1901, 2.

26. "They Want Bonds," HR, 17 October 1894, 7; "Less Disorder in Rome Than Expected," RTH, 12 October 1911, 1; "The Circus," WTC, 27 October 1882, 5.

27. "The Show," *Sylvania Telephone*, 29 September 1911, 4, RBP; "The City," ADNE, 26 November 1870, 3, RBP.

28. "'Round-A-Bout," GDN, 15 November 1885, 1; TDTE, 17 November 1894, 3; "Circus Personals," ADH, 12 October 1875, 5, RBP; a Col. Mick Edwards, a Dr. Cherry, and a Dr. Gamble also turned out for the circus in Atlanta.

29. Butsch, *American Audiences*, 34–36; Allen, *Horrible Prettiness*, 53–54.

30. "'Round-A-Bout,'" GDN, 15 November 1885, 1; "Cole's Circus," AEC, 31 October 1885, 3, RBP; "In The City," GDN, 28 October 1882, 8.

31. Evelyn Harden Jackson Diary, 1911–1912, 11 October 1911, Harden-Jackson-Carithers Collection, ms. 45, Box 5, HRBML.

32. "Local News," DN, 7 May 1920, 3; Robinson, *Old Wagon Show Days*, 158–59.

33. "The Big Show Well Attended," CES, 12 November 1898, 3, RBP; "Fun at the Circus," AC, 3 November 1891, 9, RBP.

34. Mischler, "Greatest Show on Earth," 108; "Circus Delights All Sorts and Conditions of Atlanta People," AC, 3 November 1896, 7.

35. "Notes from John Robinson's Ten Big Shows," BB 13 (29 June 1901): 4. The incident with Cole took place in Warren, Pennsylvania, but this type of street theater was repeated at every tour stop, including the southern dates. See, for example, Hugh F. Hoffman, *John Robinson's Route*, 100, RLPLRC. Also refer to "Main's Big Show Carries Old Time Circus Parade," AN, 13 October 1902, 7, RBP; Davis, *Circus Age*, 173.

36. "Fun at the Circus," AC, 3 November 1891, 9, RBP.

37. Thompson, *On the Road With a Circus*, 179–80; "The Great Eastern Circus," SMN, 18 November 1873, 3; "John Robinson Circus and Menagerie," CDS, 1 January 1873, 3, RBP; William D. Piersen, "African-American Festive Style," in Caponi, *Signifyin(g), Sanctifyin', and Slam Dunking*, 421.

38. On snack stands see photos in "African-American" folder, Small Collections, RLPLRC; Ringling, "Plantation Darkey," 113–14, RLPLRC; "John Robinson's Tour of 1903, Second Part," in Wheeler, *John Robinson's Route 1903: The Story of the Trip*, 3, JRCCR; Thompson, *On the Road with a Circus*, 50; Susan Fan Tate Oral Interview, Athens-Clarke Heritage Foundation Oral History Project, 1976, 9, ms. 2209, Box 1, Folder 51, HRBML; Tate, *Remembering Athens*, 41.

39. Cooper and Terrill, *American South*, 590; George Ade, "With the Elephant and the Clown in Dixie," in *The Red Wagon Annual: A Circus Year Book of Ringling Brothers World's Greatest Shows, Souvenir 1899*, (n.p., n.d.), 29, RLPLRC.

40. Marsh, *Hitch Up the Buggy*, 73; "The Circus," *Bainbridge Democrat*, 23 October 1890, 2. Also see the photo of the social scene around some snack stands (Circus World Museum RB-np-16-47) in this book's photo section.

41. Ringling, "Plantation Darkey," 113, RLPLRC; Robinson, *Old Wagon Show Days*, 57. For the showman's sense that snack stands were essential for creating a festive atmosphere on Circus Day, see "Some of Bailey's Plans," BB 13 (26 January 1901): 8.

42. "The Circus," *Bainbridge Democrat*, 23 October 1890, 2; "Circus Scored a Great Success," CES, 19 October 1904, 5, RBP; "The Country Darkey," AR, 20 November 1885, 4, RBP.

43. Ringling, "Plantation Darkey," 110–11, RLPLRC; "Editorials," AI, 12 October 1907, 4; "The Circus," *Macon County Citizen*, 19 November 1909, 5, RBP.

44. Robinson, *Old Wagon Show Days*, 59–60; Ringling, "Plantation Darkey," 112, RLPLRC; "The Circus! Details and Incidents of the Sawdust Arena," GDN, 30 October 1883, 1, RBP; West, "'Before We Reach the Heavenly Fields'," 343–44; J. A. Jackson, "The Negro of the Outdoor Show," BB 33 (19 March 1921): 17.

45. "Town and Country," VT, 10 February 1894, 8, RBP; Balinda (Estella) Merriam

Spencer Diary, Season 1889 (typescript), 28, RLPLRC. For other examples of circuses and revivals playing in opposition to each other, see "The John Robinson Shows," BB 17 (28 October 1905): 21; Dolly Varden, "Dolly Varden's Letter," BB 19 (31 August 1907): 24; Eddie Deck, "Sells-Floto Triumphs in South," BB 29 (13 October 1917): 28–29; *Beneath White Tents*, 158, RLPLRC.

46. "The Tent Meeting," HR, 20 September 1894, 2; "Rents in a Gospel Tent," SMN, 19 November 1890, 2; "Gospel Meetings," WTC, 15 November 1890, 3; "The Gospel Meetings," WTC, 22 November 1890, 3. Also see "Gave Rome the Go By," AC, 17 October 1895, 3; Hoffman, comp., *John Robinson's Route*, 109–10, RLPLRC.

47. "To See the Show," CES, 1 December 1877, 4, RBP; BG, 16 November 1882, 3; "An Editor at the Circus," *Dublin Post*, 2 November 1881, 2.

48. "A Few Words of Warning," GDN, 14 November 1885, 4.

49. "'Round-A-Bout," GDN, 15 November 1885, 1; "The Police Were Active," ATR, 10 October 1894, 5, RBP; marginal notation in *[John Robinson Circus] Cash Account Journal, 24 July to 17 November 1911*, 7 November 1911 [p. 184], Series VIII, Item 18, JRCCR. Also see "'Circus Drunks' Just Half Bad, Says Judge," AG, 29 October 1913, 7, RBP.

50. "Local Leaflets," MJ, 26 November 1885, 3; Szymanski, "Beyond Parochialism," 119; *Reddick v. The State*, 15 Ga. App. 437, 83 S. E. 675 (1914); "Circus at Alapaha," *Berrien County Pioneer*, 7 November 1890, 3, RBP; "Short Stops," *Early County News*, 30 November 1905, 3, RBP. Also see Root, *Ways of the Circus*, 93.

51. "Georgia Items," ANEG, 22 November 1872, 2; Thompson, *On the Road with a Circus*, 161–62; Larsen, *Urban South*, 135–38. Also see "Two Thousand People Turned Away From Robinson's Circus," SMN, 14 October 1904, 3, and "Howes' Great London Circus," AC, 26 September 1875, 3

52. "Monday's Circus," VT, 22 November 1890, 5; "Circus Day at Valdosta," SMN, 18 November 1890, 3; "Home News," *Newnan Herald and Advertiser*, 20 November 1896, 7, RBP; "Circus Day," CDES, 23 February 1878, 4; "May Result in Death," ATR, 30 November 1897, 4, RBP. On the decline of violence against circus men in the South, see Kelly, *Clown*, 95.

53. "May Result in Death," ATR, 30 November 1897, 4, RBP.

54. "Circus Day in Cordele," VT, 7 December 1897, 1, RBP.

55. "Stabbing Affrays at Rome," AC, 3 October 1900, 2; "Circus Brings a Carnival of Lawlessness," RTH, 22 September 1921, 1.

56. Root, *Ways of the Circus*, 92; Chipman, *"Hey Rube,"* 13; "Monday's Circus," VT, 22 November 1890, 5; "In the City," GDN, 28 October 1882, 8.

57. "Less Disorder in Rome Than Expected," RTH, 12 October 1911, 1; "One Arrest Circus Day," *Moultrie Daily Observer*, 13 November 1906, 1, RBP; "Big Crown [sic] Saw Big Show," *Crawford County News*, 19 November 1909, 1, RBP. On the development of professional police forces in the New South, see Larsen, *Urban South*, 135–41.

58. "Circus Day in Cordele," VT, 7 December 1897, 1, RBP; "The Circus," WTC, 27 October 1882, 5.

59. Robinson, *Old Wagon Show Days*, 149–50.

60. "The Circus," SDNH, 15 November 1866, 3; Slout, *Olympians*, 389–90. For examples of circus animal escapes in the South, see "Matinee in a Menagerie," AC, 18

December 1875, 2, and "Big Snake; Wild Man Cause Stir at Millen," AC, 7 October 1906, B8.

61. "Georgia and Florida," SMN, 30 November 1887, 6; Williams, *History of Tift County*, 360.

62. Cole, *Hair Straight'ner*, 64; "Georgia and Florida," SMN, 22 October 1895, 6; "Elephant Got Away," *Augusta Chronicle*, 20 December 1907, 10, RBP. For an exception to this way of thinking, see "The Circus," *Jesup Sentinel*, 27 October 1880, 3.

63. "Elephant Gypsy Goes Wild and is Killed Near Here," VT, 25 November 1902, 5, RBP; "Elephant Throws Valdosta Into a Panic After Killing Driver," AJ, 24 November 1902, 2, RBP. Gypsy had a history of violence. In 1897, Gypsy killed her trainer and another man in Chicago. Gypsy's "execution" was stopped by that city's Humane Society. See "The Nickel Plate Show," TDTE, 8 December 1897, 3.

64. "Elephant Gypsy Goes Wild and is Killed Near Here," VT, 25 November 1902, 5, RBP; "Elephant Throws Valdosta Into a Panic After Killing Driver," AJ, 24 November 1902, 2, RBP.

65. "Elephant Gypsy Goes Wild and is Killed Near Here," VT, 25 November 1902, 5, RBP; "Elephant Throws Valdosta Into a Panic After Killing Driver," AJ, 24 November 1902, 2, RBP; "Some More Elephant Talk," VT, 29 November 1902, 5; "Elephant Talk Continued," VT, 9 December 1902, 5. Also see "Killed Her Keeper," SMN, 24 November 1902, 1; "Chase of Elephant at Valdosta," SMN, 25 November 1902, 2. On souvenir-gathering in the aftermath of lynchings, see Litwack, *Trouble in Mind*, 280–91.

66. "The Circus," SMN, 11 October 1884, 4; "The Elephant and the Clown," SMN, 12 October 1884, 8.

Chapter 6. Performers in Bleachers: Audience Behavior and Social Interaction in Turn-of-the-Century Circus Tents

1. "Incidental Scenes on the Streets and Under the Canvas," CES, 9 December 1876, 4, RBP.

2. Kasson, *Rudeness and Civility*, 3–7. Also see Howe, "American Victorianism as a Culture," 507–32, and Levine, *Highbrow/Lowbrow*, 195–97.

3. Harris, *Humbug*, 240–41; Kasson, *Rudeness and Civility*, 248; Trachtenberg, *Incorporation of America*, 231; Butsch, *Making of American Audiences*, 120. For the 1872 date for the first ever two-ring show, see Fred Dahlinger, "Circus Big Tops," unpublished paper, 1999, RLPLRC. Cf. Slout, *Royal Coupling*, 47, 58, 60; and Davis, *Circus Age*, 20–21.

4. "A Great Show," AJ, 25 October 1890, 11.

5. Schultz, *Rural Face of White Supremacy*, 67. For examples of how African Americans sought to stake out social, cultural, and economic spaces for themselves despite the burdens of Jim Crow, see Hunter, *To 'joy my Freedom*, and Jones, *Labor of Love*. Two works that emphasize the bleaker aspects of life in the Jim Crow South are Litwack, *Trouble in Mind*, and McMillen, *Dark Journey*.

6. "A Study in Black in White," BB 29 (28 April 1917): 48; "The Circus Parade," BB 19 (16 March 1907): 76; Jack Warren, "John Robinson's Ten Big Shows," BB 20 (26 September 1908): 20; "The Circus—Last Day," SMN, 11 November 1871, 3.

7. On midways refer to Fox and Parkinson, *Circus in America*, 204, and "The Circus Has Come and Gone," CES, 10 November 1896, 5, RBP.

8. Kirk, *Locust Hill*, 88; "1,000 Eyes are Needed," *Baltimore American*, 17 May 1907, clipping in *Barnum and Bailey Press Clipping Book 1906–07*, RMC. On the development of sideshow banner lines see Pfening, "Side Shows and Bannerlines," 16–22.

9. "The Great Wallace Circus," CES, 31 October 1901, 6, RBP; P. M. Silloway, "The Modernized Circus," BB 38 (2 October 1926): 84; "The Ringling's Big Show," SMN, 7 November 1896, 8. Also see *Beneath White Tents*, 74, RLPLRC.

10. Woodward, *Strange Career*, 99–100; "Two Cyclones Couldn't Spoil Best Season of Greatest Show on Earth," *Bridgeport (CT) Farmer*, 21 November 1906, in *Barnum and Bailey Press Clipping Book 1906–07*, RMC. Contrast with the discussion of separate seating areas, entrances, and ticket windows offered by southern movie houses in the early twentieth century in Litwack, *Trouble in Mind*, 233.

11. Davis, *Circus Age*, 3; "Great Eastern Expert," ADCS, 28 October 1873, 4; "John Robinson's Circus," CST, 15 December 1867, 3, RBP. On the celebrity of ticket agents see Slout, *Royal Coupling*, 33–34;"Barnum's Show," AC, 13 October 1886, 8; unattributed and undated "Billy Vogt" clipping in *Ringling Bros. Press Clipping Book, 1896*, RMC.

12. Bogdan, *Freak Show*, 86–87; Kunhardt, Kunhardt, and Kunhardt, *Barnum*, 325; BB 25 (11 October 1913): 26; "At Police Headquarters," AC, 13 October 1886, 5.

13. Gollmar, *My Father Owned a Circus*, 154–55. Also see Dolly Varden, "Dolly Varden's Letter," BB 19 (19 October 1907): 24, and "Circuses," NYC, 12 December 1868, 287.

14. "Circus Side Scenes," AC, 16 October 1894, 7, RBP. On the nineteenth-century fear of "confidence men," see Halttunen, *Confidence Men*.

15. Robert Bogdan, "The Social Construction of Freaks," in Thomson, *Freakery*, 27; "1,000 Eyes are Needed," *Baltimore American*, 17 May 1907, clipping in *Barnum and Bailey Press Clipping Book 1906–07*, RMC.

16. Clifford E. Watkins, "Marching Bands," in Salzman, Smith, and West, *The Encyclopedia of African American Culture and History*, 3:1688–89; Joseph T. Bradbury interview.

17. Jackson, "The Negro of the Outdoor Show," BB 33 (19 March 1921): 17; "A Ten Minute Potpourri About Things in General," in Hoffman, *John Robinson's Route*, 20, RLPLRC; "Best Circus Ever Shown," CES, 7 October 1911, 8, RBP. Also see Jack Moore, "Hagenbeck-Wallace Shows," BB 26 (12 September 1914): 22.

18. O. A. Peterson, "Musical Musings," BB 32 (25 December 1920): 35; Watkins, "Marching Bands," 1690; "P. G. Lowery's Band," BB 34 (25 March 1922): 45.

19. "Cole's Success," SMN, 10 November 1885, 8.

20. Jordan, *White Over Black*, 3–43; Bogdan, *Freak Show*, 176–99; "The Circus," SMN, 12 November 1879, 3; Williams, *History of Tift County*, 357; Floyd King, "Ticket-Wagon Magnets of Other Days," BB 26 (18 December 1915): 51, 146. More generally, see Lindfors, "Circus Africans," 9–14.

21. Joseph T. Bradbury interview.

22. Davis, *Circus Age*, 118; *Beneath White Tents*, 72, RLPLRC; Robert Bogdan, "The Social Construction of Freaks," in Thomson, *Freakery*, 27; Charles Andress, "Circus Shadowgraphs," BB 26 (18 July 1914): 31; Parkinson and Fox, *Circus in America*, 204;

"It Was Such a Day As Will Be Handed Down in History," *Hagerstown (MD) Evening Globe*, 19 May 1907 clipping in *Barnum and Bailey Press Clipping Book 1906–07*, RMC; Bogdan, *Freak Show*, 14.

23. "Circus Side Scenes," AC, 16 October 1894, 7, RBP; "Bloody Heads at the Circus," AC, 10 November 1898, 10, RBP; "Pulled an Attraction," TDTE, 19 November 1895, 1; "Local Happenings," TDTE, 20 November 1895, 1.

24. "A Hog Genius," *Rome Weekly Commercial*, 15 September 1875, 3. Of course, as David Carlyon points out, few people outside of show business knew that pigs could "learn in days what might take a horse two or three years" to master and that these types of performances depended wholly on subtle cues used by the handler to prompt their porcine partners to react to the cards. Consult Carlyon, *Dan Rice*, 32–38, esp. 34, and Ricky Jay, *Learned Pigs*, 8–27.

25. Adrian D. Sharpe, "Circus Grift on the Yankee Robinson Circus," *Bandwagon* 14 (Nov.–Dec. 1970): 35. Also see Orin C. King, "The World in a Nut Shell: Wallace & Co., 1890 & 1891," *Bandwagon* 28 (March–Apr. 1984): 21–26, and Thayer, *Traveling Showmen*, 65–68.

26. Davis, *Circus Age*, 61; "Howe's New London Show," *(Sumner) Worth Local*, 12 January 1889, 2, RBP.

27. John Hanners, "The Dark Side of the American Circus," 8, undated article in "Grift" folder, vertical files, RLPLRC; King, "The World in a Nut Shell," 23; "Big Show Was a Big Fake," *Statesboro News*, 8 December 1905, 1, RBP; "Town Topics," *Vienna News*, 2 November 1899, 8, RBP; Sharpe, "Circus Grift," 32; Geo. H. Irving, "The Fixer," BB 35 (24 March 1923): 77. For a Georgia lawman refusing to condone gambling, see "Objectionable Features Cut out of Show," GDNS, 17 October 1913, 1, RBP.

28. "The Shell Trick Man," *Dawson News*, 30 November 1892, 1; Bogdan, *Freak Show*, 81–83.

29. "Items in Three States," SMN, 24 November 1890, 6. For a discussion of the era's gaming techniques, see Quinn, *Gambling and Gambling Devices*.

30. "News and Gossip," *Middle Georgia Progress*, 1 December 1896, 1, RBP; "The Shell Trick Man," *Dawson News*, 30 November 1892, 1, RBP; "Howe's New London Show," *(Sumner) Worth Local*, 12 January 1889, 2, RBP. Also see "Local News," DN, 30 October 1908, 3, RBP.

31. "Chases Circus Till He Recovers Money," AG, 29 October 1913, 1, RBP; "The Shell Trick Man," *Dawson News*, 30 November 1892, 1, RBP; Clark, *Southern Country Editor*, 159.

32. Isaac, *Transformation of Virginia*, 88–114; Breen, "Horses and Gentlemen," 239–57; Grady McWhiney, "Gambling," in Wilson and Ferris, *Encyclopedia of Southern Culture*, 1224–25; Ownby, *Subduing Satan*, 84–88, 116–18; Holliman, "American Sports," 112–16. Georgia's Constitution banned gambling in 1877; refer to Grinols, *Gambling in America*, 14–16, and more generally, Click, *Spirit of the Times*, 70–71.

33. Wyatt-Brown, *Southern Honor*, 344–45; Greenberg, *Honor & Slavery*, 143. On the practice and rules of dueling, see Wilson, *The Code of Honor*; Paul Finkleman, "Dueling," in Wilson and Ferris, *Encyclopedia of Southern Culture*, 1503–4.

34. "Georgia and Florida," SMN, 3 December 1892, 6; "Circus Train Held by Armed Men," AC, 20 September 1897, 1, (thanks to Richard J. Reynolds III of the Circus

Historical Society for this reference); "Show Was Attached," *Statesboro News*, 8 December 1905, 4, RBP. Also see "Tackled the Shell Game," VT, 1 December 1900, 5, RBP.

35. Gordon M. Carver, "The First Mugivan and Bowers Circus—Great Van Amburg and Howes Great London Shows: Part Two, Season of 1910," *Bandwagon* 28 (July–Aug. 1984): 19; Allen, *Horrible Prettiness*, 225; R. H. Lafferty, "Outdoor Forum," BB 34 (23 September 1922): 96; Joseph T. Bradbury interview.

36. Davis, *Circus Age*, 126–27; Isenberg, *My Town and the Big Top*, 82; Lafferty, "Outdoor Forum," 96.

37. Gilmore, *Gender and Jim Crow*, 72; "The Show," *Sylvania Telephone*, 29 September 1911, 4, RBP; Davis, *Circus Age*, 126–28.

38. Sidney Lewis of the *Sparta Ishmaelite* quoted in Clark, *Southern Country Editor*, 158; "Big Show Was a Big Fake," *Statesboro News*, 8 December 1905, 1, RBP; "Next to Godliness," BB 33 (9 April 1921): 44; Charles Ringling, "The Audience," BB 34 (18 March 1922): 6; "To All Outdoor Showmen, Greetings!" BB 34 (19 August 1922): 7; Charles Ringling, "Let's Get Together for a 'Graftless' 1923," BB 34 (7 October 1922): 53; "Cleaning House in Circusland," BB 35 (7 April 1923): 72; "The Autobiography of a Confidence Man," *New York Tribune*, 24 September 1922, 1; "The Shady Side of the Circus," *New York Tribune*, 1 October 1922, 1; Hanners, "The Dark Side of the American Circus," 11, RLPLRC.

39. Edward T. Bishop Diary, 28 July 1877, Bishop Family Papers, HRBML; "It is a Good Show," AC, 3 October 1889, 8, RBP.

40. "John Robinson's Great Show," AC, 19 October 1876, 4. RBP. Also consult "Barnum's Show," AC, 13 October 1886, 8. Of course, the grand irony here is that blacks and whites had viewed many of these very same animals in a circus context without such segregation practices, see page 79 in this book.

41. "Howes' Great London Circus," ACC, 1 April 1877, 2; "Circus Going," ADH, 16 October 1875, 7, RBP; "Barnum & Bailey," AC, 14 October 1906, 8D; "Circus Comes for Two Days," AC, 19 October 1906, 10. Also see Durand, *Great Southern*, 7, RLPLRC.

42. "Big Circus in All Its Glory Arrives in Town Again and Attracts Sightseeing Crowds," *Louisville (KY) Herald*, 13 May 1907, in *Ringling Bros. Press Clipping Scrapbook, 1906–1907*, RMC; "Old John Robinson," ADH, 28 November 1872, 3, RBP; "The Circus," TDTE, 3 December 1897, 1. Also see SMN, 18 October 1881, 4.

43. "The Circus," ANEG, 29 November 1872, 3; "Old John Robinson's Great Show," ADH, 27 November 1872, 3, RBP; Ade, "With the Elephant and the Clown," 29, RLPLRC.

44. Susan Fan Tate Oral Interview, Athens-Clarke Heritage Foundation Oral History Project, 1976, 9, ms. 2209, Box 1, Folder 51, HRBML; Joseph T. Bradbury interview; "At the Circus," GDN, 29 October 1882, 1; "Georgia Affairs," SMN, 13 November 1882, 1.

45. "The Great and Only New York Show," ADCS, 15 October 1873, 4; "Vast Crowd at Circus," ATR, 30 November 1897, 4, RBP; "Old John Robinson," ADCS, 22 November 1871, 2.

46. "It was Circus Day all of Yesterday," AC, 10 November 1898, 9, RBP; Slout, *Royal Coupling*, 58; *Beneath White Tents*, 95, RLPLRC; Rial, "What the Modern Circus Represents," 10.

47. Davis, *Circus Age*, 33; "The Circus Here To-Day," SMN, 10 October 1894, 8;

"S. H. Barrett's New United Monster Shows," SMN, 20 November 1887, 4; "Barnum & Bailey Greatest Show on Earth," AC, 14 October 1906, 8D.

48. "Circuses," NYC, 4 January 1873, 319; Davis, *Circus Age*, 32.

49. Woodward, *Strange Career*, 31–65; Willson, *Where the World Folds Up at Night*, 61; Hosch, *Nevah Come Back No Mo'*, 192.

50. "Punch" Wheeler, *John Robinson 10 Big Shows 1902 Route Book* (n.p., n.d.), 83, RLPLRC; Circus Solly, "Under the Marquee," BB 30 (14 September 1918): 62.

51. "Editorials," AI, 12 October 1907, 4; Jackson, "The Negro of the Outdoor Show," 17.

52. Marsh, *Hitch Up the Buggy*, 73; *Beneath White Tents*, 100–101, RLPLRC.

53. Herman Joseph, "Ringling—B & B Jottings," BB 30 (24 May 1919): 40; "Hagenbeck-Wallace," BB 21 (30 April 1910): 21. For a variation on this theme, consult "Pink Lemonade and Elephants Come to Rome Again," RTH, 12 October 1911, 1.

54. "Sparks Show Seen By Immense Crowd," SMN, 6 November 1917, 8; "Sells-Floto Has Wonderful Start in Coliseum, Chicago," BB 31 (10 April 1920): 5; Fletcher Smith, "Sparks Shows Has Auspicious Opening," BB 32 (10 April 1920): 88; Circus Solly, "Under the Marquee," BB 31 (24 July 1920): 55; Joseph T. Bradbury interview; "All Ages are United in Enjoying the Opening Circus Performance," MDT, 3 April 1921, 8; "Sparks Show Seen By Immense Crowd," SMN, 6 November 1917, 8. On masquerading and carnival, see Bakhtin, *Rabelais and His World*, 103, 247–48.

55. "The Circus," TDTE, 19 November 1895, 1. For other descriptions of the camera trick, see "It Was Circus Day All of Yesterday," AC, 10 November 1898, 9, RBP; "The Big Show Well Attended," CES, 12 November 1898, 3, RBP; and Root, *Ways of the Circus*, 246.

56. "Big Circus Pleased Two Large Audiences," AC, 12 November 1901, 9, RBP; "Old Time Circus in Walter Main's," AJ, 12 November 1901, 12, RBP; "Gentry Show is Very Entertaining," SMN, 28 October 1915, 10; "Gentry's Dog Show in Town," AC, 11 November 1898, 7. Also refer to "Sparks Show Seen By Immense Crowd," SMN, 6 November 1917, 8.

57. "Married in a Tent," AC, 21 October 1890, 5; "Married at a Circus," AJ, 21 October 1890, 5, RBP. For an ad for this circus, see SMN, 25 December 1890, 2.

58. "The Big Show Well Attended," CES, 12 November 1898, 3, RBP; "The Great Show Today," AC, 12 October 1886, 8; "Wait," SMN, 1 November 1896, 17; "The Circus Yesterday," AC, 8 October 1880, 4, RBP; "Howe's Great London Circus," AC, 26 September 1875, 3; "Shows Greater and Better than Ever," CES, 6 April 1910, 3, RBP. Also see SMN, 2 November 1898, 6.

59. "Sells' Circus," *Milledgeville Union-Recorder*, 25 September 1894, 3, RBP; Daniel, *Standing at the Crossroads*, 52–54.

60. *Partee v. The State*, 19 Ga. App. 752, 92 S. E. 306 (1917); DN, 1 October 1897, 3, RBP.

61. "Atlanta, Ga.," BB 14 (25 October 1902): 10; "Show Tent Packed to Bursting Point," AGN, 1 October 1907, 5, RBP. On oversold tents also see "Great Throngs See the Circus," AN, 2 November 1905, 11, RBP; "Big Houses in Atlanta," BB 31 (22 November 1919): 52.

62. "An Editor at the Circus," *Dublin Post,* 2 November 1881, 2. Also refer to "Matters and Things Laconically Noted," SMN, 12 November 1879, 3.

63. "Society," SMN, 4 November 1906, 14; "An Editor at the Circus," *Dublin Post,* 2 November 1881, 2; *Crawford v. State,* 146 Miss. 540, 112 So. 681 (1927). Also see "Circus is Near," MDT, 3 April 1923, 6.

64. Thomas, *Fifty Years,* 79.

65. "Old Time Circus in Walter Main's," AJ, 12 November 1901, 12, RBP; *Beneath White Tents, 131,* RLPLRC; *Program of the Performers and Exhibits of Barnum & Bailey Greatest Show on Earth, Season 1914,* 14, Circus Ephemera Collection, ms. 2717, Box 1, Folder 1, HRBML.

66. "It is a Good Show," AC, 3 October 1889, 8, RBP; "Buckley and His Hippodrome," CES, 12 November 1874, 4, RBP; "Great Spectacle," CES, 10 October 1912, 8, RBP.

67. "Near Panic Caused," CES, 26 October 1913, 1 and 3, RBP. The total number of dead in Hartford is sometimes given as 168. Refer, for example, to Hammarstrom, *Big Top Boss,* 108. For a full account of the Hartford tragedy, see O'Nan, *Circus Fire.*

68. Harris, *Humbug,* 240–41; Kasson, *Rudeness and Civility,* 248.

Chapter 7. It's Showtime: The Cultural Content of the Circus, 1880–1920

1. "Great Throngs See the Circus," AN, 2 November 1905, 11, RBP; "Sells Brothers," AC, 13 October 1895, 26; "Barnum & Bailey," AC, 14 October 1906, 8D.

2. Harris, *Humbug,* 245.

3. Clark, *Southern Country Editor,* 162; Levine, *Highbrow/Lowbrow,* 1–9, 60, 85–104; Allen, *Horrible Prettiness,* 46–73; Peiss, "Leisure," in Butsch, *For Fun and Profit,* 108–10; Kibler, *Rank Ladies,* 1–21.

4. "The Circus: A Picture of an Impression," AC, 2 October 1900, 9, RBP; "It is a Good Show," AC, 3 October 1889, 3, RBP.

5. "Notes from the John Robinson's Ten Big Shows," BB 13 (20 July 1901): 5; Smith, "Spec-ology," 51.

6 ."Barnum & Bailey," SMN, 19 October 1890, 10; Conover, *John Robinson,* 29; SMN, 16 October 1892, 7; "Adam Forepaugh Shows," SMN, 16 October 1892; Higashi, *Cecil B. DeMille,* 182, 207–8.

7. Davis, *Circus Age,* 199–200.

8. Higashi, *DeMille,* 180–82; Spain, *At Ease in Zion,* 201–2; Kasson, *Buffalo Bill's Wild West,* 55–63; Robinson, *Old Wagon Show Days,* 156–58.

9. Smith, "Spec-ology," 51; "Circus is Here," *Augusta Chronicle,* 30 October 1890, 6; "Barnum Will Not Show," SMN, 30 October 1890, 8.

10. Conover, *John Robinson,* 29; "Barnum has Gone and Everybody Was Pleased Immensely," AC, 26 October 1890, 29, RBP.

11. "Barnum has Gone and Everybody Was Pleased Immensely," AC, 26 October 1890, 29, RBP; "Barnum & Bailey," SMN, 19 October 1890, 10.

12. "A Great Show," AJ, 25 October 1890, 11, RBP.

13. "Adam Forepaugh Shows," SMN, 16 October 1892, 7.

14. "Barnum has Gone and Everybody Was Pleased Immensely," AC, 26 October

1890, 29, RBP; "A Big Crowd," AC, 29 October 1892, 4, RBP; "Columbus Stirred Up by the Circus," CES, 21 October 1892, 4, RBP.

15. "Two Thousand People Turned Away from Robinson's Circus," SMN, 14 October 1904, 3; Conover, *John Robinson*, 30–31; "The Circus [Has] Come to Town," SMN, 12 November 1901, 7; Robinson, *Old Wagon Show Days*, 156; "John Robinson's Shows in Savannah [in] Two Days," SMN, 13 October 1904, 7.

16. "John Robinson Show," *Henry County Weekly*, 17 November 1899, 8; "Two Thousand People Turned Away from Robinson's Circus," SMN, 14 October 1904, 3.

17. "Two Thousand People Turned Away from Robinson's Circus," SMN, 14 October 1904, 3; Robinson, *Old Wagon Show Days*, 156–58; Conover, *John Robinson*, 29–32.

18. "The Day with the Circus," SMN, 15 November 1896, 8. Also see "The Realm of Recreation," BB 32 (20 March 1920): 198.

19. Harry Semon, "Women of the Circus," BB 16 (9 July 1904): 14; Davis, *Circus Age*, 105–7. Also refer to Bergengren, "Taking The Circus Seriously," 678.

20. Thayer, *Traveling Showmen*, 94; Clark, *Southern Country Editor*, 161.

21. Edward T. Bishop Diary, 28 July 1877, Bishop Family Papers, HRBML.

22. Hosch, *Nevah Come Back No Mo'*, 193–94.

23. "The Circus: A Picture of an Impression," AC, 2 October 1900, 9, RBP; "Circus Criticism," ADS, 8 December 1872, 8, RBP; Hosch, *Nevah Come Back No Mo'*, 192.

24. Davis, *Circus Age*, 107–10; "Nine Famous Nelsons," SMN, 3 November 1896, 6; "Ringling Bros' World Greatest Shows," SMN, 29 October 1896, 5; "Show Pleased Big Audiences," CES, 11 October 1910, 8, RBP. Also see "Circus the Best Ever Seen Here," SMN, 25 October 1904, 7.

25. "Robinson's Circus and Elks Have Taken Town By Storm," AC, 4 October 1910, 2, RBP. On costuming, compare the garb pictured in Kasson, *Amusing the Million*, 49, with Verney, *Here Comes the Circus*, 210, and Barth and Siegel, *Step Right This Way*, 98–99.

26. "The Circus," ACS, 17 January 1877, 4. Also see "The Great London Show," AC, 14 December 1878, 1, RBP.

27. "Show Pleased Big Audiences," CES, 11 October 1910, 8, RBP.

28. Ownby, *Subduing Satan*, 59–60; Cotkin, *Reluctant Modernism*, 4; Carlyon, *Dan Rice*, 190–93, 226–28; Fichman, *Evolutionary Theory*, 98–101; Davis, *Circus Age*, 152–53.

29. "The Day with the Circus," SMN, 15 November 1896, 8; "Crowds Were Turned Away From Robinson's Circus," SMN, 5 November 1906, 4.

30. "Delights of Circus Day Made Many Hearts Happy," AC, 20 October 1906, 10; "A Heap O' Houp La," AC, 21 December 1878, 1, RBP.

31. "Ringling Brothers Circus Parades Through Streets," AG, 10 October 1910, 2, RBP; "John H. Sparks' Shows Open Season," BB 25 (19 April 1913): 22; Schroeder, "The Day They Hanged Mary the Elephant," 20; C. J. Ver Halen, "Ringling Bros.' Show Opens in Chicago," BB 23 (8 April 1911): 3; "Barnum's Show," AC, 13 October 1886, 8.

32. "At the Mercy of a Lion," MT, 11 November 1897, 6, RBP; "The Elephant on a Rampage," AC, 6 June 1869, 3.

33. "The Great and Only New York Show," ADCS, 15 October 1873, 4; "Big Parade

to Please Children," AC, 1 October 1900, 7; "Howe's Big Show Pleases Griffin," *Griffin Times*, 9 November 1912, 2, RBP.

34. "Old John Robinson's Circus," CES, 9 December 1876, 4, RBP; "Coup's Circus and Menagerie," AC, 12 April 1882, 7, RBP.

35. "The Circus," ADCS, 17 January 1877, 4; "Circus Day Drew Thousands to City," CES, 26 October 1906, 2, 6, RBP; "Circus is Gone," AJ, 18 May 1897, 6, RBP.

36. "The Circus," ADNE, 9 November 1867, 3, RBP; Slout, *Olympians*, 745.

37. "The Great Show," CST, 14 December 1867, 3, RBP; "Circuses," NYC, 6 January 1872, 315; Robinson, *Old Wagon Show Days*, 42; Slout, *Olympians*, 745.

38. "A Famous Equestrian," SMN, 19 October 1886, 8; "The Circus Yesterday," AC, 8 October 1880, 4, RBP; "Sights Under Canvas," SMN, 19 October 1886, 8.

39. Isaac, *Transformation*, 98–101; Holliman, "American Sports," 111–21; Ownby, *Subduing Satan*, 191; Wyatt-Brown, *Southern Honor*, 341–43; "The Grandest Yet Seen," AC, 11 October 1886, 5; "The Great Show Today," AC, 12 October 1886, 8; "Scenes at the Circus," SMN, 16 October 1886, 8; "Coup's Circus and Menagerie," SMN, 18 October 1881, 4. On nineteenth-century horse racing see Eisenberg, *The Great Match Race*.

40. "Buckley and His Hippodrome," CES, 12 November 1874, 4, RBP; "Columbus Stirred Up by the Circus," CES, 21 October 1892, 4, RBP; "Scenes at the Circus," SMN, 16 October 1886, 8.

41. Bradford Byrd, "Ringling Brothers Put on a Great Show," AG, 11 October 1910, 4, RBP; "A Welcome Visitor," AC, 7 October 1886, 8; "Thousands Saw the Show," SMN, 11 October 1894, 8.

42. "Scenes at the Circus," SMN, 16 October 1886, 8; "A Large Crowd Saw a Splendid Circus," CES, 20 May 1897, 8, RBP; "Wallace Show has a Day of Tribulation," AJ, 17 October 1901, 2, RBP.

43. Apps, *Ringlingville*, 146–47. For early bicycle performances under canvas see "The Great Forepaugh Show," SMN, 21 October 1881, 4. An early street "velocipede" race is detailed in "The Big Circus," ASW, 17 March 1869, 3.

44. Kern, *Culture of Time and Space*, 109–30; "Cole Brothers," SMN, 25 November 1906, 35; "Barnum & Bailey," AC, 14 October 1906, 8D.

45. "The Great Forepaugh and Sells Brothers," SMN, 24 October 1902, 6; "Circus Comes To-Morrow," SMN, 24 October 1902, 6; "Savannahians Saw Circus in a Downpour," SMN, 26 October 1902, 12; "Circus Performer Has Fall in Albany," CES, 2 November 1902, 7, RBP; "Adam Forepaugh and Sells Brothers," SMN, 9 October 1904, 28.

46. "Circus Scored a Great Success," CES, 19 October 1904, 5, RBP; "When the Circus Comes to Town," CES, 5 November 1902, 3, RBP; "Circus the Best Ever Seen Here," SMN, 25 October 1904, 7.

47. Preston, *Automobile Age Atlanta*, 50.

48. Davis, *Circus Age*, 103–4; "Immense Crowds at Circus Performances," *Louisville (KY) Times*, 14 May 1907, clipping in *Barnum and Bailey Press Clipping Book 1906–07*, RMC; Percy H. Whiting, "Dictionary is Torn to Threads in Doing Justice to Circus," AG, 20 October 1906, 13, RBP.

49. "Barnum & Bailey Still Greatest on Earth," AJ, 20 October 1906, 2, RBP; "Thousands Delighted With Barnum & Bailey's Big Show," SMN, 4 November 1906, 19.

50. "Injured in Dip of Death," BB 18 (17 February 1906): 20; "Circus Performer Has Fall in Albany," CES, 2 November 1902, 7, RBP.

51. "Barnum & Bailey Still Greatest on Earth," AJ, 20 October 1906, 2, RBP.

Chapter 8. Sparks Circus and the Reinvention of Circus Day

1. "Editorial Comment," BB 31 (8 November 1919): 42; "Circus Season Virtually Brought to Close," BB 30 (19 October 1918): 26; Tindall and Shi, *America*, 2: 1017–18, 1074; Fletcher Smith, "The Rejuvenation of the South," BB 36 (11 October 1924): 75; R. M. Harvey, "Prohibition and Circuses," BB 29 (24 March 1917): 21, 203; "Dancing Association Seeks to Lift Methodist Ban on Amusements," BB 32 (28 August 1920): 92; "Editorial Comment," BB 36 (7 June 1924): 48; "50,000 Persons See Big Circus," AG, 18 October 1920, 10, RBP.

2. "Editorial," BB 16 (19 November 1904): 10; "Circus Gossip," BB 16 (19 November 1904): 17; "Good-Bye to Parade," BB 17 (22 April 1905): 10; "Abandonment of the Parade," BB 18 (23 June 1906): 20; "Passing of the Street Parade is Explained," GDN, 2 April 1913, 1; Fletcher Smith, "About Circus Parades," BB 38 (20 March 1926): 87, 178; "New Signals Main Reason For Eliminating Parades," BB 38 (3 April 1926): 60; James F. Donaldson, "Does the Circus Need the Parade?" BB 38 (24 July 1926): 43; Circus Solly, "Under the Marquee," BB 32 (31 January 1920): 65; Fred High, "Should A Circus Pay a License?" BB 32 (14 August 1920): 39; Tony C. Edmondson, "Favors More Liberal Circus Licenses," BB 32 (28 August 1920): 30; "Farrington on Circus License," BB 32 (4 September 1920): 32; "Circus Licenses," BB 32 (11 September 1920): 34; "Editorial Comment," BB 38 (16 January 1926): 48.

3. Slout, *Olympians*, 36, 45, 130, 151, 317, 581, 613–14; Weeks, *Ringling*, xv–xvii; Chindahl, *History*, 128, 159–60; Murray, *Circus from Rome to Ringling*, 298–99; P. M. Silloway, "The Modernized Circus," BB 38 (2 October 1926): 84.

4. J. Steven Picou, "Football," in Wilson and Ferris, *Encyclopedia of Southern Culture*, 1221–24; John E. DiMeglio, "Baseball," in Wilson and Ferris, *Encyclopedia of Southern Culture*, 1210–11; Blewett, *The A-Z of World Boxing*, 41–42; Gorn, *The Manly Art*, 248; Gomery, *Shared Pleasures*, 34–56; Fuller, *At the Picture Show*, 29–34; Wood, "Spectacles of Suffering," 231–34; Kann, *The Film Daily 1929 Year Book*, 595–96; James P. Cunningham, "5,251 U. S. Houses Wired," *Film Daily*, 8 August 1929, 10–11; Tindall and Shi, *America*, 2:1076–77; Holmes, "1890–1940," in Coleman, *History of Georgia*, 336; Workers, comp., *Atlanta: A City of the Modern South*, 103–6; Kasson, *Amusing*, 3–9, 112; Chindahl, *History*, 158–64; "Editorial Comment," BB 37 (28 November 1925): 68.

5. Mischler, "Greatest Show on Earth," 283.

6. Apps, *Ringlingville USA*, xx.

7. Kasson, *Amusing*, 112; Link, *Paradox of Southern Progressivism*, 112–17.

8. Brownell, "Urban South," in Brownell and Goldfield, *The City in Southern History*, 142–50; Brownell, *Urban Ethos in the South*, 39–60.

9. Bradbury, "Central City Park," 5; "Introductory Brief History of Sparks Family and Title," 4–5; Robert L. Parkinson, "The Sparks Circus, (1894–1931)," typescript in

"Sparks Circus, 1889–1931" vertical file, RLPLRC; Bradbury, "The Old Circus Album," 39; "In Winterquarters," BB 24 (19 March 1912): 23; Route Sheet of Sparks Circus, 1919, RLPLRC.

10. Bradbury, "Central City Park," 5; "Throngs at Park to Watch Circus," MDT, 15 December 1919, 3; "Animals, Fliers and Weather Lure Crowds," MDT, 14 March 1921, 10; "Crowds Drawn to Park to See Preparations for Circus Day," MDT, 26 March 1923, 9. Also see "The Dog and Pony Show Has Arrived," MT, 3 December 1900, 3, RBP and "Circus May Move On," SMN, 31 December 1900, 8.

11. U.S. Bureau of the Census, *Fourteenth Census of the United States*, 193; Holmes, "1890–1940," in Coleman, *History of Georgia*, 274; "Macon Circus Sunbeams," BB 29 (24 March 1917): 225; "Sparks Circus Again Elects to Keep Headquarters Here," MDT, 13 March 1923, 12.

12. "Sun Bros.' Shows," BB 30 (9 November 1918): 26; "A Big Circus," SMN, 24 November 1900, 6; "Circus May Move On," SMN, 31 December 1900, 8; "Circus Will Remain Here," SMN, 2 January 1901, 8; "Circus in Winter Quarters," SMN, 14 January 1901, 8; "Circus Preparing to Move," SMN, 25 March 1901, 8; "Sun Brothers Last Stand," BB 22 (26 November 1910): 21; "Sun Bros.' Season," BB 22 (17 December 1910): 20; "Sun Bros.' Circus," BB 26 (25 April 1914): 30; The "Professor," "Seat Plank Chatter from Macon, GA.," BB 27 (30 January 1915): 22–23.

13. "Sparks' Circus," BB 32 (6 March 1920): 60.

14. "Circus Day Drew Thousands to City," CES, 26 October 1906, 6, RBP; "Great Circus Pleases Many in Columbus," CES, 15 November 1919, 2, RBP; "Hundreds Were Disappointed at Not Seeing a Parade," GDN, 30 October 1908, 1, RBP.

15. "Editorial," BB 16 (19 November 1904): 10; "Circus Gossip," BB 16 (19 November 1904): 17; Brownell, "Urban South," in Brownell and Goldfield, *The City in Southern History*, 156; Smith, "About Circus Parades," 187; "Crowds at Circus Grounds Disappointed," Little Rock, Arkansas undated newspaper clipping, ca. 13 October 1907, in *Barnum and Bailey Press Clipping Book 1906–07*, RMC; Donaldson, "Does the Circus Need the Parade?" 43; "City Marshal Levies on Largest Elephant," SMN, 5 November 1909, 5; "Damaged Streets," BB 21 (20 November 1909): 18; "Street Tax," BB 31 (6 December 1919): 54; "John Robinson Circus," BB 36 (22 November 1924): 72. Also see "Too Big to Parade," *Cumberland (MD) News*, 17 May 1907, in *Barnum and Bailey Press Clipping Book 1906–07*, RMC.

16. Fletcher Smith, "Does Circus Opposition Pay?" BB 36 (18 October 1924): 51; Preston, *Automobile Age Atlanta*, 51, 113–18; Goldfield, *Cotton Fields and Skyscrapers*, 154; Circus Solly, "Under the Marquee," BB 26 (12 December 1914): 23; "Passing of the Street Parade is Explained," GDN, 2 April 1913, 1.

17. Charles E. Ringling, "Minus the Circus Parade," BB 36 (13 December 1924): 6.

18. Donaldson, "Does the Circus Need the Parade?" 43.

19. "Introductory Brief History of Sparks Family and Title," 4–5; The "Professor," "Sun Bros.' Show Notes," BB 21 (11 December 1909): 43.

20. "Sparks Shows Have Auspicious Opening," BB 32 (10 April 1920): 5.

21. "Sparks Circus Ticket Cut is Granted Local School Kiddies," MDT, 28 March 1922, 8; "Circus to Open Here on April 1," MDT, 19 March 1922, 8; "Cut Price Tickets to Circus Distributed to More than 9,000 Kids," MDT, 30 March 1922, 10; "Capacity

Crowds Greet Sparks' Show Opening," BB 34 (8 April 1922): 5, 16; "Circus Day in Macon Tomorrow," MT, 31 March 1922, 1A.

22. "Capacity Crowds Greet Sparks' Show Opening," BB 34 (8 April 1922): 5, 16; "Circus Performances Draw a Record Crowd as Sparks Opens Here," MDT, 2 April 1922, 1, 12; "Mercer's Band Will Parade With Circus," MDT, 29 March 1922, 7.

23. "Capacity Crowds Greet Sparks' Show Opening," BB 34 (8 April 1922): 5, 16; "Circus Performances Draw a Record Crowd as Sparks Opens Here," MDT, 2 April 1922, 1, 12; "Sparks Circus Ticket Cut is Granted Local School Kiddies," MDT, 28 March 1922, 8.

24. Oliver Orr, "Two Capacity Audiences at Opening of Sparks' Circus," BB 35 (14 April 1923): 74; "Consignment of Animals," BB 35 (24 March 1923): 74; "Sparks Circus Begins its Tour After Opening Season in Macon," MDT, 6 April 1923, 3.

25. "Consignment of Animals," BB 35 (24 March 1923): 74; Circus Solly, "Under the Marquee," BB 35 (21 April 1923): 76; "Sparks Circus to Open at Macon, GA, April 3," BB 36 (22 March 1924): 82; "Sparks Circus to Help Macon," MDT, 28 March 1926, 6; *Macon Telegraph* quoted in "Charles Sparks Commended," BB 34 (15 April 1922): 66.

26. "Gala Day is Planned When Sparks' Circus Opens Here Saturday," MDT, 27 March 1921, 8; "Sparks Circus Again Elects to Keep Headquarters Here," MDT, 13 March 1923, 12; "Sparks Circus Arrives Today," SMN, 30 November 1924, 10; "Sparks Circus Preparing For Its Fortieth Journey," MDT, 9 April 1930, 19; "Sparks Circus Returns to Macon, Ga., Quarters," BB 36 (13 December 1924): 106; "Sparks' Circus," BB 37 (12 December 1925): 146.

27. *Macon Telegraph* editorial reprinted as "Our Own Circus," BB 37 (25 April 1925): 65.

28. *Macon Telegraph* quoted in "Sparks Circus is Big Advertiser of Macon," BB 36 (19 July 1924): 112; "Sparks Three Ring Circus," MDT, 31 March 1922, 8; C. G. Sturtevant, "A Boom in Circus Magazine Writing," BB 36 (13 September 1924): 75, 95; C. G. Sturtevant, "A Year in Circus Writing," BB 37 (12 November 1925): 93; "Sparks Circus Starts Season," BB 37 (18 April 1925): 5; "Our Own Circus," BB 37 (25 April 1925): 65; Circus Solly, "Under the Marquee," BB 35 (21 April 1923): 76.

29. "Sparks Circus Returns to Macon, Ga., Quarters," BB 36 (13 December 1924): 106; "Sparks' Circus," BB 37 (12 December 1925): 146; "Sparks Three Ring Circus," MDT, 31 March 1922, 8; "Sparks Circus Returns to Macon, Ga., Quarters," BB 36 (12 December 1924): 106.

30. "Sparks and Gentry Bros. Open Their Circus Season," BB 38 (24 April 1926): 5, 85; "Sparks Circus Has Gala Opening," BB 39 (16 April 1927): 5; "Sparks Circus Notes," BB 40 (7 April 1928): 58.

31. "Sparks Circus For Atlanta," BB 34 (25 March 1922): 68; Circus Solly, "Under the Marquee," BB 34 (15 April 1922): 67; Eddie Jackson, "Sparks' Circus," BB 34 (22 April 1922): 64; "Sparks Circus Makes a Big Hit," AJ, 4 April 1922, 3, RBP; Eddie Jackson, "Sparks' Circus," BB 34 (22 April 1922): 64; "Sparks Not Enlarging," BB 36 (15 November 1924): 72.

32. "Sparks Circus Will Arrive Here Today," SMN, 9 December 1923, 2.

33. The Ringling Brothers and Barnum and Bailey Circus had played Savannah on November 21, 1919. See "Thousands Visit Circus," SMN, 22 November 1919, 12.

34. "Elks Big Circus Pitches its Tents," SMN, 10 December 1923, 10; "Prohibitive License in Savannah Continued," BB 38 (23 January 1926): 65. Also consult Chas. Bernard, "Sparks Circus Has Big Day at Savannah, GA.," BB 35 (22 December 1923): 76.

35. John F. Battle Jr., "Sparks Circus, Bigger than Ever, Delights Big Crowds," *Augusta Chronicle*, 10 April 1926, 10; Henry Averill, "Sparks Circus Pleases Crowds," CES, 27 September 1927, 5, RBP.

36. "Remember," *Dawson News*, 30 September 1924, 7.

37. Carver, "Sparks Circus Season of 1928," 10; "Shell Game," BB 34 (16 September 1922): 9; "Circuses," BB 34 (23 September 1922): 70; "Outdoor Forum," BB 34 (4 November 1922): 88; "Alleges He was Shortchanged," BB 35 (16 June 1923): 114; "Circus Brings a Carnival of Lawlessness," RTH, 22 September 1921, 1.

38. "Capacity Crowds Greet Sparks' Show Opening," BB 34 (8 April 1922): 5, 16; *Macon Telegraph* quoted in Circus Solly, "Under the Marquee," BB 35 (21 April 1923): 76; Battle, "Sparks Circus," 10. Also see "Circus Solly Says," BB 34 (23 September 1922): 119; "A Clean Circus," BB 34 (11 November 1922): 75; Circus Solly, "Under the Marquee," BB 34 (18 November 1922): 73.

39. Carver, "Sparks Circus Season of 1928," 7; "A Warning to the Public," CES, 10 September 1926, 2.

40. "Billy Sunday Boosts Circus," BB 38 (1 May 1926): 60; "Fine Spring Business for Sparks Circus," BB 38 (8 May 1926): 58.

41. Battle, "Sparks Circus," 10.

42. Circus Sy, "Under the Marquee," BB 36 (15 November 1924): 74; "Good Performances of Sparks' Circus," CES, 7 April 1923, 10, RBP.

43. Bradbury, "Sparks Circus: Season of 1929," 4–5; "Gentry Buys Sparks Circus," BB 40 (1 December 1928): 3; "Under the Marquee," BB 40 (15 December 1928): 58; Bradbury, "Central City Park," 6; Weeks, *Ringling*, 218–19; "Sparks Circus—Season of 1930," Route Sheet, RLPLRC.

44. On the "safe and sane" holiday movement see Litwicki, *America's Public Holidays*.

Conclusion

1. "Novelties for Klan Circus," *Sunday American*, 5 April 1925, 3B, RBP; "Rich 'Sell Out' For Circus Tickets," AG, 6 April 1925, 6, RBP; "Workmen Rear Tent For Klan Circus," AG, 13 April 1925, 5, RBP; "Klan Circus Sets Attendance Records," AG, 16 April 1925, 7, RBP.

2. On the Klan and these issues, see Chalmers, *Hooded Americanism*, 28–38, and Feldman, *Politics, Society, and the Klan in Alabama*, 21–50, 92–115.

3. Slout, *Royal Coupling*, 44–45.

4. Hammarstrom, *Big Top Boss*, 27–37, 107–11, 133, 220–26; Eckley, *American Circus*, 185–200, Henry Ringling North quote appears on 198.

5. Davis, *Circus Age*, 229.

6. Gregory J. Renoff, personal observation, Red Unit, 133rd Edition, Ringling Brothers and Barnum & Bailey Circus, Civic Center, Hartford, Connecticut, 17 May 2003;

Marlon Manuel, "The Greatest Shows on Earth," *Atlanta Journal-Constitution*, 25 February 2003, E1.

7. Kenneth Feld quoted in Glenn Collins, "In a Daring Leap, Ringling Loses its Three Rings," NYT, 31 December 2005; Edward Rothstein, "Ringling Brothers and Barnum & Bailey Circus Play Madison Square Garden," NYT, 29 March 2006.

8. Wendy Cole, "Under the Small Top," *Time* 163 (5 April 2004): 81–82.

9. Bradbury, "Central City Park," 6–7; "Three-Ring Cinema: Looking at Life Under the Big Top," *Atlanta Journal and Atlanta Constitution*, 24 February 2000, E4.

10. Shandra Hill, "One-Ring Success," *Atlanta Journal and Atlanta Constitution*, 11 March 1999, JD6; Cherise M. Williams, "Out on a Limb and Lovin' It," *Atlanta Journal-Constitution*, 24 June 2004, P40; Jane H. Lii, "Black Circus Seeks to Stir And Inspire," NYT, 1 June 1997; Marlon Manuel, "Drumroll, Please," *Atlanta Journal-Constitution*, 25 February 2003, E1; Julian E. Barnes, "Circus Acts for the Streetwise," NYT, 27 April 2000, A25.

11. Sean Lengell, "Ybor City's Cafe Owners Prepare to Share the Sidewalk," *Tampa Tribune*, 3 September 2005.

12. Chris Jenkins, "Playing in NASCAR's Infield," *USA Today*, 15 October 2002; John Scheinman, "Luxury Viewing to be Set Up For Preakness Infield," *Washington Post*, 26 February 2005, D1; Gregory J. Renoff, personal observation, Preakness Stakes, Pimlico Race Course, Baltimore, Maryland, 21 May 1989 and 19 May 2007.

BIBLIOGRAPHY

Manuscript Collections

Brisendine, Robert, Papers, 1899–2002. Manuscript, Archives, and Rare Book Library, Emory University, Atlanta, Georgia.
Hargrett Rare Book and Manuscript Library, University of Georgia, Athens.
Harvard Theater Collection, Houghton Library, Harvard University, Cambridge, Mass.
John Robinson Circus Company Records, Cincinnati Historical Society Library, Cincinnati Museum Center, Cincinnati, Ohio.
Ringling Museum of the Circus, John and Mable Ringling Museum of Art, Sarasota, Florida.
Robert L. Parkinson Library and Research Center, Circus World Museum, Baraboo, Wisconsin.

Author Interviews

Bradbury, Joseph T. Atlanta, Georgia, 1 March 2001.

Government Documents

Clark, R. H., T. R. R. Cobb, and D. Irwin. *The Code of the State of Georgia*. Atlanta: Crusader Book and Job Office, 1861.
Foster, Arthur. *A Digest of the Laws of the State of Georgia*. Philadelphia: C. Sherman & Co., 1831.
Journal of House of Representatives of the State of Georgia at the Regular Session of the General Assembly at Atlanta, Wednesday, June 26, 1907. Atlanta: Franklin-Turner, 1907.
U.S. Bureau of the Census. *Fourteenth Census of the United States Taken in the Year 1920*, Vol. 1, *Population*. Prepared under the supervision of William C. Hunt. Washington, D.C.: GPO, 1921.
U.S. Bureau of the Census. *Negro Population 1790–1915*. Washington, D.C.: GPO, 1918.
U.S. Bureau of the Census. *Thirteenth Census of the United States Taken in the Year*

1910, Vol. 2, *Population*. Prepared under the supervision of William C. Hunt. Washington, D.C.: GPO, 1913.

U.S. Department of the Interior. *Ninth Census: The Statistics of the Population of the United States*, Vol. 1. Compiled under the direction of Francis A. Walker. Washington, D.C.: GPO, 1872.

U.S. Department of the Interior. *Report on the Population of the United States at the Eleventh Census: 1890, Part I*. Prepared under the supervision of Robert B. Porter. Washington, D.C.: GPO, 1895.

Newspapers and Periodicals

American Quarterly
Americus Recorder
Americus Times Recorder
Athens North-East Georgian
Athens Southern Banner
Athens Southern Watchman
Atlanta Christian Index and South-Western Baptist
Atlanta Constitution
Atlanta Daily Era
Atlanta Daily Herald
Atlanta Daily New Era
Atlanta Daily Sun
Atlanta Evening Capitol
Atlanta Georgian
Atlanta Georgian and News
Atlanta Independent
Atlanta Intelligencer
Atlanta Journal
Atlanta News
Augusta Chronicle
Augusta Chronicle and Constitutionalist
Augusta Chronicle & Sentinel
Augusta Daily Chronicle & Sentinel
Bainbridge Democrat
Barnesville Gazette
Berrien County Pioneer
Billboard
Bulloch Times
Cartersville News and Courant
Charlotte (NC) Journal
Clinton (MS) Baptist Record
Columbus Daily Enquirer-Sun
Columbus Daily Sun
Columbus Daily Sun & Times

Columbus Enquirer
Columbus Enquirer-Sun
Columbus Sun and Times
Columbus Sunday Herald
Columbus Times
Crawford County News
Daily Atlanta Intelligencer
Daily Savannah Republican
Dalton North Georgia Citizen
Dawson News
Dublin Post
Dublin Times
Early County News
Fitzgerald Leader-Enterprise
Fitzgerald Leader-Enterprise and Press
Georgia Historical Quarterly
Griffin Daily News
Griffin Daily News and Sun
Griffin Weekly News
Henry County Weekly
Hustler of Rome
Jackson Herald
Jesup Sentinel
Jones County News
LaGrange Reporter
Lexington (KY) Western Luminary
Macon County Citizen
Macon Daily Telegraph
Macon Telegraph
Marietta Journal
Memphis Daily Bulletin
Memphis Commercial Appeal
Milledgeville Federal Union
Milledgeville Union & Recorder
Milledgeville Union-Recorder
Monroe Advertiser
Moultrie Weekly Observer
Newnan Herald
Newnan Herald and Advertiser
New York Clipper
New York Tribune
Norfolk (VA) Gazette
Ocilla Star
Oglethorpe Echo
Daily Richmond (VA) Examiner

Rome Tribune-Herald
Rome Weekly Commercial
Sandersville Herald
Sandersville Middle Georgia Progress
Savannah Daily Herald
Savannah Daily News & Herald
Savannah Morning News
Statesboro News
Sumner Worth Local
Swainsboro Forest Blade
Sylvania Telephone
Thomaston Herald
Thomaston Middle Georgia Times
Thomasville Daily Times Enterprise
Tifton Gazette
Toccoa Record
Valdosta Daily Times
Valdosta Times
Vienna News
Wayne County News
Waynesboro True Citizen
Waynesboro True Citizen Extra

Books, Articles, Dissertations, and Theses

Adams, Bluford. *E Pluribus Barnum: The Great Showman and the Making of U.S. Popular Culture.* Minneapolis: University of Minnesota Press, 1997.

Allen, Robert C. *Horrible Prettiness: Burlesque and American Culture.* Chapel Hill: University of North Carolina Press, 1991.

Altick, Richard D. *The Shows of London.* Cambridge, Mass.: Belknap Press of Harvard University Press, 1978.

Apps, Jerry. *Ringlingville USA: The Stupendous Story of Seven Siblings and Their Stunning Circus Success.* Madison: Wisconsin Historical Society, 2004.

Atherton, Lewis Eldon. *Main Street on the Middle Border.* Bloomington: Indiana University Press, 1954.

Avary, Myrta Lockett. *Dixie After the War: An Exposition of Social Conditions Existing in the South, During the Twelve Years Succeeding the Fall of Richmond.* 1906. Reprint, New York: Da Capo Press, 1970.

Avery, Isaac Erwin. *Idle Comments.* Charlotte, N.C.: Stone Publishing, 1912.

Ayers, Edward L. *The Promise of the New South: Life After Reconstruction.* New York: Oxford University Press, 1992.

Bakhtin, Mikhail. *Rabelais and His World.* Translated by Helene Iswolsky. Bloomington: Indiana University Press, 1984.

Barnum, P. T. *Struggles and Triumphs: Or, The Life of P. T. Barnum.* 2 vols. 1869. Reprint, New York: Knopf, 1927.

Barth, Miles, and Alan Siegel. *Step Right This Way: The Photographs of Edward J. Kelty.* New York: Word Wise Press, 2002.

Bartley, Numan V. *The Creation of Modern Georgia.* Athens: University of Georgia Press, 1983.

Battle, Kemp Plummer. *Memories of an Old-Time Tar Heel.* Edited by William James Battle. Chapel Hill: University of North Carolina Press, 1945.

Bell, N. J. *Southern Railroad Man: Conductor N. J. Bell's Recollections of the Civil War Era.* Edited by James A. Ward. DeKalb: Northern Illinois Press, 1993.

Bergengren, Ralph. "Taking The Circus Seriously." *Atlantic Monthly* 103 (1909): 672–79.

Bernstein, Iver. *The New York City Draft Riots: Their Significance for American Society and Politics in the Age of the Civil War.* New York: Oxford University Press, 1990.

Bertelson, David. *The Lazy South.* New York: Oxford University Press, 1967.

Bierce, Ambrose. *The Devil's Dictionary.* 1911. Reprint, Mineola, N.Y.: Dover Publications, 1993.

Blassingame, John W. *The Slave Community: Plantation Life in the Antebellum South.* New York: Oxford University Press, 1972.

Blewett, Bert. *The A–Z of World Boxing: An Authoritative and Entertaining Compendium of the Fight Game from its Origins to the Present Day.* London: Robson Books, 1996.

Bogdan, Robert. *Freak Show: Presenting Human Oddities for Amusement and Profit.* Chicago: University of Chicago Press, 1988.

Boles, John B., ed. *A Companion to the American South.* Malden, Mass.: Blackwell Publishers, 2002.

Boles, John B., and Evelyn Thomas Nolen, eds. *Interpreting Southern History: Historiographical Essays in Honor of Sanford W. Higginbotham.* Baton Rouge: Louisiana State University Press, 1987.

Bonner, James Calvin. *Georgia's Last Frontier: The Development of Carroll County.* Athens: University of Georgia Press, 1971.

———. *Milledgeville: Georgia's Antebellum Capital.* Athens: University of Georgia Press, 1978.

Botkin, B. A. *Lay My Burden Down: A Folk History of Slavery.* New York: Delta Books, 1994.

Bradbury, Joseph T. "Central City Park, Macon, Georgia, One of America's Historic Circus Spots." *White Tops* 34 (1961): 3–7.

———. "The Old Circus Album: A Historic Look at the Shows of the Past." *White Tops* 59 (1986): 39–42.

———. "Sparks Circus: Season of 1929." *Bandwagon* 28 (1984): 4–5.

Brannen, Dorothy. *Life in Old Bulloch: The Story of a Wiregrass County in Georgia.* Gainesville, Ga.: Magnolia Press, 1987.

Branson, E. C. "Farm Tenancy in the Cotton Belt: How Farm Tenants Live." *Journal of Social Forces* 1 (1923): 213–21.

Breen, T. H. "Horses and Gentlemen: The Cultural Significance of Gambling among the Gentry of Virginia." *William and Mary Quarterly* 34 (1977): 239–57.

Brown, Richard. *Modernization: The Transformation of American Life, 1600–1865.* New York: Hill and Wang, 1976.

Brownell, Blaine A. *The Urban Ethos in the South, 1920–1930.* Baton Rouge: Louisiana State University Press, 1975.

Brownell, Blaine A., and David R. Goldfield, eds. *The City in Southern History: The Growth of Urban Civilization in the South.* Port Washington, N.Y.: Kennikat Press, 1977.

Bryant, Jonathan M. "'A county where plenty should abound': Race, Law, and Markets in Greene County, Georgia, 1850–1885." Ph.D. diss., University of Georgia, 1992.

Buck, Paul Herman. *The Road to Reunion, 1865–1900.* Boston: Little, Brown and Co., 1937.

Bull, Jacqueline P. "The General Merchant in the Economic History of the New South." *Journal of Southern History* 18 (1952): 37–59.

Burton, Orville Vernon, and Robert C. McMath Jr., eds. *Toward a New South? Studies in Post–Civil War Southern Communities.* Westport, Conn.: Greenwood Press, 1982.

Butsch, Richard, ed. *For Fun and Profit: The Transformation of Leisure into Consumption.* Philadelphia: Temple University Press, 1990.

———. *The Making of American Audiences: From Stage to Television, 1750–1990.* Cambridge: Cambridge University Press, 2000.

Carlyon, David. *Dan Rice: The Most Famous Man You've Never Heard Of.* New York: Public Affairs, 2001.

Carter, Jimmy. *An Hour Before Daylight: Memories of a Rural Boyhood.* New York: Touchstone, 2001.

Carver, Gordon M. "The First Mugivan and Bowers Circus—Great Van Amburg and Howes Great London Shows: Part Two, Season of 1910." *Bandwagon* 28 (1984): 13–20.

———. "Sparks Circus Season of 1928." *Bandwagon* 23 (1979): 3–10.

Chalmers, David M. *Hooded Americanism: The First Century of the Ku Klux Klan, 1865–1965.* Garden City, N.Y.: Doubleday & Co., 1965.

Chindahl, George L. *A History of the Circus in America.* Caldwell, Idaho: Caxton Printers, 1959.

Chipman, Bert J. *"Hey Rube."* Edited by Harry B. Chipman. Hollywood, Calif.: Hollywood Print Shop, 1933.

Clark, Thomas D. *Pills, Petticoats and Plows: The Southern Country Store.* Indianapolis: Bobbs-Merrill Co., 1944.

———. *The Southern Country Editor.* Indianapolis: Bobbs-Merrill Co., 1948; Gloucester, Mass.: Peter Smith, 1964.

Click, Patricia C. *The Spirit of the Times: Amusements in Nineteenth Century Baltimore, Norfolk, and Richmond.* Charlottesville: University Press of Virginia, 1989.

Cohen, William. *At Freedom's Edge: Black Mobility and the Southern White Quest for Racial Control, 1861–1915.* Baton Rouge: Louisiana State University Press, 1991.

Cole, Marjorie Daniel. *Hair Straight'ner and Curlin' Irons: Kinfolk and Neighbors in Rural Georgia, 1910–1930.* Concord, Mass.: Concord River Press, 1998.

Coleman, Kenneth, ed. *A History of Georgia.* 2nd ed. Athens: University of Georgia Press, 1991.

Conklin, George, and Harvey Woods Root. *The Ways of the Circus; Being the Memories and Adventures of George Conklin, Tamer of Lions.* New York: Harper and Brothers, 1921.

Conover, R. E. *Give 'em a John Robinson.* Xenia, Ohio: n.p., 1965.

Conway, Alan. *The Reconstruction of Georgia.* Minneapolis: University of Minnesota Press, 1966.

Cooper, William J., Jr., and Thomas E. Terrill. *The American South: A History.* New York: Knopf, 1990.

Cotkin, George. *Reluctant Modernism: American Thought and Culture, 1880–1900.* New York: Twayne Publishers, 1992.

Coulter, E. Merton. *College Life in the Old South.* New York: Macmillan Co., 1928.

Coup, William Cameron. *Sawdust & Spangles: Stories & Secrets of the Circus.* Washington, D.C.: Paul A. Ruddell, 1901.

Crofts, Daniel W., ed. *Cobb's Ordeal: The Diaries of a Virginia Farmer, 1842–1872.* Athens: University of Georgia Press, 1997.

———. *Old Southampton: Politics and Society in a Virginia County, 1834–1869.* Charlottesville: University of Virginia Press, 1992.

Crowley, John G. *Primitive Baptists of the Wiregrass South, 1815 to the Present.* Gainesville: University Press of Florida, 1998.

Culhane, John. *The American Circus: An Illustrated History.* New York: Henry Holt and Co., 1989.

Current, Richard N. *Those Terrible Carpetbaggers: A Reinterpretation.* New York: Oxford University Press, 1988.

Dabney, Virginius. *Across the Years: Memories of a Virginian.* Garden City, N.Y.: Doubleday, 1978.

Dailey, Jane, Glenda Elizabeth Gilmore, and Bryant Simon, eds. *Jumpin' Jim Crow: Southern Politics from the Civil War to Civil Rights.* Princeton, N.J.: Princeton University Press, 2000.

Daniel, Pete. *Standing at the Crossroads: Southern Life Since 1900.* New York: Hill and Wang, 1986.

Davis, Allison, Burleigh B. Gardner, and Mary R. Gardner. *Deep South: A Social Anthropological Study of Caste and Class.* Chicago: University of Chicago Press, 1941.

Davis, Janet. *The Circus Age: Culture and Society Under the American Big Top.* Chapel Hill: University of North Carolina Press, 2002.

Degler, Carl N. *Place Over Time: The Continuity of Southern Distinctiveness.* Baton Rouge: Louisiana State University Press, 1977.

DeMott, Josephine. *The Circus Lady.* New York: Thomas Y. Crowell Co., 1925.

Dittmer, John. *Black Georgia in the Progressive Era.* Urbana: University of Illinois Press, 1977.

Dollard, John. *Caste and Class in a Southern Town.* New Haven: Yale University Press, 1937.

Dore, Gustave. *The Dore Bible Illustrations.* Edited by Millicent Rose. New York: Dover Publications, 1974.

Dormon, James H., Jr. *Theater in the Ante Bellum South, 1815–1861.* Chapel Hill: University of North Carolina Press, 1967.
Dorsey, James E. *The History of Hall County, Georgia,* Volume I: *1818–1900.* Gainesville, Ga.: Magnolia Press, 1991.
Doyle, Don H. *New Men, New Cities, New South: Atlanta, Nashville, Charleston, and Mobile, 1860–1910.* Chapel Hill: University of North Carolina Press, 1990.
Drage, Edmund. *Hurrah for Hampton: Black Red Shirts in South Carolina During Reconstruction.* Fayetteville: The University of Arkansas Press, 1998.
Dumenil, Lynn. *The Modern Temper: American Culture and Society in 1920s.* New York: Hill and Wang, 1995.
Dyer, Thomas G. *The University of Georgia: A Bicentennial History, 1785–1985.* Athens: University of Georgia Press, 1985.
Eckley, Wilton. *The American Circus.* Boston: Twayne Publishers, 1984.
Edwards, Richard Henry. *Popular Amusements.* New York: Association Press, 1915.
Eisenberg, John. *The Great Match Race: When North Met South in America's First Sports Spectacle.* Boston: Houghton Mifflin Co., 2006.
Emerson, Ken. *Doo-dah! Steven Foster and the Rise of American Popular Culture.* New York: Simon and Schuster, 1997.
Escott, Paul D., ed. *North Carolina Yeoman: The Diary of Basil Armstrong Thomasson, 1853–1862.* Athens: University of Georgia Press, 1996.
Ezell, John Samuel. *The South Since 1865.* 2nd ed. New York: Macmillan Publishing Co., 1975.
Fawcett, James Waldo. "The Circus in Washington." *Records of the Columbia Historical Society of Washington, D.C.* 50 (1950): 265–71.
Feldman, Glenn. *Politics, Society, and the Klan in Alabama, 1915–1949.* Tuscaloosa: University of Alabama Press, 1999.
Fellows, Dexter W., and Andrew A. Freeman. *This Way to the Big Show: The Life of Dexter Fellows.* New York: Viking Press, 1936.
Fichman, Martin. *Evolutionary Theory and Victorian Culture.* Amherst, N.Y.: Humanity Books, 2002.
Fields, Barbara J. "Ideology and Race in American History." In *Region, Race, and Reconstruction: Essays in Honor of C. Vann Woodward,* edited by J. Morgan Kousser and James M. McPherson, 143–77. New York: Oxford University Press, 1982.
———. *Slavery and Freedom on the Middle Ground: Maryland During the Nineteenth Century.* New Haven, Conn.: Yale University Press, 1985.
Foner, Eric. *Reconstruction: America's Unfinished Revolution, 1863–1877.* New York: Harper and Row, 1988.
Foster, Gaines M. *Ghosts of the Confederacy: Defeat, the Lost Cause, and the Emergence of the New South.* New York: Oxford University Press, 1987.
Fox, Charles Philip, and Tom Parkinson. *The Circus in America.* Waukesha, Wisc.: Country Beautiful, 1969.
Fox, Richard Wightman, and T. J. Jackson Lears, eds. *The Culture of Consumption: Critical Essays in American History, 1880–1980.* New York: Pantheon Books, 1983.
Franklin, John Hope. "History of Racial Segregation in the United States." *Annals of the American Academy of Political and Social Science* 304 (1956): 1–9.

———. *The Militant South, 1800–1861*. Cambridge, Mass.: Harvard University Press, 1956.

"A Freedmen's Bureau Diary by George Wagner." *Georgia Historical Quarterly* 48 (1964): 196–214.

Fuller, Kathryn H. *At the Picture Show: Small Town Audiences and the Creation of Movie Fan Culture*. Washington: Smithsonian Institution Press, 1996.

Gallagher, Gary W., and Alan T. Nolan. *The Myth of the Lost Cause and Civil War History*. Bloomington: Indiana University Press, 2000.

Garrett, Franklin M. *Atlanta and Environs: A Chronicle of Its People and Events*. 2 vols. Athens: University of Georgia Press, 1982.

Genovese, Eugene D. *The Political Economy of Slavery: Studies in the Economy and the Society of the Slave South*. New York: Pantheon Books, 1965.

———. *Roll, Jordan, Roll: The World the Slaves Made*. New York: Vintage Books, 1976.

Georgia Department of Archives and History. *Vanishing Georgia*. Athens: University of Georgia Press, 1982.

Gilmore, Glenda Elizabeth. *Gender and Jim Crow: Women and the Politics of White Supremacy in North Carolina, 1896–1920*. Chapel Hill: University of North Carolina Press, 1996.

Gladden, Washington. "Christianity and Popular Amusements." *Century Illustrated Monthly Magazine* 29 (1885): 384–92.

Glenroy, John H. *Ins and Outs of Circus Life or, Forty-Two Years Travel of John H. Glenroy, Bareback Rider, Through United States, Canada, South America and Cuba*. Boston: Wing & Co., 1885.

Goldfield, David R. *Cotton Fields and Skyscrapers: Southern City and Region, 1607–1980*. Baton Rouge: Louisiana State University Press, 1982.

Gollmar, Robert H. *My Father Owned a Circus*. Caldwell, Idaho: Caxton Printers, 1965.

Gomery, Douglas. *Shared Pleasures: A History of Movie Presentation in the United States*. Madison: University of Wisconsin Press, 1992.

Goodson, Steve. *Highbrows, Hillbillies, and Hellfire: Public Entertainment in Atlanta, 1880–1930*. Athens: University of Georgia Press, 2002.

Gorn, Elliott J. "'Gouge and Bite, Pull Hair and Scratch': The Social Significance of Fighting in the Southern Backcountry." *American Historical Review* 90 (1985): 18–43.

———. *The Manly Art: Bare-Knuckle Prize Fighting in America*. Ithaca, N.Y.: Cornell University Press, 1986.

Grant, Donald L. *The Way It Was in the South: The Black Experience in Georgia*. New York: Birch Lane Press, 1993.

Greenberg, Kenneth S. *Honor & Slavery: Lies, Duels, Noses, Masks, Dressing as a Woman, Gifts, Strangers, Humanitarianism, Death, Slave Rebellions, The Proslavery Argument, Baseball, Hunting, and Gambling in the Old South*. Princeton, N.J.: Princeton University Press, 1996.

Greenwood, Isaac J. *The Circus: Its Origin and Growth Prior to 1835*. 1898. Reprint, Washington, D.C.: Hobby House Press, 1962.

Grinols, Earl L. *Gambling in America: Costs and Benefits.* Cambridge: Cambridge University Press, 2004.

Gutman, Herbert G. *Work, Culture, and Society in Industrializing America: Essays in American Working Class and Social History.* New York: Knopf, 1976.

Hahn, Steven. *The Roots of Southern Populism: Yeoman Farmers and the Transformation of the Georgia Upcountry, 1850–1890.* New York: Oxford University Press, 1983.

Hallock, E. S. "The American Circus." *Century Magazine* 70 (1905): 568–85.

Halttunen, Karen. *Confidence Men and Painted Women: A Study of Middle-Class Culture in America, 1830–1870.* New Haven, Conn.: Yale University Press, 1982.

Hammarstrom, David Lewis. *Big Top Boss: John Ringling North and the Circus.* Urbana: University of Illinois Press, 1992.

Harris, Neil. *Humbug: The Art of P. T. Barnum.* Boston: Little, Brown, and Co., 1973.

Heyrman, Christine Leigh. *Southern Cross: The Beginnings of the Bible Belt.* New York: Knopf, 1997.

Higashi, Sumiko. *Cecil B. DeMille and American Culture: The Silent Era.* Berkeley: University of California Press, 1994.

Hill, Samuel S., Jr., ed. *Religion and the Solid South.* Nashville, Tenn.: Abingdon Press, 1972.

Hogan, William Ransom, and Edwin Adams Davis, eds. *William Johnson's Natchez: The Ante Bellum Diary of a Free Negro.* 2 vols. Port Washington, N.Y.: Kennikat Press, 1968.

Hoh, LaVahn G., and William H. Rough. *Step Right Up! The Adventure of Circus in America.* White Hall, Va.: Betterway Publications, 1990.

Holliman, Jennie. "American Sports (1785–1835)." Ph.D. diss., Columbia University, 1931.

Holmes, Yulssus Lynn. *Those Glorious Days: A History of Louisville as Georgia's Capital, 1796–1807.* Macon, Ga.: Mercer University Press, 1996.

Hope, W. Martin, and Jason H. Silverman. *Relief and Recovery in Post–Civil War South Carolina: A Death by Inches.* Lewiston, N.Y.: Edwin Mellen Press, 1997.

Horowitz, Daniel. *The Morality of Spending: Attitudes Toward the Consumer Society in America, 1875–1940.* Baltimore: Johns Hopkins University Press, 1985; Chicago: Elephant Paperbacks, 1992.

Hosch, Clarence Robert. *Nevah Come Back No Mo': Boyhood Memories of the Foothills of North Georgia.* Jericho, N.Y.: Exposition Press, 1968.

Howe, Daniel Walker. "American Victorianism as a Culture." *American Quarterly* 27 (1975): 507–32.

Howell, Mark D. *From Moonshine to Madison Avenue: A Cultural History of the NASCAR Winston Cup Series.* Bowling Green, Ohio: Bowling Green State University Popular Press, 1997.

Howells, W. D. *A Boy's Town.* New York: Harper & Brothers, 1890.

Hull, Augustus Longstreet. *Annals of Athens, Georgia, 1801–1901.* Athens: Banner Job Office, 1906.

Hunter, Tera W. *To 'joy My Freedom: Southern Black Women's Lives and Labors after the Civil War.* Cambridge, Mass.: Harvard University Press, 1997.

Hynds, Ernest C. *Antebellum Athens and Clarke County, Georgia.* Athens: University of Georgia Press, 1974.

Inge, M. Thomas, and Edward J. Piacentino, eds. *The Humor of the Old South.* Lexington: University Press of Kentucky, 2001.

"Introductory Brief History of Sparks Family and Title." *Bandwagon* 8 (1964): 4–8.

Isaac, Rhys. *The Transformation of Virginia, 1740–1790.* New York: W. W. Norton, 1982.

Isbell, Robert L. *The World of My Childhood.* Hudson, N.C.: W & H Graphics, 1955.

Isenberg, Arthur V. *My Town and the Big Top.* (self-published, 1954).

Jay, Ricky. *Learned Pigs & Fireproof Women.* New York: Villard Books, 1986.

Jensen, Faye Lind. "Power and Progress in the Urban South: Columbus, Georgia, 1850–1885." Ph.D. diss., Emory University, 1991.

Johnson, Paul E. *Sam Patch, The Famous Jumper.* New York: Hill and Wang, 2003.

———. *A Shopkeeper's Millennium: Society and Revivals in Rochester, New York, 1815–1837.* New York: Hill and Wang, 1978.

Jones, Jacqueline. *Labor of Love, Labor of Sorrow: Black Women, Work and the Family, from Slavery to the Present.* New York: Basic Books, 1985.

Jones, Robert F. "Make or Break." *Sports Illustrated,* September 2, 1974.

Jordan, Winthrop D. *Tumult and Silence at Second Creek: An Inquiry into a Civil War Slave Conspiracy.* Baton Rouge: Louisiana State University Press, 1993.

———. *White Over Black: American Attitudes Toward the Negro, 1550–1812.* Chapel Hill: University of North Carolina Press, 1968.

Kann, Maurice D., ed. *The Film Daily 1929 Year Book.* New York: John W. Alicoate, 1929.

Kasson, John F. *Amusing the Million: Coney Island at the Turn of the Century.* New York: Hill and Wang, 1978.

———. *Rudeness and Civility: Manners in Nineteenth Century Urban America.* New York: Hill and Wang, 1990.

Kasson, Joy S. *Buffalo Bill's Wild West: Celebrity, Memory, and Popular History.* New York: Hill and Wang, 2000.

Kelly, Emmett, with F. Beverly Kelly. *Clown.* New York: Prentice Hall, 1954.

Kern, Stephen. *The Culture of Time and Space, 1880–1918.* Cambridge, Mass.: Harvard University Press, 1983.

Kibler, M. Alison. *Rank Ladies: Gender and Cultural Hierarchy in American Vaudeville.* Chapel Hill: University of North Carolina Press, 1999.

King, Orin C., "The World in a Nut Shell: Wallace & Co., 1890 & 1891." *Bandwagon* 28 (1984): 21–26.

Kirk, Mary Wallace. *Locust Hill.* University: University of Alabama Press, 1975.

Kitchen, Robert. "19th Century Circus Bands and Music." *Bandwagon* 29 (1985): 14–17.

Konvitz, Milton R. "The Extent and Character of Legally-Enforced Segregation." *Journal of Negro Education* 20 (Summer 1951): 425–35.

Kunhardt, Philip B., Jr., Philip B. Kunhardt, and Peter W. Kunhardt. *P. T. Barnum: America's Greatest Showman.* New York: Knopf, 1995.

Lang, Robert, ed. *The Birth of a Nation: D. W. Griffith, Director.* New Brunswick, N.J.: Rutgers University Press, 1994.

Larsen, Lawrence H. *The Rise of the Urban South.* Lexington: University Press of Kentucky, 1985.

Leach, William. *Land of Desire: Merchants, Power, and the Rise of a New American Culture.* New York: Pantheon Books, 1993.

Lears, Jackson. *Fables of Abundance: A Cultural History of Advertising in America.* New York: Basic Books, 1994.

Leavitt, M. B. *Fifty Years in Theatrical Management.* New York: Broadway Publishing, 1912.

Levine, Lawrence W. *Highbrow/Lowbrow: The Emergence of Cultural Hierarchy in America.* Cambridge, Mass.: Harvard University Press, 1986.

Lindfors, Bernth. "Circus Africans." *Journal of American Culture* 6 (1983): 9–14.

Link, William A. *The Paradox of Southern Progressivism, 1880–1930.* Chapel Hill: University of North Carolina Press, 1992.

Litwack, Leon F. *Been in the Storm So Long: The Aftermath of Slavery.* New York: Knopf, 1979.

———. *Trouble in Mind: Black Southerners in the Age of Jim Crow.* New York: Knopf, 1998.

Litwicki, Ellen M. *America's Public Holidays, 1865–1920.* Washington, D.C.: Smithsonian Institution Press, 2000.

Livingston, James. *Pragmatism and the Political Economy of Cultural Revolution, 1850–1940.* Chapel Hill: University of North Carolina Press, 1994.

Lott, Eric. *Love and Theft: Blackface Minstrelsy and the American Working Class.* New York: Oxford University Press, 1995.

Loveland, Anne C. *Southern Evangelicals and the Social Order, 1800–1860.* Baton Rouge: Louisiana State University Press, 1980.

Mandle, Jay R. *The Roots of Black Poverty: The Southern Plantation after the Civil War.* Durham, N.C.: Duke University Press, 1978.

Marsh, Blanche. *Hitch Up the Buggy.* Greenville, S.C.: A Press, 1977.

Martell, Joanne. *Millie-Christine: The Remarkable Journey of Siamese Twins from Slavery to Freedom.* Winston-Salem, N.C.: John F. Blair, 2000.

Marx, Leo. *The Machine in the Garden: Technology and the Pastoral Ideal.* New York: Oxford University Press, 1964.

Matheny, Martha. "The Circus in Tallahassee, 1831–1920." M.A. thesis, Florida State University, 1973.

Mathews, Donald G. *Religion in the Old South.* Chicago: University of Chicago Press, 1977.

Maurer, David W. "Carnival Cant: A Glossary of Circus and Carnival Slang." *American Speech* 6 (1931): 327–37.

McMillen, Neil R. *Dark Journey: Black Mississippians in the Age of Jim Crow.* Urbana: University of Illinois Press, 1989.

McPherson, James M. *Ordeal By Fire.* Vol. 2, *The Civil War.* New York: Knopf, 1982.

McWhiney, Grady, Warner O. Moore Jr., and Robert F. Pace, eds. *"Fear God and Walk Humbly": The Agricultural Journal of James Mallory, 1843–1877.* Tuscaloosa: University of Alabama Press, 1997.

Methodist Episcopal Church. *The Doctrines and Discipline of the Methodist Episcopal Church, 1876: With an Appendix.* New York: Nelson and Phillips, 1876.

Middleton, George. *Circus Memoirs: Reminiscences of George Middleton as Told to and Written by his Wife.* Los Angeles: G. Rice & Sons, 1913.

Milburn, George. "Circus Words," *American Mercury* 24 (1931): 351–54.

Mishler, Doug A. "The Greatest Show on Earth: The Circus and the Development of Modern American Culture, 1860–1940." Ph.D. diss., University of Nevada, Reno, 1994.

Nasaw, David. *Going Out: The Rise and Fall of Public Amusements.* Cambridge, Mass.: Harvard University Press, 1993.

"19th Century Animal Booklets." *Bandwagon* 30 (1986): 30–31.

Nisbett, Richard E., and Dov Cohen. *Culture of Honor: The Psychology of Violence in the South.* Boulder, Colo.: Westview Press, 1996.

O'Nan, Stewart. *The Circus Fire: A True Story.* New York: Doubleday, 2000.

Ownby, Ted. *American Dreams in Mississippi: Consumers, Poverty, & Culture.* Chapel Hill: University of North Carolina Press, 1999.

———. *Subduing Satan: Religion, Recreation, and Manhood in the Rural South, 1865–1920.* Chapel Hill: University of North Carolina Press, 1990.

Owsley, Frank L. *Plain Folk of the Old South.* Baton Rouge: Louisiana State University Press, 1949.

Packard, Jerrold M. *American Nightmare: The History of Jim Crow.* New York: St. Martin's Press, 2002.

Peiss, Kathy. *Cheap Amusements: Working Women and Leisure in Turn-of-the-Century New York.* Philadelphia: Temple University Press, 1986.

Perman, Michael, ed. *Major Problems in the Civil War and Reconstruction.* Boston: Houghton Mifflin, 1998.

Pfening, Fred D., Jr. "Side Shows and Bannerlines." *Bandwagon* 29 (1985): 16–22.

Phillips, Ulrich Bonnell. *The Slave Economy of the Old South: Selected Essays in Economic and Social History.* Baton Rouge: Louisiana State University Press, 1968.

Piersen, William D. "African-American Festive Style." In *Signifyin(g), Sanctifyin', and Slam Dunking: A Reader in African American Expressive Culture*, edited by Gena Dagel Caponi, 417–33. Amherst: University of Massachusetts Press, 1999.

Porter, Katherine Anne. "The Circus." *Southern Review* 1 (1935): 36–41.

Powell, Arthur G. *I Can Go Home Again.* Chapel Hill: The University of North Carolina Press, 1943.

Preston, Howard L. *Automobile Age Atlanta: The Making of a Southern Metropolis, 1900–1935.* Athens: University of Georgia Press, 1979.

"Public Amusements and Social Enjoyments." *De Bow's Review* 29 (1860): 330–34.

Quinn, John Philip. *Gambling and Gambling Devices.* 1912. Reprint, Montclair, N.J.: Patterson Smith Publishing, 1969.

Rabinowitz, Howard N. *The First New South: 1865–1920.* Arlington Heights, Ill.: Harlan Davidson, 1992.

———. "From Exclusion to Segregation: Southern Race Relations, 1865–1890." *Journal of American History* 63 (1976): 325–50.

———. *Race Relations in the Urban South, 1865–1890.* Urbana: University of Illinois Press, 1980.

Ransom, Roger L., and Richard Sutch. *One Kind of Freedom: The Economic Consequences of Emancipation.* Cambridge: Cambridge University Press, 1977.

Reddin, Paul. *Wild West Shows.* Urbana: University of Illinois Press, 1999.

Register, Woody. *The Kid of Coney Island: Fred Thompson and the Rise of American Amusements.* Oxford: Oxford University Press, 2001.

Reid, Whitelaw. *After the War: A Tour of the Southern States, 1865–66.* Edited by C. Vann Woodward. 1866. Reprint, New York: Harper & Row, 1965.

Reidy, Joseph P. *From Slavery to Agrarian Capitalism in the Cotton Plantation South: Central Georgia, 1800–1880.* Chapel Hill: University of North Carolina Press, 1992.

Renoff, Gregory James. "From Systematic Farming to Systematic Management: The Agrarian Origins of the Systematic Ideal in the Old South." M.A. thesis, University of Mississippi, 1996.

Robertson, Ben. *Red Hills and Cotton.* Chapel Hill: University of North Carolina Press, 1960.

Robinson, Gil. *Old Wagon Show Days.* Cincinnati: Brockwell, 1925.

Roediger, David. *The Wages of Whiteness: Race and the Making of the American Working Class.* New York: Verso, 1991.

Rogers, William Warren. *Thomas County, 1865–1900.* Tallahassee: Florida State University Press, 1973.

Root, Harvey W. *The Ways of the Circus; Being the Memoirs and Adventures of George Conklin, Tamer of Lions.* New York: Harper and Brothers, 1921.

Rosenzweig, Roy. *Eight Hours for What We Will: Workers & Leisure in an Industrial City, 1870–1920.* Cambridge: Cambridge University Press, 1983.

Russell, James M. *Atlanta, 1847–1890: City Building in the Old South and the New.* Baton Rouge: Louisiana State University Press, 1988.

Ryan, Mary. *Women in Public: Between Banners & Ballots, 1825–1880.* Baltimore: Johns Hopkins University Press, 1989.

Salzman, Jack, David Lionel Smith, and Cornel West, eds. *The Encyclopedia of African American Culture and History.* New York: Simon & Schuster, 1996.

Sams, Anita B. *Wayfarers in Walton: A History of Walton County, Georgia, 1818–1967.* Doraville, Ga.: Foote & Davies, 1967.

Saxon, A. H. *P. T. Barnum: The Legend and the Man.* New York: Columbia University Press, 1989.

Saxon, Lyle. *Old Louisiana.* New York: Century Co., 1929.

Schroeder, Joan Vannorsdall. "The Day They Hanged Mary the Elephant." *Blue Ridge Country*, May–June 1997, 18–21.

Schultz, Mark. *The Rural Face of White Supremacy: Beyond Jim Crow.* Urbana: University of Illinois Press, 2005.

Scott, W. W. "Some Personal Memories of General Robert E. Lee." *William and Mary Quarterly* 6 (1926): 277–88.

Shannon, Jasper Berry. *Toward a New Politics in the New South.* Knoxville: University of Tennessee Press, 1949.

Sharpe, Adrian D. "Circus Grift on the Yankee Robinson Circus." *Bandwagon* 14 (1970): 31–36.
Sherwood, Robert Edmund. *Here We Are Again: Recollections of an Old Circus Clown.* Indianapolis: Bobbs-Merrill Co., 1926.
———. *Hold Yer Hosses! The Elephants are Coming.* New York: Macmillan Co., 1932.
Shettles, Elijah L. *Recollections of a Long Life.* Edited by Archie P. McDonald. Nashville, Tenn.: Blue & Gray Press, 1973.
Shippee, Lester B., ed. *Bishop Whipple's Southern Diary, 1843–1844.* Minneapolis: University of Minnesota Press, 1937.
Shuler, Edward Leander. *Blood Mountain: A Historical Study About Choestoe and Choestoeans.* Jacksonville, Fla.: Convention Press, 1953.
Silber, Nina. *The Romance of Reunion: Northerners and the South, 1865–1900.* Chapel Hill: University of North Carolina Press, 1993.
Slout, William L. *Chilly Billy: The Evolution of a Circus Millionaire.* San Bernardino, Calif.: Emeritus Enterprise Books, 2000.
———. *Clowns and Cannons: The American Circus During the Civil War.* San Bernardino, Calif.: Emeritus Enterprise Books, 1997.
———. *Olympians of the Sawdust Circle: A Biographical Dictionary of the Nineteenth Century American Circus.* cd-rom. San Bernardino, Calif.: Emeritus Enterprise Books, 2002.
———. *A Royal Coupling: The Historic Marriage of Barnum and Bailey.* San Bernardino, Calif.: Emeritus Enterprise Books, 2000.
Slovenko, Ralph, and James A. Knight, eds. *Motivations in Play, Games, and Sports.* Springfield, Ill.: Charles C. Thomas Publishing, 1967.
Smith, John David, ed. *When Did Southern Segregation Begin?* New York: Bedford/St. Martin's, 2001.
Sorkin, Michael. *Variations on a Theme Park: The New American City and the End of Public Space.* New York: Hill and Wang, 1992.
Spain, Rufus B. *At Ease in Zion: A Social History of Southern Baptists, 1865–1900.* Nashville, Tenn.: Vanderbilt University Press, 1961.
Sparks, Randy J. *On Jordan's Stormy Banks: Evangelicalism in Mississippi, 1773–1876.* Athens: University of Georgia Press, 1994.
Stallybrass, Peter, and Allon White. *The Politics and Poetics of Transgression.* Cornell, N.Y.: Cornell University Press, 1986.
Steiner, W. H. "Changing Composition of the Savannah Business Community." *Southern Economic Journal* 10 (1944): 303–10.
Susman, Warren. *Culture as History: The Transformation of American Society in the Twentieth Century.* New York: Pantheon, 1984.
Szymanski, Ann-Marie. "Beyond Parochialism: Southern Progressivism, Prohibition, and State Building." *Journal of Southern History* 69 (2003): 107–36.
Tate, Susan Frances Barrow. *Remembering Athens.* Edited by Charlotte Thomas Marshall and George O. Marshall Jr. Athens, Ga.: Athens Historical Society, 1996.
Taylor, A. A. "The Negro Population." *Journal of Negro History* 11 (1926): 273–93.

Telfair, Nancy. *A History of Columbus, Georgia, 1828–1928.* Columbus: Historical Publishing Co., 1929.

Temple, Sarah Blackwell Gober. *The First Hundred Years: A Short History of Cobb County, in Georgia.* Atlanta: Walter W. Brown Publishing Co., 1935.

Thayer, Stuart. *Annals of the American Circus, 1793–1860.* Seattle: Dauven & Thayer, 2000.

———. "The Birth of the Blues: Early Circus Seating." *Bandwagon* 29 (1985): 24–26.

———. "Legislating the Shows: Vermont, 1824–1933." *Bandwagon* 25 (1981): 20–22.

———. "Notes on the History of Circus Tents." *Bandwagon* 30 (1986): 28–30.

———. "Some Class Distinctions in the Early Circus Audience." *Bandwagon* 24 (1980): 20–21.

———. *Traveling Showmen: The American Circus Before the Civil War.* Detroit: Astley & Ricketts, 1997.

———. "Trouping in Alabama in 1827." *Bandwagon* 26 (1982): 20–21.

Thigpen, S. G. *A Boy in Rural Mississippi.* Kingsport, Tenn.: Kingsport Press, 1966.

Thomas, J. J. *Fifty Years on the Rail.* New York: Knickerbocker Press, 1912.

Thomason, Michael V. R. *Trying Times: Alabama Photographs, 1917–1945.* University: University of Alabama Press, 1985.

Thompson, C. Mildred. *Reconstruction in Georgia: Economic, Social, Political.* New York: Columbia University Press, 1915.

Thompson, E. P. "Time, Work-Discipline and Industrial Capitalism." *Past and Present* 38 (1967): 56–97.

Thompson, W. C. *On the Road with a Circus.* New York: New Amsterdam Book Co., 1905.

Thomson, Rosemarie Garland, ed. *Freakery: Cultural Spectacles of the Extraordinary Body.* New York: New York University Press, 1996.

Thornburg, Miles O. *Thread of My Life.* Charlotte, N.C.: William Loftin Publishers, 1958.

Tindall, George Brown. *The Emergence of the New South, 1913–1945.* Baton Rouge: Louisiana State University Press, 1967.

Tindall, George Brown, and David E. Shi. *America: A Narrative History.* 3rd ed. New York: W. W. Norton, 1992.

Trachtenberg, Alan. *The Incorporation of America: Culture and Society in the Gilded Age.* New York: Hill and Wang, 1982.

Trowbridge, John T. *The Desolate South, 1865–66: A Picture of the Battlefields and of the Devastated Confederacy.* 1866. Reprint, New York: Duell, Sloan and Pearce, 1956.

Truzzi, Marcello. *Sociology and Everyday Life.* Englewood Cliffs, N.J.: Prentice Hall, 1968.

Turnour, Jules. *The Autobiography of a Clown.* New York: Moffat, Yard and Co., 1910.

Twain, Mark. *The Adventures of Huckleberry Finn.* 1885. Reprint, Mineola, N.Y.: Dover Publications, 1994.

Vaughan, David Wynn. "A Brief History of the Georgia Military Institute and a Study of Its Uniform, 1851–1864." *Military Images* 26 (2004): 32–36.

Verney, Peter. *Here Comes the Circus*. New York: Paddington Press, 1978.

Waldstreicher, David. *In the Midst of Perpetual Fetes: The Making of American Nationalism, 1776–1820*. Chapel Hill: University of North Carolina Press, 1997.

Waller, Gregory A. *Main Street Amusements: Movies and Commercial Entertainment in a Southern City, 1896–1930*. Washington, D.C.: Smithsonian Institution Press, 1995.

Washington, Forrester B. "Recreational Facilities for the Negro." *American Academy of Political and Social Science Annals* 140 (1928): 272–82.

Weeks, David C. *Ringling: The Florida Years, 1911–1936*. Gainesville: University Press of Florida, 1993.

Weiner, Jonathan M. *Social Origins of the New South: Alabama, 1860–1885*. Baton Rouge: Louisiana State University Press, 1978.

West, Jennifer Boone. "'Before We Reach the Heavenly Fields': Religion and Society in Wilkes County, Georgia, 1783–1881." Ph.D. diss., Emory University, 1991.

Wetherington, Mark V. *The New South Comes to Wiregrass Georgia, 1860–1910*. Knoxville: University of Tennessee Press, 1994.

Whitehead, Margaret Laney, and Barbara Bogart. *City of Progress: A History of Columbus, Georgia*. Columbus, Ga.: Columbus Office Supply Co., 1978.

Wiebe, Robert. *The Search for Order, 1877–1920*. New York: Hill and Wang, 1967.

Williams, Ida Belle. *History of Tift County*. Macon, Ga.: J. W. Burke Co., 1948.

Wills, Gregory A. *Democratic Religion: Freedom, Authority, and Church Discipline in the Baptist South, 1785–1900*. New York: Oxford University Press, 1997.

Willson, Dixie. *Where the World Folds Up at Night*. New York: D. Appleton & Co., 1932.

Wilson, Charles Reagan. *Baptized in Blood: The Religion of the Lost Cause, 1865–1920*. Athens: University of Georgia Press, 1980.

Wilson, Charles Reagan, and William Ferris, eds. *Encyclopedia of Southern Culture*. Chapel Hill: University of North Carolina Press, 1989.

Wilson, John Lyde. *The Code of Honor; or Rules for the Government of Principals and Seconds in Duelling*. Charleston, S.C.: James Phinney, 1858.

Wingo, Horace Calvin. "Race Relations in Georgia 1872–1908." Ph.D. diss., University of Georgia, 1969.

Winston, Robert Watson. *It's a Far Cry*. New York: Henry Holt, 1937.

Wood, Amy Louise. "Spectacles of Suffering: Witnessing Lynching in the New South, 1880–1930." Ph.D. diss., Emory University, 2002.

Woodman, Harold D. *King Cotton and His Retainers: Financing and Marketing the Cotton Crop of the South, 1800–1925*. Lexington: University of Kentucky Press, 1968.

———. "Sequel to Slavery: The New History Views the Postbellum South." *Journal of Southern History* 43 (November 1977): 523–54.

Woodward, C. Vann. *Origins of the New South, 1877–1913*. Baton Rouge: Louisiana State University Press, 1951.

———. *The Strange Career of Jim Crow*. 3rd ed., revised. New York: Oxford University Press, 1974.

Workers of the Writers Program of the Works Progress Administration in the State of Georgia, comp. *Atlanta: A City of the Modern South*. New York: Smith & Durrell, 1942.

Wyatt-Brown, Bertram. *Southern Honor: Ethics and Behavior in the Old South*. New York: Oxford University Press, 1982.

Young, Ida, Julius Gholson, and Clara Nell Hargrove. *History of Macon, Georgia*. Macon: Lyon, Marshall & Brooks, 1950.

INDEX

A. B. Rothschild and Company's Great Royal Victoria Menagerie, Caravan and Circus, 116
accommodations, for families, 20–21
Ackerman, Amos T., 94
advance man, 17
advertising: bills and posters, 17, 18, 59, 87, 88, 139; joint with merchants, 68, 70, 80; modern, 2; in newspapers, 187n13. *See also under* Atlanta
African Americans: assaulted by police, 128; attendance of, at circus, 20, 99, 110–11; in bands, 114; businesses and, 72; as clowns, 25, 97–98; in contests, 126; economic impact on, 78–79; elopements of, 100; as exhorters, 137; and failure of segregation, 196n40; menagerie and, 121; migration of, to towns, 54; opposition of, to circus, 71–72; and parades, 97; as performers, 114, 144; religion and, 100–101; seating of, 21, 124; and slavery, 20; and snack stands, 7, 87, 97, 98–100; UniverSoul Circus, 171; violence and, 93, 104, 105, 107, 128. *See also* Jim Crow; segregation; slavery
Albany, Ga., 105, 148
alcohol, 30, 87–89, 92, 93, 101–3
Allen, Robert C., 62
American Circus Corporation (ACC), 151–52, 161, 163
Americus, Ga., 83, 89, 90, 100, 102–3, 122
Americus Recorder, 90, 103
Ames, Clark T., 41, 42
Ames Circus, 42, 50, 52, 143
Andrew Haight's Great Southern Show, 64

Andrews, Billy, 46, 48
Andrews, L. F. W., 49
animals: acts, 142; Darwinist beliefs about, 141–42; escapes by, 87, 105–6, 194n60; feeding of, 121–22; labor by, 18; racing of, 142; tricks by, 116, 141, 142. *See also entries for specific animals*
Athens, Ga.: attendance at circus in, 60, 61, 77, 78, 91, 120; churches and ministers in, 50, 53, 60–61; college in, 27; farmers in, 75; grifting in, 93; interest in circus in, 88, 90; menagerie in, 122; parade in, 92, 94; performances in, 162; sideshow in, 114; snack stands in, 98
Atlanta: advertising in, 40, 70, 87; African Americans, 71–72, 97; animals, 63, 64, 122, 143–44; attendance at circus in, 55–56, 90, 150; audience interaction in, 94–97; autos in, 147; business with circus, 42, 44; charity in, 51, 52; church in, 136; as commerce center, 3; Confederate Cemetery in, 52; economy in, 3, 4, 70; Haight Brothers' Circus in, 45–46; localism in, 43, 160, 164, 165; merchant elite of, 68, 69, 70, 72, 73, 75; modern circus in, 171; parades in, 91, 92, 93, 156, 165, 168; people of, 21, 128; railroad in, 4, 36; segregation in, 112, 121; spectacle in, 133, 135, 136; "Stonewall" at, 41; taxes in, 80, 82; violence in, 115; wintering in, 83, 170; women performers in, 139, 140, 146; zoo in, 79
Atlanta Constitution: on animals, 142; approval of, 67; on city council, 90; as

227

Atlanta Constitution (continued)
　　democratic, 2; on off-season activities, 45; on performers, 47, 67, 136; on Robinson, 40; on spectacle, 136
Atlanta Daily Herald, 45–46, 56, 71, 94, 121
Atlanta Daily New Era, 41, 43–44
Atlanta Georgian, 142
Atlanta Independent, 71, 72
Atlanta Intelligencer, 52
Atlanta Journal, 110, 132, 136, 148
Atlanta News, 132
Atlanta Sun, 55–56
Augusta, Ga.: advertising in, 70; animals in, 106, 122, 143; boat service to, 16; children in, 64; financiers in, 112; rail service to, 36
Augusta Daily Chronicle and Sentinel, 40, 112, 122, 140, 161, 162
autos: blocked parades, 150, 156, 166; led parades, 160; registered, 147; travel to show by, 155; tricks by, 132–33, 147, 148, 149

Bachler, Jerome, 22
Bailey, Hackaliah, 13
Bailey, James A., 69, 151, 168
Bailey and Company, 25
Bainbridge, Ga., 86, 91, 96, 99
Bakhtin, Mikhail, 2, 86
bands: opening, 21, 133; in parades, 19, 95, 96, 102, 157–58, 160; in program, 133; in sideshow, 114
bankruptcy, 189n33
banned circuses, 15
Barnesville, Ga., 65, 88, 91, 101, 122
Barnum, P. T., 30, 44, 57, 63, 69, 167
Barnum and Bailey Circus: animals in, 121, 141–42, 143–44; attendance at, 90; and autos, 148; economics of, 70, 73; fire at, 130; parade for, 155; politics and, 64; posters for, 87; seating at, 20; sideshow band for, 114; spectacle of, 135–36; taxes on, 82; tents of, 123; violence and crime and, 112–13; women and, 147. *See also* Ringling Brothers and Barnum and Bailey Circus
Barnum and London Show, 63, 142
Barrett, S. H., 77
Barrett & Co., 101, 122
Battle, Kemp Plummer, 11
Beale Street, Memphis, Tenn., 171

Beecher, Henry Ward, 63
behavior: drunken, 115; excessive, 7; rowdy, 109–10, 126, 129–30; uninhibited, 6. *See also* violence
bicycles, 89, 132–33, 146–47
Bierce, Ambrose, 109
Big Apple Circus, 171
Billboard Magazine, 80, 115, 119, 124, 125, 157
Bird, Calvin, 115
Bishop, Edward T., 60–61, 88, 92, 120, 138–39
blacks. *See* African Americans
Blakely, Ga., 76
bleachers, 19, 123, 128; "country bloods" in, 109; females in, 25; fire started in, 130; noise from, 21; protest of immorality from, 129
boats, 16, 35
Bradbury, Joseph, 114, 115, 119, 125
brawls, 29, 31, 32, 37
Brown, J. Purdy, 15, 16, 26, 28
Bryant, William Cullen, 63, 64
Buckley's Circus, 130
Burk, T. K., 126
Butler, Miss (stunt driver), 147–48
Butsch, Richard, 30

C. W. Noyes Circus, 39. *See also* Thayer and Noyes' United States Circus
camp followers, card sharps, and swindlers, 19–20, 30, 77, 113. *See also* grifting
Carlisle, Ga., 20
Carlyon, David, 24, 25
carnivalesque atmosphere, 2, 126
Carroll, W. B., 44–45
cars. *See* autos
Carter, Jimmy, 1
Cartersville, Ga., 87
Castello, Dan, 33–34, 36, 37, 57. *See also* Dan Castello's Great Show
Cedartown, Ga., 80
celebrities, endorsements by, 63
charity: circus's appeal to those on, 72; Elks and, 160; females and, 52, 66; politicians and, 51, 151, 163, 164; shows for, 51–52; Shriners and, 164
Charlotte Observer, 63
Christian Index, 52

churches: African American, 100; circus response to opposition from, 50, 52, 59, 63–65, 87; doctrine of, against circus-going, 49; as less attractive than circus, 1, 61; and members' guilt over circus-going, 60–61; ministers versus members of, 60, 62, 66; on wickedness of circus, 15, 26–27, 50, 57, 62
Circus Age, The (Davis), 3, 134, 138
Circus Maximus, 135–36
Circus Memoirs (Middleton), 33
cities. *See entries for specific cities*
Clark, W. C., 66
classes: appeal of circus to all, 1, 133; distinctions among, 2–6, 21, 62, 63, 91, 109; interaction of, 56, 92, 95; separation of, 115
Clinton (Mississippi) Baptist Record, 62
clowns, 12, 24–26, 28; animals and, 142; as beginning act, 124–25; cross-dressing, 125–26; Dan Rice, 24, 25, 37, 38; females and, 25, 27–28; insolence of, 50, 56; Johnny Lowlow, 40; "Mack," 96–97; in parades, 96, 97, 193n35; vulgarity of, 15, 178n50
Cole, William W., 69, 79, 114, 151
Cole Brothers Show, 120
colleges: as opposed to circus, 27, 65; as supportive of circus, 157, 158
Collins, Steven, 51
Columbus, Ga., 36, 41, 55–57, 109, 112, 147; African Americans in, 87, 114; alcohol issues in, 101–2; and animals, 141, 143, 145, 146; crowd segregation in, 55, 91; economics of, 72, 73, 74; and menagerie, 16; merchants in, 92; ministers and laity differences in, 60, 62, 66; and parades, 88–89; and spectacle, 87, 95, 136; taxes in, 80–81, 82; violence averted in, 33–34; visitors to, from rural areas, 74–75, 86–88, 89, 145, 146
Columbus Daily Sun, 55, 72, 85
Columbus Enquirer-Sun: on African Americans, 99–100; on parades, 155; on performer, 148; on Robinson, 41; social concerns expressed by, 103, 144, 161, 162, 173; on Sparks, 162; on spectacle, 136
Columbus Sun and Times, 36, 49, 144
con men. *See* camp followers, card sharps, and swindlers

Confederate Cemetery, Atlanta, 52
Conklin, Pete, 37
consumerism, 2, 3, 7; eclipsed by civic pride, 158; helped by circus, 70, 73, 84; hurt by circus, 73
Cordele, Ga., 103, 104, 116
Cordele Daily Sentinel, 103
"country bloods," 92, 109
Coup, William Cameron, 12, 57, 151
Coup Circus, 143
Crawford County News, 104
crime, 78, 112, 127. *See also* grifting; pickpockets; violence
cross-dressing clowns, 125–26
culture: challenge to, 140; trends in, 2, 3, 7, 133, 165
Cuthbert, Ga., 80, 81

Dahlonega, Ga., 57, 90
Dahlonega Nugget, 78, 85, 95, 128
Dalton, Ga., 75, 80
Dalton North Georgia Citizen, 67
Dan Castello's Great Show, 35, 51, 55, 57, 105
Dan Rice Circus, 20, 35
Davis, Janet, 3, 134, 138
Dawson, Ga., 42, 118, 161
DeBow's Review, 150
decorum. *See* Victorian decorum and standards
DeHaven, George W., 44, 45
DeMille, Cecil B., 132, 134
devil costume, 24
Devil's Dictionary, The (Bierce), 109
Diavolo (bicyclist), 146, 147
Dore, Gustave, 59
Doris, John B., 75
drinking. *See* alcohol
drunken rider act, 26
Dublin, Ga., 78, 82

economy: cities and, 71–72; after Civil War, 67–68; impact of, on farmers, 70, 75; impact of, on locals, 3, 47, 78; impact of, on merchants, 46, 70–71, 72–77, 80, 84; and money transfer to towns, 75–76; and poor people, 7, 71; and supplies for circus, 64–70; and winter quarters, 68–69, 83. *See also entries for specific cities*; politics and politicians
educational value of circus, 14, 58, 63–66

Egyptian Caravan. *See* Haight and Wooten Circus
Eldred, G. N., 27
elephants: escape by, 106–7, 143; sale of, 13, 42; tricks by, 140, 141, 142; used as labor, 18
Elks Lodge, 74, 159, 160
Emmons, William, 20
endorsements: by celebrities, 63; by politicians, 51, 63
equestrians. *See* horses
excursions. *See* railroads

families, seating accommodations for, 20–21
fees and licenses, 47, 68, 80–83, 150–51. *See also* taxation
Feld, Kenneth, 170
Feld Entertainment, 169–71
females: circus attendance by, 28, 52, 53, 56, 66; as dancers, 119–20; as equestrians, 23, 134; jokes about, 25; in New South, 120; as performers, 138, 139, 146, 147; seating of, 25, 28
fire, 130, 169
Fitzgerald, Ga., 81, 91
flag, American, and reception of circus in South, 33, 36, 38
foods, 98–99. *See also* snack stands
Forepaugh, Adam, 69, 79, 136, 168
Forepaugh and Sells Brothers Shows, 76, 137–38, 146. *See also* Sells Brothers
Forepaugh Circus, 79, 96, 97, 136
Forsyth, Ga., 88
Franklin, John Hope, 31
Franklin Brothers Circus, 91
Franklin College, 27
Fraternal Circus Company, 165
French Quarter, New Orleans, 171

G. N. Eldred's Great Southern Show, 27
gambling, 20, 77, 78, 84, 116–20, 162. *See also* violence
Gate City. *See* Atlanta
Gaul, H. K., 19
Gentry, Henry B., 163
Gentry Brothers' Circus, 126
Georgia House of Representatives, 55
Georgia Military Institute, 27
Georgia State Fair, 74

Gilded Age, 79, 84, 133, 146, 169
Goodson, Steve, 6
Gorn, Elliott, 31
Grant Park, 79
Gray, Ga., 78
Great Eastern Circus, 52, 63, 88, 112
Great Eastern Menagerie, Museum, Aviary, Circus, and Roman Hippodrome. *See* Haight and Wooten Circus
Great Southern Circus. *See* John Robinson Circus
Great Southern Show. *See* Haight, Andrew
Great Southern Zoological and Callisthenic Aggregation, 46, 47
Great Southwestern Circus, 40
Great Union Combination Circus, 41
Great Van Amburg Circus. *See* Van Amburg's Consolidated Show
Great Western Circus, 22
Greenberg, Kenneth S., 118
Greensboro, Ga., 57
Griffin, Ga.: advertising in, 76, 80; African Americans in, 88; and alcohol, 102; attendance at circus in, 86–88; economics of, 75, 85; parade in, 85, 91, 94; poor performance in, 78; showing horses in, 143
Griffin Daily News, 67, 79, 85, 94, 101–2
grifting, 93, 113; ACC and, 163; gambling and, 117, 119; reaction to, 77, 119; rejection of, 152; in shows, 116–18; in sideshows, 113–20, 161, 163, 197n27; Sparks's view of, 163; techniques used for, 117–19, 161; ticket sellers and, 113; and violence, 30
gymnastic acts, 12, 15, 22, 46, 47

Hadden, David P., 64
Hagenbeck-Wallace Circus, 82, 128, 141, 151, 161
Haight, Andrew: advertising by, 43; charity by, 52; as circus operator, 42, 44–46, 47, 48, 64, 181n31; as northerner, 42
Haight, Jacob, 45
Haight and Chambers, 51, 52, 180n9
Haight and Wooten Circus (also called Haight and Company's Circus, Museum and Menagerie; The Great Eastern Menagerie, Museum, Aviary, Circus, and Roman Hippodrome; The Egyptian Caravan;

230 INDEX

Haight and Company's Empire City Circus), 42, 43–45, 46, 58
Hampton, Ga., 88
Handy, Ga., 87
Harden, Evelyn Jackson, 91, 92, 93, 94–95
Harris Nickel Plate Show, 83, 106, 119, 142
hayseeds. *See* rubes, hayseeds, and rural southerners
Herr Lengel (lion tamer), 105
"Hey Rube," 39. *See also* violence
Hill, Samuel S., 15
hippodrome races, 110, 129–30, 133, 145, 146
historical spectacles (specs), 132, 133, 134–37, 149
horses: and equestrianism, 12, 22, 23, 26, 133, 139; in parades, 19, 21; racing of, 11, 145–46; thoroughbreds, 122; used as labor, 18
Hosch, Clarence, 139
Howes' Great London Circus, 50, 64, 121, 127, 142, 143. *See also* S. B. Howes' European Circus
Huckleberry Finn (Twain), 26, 67
humbug, 34, 39, 40–41, 44, 48, 78
humor, in Old South, 24–25. *See also* clowns
Hunterson, John, 145

interaction: among audience members, 86–87, 130; between audiences and performers, 97–98, 114–15, 125, 126, 130. *See also* clowns

J. B. White's Dry Goods, 70
J. Purdy Brown's New York Circus, 26, 28
James Robinson Championship Circus, 53
Jefferson, Ga., 66, 82
Jesup, Ga., 65
Jim Crow, 88, 111, 112, 124, 128. *See also* segregation
John B. Doris' New Monster Show, 75
John Robinson and Franklin Brothers, 91, 103
John Robinson Circus: advertising for, 17; animals in, 23–24, 64, 121–23, 141, 143–44; annual Georgia tour by, 67; attack on, 44; audiences for, 109; beginning of, 121; decency and, 58; drinking at, 102–4; economic impact of, on cities, 67, 71, 76–77, 83; parades for, 96, 97; religion and, 27, 58–59, 65, 101; response of, to sectionalism, 40–45; rural response to, 88; seating and segregation at, 88, 110, 124; sold to ACC, 151, 161; as spectacle, 111, 136, 137; taxes and regulation of, 81, 82, 83; violence at, 38, 39, 105; women and, 55
Johnson, William, 20
June, Titus, Angevine and Company, 14

Kasson, John, 6, 109
Kiralfy, Imre, 135
Ku Klux Klan (KKK), 165

Ladies Memorial Association of Atlanta, 52
LaGrange, Ga., 26, 66, 76, 102
Lake and Company, 35
Lavonia, Ga., 127–28
Lawton, "Happy" Jack, 41, 46
Lears, Jackson, 86
Leavitt, M. B., 17, 18
Lee, Robert E., 37, 42
leisure, commercialization of, 2
Lengel, Herr (lion tamer), 105
Lent's Circus, 71, 77, 78
licenses and fees, 47, 68, 80–83, 150–51
lions (animals): attacks by, 142–43; loose, 105; tricks by, 140–41
Lions (organization), 142
Lipman, Mike, 38
Longfellow, Henry W., 63
Lost Cause, 35, 42. *See also* sectionalism
Lowery, P. G., 114
Lowlow, Johnny, 40
lynching, 104, 105, 107, 195n65. *See also* violence

Macon, Ga., 4, 36, 45, 54; African Americans in, 54; businessmen in, 69; and charity, 51, 154; economics of, 78, 154; lion in, 142; parades in, 155–58; wagon transportation to, 16; as winter quarters, 9, 83. *See also* Sparks Circus
Macon Daily Telegraph, 125
Macon Georgia Citizen, 49–50
Macon Telegraph, 157, 158, 159, 162
Mardi Gras, 171
Marietta, Ga., 89, 102, 160
Marietta Journal, 102
mass entertainment, 1, 2–3, 84
Mathews, Donald G., 57

McDonough, Ga., 82, 88
McPherson, William, 22
menageries, 5, 13–16, 21, 121, 122, 176n9
merchant class, 4, 68–75, 92, 93, 95, 155. *See also* advertising; economy
Methodist Book of Discipline, 150
middle class: appeal of circus to, 5, 6; attendance at circus justified by, 66; criticisms by, 8, 26, 27, 28, 50; and parades, 94; uneasiness of, 63, 109, 124; vice and, 120; violence and, 103
Middleton, George, 33
Mighty Haag Circus, 100
Mike Lipman's Colossal Combination Circus, 38
Miles, R. E. J., 44–45
military, 22, 33–34, 36–37, 39
Milledgeville, Ga., 40, 102, 119, 127
ministers: difference from laity on circus, 27, 59–62, 66; used by circuses, 63–65. *See also* churches; wedding at circus
Minting (unicyclist), 147–48
Monroe, Ga., 79
Monroe Advertiser, 76
morality: appropriate conduct and, 4, 15; contradictions in, 4; crime and, 93, 117; equality and, 87, 166; and evils, views of, 28, 60; and ideals, 57; impact of circus on, 3; organizations for, 160; power and, 6; and priorities, 27; race and, 124; social conservatives and, 4, 52, 62, 66; and social tensions, 87, 118; spectrum of, 53, 54, 55, 56, 91; and transformations, 7, 66, 86, 152. *See also* Victorian decorum and standards
Mozart, Harry, 142
music. *See* bands

name changes, postwar, 34
Nasaw, David, 6
NASCAR, 145, 146, 172
Nathans, Emma, 22
national rail system. *See* railroads
Newnan, Ga., 46, 47, 82, 88, 103
Newnan Herald, 46
New Orleans Academy of Music, 39
New Orleans Mammoth Circus and Menagerie, 41
New South: African Americans in, 98; lynching in, 103; Old South contrasted with, 4, 7, 12, 24–25, 83–84, 133, 166; police in, 194n57; profit in, 66, 84, 188n22; race, class, and religion in, 5, 7, 57, 62, 93, 110; segregation in, 111; southernism in, 43; violence in, 103, 104, 105, 127; womanhood in, 120
New York Circus and Arena Company, 16
New York Clipper, 47, 80, 123, 144; and southernism, 36, 37–38, 39
Norman Brothers' Circus, 78
North, Henry Ringling, 169
North, John Ringling, 169
Noyes, C. W., 39

O'Brien, John, 144
Oglethorpe, Ga., 100
Old South, 26; bawdy shows in, 5; females and, 5–6; New South contrasted with, 4, 7, 12, 24–25, 83–84, 133, 166; size of shows in, 166, 167; violence in, 11
O'Rourke, James, 106–7
Orton Circus, 38
Ownby, Ted, 60
Owsley, Frank L., 23

P. T. Barnum's Great Traveling Museum, Menagerie, Caravan and Hippodrome, 57
pageants, 133–34. *See also* specs
parades, 15, 12, 28, 72, 73; African Americans at, 97, 98, 99, 100, 105; animals in, 19; ending of, 150, 151, 155–56, 165, 168; socializing at, 97, 105, 107, 111, 114, 164–65; spectacle of, 18–19, 90–94, 95, 156; violence at, 87, 92, 166. *See also under* Sparks
Parks, H. H., 50, 60
peddlers, 19. *See also* camp followers, card sharps, and swindlers
Peiss, Kathy, 6
pickpockets, 30, 93, 120
Plains, Ga., 1
police, 30, 96, 97, 155; and animals, 105, 106–7; crowd control by, 112, 127; and drinking, 102; enforcement by, 104, 128; failure of, to protect circus, 39; and grifting, 119; in New South, 194n57; private, 102–3; and segregation, 112, 128
politics and politicians: appeal to, 51, 73, 90, 134; business alliance with, 3, 7, 69, 151,

232 INDEX

158, 188n22; control by, 15, 51, 74, 81, 82; economics and, 67, 69, 167; endorsements by, 51, 63; mocking of, 24; opposition of, to circus, 34, 73, 74; religion and, 15; sectionalism and, 34, 41, 45, 48, 72; winter quarters and, 9, 47

popular culture, 2, 17, 35, 50–51

Porthos (bicyclist), 147

posters. *See* advertising

Preakness Stakes, 172

Professor Sanders the Boneless Man, 47

Pullman, Giles, 79

racial interaction: circus and, 2, 3, 12; at entrances to circus, 54, 55, 112; etiquette of, 54, 91, 99

railroads: advertising by, 159; arrival of, in towns, 1, 2, 5, 6; in Atlanta, 4, 136; importance of, 83, 167; national system of, 2, 17, 74, 83, 86, 154; north-south movement of, 36; rebuilding of, in Georgia, 4, 7, 167; shift from wagons to, 2; shift to trucks from, 170; size of trains on, 44, 85, 153; southern network of, 68; and taxes, 81, 189–90n40; town expansion and, 167; towns without, 68, 74, 170; travel on, 45, 47, 73, 88; violence connected with, 102; and winter quarters, 154

Reconstruction: evangelicals and, 56; military and, 36; movement to towns during, 4; northerners and, 3; southern values and, 48; southernism and, 8, 35, 36, 39, 42; violence and, 8

"Regulators" (returned rebel soldiers), 37, 38

reserved seating. *See* seating: reserved

Rice, Dan, 24, 25, 35–37, 38. *See also* Dan Rice Circus

Ricketts, John Bill, 12, 13, 16

Ringling, Alf, 98, 99

Ringling, Charles, 120, 156

Ringling, John, 163

Ringling Brothers and Barnum and Bailey Circus: animals in, 63, 142; attendance at, 89–90; audience size at, 132, 150; autos in, 147; clowns in, 125; ethics of, 116; fashion of, 139; fire at, 130; food at, 70, 98–99; interactions of audience with, 122, 125; modern, 168, 169, 170; parade for, 95; and politicians, 90; races at, 129, 145; Sparks purchase by, 163; tent size of, 123; ticketing at, 112; winter quarters of, 163. *See also* Barnum and Bailey Circus

ringmaster, 22, 24–25, 26, 49, 126, 171

road conditions, 18, 22, 167

Roberta, Ga., 91, 104

Robinson, Gil: on circus life, 18, 23, 24, 31, 144; on lynching, 104; as manager, 17; on snack stands, 99

Robinson, James, 23, 39–40, 144

Robinson and Eldred's Grand New York Circus, 19, 21, 26

Rocky Mount, N.C., 45

Rocky Mount Mail, 45

Roman riding, 23

Rome, Ga.: animals in, 116; churches in, 101; crime in, 93, 104, 161; crowds in, 91; decency in, 162; modern circus in, 170; parade in, 86

Rothschild, A. B., 116

rubes, hayseeds, and rural southerners, 29, 69, 125, 133

S. B. Howes' European Circus, 33, 36, 151. *See also* Howes' Great London Circus

S. H. Barrett Show, 77

Sanders, "Professor" ("the Boneless Man"), 47

Sandersville Herald, 61

Savannah, Ga.: advance ticketing in, 53; African Americans in, 21, 97, 115; animals in, 5, 16, 57, 105, 141, 144–45; autos in, 148; bicycles in, 147; boats in, 16; business opposition to circus in, 68, 73; charity in, 51, 160; churches in, 57; clowns in, 125–26; crowds in, 112; economics of, 71, 73, 74–75, 161; first circus in Georgia in, 16; interactions in, 92, 126; parade in, 97, 111; politics of, 52, 81; Retail Merchant's Association (RMA) in, 73–74; school closing in, for circus, 89; as seaport, 4; taxes in, 73, 81, 82; travel to, 16, 89; as winter quarters, 83

Savannah Daily Herald, 52

Savannah Female Orphan Asylum, 51

Savannah Morning News, 59, 90, 107, 125, 129; on cross dressing, 126; on economy, 69–70, 74, 160–61; on social aspects, 129; on southernism, 41, 42, 44; on spectacle, 137; on ticket sales, 53; turpitude charges by, 137–38

Schultz, Mark, 110–11
seating: of African Americans, 21, 124, 126; in bleachers, 123; by class, 110; in contrast to movies, 196n10; of elites, 21; of females, 28; lack of, 5; in pit, 21; reserved, 20, 21, 52, 55, 123, 124, 126; segregated, 5, 54, 110, 184; violence over, 127
sectionalism, 3, 35, 37, 45, 47, 48. *See also* southernism
segregation, 3, 111, 115, 124; in bands, 14; of seating, 5, 54, 110, 184; on trains, 88. *See also* Jim Crow
Sells, Lewis, 79, 151
Sells, William, 83, 151
Sells and Rentfrow Circus, 77, 119
Sells Brothers, 80, 85, 101, 120, 127, 132. *See also* Forepaugh and Sells Brothers Shows
Sells-Floto Circus, 115, 151, 161
Sheak, William, 65
Sherwood, Robert, 18, 22, 25
Shriners, 154, 157, 160
sideshows: barkers at, 87, 111, 113; dancers at, 1, 5, 110, 114–15, 119–20; features of, 113; gambling at, 77, 84, 117–18; grift in, 113–20, 161, 163, 197n27; interactive nature of, 115, 116, 120, 121, 130; music for, 114, 123, 159; oddities in, 20, 110, 116; segregated bands for, 114; violence in, 115
Sizer, Mrs. (equestrian), 23
Skillman, Thomas, 26, 28, 29
slavery, 5, 20, 25, 27, 28, 54–55
Slout, William, 144
snack stands, 7, 10, 87, 98–101, 111, 108, 171
social concerns, 7, 25, 99, 166; equality, 87; interaction, 1, 86–92, 93–94, 109, 129
Somers, N.Y., 13–14, 15
southernism, 3, 5, 11–12, 15, 25, 35. *See also* sectionalism
Sparks, Charles: and ACC, 163; charity by, 160; and civic interest, 156, 158, 160; Macon and, 153, 154, 159–60, 161, 163, 164; and parade, 154, 156, 164; and politics, 160, 164; public approval for, 151–52, 154; and religion, 162; retirement of, 163; and Savannah, 160; as showman, 152, 153–54, 164
Sparks, Clifton, 159, 160, 164
Sparks Circus: charity shows by, 151, 154–55, 158, 160; community ties of, 153, 157, 158, 159–60; economic benefits of, 158, 160–61; as ending grift, 152, 161, 162; moral approbation for, 152; and parades, 157–58, 164; political ties of, 151–53, 157, 161; and propriety, 157; as publicity for Macon, 159; quality of shows of, 162; support of churches by, 162; winter quarters of, 153–55
Sparta Ishmaelite, 120
specs (historical spectacles), 132, 133, 134–37, 149
Statesboro, Ga., 65, 77, 89
Statesboro News, 120
Stickney, Sam, 44–45
Stockbridge, Ga., 81
Stone and McCollum's Mammoth Great Western Circus, 19, 21, 28
Stone and Murray Combination Circus, 53
Stone, Rosston and Murray Circus, 36, 39, 51–52, 55, 56
Sun Brothers, 127, 154, 156
Sunday, Billy, 152, 162
Swainsboro Forest Blade, 76
Sylvania, Ga., 93, 120

T. K. Burk Circus, 126
Tampa, Fla., 171
Tate, Susan Fan, 98, 122
taxation, 46, 50–51, 73, 74, 80–83; on railcars, 81, 189–90n40
tents: portable canvas, 11–12, 16; size of, 20, 123; use of multiple, 44, 58–59, 123, 184n24
Thayer, Stuart, 13, 16, 21
Thayer and Noyes' United States Circus, 34, 36, 39, 55
Thomasson, Basil Armstrong, 27
Thomasville, Ga., 88, 89, 90, 104, 116, 122
Thomasville Daily Times, 94
Thomasville Daily Times Enterprise, 61, 91
Thompson, W. C., 39, 98
Thrasher, A. B., 126
ticketing: advance selling, 52, 53, 54, 70, 157, 183n11; agents, 9, 19; charity, 64, 66, 160; failure to use, 53; grifting and, 112–13, 115, 118; prices, 123; segregation and, 112, 124, 196n10; speed of sale, 112; violence and, 92, 104; wagon, 5, 16, 19, 50, 53–54, 111–12
Tifton, Ga., 77, 105
Tifton Gazette, 61

trains. *See* railroads
travel, 2, 155. *See also* railroads; road conditions; wagons, travel by
Tri-County Fair, 74
Tuttle, Jerome, 40
Twain, Mark, 1, 26, 67

United States Army, 33–34, 45
UniverSoul Circus, 171
USA Today, 172

Valdosta, Ga., 83, 93, 102, 103, 104, 106
Valdosta Times, 101, 103–4, 106, 107
Van Amburg's Consolidated Show (also called Great Van Amburg Circus), 59, 77, 83, 119, 120
Victorian decorum and standards, 9, 50, 71, 109, 127, 130. *See also* morality
violence: alcohol as cause of, 30, 87, 102, 150; animals and, 195n63; class and, 102–3; crowd and, 104; females and, 104, 115; forcible response to, 30, 31; grifting as cause of, 30; police and, 104; race and, 93, 104–5, 128; in railroad towns, 102; over seating, 127; in South, 29, 103; in stands, 129; in theaters, 30; use of southernism to defuse, 8, 48; and Yankees, 30, 32, 33. *See also* brawls; lynching

W. C. Clark's Show, 66
W. W. Cole's New Colossal Shows, 114
wagons, travel by, 16, 17, 20, 128, 153
Wallace Circus, 146
Waller, Gregory, 6
Walter L. Main Circus, 126
Waring and Company's Great Zoological Exhibition, 14
Washington, George, 20
Waynesboro, Ga., 80, 93, 101, 103
weather, 17, 18, 71, 83
wedding at circus, 126–27
Welch, Nathans and Company's National Circus, 22
Willis, Lewis, 144
Willson, Dixie, 124
winter quarters, 9, 47, 68–69, 83, 153–55, 163, 170
women. *See* females
Wooten, P. Bowles, 42, 44, 46, 47, 48, 161
Wyatt-Brown, Bertram, 118

Yankee Robinson Circus, 52, 117

Zebold, George W., 112
Zebulon, Ga., 88
Zoological Institute, 14
zoos, 14, 79, 121, 122, 154

www.ingramcontent.com/pod-product-compliance
Lightning Source LLC
Chambersburg PA
CBHW011755220426
43672CB00018B/2972